Transference

Jacques Lacan

Transference

The Seminar of Jacques Lacan
Book VIII

Edited by Jacques-Alain Miller

Translated by Bruce Fink

polity

First published in French as *Le Séminaire de Jacques Lacan, Livre VIII, Le transfert* (c) Éditions du Seuil, 1991; revised edition published in 2001.

English edition © Polity Press, 2015
This paperback edition © Polity Press 2017

7

Polity Press
65 Bridge Street
Cambridge CB2 1UR, UK

Polity Press
350 Main Street
Malden, MA 02148, USA

ISBN-13: 978-0-7456-6039-4
ISBN-13: 978-1-5095-2360-3 (pb)

A catalogue record for this book is available from the British Library.

Library of Congress Cataloging-in-Publication Data

Lacan, Jacques, 1901-1981, author.
  [Transfert, 1960-1961. English]
  Transference / Jacques Lacan ; translated by Bruce Fink.
     p. ; cm. -- (The seminar of Jacques Lacan ; bk. 8)
  First published as Le transfert, 1960-1961 / Jacques Lacan. 2nd ed. corrected. 2001.
  Includes bibliographical references and index.
  ISBN 978-0-7456-6039-4 (hardcover : alk. paper) -- ISBN 0-7456-6039-8 (hardcover : alk. paper)
  I. Fink, Bruce, 1956- , translator. II. Title. III. Series: Lacan, Jacques, 1901-1981. Séminaire de Jacques Lacan. English ; bk. 8.
  [DNLM: 1. Transference (Psychology)--Lectures. WM 460 L129s 2015a]
  RC506
  616.89'17--dc23
                              2014047150

Typeset in 10.5 on 12 pt Times NR MT by
Servis Filmsetting Ltd, Stockport, Cheshire
Printed and bound in the UK by CPI Group (UK) Ltd, Croydon, CR0 4YY

The publisher has used its best endeavours to ensure that the URLs for external websites referred to in this book are correct and active at the time of going to press. However, the publisher has no responsibility for the websites and can make no guarantee that a site will remain live or that the content is or will remain appropriate.

Every effort has been made to trace all copyright holders, but if any have been inadvertently overlooked the publisher will be pleased to include any necessary credits in any subsequent reprint or edition.

For further information on Polity, visit our website: www.politybooks.com

Contents

THE OEDIPAL MYTH TODAY
A COMMENTARY ON THE COÛFONTAINE TRILOGY BY PAUL CLAUDEL

CAPITAL I AND LITTLE *a*

Translator's Note

All quotations from Plato's *Symposium* are from the excellent rendition by Alexander Nehamas and Paul Woodruff in *Plato on Love: Lysis, Symposium, Phaedrus, Alcibiades, with Selections from Republic and Laws*, edited by C. D. C. Reeve (Indianapolis, IN, and Cambridge, England: Hackett Publishing Company, 2006). Since Lacan sometimes quotes from Léon Robin's translation into French, and sometimes provides his own rendition or paraphrasing, I do not always supply the exact translation found in *Plato on Love*, adapting it instead to fit what Lacan seems to me to be trying to convey. Indeed, it is not always easy to know when Lacan is providing his own rendition of the Greek and when he is putting words in a character's mouth that correspond to his own interpretation of the import of that character's speech.

I have relied for the Greek on the Loeb Classical Library edition (Cambridge, MA: Harvard University Press, 1983) and on the Greek spellings and transliterations provided by Rachel Rue, Ph.D., who was kind enough to scour the manuscript for me.

All references here to Lacan's *Écrits* (Paris: Seuil, 1966) are to the French pagination included in the margins of *Écrits: The First Complete Edition in English* (New York and London: W. W. Norton & Co., 2006), translated by B. Fink in collaboration with R. Grigg and H. Fink. When I refer to Lacan's seminars, I provide the pagination of the French editions, followed – after a slash – by the page number in the English editions (published by Norton), when they exist; in the case of Seminar III, I give only the French page numbers, as they are included in the margins of the English edition. All but one of the extant seminars in French were published by Éditions du Seuil in Paris. *Le séminaire, Livre VI: Le désir et son interprétation (1958–1959)* [*The Seminar, Book VI: Desire and Its Interpretation*], was published in 2013 by La Martinière in Paris.

References to Freud's work here are always to *The Standard*

Edition of the Complete Psychological Works of Sigmund Freud (24 volumes), published in London by the Hogarth Press, abbreviated here as *SE*, followed by the volume number and page(s).

Note that throughout this Seminar I have translated *l'analysé* as "the analysand" (instead of as the more cumbersome "person analyzed"), even though Lacan had not yet begun to use *l'analysant* here.

Le réel means both reality and the real (Lacan defining the latter in opposition to the imaginary and the symbolic). It is not always clear which is intended at which point in his work, so whenever I translate *le réel* as "reality" instead of as "the real," I include the French in brackets.

Despite assistance from Rachel Rue, from my wife, Héloïse Fink, and from Russell Grigg and Dan Collins, numerous errors no doubt remain here. Lacan's incredibly broad background and in-depth knowledge of numerous fields are such that I have surely misunderstood specialized terminology, overlooked references to specific authors, and just generally misinterpreted the French – Lord knows it is easy enough to do given Lacan's singular style! His oral work presents additional problems, given the number of homophonies French allows for; I have attempted to address some of these (along with alternative readings and translations, as well as likely sources of Lacan's discussions) in my endnotes. The latter are keyed to the pagination of the present English edition. Numbers found in the margins here correspond to the pagination of the 2001 French edition.

Readers who believe they have found mistakes of whatever kind are encouraged to send comments to me at <brucefinkanalyst@ gmail.com>. I consider this translation to be, like my others (for which updates can be found in the form of PDFs at <http:// brucefink.com/bruce-fink-library/>), a work in progress, and hope to improve on the text here in future editions.

Abbreviations Used in the Text and Notes

Écrits *Écrits: The First Complete Edition in English*
GW *Gesammelte Werke* by Sigmund Freud (Frankfurt am Main: S. Fischer Verlag)
IJP *International Journal of Psychoanalysis*
IPA International Psychoanalytical Association
PQ *Psychoanalytic Quarterly*
PUF Presses Universitaires de France
RFP *Revue Française de Psychanalyse*
SE *Standard Edition of the Complete Psychological Works of Sigmund Freud*

Words followed by an asterisk (*) are found in English in the original.

Book VIII

Transference

1960–1961

INTRODUCTION

I

IN THE BEGINNING WAS LOVE

Plato's *Schwärmerei*.
Socrates and Freud.
A critique of intersubjectivity.
The beauty of bodies.

I announced that this year I would discuss transference "in its subjective disparity, its supposed situation, and its excursions into the realm of technique."

"Disparity" is not a term I chose lightly. It essentially highlights the fact that transference involves much more than the simple notion of a dissymmetry between subjects. Right from the outset, "disparity" implies that I reject the idea that intersubjectivity alone can furnish the framework within which the phenomenon of transference is situated. Different languages offer more or less apt words with which to express the kind of disparity I have in mind. I have been trying to find something equivalent to the word "odd"* to qualify the essentially uneven [*impair*] nature of transference. There is no term in French with which to designate it, apart from *imparité*, which is not currently in use.

"Its supposed situation," my title continues, referring thereby to the attempt that has been made in recent years in analysis to organize what takes place during treatment around the notion of situations. "Supposed" is included there to alert you to the fact that I do not endorse this attempt, or at least that I propose to correct it. I do not think one can purely and simply say of analysis that it constitutes a situation. If it is a situation, then it is a situation that can also be said not to be a situation, or again that it is a rather artificial [*fausse*] situation.

As for "technique," everything that is proffered on that score must be viewed in relation to the principles, or at least to the search for principles, already evoked by my title, with its allusion to differences

in approach. To put it in a nutshell, a correct topology is required
here and, consequently, a rectification of what is commonly implied
by our everyday use of the theoretical notion of transference. The
goal is to relate this notion to an experience. We are, however,
extremely familiar with this experience, at least insofar as each of us
has practiced analysis in one form or another.

It has taken me a long time to come to this crux of our experience. Depending on when one takes this seminar – in which I have
been guiding a number of you for some years – to have begun, it is
in either its eighth or tenth year that I am finally broaching transference. You will see that this long delay was not accidental.

Let us thus begin.

1

"In the beginning –"

You all immediately infer that I am paraphrasing the sentence,
"In the beginning was the Word" [John 1:1].

"*Im Anfang war die Tat*," says another.

A third sustains that first – that is, at the beginning of the human
world – there was praxis.

This gives us three apparently incompatible statements. But, in
fact, from the perspective of analytic practice [*expérience*], what
counts is not their value as statements but rather their value as enun-
ciations or announcements – that is, the respect in which they bring
out the *ex nihilo* character of all creation and demonstrate its intimate connection with the evocative power of speech. In this respect,
all three obviously prove to come under the first statement, "In the
beginning was the Word."

I am mentioning this so as to distinguish it from what I am saying,
and from the point from which I am setting out to grapple with this
most opaque term, this core of our experience: transference.

I intend to start, I would like to start, I will try to start today –
beginning with all the necessary clumsiness – with the fact that
the term "in the beginning" certainly has another meaning in
psychoanalysis.

In the beginning of analytic practice was, let us recall, love. This
beginning was not akin to the self-transparency of enunciation that
gave meaning to the three sentences mentioned before. It was a dense,
jumbled [*confus*] beginning. A beginning not of creation but rather of
training. I will come later to the historic moment at which, in the
encounter between a man and a woman, Josef Breuer and Anna O.,
recounted in the inaugural case of the *Studies on Hysteria*, what was

already a form of psychoanalysis emerged – Anna herself named it the "talking cure,"* referring to it also as "chimney sweeping."*

Before coming to that, I want to familiarize those of you who weren't here last year with some of the terms around which our exploration of what I called the ethics of psychoanalysis revolved.

Last year I endeavored to explain to you – to refer back to the word "creation" I mentioned a moment ago – the creationist structure of the human *ethos* as such, that is, the *ex nihilo* that subsists at its core, constituting "the core of our being," to borrow Freud's expression (*Kern unseres Wesen*). I wanted to show that this *ethos* wraps around the *ex nihilo* as subsisting in an impenetrable void.

To broach the subject, and to designate this characteristic of impenetrability, I began, as you may remember, with a critique whose aim it was to explicitly reject what you will allow me – or at least those of you who were here will allow me – to call Plato's *Schwärmerei*.

For those of you who don't know it, in German *Schwärmerei* means daydream or fantasy involving some enthusiasm, especially related to superstition. In short, it implies a negative assessment [of superstition] that was made at a later date from the perspective of a religious orientation. The word *Schwärmerei* is clearly inflected in this way in Kant's texts. Well, Plato's *Schwärmerei* consists in having projected the idea of the Sovereign Good onto the impenetrable void.

Such is the path that, with more or less success of course, I deliberately tried to trace out: what happens to us when we reject Plato's notion of the Sovereign Good as occupying the center of our being?

In order to relate that discussion to our practice, I naturally proceeded, with a critical aim, on the basis of what might be called Aristotle's conversion from Platonism. Aristotle is indubitably outmoded as far as ethics is concerned, but from our temporal vantage point, where we are obliged to show the historical fate of ethical notions starting from Plato, it is clearly essential to refer to Aristotle.

14

In tracing what Aristotle's *Nicomachean Ethics* provides by way of a decisive step in the construction of ethical reflection, it is difficult not to see that, while Aristotle maintains the notion of the Sovereign Good, he profoundly changes its meaning. Through an inverse reflective shift, he turns the Sovereign Good into contemplation of the stars, the world's outermost sphere. And it is precisely because this sphere – which to Aristotle was an absolute, uncreated, and incorruptible entity – has been decisively exploded in our time into a shimmering expanse of galaxies, the last word in our cosmological investigations, that Aristotle can be taken as a crucial reference point for the notion of the Sovereign Good in Antiquity.

We were led into a tight spot by his step, the same tight spot as countless others who have attempted to take ethical reflection further. We had to either accept or reject what ethical reflection or thought has never been able to shake off – namely, that there is no good, *bon*, *Gute*, or pleasure that is not based on the Good [*Bien*]. It was up to us to seek the principle of *Wohltat*, right action [*bien agir*], and what it implies allows us to say that it is perhaps not simply good deeds, even if they are raised to the Kantian power of a universal maxim.

If we are to take seriously the fallacy of so-called moral satisfactions that Freud pointed out, insofar as an aggressiveness lurks within them that succeeds in stealing from he who carries out such deeds his own jouissance, while his misdeeds [*méfait*] have endless repercussions on his social partners – what these long conditionals and circumstantials indicate is the exact equivalent of *Civilization and Its Discontents* in Freud's work – we must ask ourselves by what means we are to honestly handle desire. In other words, how are we to keep desire in our deeds – that is, to preserve the relationship between desire and action? In action, desire ordinarily achieves its demise [*collapsus*] rather than its fulfillment, and, at best, a deed presents desire with its mere feat, its epic, heroic exploit [*geste*]. How, I ask, are we to maintain what might be called a simple or salubrious relationship between desire and action?

Let's not mince words about the meaning of "salubrious" in the context of Freudian practice. It means unburdened, as unburdened as possible of the infection that, to my mind – but not to mine alone, to everyone's from the moment they begin to engage in ethical reflection – is the seething ground [*fond grouillant*] of every social institution as such.

This assumes, of course, that psychoanalysis, in its very user's guide, does not respect the opaque spot [*taie*], newly invented cataract, moral wound [*plaie*], or form of blindness constituted by a certain practice deriving from the so-called sociological point of view. I could recount here what a recent meeting showed me about the vacuity and scandalousness to which sociological research leads – research that claims to reduce an experience like that of the unconscious to two, three, or maybe four sociological models – but my irritation, which was very great at the time, has subsided, and I will leave the authors of such exercises in futility to the truisms that will welcome them with open arms.

I should point out that in speaking of sociology in such terms, I am obviously not referring to the level at which Lévi-Strauss' thought is situated – I refer you to his inaugural lecture at the Collège de

France – for he explicitly engages in an ethical meditation on social practice. His twofold reference to a cultural norm on the one hand, that is more or less mythically situated in the Neolithic era, and to Rousseau's political meditations on the other, is sufficiently indicative here. But let us set this aside – it is of no concern to us in the present context.

I will merely recall here that it was by examining Sade's savage reflections regarding ethics, and by following the insulting paths of Sadean jouissance, that I showed you one of the possible means of access to the properly tragic frontier where Freud's *Oberland* [highland] lies. It is at the heart of what some of you dubbed the "between-two-deaths" – a perfect expression for designating the field in which everything that happens in the universe traced out by Sophocles is articulated, and not just in the adventure of *Oedipus Rex* – that a phenomenon is situated about which I think I can safely say that we have introduced a guidepost in the ethical tradition, that is, in reflection on motives and motivations for doing the Good. I designated this guidepost as beauty insofar as it dresses up – or rather functions as a final barrier to access to – the final or mortal thing, at the point where Freud's thought made its ultimate admission with the term "death drive."

Please excuse this long detour. It was but a short summary by which I thought I should outline what we stated last year. This detour was necessary to remind you where we left off concerning the function of beauty, as it will be a springboard for what I will have to say this year. Indeed I need not, for most of you, mention what is constituted by the term "the beautiful" or "beauty" as it is inflected in what I called Plato's *Schwärmerei*. 16

As a hypothesis, we are provisionally going to assume that the latter constitutes – at the level of an adventure that, if it is not psychological, is at least individual – the effect of a form of mourning that we can qualify as immortal, because it is at the very source of everything that has been articulated since then in our tradition concerning the idea of immortality: the immortal mourning for he who accepted the wager of sustaining his question, the same question raised by everyone who speaks, so much so that he received this question from his own daemon in an inverted form, to use our own expression. I am talking about Socrates, Socrates thus placed at the origin – and why not say so right away? – of the longest transference, giving this expression its fullest import, that history has ever known.

I hope to get you to sense this – Socrates' secret will be behind everything I will have to say about transference this year.

2

This secret was admitted to by Socrates. But it is not because one admits to having a secret that it stops being a secret. Socrates claims to know nothing, except how to recognize what love is, how to infallibly recognize, he tells us – I am referring to Plato's account in the *Lysis*, 204c – when he meets a couple, who is the lover and who is the beloved.

Socrates often refers to love and this brings us back to our point of departure, as I intend to highlight it today. Indeed, however prudish or improper it was to keep partially veiled the inaugural incident that dissuaded the eminent Breuer from following through on his first sensational experiment with the talking cure,* it is clear that it was a love story. It is equally clear that it was not unrequited – in other words, love was not felt solely by the patient.

It is not enough to say, in the exquisitely measured terms of our vocabulary, as Ernest Jones does in the first volume of his biography of Freud, that Breuer must have fallen prey to what we call a somewhat pronounced countertransference. It is clear that Breuer loved his patient. By way of proof, we need no more evidence than what, in such cases, is the true bourgeois outcome: the return to renewed conjugal fervor and the abrupt departure for Venice, which even bore fruit in the form of a new daughter being added to the family – Jones sadly tells us that her death was tied to the catastrophic invasion of Vienna by the Nazis.

There is no point ironizing about such incidents, except, of course, insofar as they present what is typical of certain so-called bourgeois ways of dealing with love. They reveal the need for or necessity of an awakening regarding the neglect of the heart that goes together so well with the kind of abnegation characteristic of bourgeois duty.

But this is not what is essential here. What difference does it make whether Breuer resisted or not? What we should instead celebrate about that moment is that it foreshadowed the break between Freud and Breuer 10 years before it occurred. The latter's work with Anna O. took place in 1882, and it took 10 years for Freud's experience to result in the *Studies on Hysteria,* written with Breuer, and 15 years for them to go their separate ways. It's all there. Little Eros, whose mischievousness struck the one like a bolt from the blue and forced him to take flight, found his master in the other, Freud. Why?

I could say – if you'll allow me to strike a lighter note for a moment – that it was because all possibility of retreat had been cut off for Freud. This fact arises from the same context as the one we know of now that his correspondence with his fiancée has been published – the intransigent love he espoused. He would meet ideal

17

women, who responded to him physically like porcupines, *Sie streben dagegen*, he wrote in the dream of Irma's injection, where the allusions to his own wife are neither obvious nor admitted to – "they always rub me the wrong way." The *Frau Professor* [the Professor's wife] appeared in every case as an element of the permanent picture Freud provided us with of his thirst, and she was occasionally a source of marvel to Jones who, if my informants are to be trusted, himself knew what it meant to be submissive.

This would constitute a curious common denominator between Freud and Socrates, Socrates having had, as you know, dealings at home with an unmanageable shrew. The difference between the two, insofar as it was palpable, is that outlined by Aristophanes between the pompous otter and the Lysistrata-like weasel [*belette*] whose powerful bite can be sensed in the dialogues in his plays – a simple difference in odor.

But enough on this topic. I reckon that it is but a secondary connection, and that this datum concerning married life is in no way indispensable, each of you should be reassured, to your proper conduct. We must look further to approach the mystery in question.

The approach adopted by Freud – unlike Breuer, and regardless of the reasons why – made him master of the fearsome little god, Eros. Like Socrates, Freud chose to serve the god in order to make use of him. It is in this "making use of" Eros – which nevertheless had to be emphasized – that our problems begin. Making use of him for what?

This is why I had to remind you of the mile markers of our work last year – making use of Eros for the Good? We know that the realm of Eros goes infinitely beyond any field the Good can cover. At the very least, we take it for granted and this is why the problems posed by transference merely begin here. It is, moreover, something that is ever fresh in my mind. It is in yours too, inasmuch as people commonly say concerning transference that you must in no way, whether premeditated or permanent, posit as the primary aim of your action your patient's own good – supposed or otherwise – but rather his eros.

I don't think I should pass up the opportunity to remind you once again here of what the Socratic and Freudian endeavors – at their most scabrous – have in common. I will do so by pointing to the similarity of their outcomes via the duplicity of the terms in the following condensed expression: Socrates, too, chose to serve Eros in order to make use of him [*pour s'en servir*], to serve Eros in using him [*en s'en servant*]. Note that it took Socrates quite far – to a far-off place that people strive to camouflage by turning it into a pure and simple accident of what I earlier called the seething ground of

the social infection. But wouldn't we be doing Socrates an injustice –
tantamount to refusing to accept his viewpoint – were we to believe
that he didn't know full well that he was going against the tide of
the whole social order within which his daily practice was situated? Wasn't his behavior truly insane and scandalous, despite the
praiseworthy light his disciples devotedly cast on it by emphasizing
its heroic facets? It is clear that they could not but record a major
characteristic of Socrates, that Plato himself qualified with a term
that has remained famous to those who have taken up the problem
of Socrates: his ἀτοπία (atopía) within the order of the city.

In the social bond, opinions have no place if they are not borne
out by all that ensures the city's equilibrium, and thus Socrates not
only did not have his place – he was no place. What is so surprising if
an act that is so powerfully unclassifiable that its aftershocks are still
felt in our own times, and that has found a place – what is so surprising about the fact that it resulted in a death sentence? It resulted, in
the clearest fashion possible, in real death, inflicted at a time chosen
in advance, with everyone's consent and for the good of all. And,
indeed, writers in the centuries that have since passed have never
been able to decide whether the sanction was just or unjust. Where
will Socrates' fate – a fate that can, without exaggerating, it seems
to me, be considered necessary, not extraordinary – take him now?

As for Freud, on the other hand, wasn't it in strict accordance
with the rigor of his path that he discovered the death drive? It too
was quite scandalous, albeit less costly to Freud himself. But does
this amount to a true difference?

Formal logic has been repeating for centuries, and its insistence
is not unfounded, that Socrates is mortal and thus that he, in any
case, had to die sooner or later. But it is not the fact that Freud died
peacefully in his bed that concerns us here. Last year, I endeavored
to show you how what I sketched out converges with Sadean aspi-
rations. The idea of eternal death must be distinguished here from
death insofar as it makes being itself into a detour – we being unable
to know whether or not it makes sense. The idea of eternal death
must be distinguished from the other death as well, the second, that
of the body, the body that uncompromisingly obeys Eros. Eros is
that by which bodies come back together, according to Plato into a
single soul, according to Freud with no soul at all, but in any case
into but one – Eros is what unites unitively.

You could, of course, interrupt me here by asking, "Where are
you leading us?" "Eros," you will grant me, "is clearly the same
in both cases, even if we can't bear it. But why are you trotting
out the two deaths – last year's old hat? Are you still mulling it
over? And what are you trying to convey with it?" The river that

separates them. "Are we dealing with the death drive or dialectic?" My answer is, "Yes." Yes, if the one brings the other with it and astonishes you.

I am willing to admit that I'm getting off track, that I need not take you through all the most far-reaching paradoxes, and that by doing so at the outset, I am making sure you are astonished – if you weren't already – by Freud if not by Socrates.

If you are unwilling to be astonished by anything, these paradoxes will undoubtedly prove simple to resolve. You merely take as your point of departure something as easy as pie, as clear as day: intersubjectivity. I intersubjectivize you, you intersubjectivize me by my chinny chin chin – the first one who laughs will get a well-deserved slap.

Doesn't everyone know by now that Freud mistakenly thought that was all there was in the sadomasochist constant? Narcissism supposedly explained everything. And people ask me, "Didn't you yourself almost endorse the same view?" It should be said that at the time I was already restive regarding the function of the narcissistic wound, but that's of no importance. People will tell me that my untimely Socrates should also have come back to [the notion of] intersubjectivity. In all, he committed but one mistake, and that was to swim against the tide of the masses, which should always be our guide. Everyone knows that one has to wait for the masses before making the slightest wave on the shore of justice, for they will necessarily arrive there tomorrow. This is how astonishment works – things get chalked up to wrongdoing [*faute*]. Errors will never be anything other than errors of judgment.

That's that, without counting my personal motives – my ever-present need to exaggerate, related to my inclination to make things sound good [*faire beau*], beauty showing up here again. It's a perverse tendency. Thus my sophistry may be superfluous. So we'll begin again by starting from scratch, and I will take up anew – coming back down to earth – the power of understatement to aim without your being even slightly astonished.

3

Isn't intersubjectivity what is most foreign to the analytic encounter? Would it resurface if we were to flee from it, convinced that it must be avoided? Freudian practice congeals as soon as intersubjectivity appears on the scene. The former flourishes only in the latter's absence.

Are the doctor and the patient, as they say in talking about us – that doozy of a relationship people get all worked up about – going to outdo each other at intersubjectivizing each other? Perhaps, but in this case it can be said that both are rather uneasy. "He's telling me that to reassure me or make me happy," thinks the one. "Is he trying to pull a fast one on me?" thinks the other. Dick and Jane relationships get off to a bad start if they start out on this footing. They are doomed, if they stay at this level, to go nowhere. Which is why doctor/patient and Dick and Jane relationships must at all costs differ from diplomatic negotiations and ambushes.

With all due respect to Henri Lefebvre, what is known as poker, theory as poker, is not discussed in von Neumann's work, despite what Lefebvre has recently claimed. This means that, owing to my benevolence, I can deduce but one thing: Lefebvre knows nothing more of von Neumann's theory than the title of the latter's book that appears in the Hermann publishing house catalogue. It is true that, at the same time, Lefebvre situates the very philosophical discussion that held us in thrall at the level of poker. If he is not within his rights to do so, I can, after all, but wish him all the credit that comes from having done so.

Returning to the thoughts of our intersubjective couple, my first concern as an analyst would be not to get myself into a situation where my patient would have to confide such reflections to me. The simplest way to spare him that is precisely to avoid any attitude which would incline him to accuse me of attempting to reassure him, much less seduce him. Even if I try to absolutely avoid any such attitude, it could happen that I let something slip out anyway – if, for example, I see the patient, at the end of his rope, adopt a certain attitude. Even in this case, I can only say something about it if I stress that I assume that he is doing so unbeknown to himself. And even then I have to be cautious in order to avoid a misunderstanding – namely, seeming to accuse him of some kind of trickery [*finasserie*], whether calculated or not.

I am not saying that it is the job of analysis to rework intersubjectivity in such a way as to raise it to a second power – as if the analyst were expecting the patient to impale himself [*s'enferrer*] so that the analyst could then roast him on the spit [*le tourner*]. No, intersubjectivity is withheld or, better still, put off indefinitely to allow another handhold [*prise*] to appear, whose essential characteristic is that it is transference itself.

The patient himself knows it; he calls for it; he wants to be found out elsewhere. You may retort that this is another aspect of intersubjectivity and that I, strangely enough, am supposedly the one who paved the way here. But whoever introduced the idea, it can only be attributed to me mistakenly.

And in fact, if I hadn't formalized the subjective alterities involved in the analytic setting in the guise of bridge players, no one could have claimed I took a step that converges with the falsely audacious schema Rickman once proffered that goes by the name of "two-body psychology."*

Such creations always have a certain modicum of success, given the state of amphibious respiration in which analytic thought maintains itself. Two conditions suffice for their success. First, that they be supposed to stem from honorable zones of scientific activity, whereby psychoanalysis can be made to seem relevant and shine anew – for what is relevant today quickly loses its luster. This is the case here, for Rickman was a man who, just after the war, had the advantageous aura of having been involved in the Russian Revolution, which was supposed to have given him plenty of experience in interpsychology. The second condition for success is not to rock the boat of analytic routine. This is how people repave a path for intellectual guidance that leads nowhere.

The name "two-body psychology"* could at least have had the virtue of awakening us to how the attraction of bodies it evokes might relate to the supposed analytic situation. But, curiously enough, the attraction of bodies is the very meaning that is elided when people use the term.

It is odd that we are obliged to turn to Socrates to realize its import. In Socrates' discourse, I mean in the dialogues in which he is made to speak, he refers constantly to the beauty of bodies. It animates, so to speak, the moment of questioning we haven't taken up yet where we still don't even know how the functions of the lover and the beloved are divided up. At least a spade is called a spade there, which allows us to make, in this regard, some useful remarks.

If something in the impassioned questioning that characterizes the beginning of the dialectical process is, in fact, related to the body, it must be stated that, in analysis, this relationship is highlighted by traits whose value derives from its particularly negative impact. Socrates' ugliness gives us the most noble example of the fact that analysts – I hope that no one here will feel that I am singling him out – aren't well known for their physical charms. But at the same time it also reminds us that ugliness in no way constitutes an obstacle to love. I must nevertheless stress the fact that the ideal physical appearance of the psychoanalyst – or, in any case, the way in which the analyst is pictured in the popular mind – also includes an obtuse denseness and a narrow-minded brutishness that truly raise the whole question of prestige.

The silver screen is the most revealing medium in this regard. To refer only to Hitchcock's most recent film [*Psycho*], consider in what

23

form the unscrambler of enigmas appears, the one who is presented there as deciding irrevocably at the end when there is no longer any other recourse. Quite frankly, he is endowed with all the features of the untouchable.

We touch here on an essential element of the convention as it concerns the analytic setting. In order for it to be violated in a way that is not revolting, the person who plays the role of analyst – sticking with film, consider here the movie *Suddenly Last Summer* – the therapist, he who pushes *caritas* [charity] to the point of kissing back an unfortunate woman who kisses him on the lips, must be a good-looking guy. In film, this is absolutely essential. True, he is also a neurosurgeon and he is promptly sent back to his trephines. The situation couldn't last.

Overall, analysis is the only praxis in which charm is a disadvantage. It would break the spell [*charme*]. Who ever heard of a charming analyst?

24   These are not irrelevant remarks, even though they may seem designed to amuse you. It is important for them to be made at the appropriate stage. It is no less notable that in guiding the patient, the very access to the body that medical examination seems to require is forgone, as a rule. This is worth pointing out. And we cannot explain why it is forgone simply by saying that it is in order to avoid excessive transferential effects. Why would such effects be any more excessive in this realm than in others? It is not due to anachronistic prudishness, traces of which subsist in rural areas, in Islamic harems, and in Portugal where, incredibly enough, doctors auscultate beautiful foreigners only through their clothing. We up the ante. Auscultation, however necessary it may seem at the outset of treatment or may be in the course of it, constitutes a breaking of the rules.

Let us look at things from a different angle. There is nothing less erotic than the reading of the body's momentary states at which certain psychoanalysts excel, for one might say that these bodily states are translated into signifying terms. The focal distance at which this reading can occur demands on the analyst's part as much aversion as interest.

Let us not too quickly decide what all of this means.

One could say that the neutralization of the body, which seems, after all, to be the first goal of civilization, is related here to a greater urgency, and that all these precautions assume that the body can be abandoned. I'm not sure about that. Here I am simply asking what this bracketing [*epoché*] is. It would show poor judgment on our part if we were not to recognize at the outset that psychoanalysis requires, right from the beginning, a high degree of libidinal sublimation at the level of collective relations. The extreme decency that one can truly claim to be maintained in the majority of cases in the analytic relationship makes us think that, if the regular confinement of the two interested parties in an enclosed space sheltered from all uninvited interruption only very rarely leads to bodily coercion [*contrainte par corps*] of one by the other, it is because the temptation to which this kind of confinement would give rise in any other occupation is lesser here than elsewhere. Let's leave it at that for the moment.

The analytic cell, even if it is comfy and cozy, is nothing but a bed for lovemaking. This is due to the fact that, despite all the attempts that have been made to reduce it to the common denominator of a situation – with all the connotations we can provide for this familiar term – entering into it is *not* a situation. As I said earlier, it is the most artificial situation going.

What allows us to understand this is precisely the reference I will try to take up next time to what is, in the social context, the situation of love itself. It is to the extent that we can home in on what Freud discussed on more than one occasion – namely, the status [*position*] of love in society, a precarious status, a threatened status, and, to come right out with it, a clandestine status – that we can appreciate why and how, in the most protected context of all, that of the analyst's office, the status of love becomes even more paradoxical.

I will arbitrarily end our discussion today on this point. It will suffice if you see from what direction I intend to broach the topic.

Breaking with the tradition that consists in abstracting from, neutralizing, and emptying of all its meaning what may be involved in the foundations of the analytic relationship, I intend to use an extreme question as my springboard: what is presupposed by the fact of isolating oneself with another in order to teach him what he is lacking?

This situation is still more redoubtable if we consider that, by the very nature of transference, he will find out what he is lacking insofar as he loves [*en tant qu'aimant*]. If I am there for his own good, it is certainly not in the comfortable old sense in which the Thomist tradition articulates it as *Amare est velle bonum alicui*, since this "good" [*bien*] is already a term that is more than just problematic. If you were willing to grant what I said last year, you know that it is outdated.

I am not there, in the final analysis, for a person's own good, but in order that he love. Does this mean that I must teach him how to love? Clearly it seems difficult to avoid this necessity. As for what it means to love and what love is, we will have to indicate that the two things are not identical. As for what it means to love and to know what it is to love, I must at least, like Socrates, be able to credit myself with knowing something about it. Now if we take a look at the psychoanalytic literature, we see that this is what people talk about the least. It seems that love in its primordial, ambivalent coupling with hate is a self-evident term. Don't think of my humorous observations today as anything other than remarks designed to tickle your funny bone.

26   A long tradition, nevertheless, exists concerning love. It has most recently led to a huge harebrained lucubration by Anders Nygren who splits it into two radically opposed terms: Eros and Agápe. But before that, people debated about nothing else for centuries. Isn't it astonishing that we analysts – who make use of love and talk about nothing else – can be said to present ourselves as truly deficient when compared to this tradition? We haven't made even a partial attempt to add to – much less revise – what has been developed over the centuries on the subject of love or provide something that might be not unworthy of this tradition. Isn't that surprising?

In order to bring this home to you, I have selected as the subject matter for my next class a text of truly monumental interest, which lies at the origin of our whole tradition concerning the structure of love – Plato's *Symposium*.

If someone who is sufficiently interested wants to dialogue with me about it, I anticipate that it can only be to our advantage to read a text that is chock full of enigmas, where everything remains to be demonstrated – especially everything that the very mass of religious lucubrations that has permeated every fiber of our being, that is present in all our experiences, owes to this extraordinary testament to Plato's *Schwärmerei*.

I'll show you what we can find in it and what we can deduce from it by way of essential landmarks, even regarding the history of the debate about what really took place in the first psychoanalytic transference. I think that, once we have put it to the test, you will have no doubt as to our ability to find all the possible keys in it.

Assuredly, these are not terms that I would easily allow to be published in a summary of our work, since they are so showy. Nor are they formulations that I would like to have repeated outside of this room to furnish fodder for the usual tomfoolery. I will expect you to take into account this year among whom we find ourselves and who we are.

November 16, 1960

THE MAINSPRING OF LOVE

A COMMENTARY ON PLATO'S *SYMPOSIUM*

II

SET AND CHARACTERS

Alcibiades.
Scholars.
The *Symposium*, a session.
Recording on the brain.
Greek love.

Today we are going to begin our examination of the *Symposium*. At least that is what I promised you.

What I spoke about last time seems to have affected you in different ways. The tasters have been sampling the vintage. "Will it be a good year?" they wonder. I can only hope no one will dwell for too long on what may appear approximate in certain of the strokes with which I am trying to sketch out our path.

Last time I tried to show you the pillars of the scene that provides the context for what I have to say about transference. It should be quite clear that my reference to the body, in particular when beauty may be one of its attributes, was not simply an opportunity to be witty regarding transference.

It has been objected that in movies, which I took as an example of widespread views about psychoanalysts' looks, it sometimes happens that the psychoanalyst is a good-looking guy, and not only in the exceptional case I mentioned. My response is that such is the case precisely when analysis is taken as an occasion for comedy.

In short, you will see that the main points I brought out last time find their justification in the path we shall have to follow today.

How shall I relate what is at stake in the *Symposium*? It isn't easy, given the style and limits imposed upon me by my position and objective, which, let it not be forgotten, is specifically that of psychoanalytic practice. To set myself the task of making a nice orderly commentary of this extraordinary text would perhaps require me to make a long detour, which would then leave us too little time for other parts of the field to which the *Symposium* seems to me to provide an illuminating introduction – this is why I chose it. It will thus be necessary to proceed in a way which is obviously not that of what one might call academic commentary.

Furthermore, I must assume that at least some of you are not truly familiar with Plato's work. I'm not saying that I consider myself thoroughly equipped in this regard either. But I do have enough experience with it, and enough of a grasp of it, to think that I can allow myself to direct a spotlight on the *Symposium* while giving proper consideration to the whole backdrop of the dialogue. Moreover, I bid those who are equipped to do so to monitor what I say, and to let me know, should the occasion arise, what might be, not arbitrary – it obviously must be – but forced or off the mark in its arbitrariness.

What's more, I have nothing against a certain roughness or newness – I even think it should be emphasized – in taking up a text like the *Symposium*. This is why you will excuse me for presenting it to you in a way that is a bit paradoxical at first, or that may seem paradoxical to you.

It seems to me that whoever reads the *Symposium* for the first time, if he is not obsessed with the fact that it is a text from a respected tradition, cannot fail to feel flabbergasted, to put it approximately.

I would go still further. If he has a bit of historical imagination, he must wonder how such a thing could have been preserved for us throughout what I would willingly refer to as the generations of monks and ignoramuses, all of them vocationally unsuited to transmit a text to us that is quite akin – due to at least one of its parts, in other words, its end, and one cannot but be struck by this fact – to (and why not just say so?) what is nowadays called a specialized literary genre, the kind that may fall within the ambit of police investigations.

Indeed, if you simply know how to read – and just once won't hurt you (I think that after my announcement the last time many of you went out and bought the text, and have thus no doubt had a look at it) – you cannot help but be struck at least by what transpires in the second part of this dialogue between Alcibiades and Socrates.

What transpires between Alcibiades and Socrates goes beyond the limits of the symposium itself.

1

What then is a symposium?

It is a ceremony with rules, a sort of ritual, intimate contest among the elite, or parlor game. The holding of such a symposium is thus not simply an occasion for Plato's dialogue, but refers to the mores and real customs variously observed in different localities in Greece, and, I might add, in certain cultural strata. The regulation imposed is by no means unusual: each person must do his share by giving a short speech on a specific topic.

A rule is announced at the beginning of this symposium that no one is to drink to excess. The reason why is ostensibly that most of the people there already have splitting headaches from having drunk a bit too much the day before, but it also makes us appreciate the importance and gravity of the elite group formed by the fellow drinkers assembled that evening. Something nevertheless happens that was not expected – pandemonium, as it were.

At a point at which the meeting is far from over, and at which a guest by the name of Aristophanes is about to say something – to rectify some point or request an explanation [212c] – a group of people turn up at the doorstep and enter, all of whom are completely smashed, namely, Alcibiades and his companions. And Alcibiades, in a rather offhand manner, takes it upon himself to preside over the symposium, and begins to speak of things whose scandalous nature I intend to bring out.

This requires our forming a certain notion of who and what Alcibiades and Socrates are, which will take us quite far afield.

For the commonly accepted account, read what Plutarch says in his *Lives of the Noble Grecians and Romans*, and you will get an idea of Alcibiades' general character. But you will have to make an effort there too, for his life is described by Plutarch in what I will call an Alexandrian atmosphere – in other words, a funny time in history where everything seems to transform characters into mere shadows of themselves. I am referring to the moralistic tone of the works that have been handed down to us from that era, involving a coming out of the shadows, or νεκυία (*nekuia*) as it's put in the *Odyssey*. Plutarch's fabrications or characters, colored by the fact of having, moreover, served as models or paradigms for the whole of the moralist tradition that followed, have a *je ne sais quoi* that reminds us of zombies. It isn't easy to make veritable blood flow anew through their veins. But try to imagine, on the basis of the one-of-a-kind career Plutarch outlines for us, who Alcibiades could have been, this man who shows up before Socrates – in other words, before he who declares elsewhere that he was Alcibiades' πρῶτος ἐραστής (*prótos erastés*), the first to have ever loved Alcibiades.

Alcibiades was a sort of early Alexander. All of his political adventures were beyond a shadow of a doubt marked with the stamp of defiance and extraordinary daring – *tour de force* – and

32

the inability to either situate or stop himself at any point. He would turn the situation around wherever he went, snatching victory from the jaws of defeat for whichever camp he aligned with, but would be chased away or exiled by everyone – precisely, it must be pointed out, because of his misdeeds.

It seems that Athens lost the Peloponnesian War because the city felt the need to call Alcibiades back from the fray right in the middle of the hostilities to make him account for an obscure event, that of the so-called mutilation of the ἑρμαῖ (*hermaî*), which, with hindsight, strikes us as just as inexplicable as it is far-fetched, but which surely involved at its root an element of profanation and, strictly speaking, insult to the gods.

Nor can we completely let Alcibiades and his companions off the hook. The people of Athens were no doubt justified in calling him to account. The practice in question was suggestive, by analogy, of some kind of black mass. We cannot but notice the context of insurrection and subversion of the polis' laws from which a character like Alcibiades emerges – a context implying a break with and contempt for the forms, traditions, laws, and no doubt religion itself.

This is the kind of disturbing background he brought with him. He also exercised, wherever he went, a truly remarkable fascination on people [*séduction*]. After the suit brought against him by the people of Athens, he sided with the enemy, Sparta, he himself having played a role in setting the two cities at odds, since prior to that he had done everything in his power to ensure that the peace talks between them fell through.

So he sided with Sparta, and right away found nothing better, nothing more worthy of his fame, than to get the queen pregnant, in plain sight of and with full cognizance of everyone. It turned out that it was well known that the king, Agis, had not slept with his wife for ten months, for reasons I'll spare you. The queen thus bore Alcibiades' child. "I didn't do it for pleasure's sake," he tells us, "but rather because it seemed a worthy undertaking to ensure a throne to my descendants, and to thus honor Sparta's throne with someone of my lineage."

As you may well imagine, such things can captivate people for a while, but are not easily forgiven. You know, of course, that Alcibiades, after having bestowed this present – along with several ingenious ideas concerning battle tactics – set up headquarters elsewhere, taking the opportunity to do so in a third camp, that of the Persians. He paid a visit to the person who represented the power of the king of Persia in Asia Minor, namely, Tissaphernes, who, Plutarch tells us, hardly liked Greeks – in fact he hated them, but he was taken with [*séduit*] Alcibiades.

From then on Alcibiades knuckled down to the business of restoring Athens' good fortune. He did so thanks to conditions whose history is also highly surprising, as it seems that it was in the thick of a network of double agents and constant double-crossing. All the warnings he sent the Athenians were immediately rerouted and passed on to Sparta and to the Persians themselves, who then informed the person in the Athenian fleet who had passed on the news, such that Alcibiades wound up being informed, in turn, that people in high places were perfectly well aware that he had betrayed them.

In any case, each of these people got on as best he could. What is clear is that in the midst of all this, Alcibiades reversed Athens' fortune. And consequently, although we cannot be absolutely sure of the particulars, which vary from one ancient historian's account to another, we should not be surprised to learn that Alcibiades returned to Athens with all the signs of an unprecedented triumph that, despite the joy of the Athenian people, marked the beginning of a swinging back of the pendulum of public opinion. For here we are dealing with someone who could not avoid being, at every turn of the way, the kind of guy about whom people could not but have an opinion.

34

His death, too, was very strange. Questions remain as to who was responsible for it. It seems that, after a series of reversals of fortune, each more astonishing than the one before – as if, in any case, regardless of the trouble he got into, he could never be defeated – a sort of immense tide of hatred ended up doing him in, employing the means that legend or myth tells us must be used with scorpions. He was surrounded by a circle of fire – but he managed to escape from it, and it was only at some distance that he could be laid low with javelins and arrows.

Such was Alcibiades' incomparable career. While I have highlighted his highly active, exceptional, powerful, penetrating mind, I would nevertheless say that this character's most salient feature was the added luster of what is said of his looks [beauté]. Not only his precocious good looks as a child, insofar as we know that it is altogether related to the history of the dominant form of love at that time in Greece, namely, love for children, but also his long-preserved attractiveness, which even late in life made him someone who seduced people as much with his looks as with his exceptional intelligence.

Such was the man. Here we see him show up at the symposium, at this contest assembling serious learned men, albeit in the context of Greek love, which I'll stress later, that already provides a backdrop of constant eroticism to the speeches on love. He tells everyone about something that can be summed up in these words: the vain efforts he made when he was young, when Socrates loved him, to get Socrates to fuck him.

He goes into it at length, furnishing plenty of details and describing it in the crassest of terms. He quite clearly wanted to make Socrates lose control, show some emotional turmoil, and yield to direct corporal come-ons – physical contact. All of this is said publicly, by a man who is drunk, no doubt, but whose words Plato doesn't consider it beneath his dignity to repeat right down to the last detail.

I'm not sure I'm getting my point across. Imagine that a book comes out, not now – for Plato brings it out some 50 years after the scene it relates took place. But imagine that a book comes out some time in the future, to avoid ruffling anyone's feathers, in which a celebrity, Kennedy, for example, a Kennedy who is simultaneously James Dean, recounts in a book designed for the elites that he did everything, when he was in college, to get ＿＿ to make love to him – I'll let you fill in the blank with someone's name. You needn't absolutely restrict yourself to teachers, since Socrates was not exactly a teacher, but he was one all the same, a rather unusual one at that. Imagine that it is someone like Massignon, and at the same time Henry Miller. That would make waves, and would spell trouble for Jean-Jacques Pauvert who would publish the book. Keep this in mind when considering that it is thanks to those who we must call the Brothers variously ignoramus that this astonishing book has been handed down to us through the centuries, such that we no doubt have the complete text. This is what I was thinking, not without some degree of admiration, in thumbing through the admirable edition Henri Estienne gave us, which includes a Latin translation. This edition is quite definitive – it is such a perfect critical edition that even now, in all other editions, whether more or less scholarly, its pagination is provided. Those of you for whom this is all a bit new should know that the little 872a's and so on you see in the margins refer to Henri Estienne's pagination dating back to 1575.

Henri Estienne certainly wasn't an ignoramus [un ignorantin], but it's a bit hard to believe that someone who was capable of devoting himself to compiling such monumental editions – though this wasn't all he did – was sufficiently open to life to fully appreciate the contents of this text, inasmuch as it is a text about love.

Other people were interested in love during the same era as Henri Estienne, and I can certainly tell you that, when I talked last year at length about sublimation as concerns love for women, the author I didn't mention was neither Plato, nor any other scholar, but rather

Marguerite de Navarre. I alluded to her without spelling it out. Keep in mind that, for the sort of banquet or symposium constituted by her *Heptaméron*, she carefully excluded the people with ink on their hands who appeared at the time as overhaulers of the contents of libraries. She wanted only cavaliers and lords, people who, when speaking of love, spoke of something they had time to experience. And in all commentaries on the *Symposium*, it is this very dimension which is often lacking, leaving something to be desired. But that is of little consequence.

36

For those who never wonder whether their understanding, as Jaspers says, extends to the limits of the concrete, perceptible, or comprehensible, the story of Alcibiades and Socrates has always been hard to swallow. By way of proof I need but mention the fact that Louis [or Loys] Le Roy, Ludovicus Regius, the first French translator of these texts that had just surfaced in Western culture from the Orient, quite simply stopped translating when he reached Alcibiades' entrance. He went no further. It seemed to him that enough fine speeches had already been made – which is, indeed, true. The scene with Alcibiades seemed to Le Roy superfluously tacked on – apocryphal.

He wasn't the only person to behave this way either. I'll spare you the details, but one day Racine received the manuscript of a translation of the *Symposium* from a lady who had worked on it, asking him to look it over. Racine, a sensitive man, considered it to be untranslatable – not just the story of Alcibiades, but the whole *Symposium*. We have his notes, which prove that he looked very closely at the manuscript that had been sent to him. But as for correcting it, for it required nothing less than total revamping – only someone like Racine could translate the Greek – he refused. It didn't tickle his fancy.

Third reference: a long time ago I was lucky enough to come across handwritten notes of a course on Plato given by Victor Brochard, which had been tucked away somewhere. They are quite remarkable: the notes were exceptionally well taken, the writing exquisite and, concerning the theory of love, Brochard referred to everything relevant – the *Lysis*, the *Phaedrus*, and above all the *Symposium*. But he plays a very cute little game of substitution when it comes to the part about Alcibiades – he shifts gears and redirects things toward the *Phaedrus*, which becomes his new focus. He doesn't take it upon himself to account for the story of Alcibiades.

This reserve on his part is rather deserving of our respect. It at least attests to his sense that there was something there that raised a question. And I prefer this to seeing it resolved by the sorts of unusual hypotheses that are not infrequently proposed.

The most amazing of them, never in a million years would you guess it – and Léon Robin rallies to it, which is astonishing – is that Plato was concerned in this last scene to make people give his master his due. Scholars have discovered that, several years after Socrates' death, a man by the name of Polycrates brought out a pamphlet in which one sees Socrates collapse under the weight of various accusations that are conveyed by three people. Polycrates is supposed to have made one of the three, Anytus, furnish an indictment whose main claim was that Socrates was responsible for what I told you about earlier – namely, the trail of corruption and scandal Alcibiades left in his wake his whole life long, including the string of problems, if not catastrophes, he created.

It must be agreed that the idea that Plato was trying to exonerate Socrates and his mores, if not his influence, by presenting us with such a scene of public confession, has truly got it all backward. What could people who come up with such hypotheses possibly be thinking? The idea that Socrates resisted Alcibiades' come-ons, and that this, in and of itself, would justify presenting this part of the *Symposium*, insofar as it was designed to improve the public's view of Socrates' mission, personally leaves me dumbfounded.

One of the two following things must be true – either we have to come to grips with a whole series of reasons Plato never mentions or else this scene in fact serves a purpose. Why does Alcibiades burst in? And why does he sit beside Socrates, who can be associated with him, who no doubt hails from a rather more distant shore, but who is the most indissolubly bound up with him in some way? Alcibiades' arrival here in the flesh is, in fact, closely related to the question of love.

Let us now see what it's about, since this is the focal point of everything at stake in the *Symposium*. It is here that will be most deeply illuminated, not so much the nature of love, but what interests us in this context – namely, the relationship between love and transference. This is why I am emphasizing the shift [*l'articulation*] between the speeches given at the symposium – at least according to the text of it that is reported to us – and Alcibiades' bursting onto the scene.

2

First I must sketch out for you the meaning of these speeches, but even before that, I must say something about the text thereof which is communicated to us – in other words, the narrative.

What is this text? And what is Plato telling us? One can raise this question right from the outset. Is it fiction or a fabrication, as many of his dialogues clearly are, being compositions that obey certain laws? Lord knows that much could be said about this. Why this genre? Why this law of the dialogue? We will have to leave certain things aside, and I will simply indicate to you that there is a whole lot to know in this vein. But the *Symposium* nevertheless has another feature that is not so very different from the way in which certain of his other dialogues are presented to us.

To give you a glimpse of what I mean, first let me say that we are going to take the *Symposium* as a sort of account of psychoanalytic sessions. For it is indeed a question of something like that. As the dialogue progresses, and the contributions by the different persons participating in the symposium lead one to the next, something happens, which is that each flash is illuminated by the one that follows, and then at the end, life – Alcibiades' presence – bursts onto the scene, this being reported to us as a raw and even disturbing fact. It is up to us to grasp the meaning of Alcibiades' speech.

Assuming then that this is what we are dealing with, we have, according to Plato, a sort of recording of it. As there were no tape recorders at the time, we'll call it a recording on the brain.

Recording on the brain is an exceedingly old practice, which under-lay for many centuries the way people who participated in serious events listened, for as long as writing hadn't taken on the dominant role in our culture that it has nowadays. Since things can be written, those that are to be remembered are remembered for us in what I've called the kilos of language – stacks of books and piles of paper. But when paper was rarer and books far more difficult to manufacture and distribute, it was essential to have a good memory, and, if I may say so, to experience everything one heard with an eye to storing it in one's memory. It is not simply at the beginning of the *Symposium*, but in all the traditions we know of, that we find evidence that the oral transmission of the sciences and wisdom was absolutely essential. It is by this pathway, moreover, that we know something of them. In the absence of writing, the oral tradition served as their medium.   39

This is what Plato is referring to when he tells us how the text of the *Symposium* comes down to us. He has someone named Apollodorus tell the story. We know this character because he existed historically. He is supposed to have come into the picture just over 30 years before the appearance of the *Symposium*, if we take its date of publication as *circa* 370 B.C. It is thus before Socrates' death that Apollodorus hears, Plato tells us, the account of what happened. And Apollodorus is supposed to have heard it from Aristodemus, who attended the supposed symposium 16 years earlier, since we are given to believe it took place in 416 B.C.

It is thus 16 years after the fact that a character extracts from his memory the verbatim text of what was supposedly said. Consequently, the least one can say is that Plato takes all the necessary steps to make us believe in this brain recording which was widely practiced, and which was always practiced in such phases of culture. He stresses the fact that "Aristodemus," I am quoting 178a, "couldn't remember exactly what everyone said," no more than Apollodorus himself did – parts of the tape were damaged and there might be gaps at certain points. Obviously none of this can definitively answer the question of historical veracity, but it nevertheless rings true. If it is a lie, it is a pretty one. And as it is, moreover, manifestly a work on love – and we will perhaps come to where the notion arises that, after all, only liars can fittingly respond to love – the *Symposium* would certainly seem to be the choice reference, concerning love, of Socrates' action. This, indeed, is conveyed to us unambiguously.

This is clearly why the *Symposium* is such an important piece of evidence. We know that Socrates himself asserts that he truly knows only about what falls under the heading of love. No doubt the *Theages*, where he says so, was not written by Plato, but it is nevertheless a dialogue by someone who wrote about what was known of Socrates and what had been handed down about him. In it, Socrates is attested to have expressly said that he knew nothing, all in all, but this little bit, σμικροῦ τινος (*smikroú tinos*), of science, μαθήματος (*mathématos*), which concerns matters of love, τῶν ἐρωτικῶν (*tón erotikón*). Socrates repeats this, and in exactly the same terms, at one point in the *Symposium* [177d].

What is the topic of the *Symposium*? The topic was proposed by the character, Phaedrus [177a–c]. He is no other than the character for whom another dialogue was named, one I referred to last year regarding beauty, in which love is also discussed, for the two are linked in Plato's thought. Phaedrus is said to be πατὴρ τοῦ λόγου (*patér toú lógou*), the father of the topic that is taken up in the *Symposium* [177d]. The topic is the following – what is the purpose of being knowledgeable about love? And we know that Socrates claims to be knowledgeable about nothing else.

It becomes still more striking when the following remark is made, a remark you will be able to fully appreciate when you go back to the text – Socrates says almost nothing in his own name. I will tell you today if we have time that this almost-nothing is important – I even think we are reaching the point where I can say so – it is no doubt essential, for it is around this almost-nothing that the scene really revolves, and that they begin, as was to be expected, to truly delve into the topic.

40

Socrates, in a sense, calibrates or adjusts the level at which things must be taken up and, in the final analysis, he does not rate love as highly as all that compared to the others present. What he says consists rather in framing [*cadrer*] things, adjusting the lights in such a way that one sees precisely the level, which is middling. If Socrates tells us something, it is assuredly that love is not divine. He doesn't rate it that highly, but it is nevertheless what he loves. In fact, he loves it and it alone.

It is worth pointing out the moment at which he begins to speak – just after Agathon. I will bring the characters in one at a time, instead of presenting them all at the outset. There is Phaedrus, Pausanias, and Aristodemus who is a party crasher – in other words, he ran into Socrates, and Socrates brought him along. There is also Eryximachus who counts as a colleague for most of you since he is a medical doctor, and Agathon who is the host. Socrates, who invited Aristodemus, arrives very late because, on the way, he had what we might call a fit [*crise*]. Socrates' fits consisted in stopping short, and standing still in some spot on one foot. That evening he stopped at the house next door where he had no business being. He remained glued there in the foyer between the umbrella stand and the coat rack, and there was no way to rouse him. One must provide a bit of atmosphere for these things. These stories are not nearly as boring as they make them out to be in junior high school.

Some day I'd like to give a talk – in which I'd take my examples from the *Phaedrus*, or from one of Aristophanes' plays – on an absolutely essential trait without which there is no way of understanding how what I will call the lit circle is situated in everything Antiquity has bequeathed us.

We live in the midst of constant light. The night is brought to us on a stream of neon. But try to imagine that up until a relatively recent era – there's no need to go back as far as Plato – night was night. When, at the beginning of the *Phaedrus*, someone comes knocking to wake up Socrates because he has to rise a little before daybreak – I hope it's in the *Phaedrus*, but that's of little importance, it's at the beginning of one of Plato's dialogues – it's a whole to-do. He gets up and finds himself truly in the dark, for he knocks things over at every step. The same thing happens at the beginning of one of Aristophanes' plays. When one is in the dark, one is truly in the dark. It is at such times that you cannot recognize the person who is touching your hand.

The *Heptaméron*, to mention what was still common in Marguerite de Navarre's era, is full of stories that turn on the fact that at that time, when you slipped into a lady's bed at night, it was considered entirely possible to pass yourself off as her husband or her lover, as long as you kept your mouth shut. It seems that went on all the time. Obviously, what I will call, with an altogether different meaning, the spreading of light, changes many things in the realm of human relations. To us, night is not a consistent reality – it cannot be poured from a ladle or form a blanket of darkness. That deprives us of certain things, many things.

All of this to return to our topic, which is that to which we must come – namely, what is signified by the lit circle in which we find ourselves, and what was at issue when love was talked about in Greece.

42

When it was talked about, well, as Mr. de La Palice would say, it was Greek love that was at issue.

3

You'll have to get used to the idea that Greek love was love for pretty boys. And . . . that's it.

It is quite clear that when people spoke of love they were speaking of nothing else. All the attempts we make to situate this in its proper context are doomed to failure. To try to see exactly what it is, we are no doubt obliged to push back the furniture in a certain way, re-establish certain perspectives, and look at it from a different angle, by saying that there wasn't necessarily only that, obviously, naturally. The fact remains that, as far as love was concerned, that's all there was.

You will tell me that love for boys is something that was universally accepted. Some of our contemporaries have been saying so for a long time, regretting that they weren't born a bit earlier. But no. The fact remains that in a whole part of Greece it was not at all thought well of, and that in a whole other part of Greece – Pausanias says so himself in the *Symposium* – it was thought well of. And as it was in the totalitarian part of Greece, among the Boeotians and Spartans, where everything that was not prohibited was compulsory, that it was not only thought well of, but the mandatory form of service, there was no getting around it. There are people who are far superior to us, says Pausanias – it's well thought of by we Athenians, but it's prohibited nevertheless, and naturally that makes it all the more invaluable [182].

All of this teaches us little, except that it was more credible, on condition that we understand more or less what it corresponded to. To get some idea of it, we must refer back to what I said last year about courtly love. It wasn't the same thing, but it served an analogous function in the society. It was quite obviously a kind of sublimation – recall that I tried last year to provide a slight rectification in your minds regarding the real function of sublimation.

It involved nothing that we can situate within the register of   43
regression on a societal scale. While it is true that psychoanalytic
theory points to fraternity among men as the basis of the social
bond – homosexuality attaching man to the neutralization of the
bond – that's not what is at issue here. It is not in the least a question of the dissolution of the social bond and a return to some sort
of innate form. It is obviously something else – it is a fact of culture.
This form of love was practiced by the masters of Greece – people
of a certain social class and milieu, people at a level at which culture
reigned supreme and was developed. This love was obviously the
great center of elaboration of interpersonal relationships.

Let me remind you, in another guise, of what I indicated at the
end of an earlier Seminar – the schema of the relationship between
perversion and culture, insofar as culture is distinct from society.
While society leads, via censorship, to a form of disintegration which
is called neurosis, perversion can be understood, contrariwise, as a
kind of elaboration, construction, or even sublimation – to use that
word – when it is a product of culture. The circle closes: perversion
contributes elements that shape [*travaillent*] society, and neurosis
favors the creation of new cultural elements.

This doesn't stop Greek love from being a perversion, however
sublimated it may be. No culturalist viewpoint can prevail here. Let
it not be retorted, on the basis of the pretext that it was an accepted,
approved, and even celebrated perversion, that it was not a perversion. Homosexuality still was what it is, a perversion. To maintain,
in order to be accommodating, that if we treat homosexuality, it's
because in our era it's something else altogether – it's no longer in
style, while at the time of the Greeks it served a cultural function,
and was as such worthy of our highest regard – is truly to skirt the
issue.

The only thing that distinguishes contemporary homosexuality from Greek perversion is, I believe – well – hardly to be found
anywhere but in the quality of its objects. High-school students
here are pimply and turned into blithering idiots by the education
they receive. In Greece, the conditions were favorable for their
being objects of homage, without it being necessary to go find these
objects in dark alleys or in the gutter. That's the whole difference.   44
But the structure is in no way different.

This is scandalous given the eminent dignity we have bestowed
upon the Greek message. People shroud themselves in this context
in fine words. "Nevertheless," they say, "don't think women weren't
paid suitable homage, for all that. Don't forget that Socrates, for
example, in the *Symposium*, while saying very little in his own name,
has a woman, Diotima, speak in his stead. Don't you see that this

proves the supreme homage was paid, even in Socrates' own words, to women?" That, at least, is what the kind souls never fail to trot out in this context. And they add, "You know, from time to time he went to visit Lais, Aspasia, and Theodota who was Alcibiades' mistress" – anything and everything they can find in the gossip of the historians. And then there's the amazing Xanthippus [Socrates' wife] to whom I alluded last week. "She was there the day of his death, you know, and she even wailed so loudly she deafened all around." There's just one hitch – it is attested to in the *Phaedo* – and it is that Socrates bids those present to get her out of there as quickly as possible and put her to bed straight away so that they can talk in peace, there being only a few hours left. If it weren't for that, the dignity of women in Greece would be safe and sound.

Personally, I don't question the importance of women in ancient Greek society. I would even say it was rather considerable, and you will see its import in what follows. The fact is that they had what I would call their true place. And not only their true place, but an altogether eminent role in love relations. We have all kinds of proof thereof. It turns out, in fact, assuming, as usual, that we know how to read – you can't read ancient authors with blinders – that they had a role that is veiled for us, but that is nevertheless eminently theirs in love: quite simply the active role. The difference between the women of Antiquity and modern women is that the women of Antiquity demanded their due – they attacked men.

This is quite palpable in many cases. Once you have opened your eyes to this point of view, you will notice many things in ancient history that otherwise seem strange. Aristophanes, who was a very fine music-hall director, did nothing to conceal how the women of his time behaved. There has never been anything more characteristic and direct concerning women's doings, and this is precisely why learned love [*l'amour savant*], so to speak, sought refuge elsewhere. We have here one of the keys to the question, and it is not such as to surprise psychoanalysts terribly much.

All of this may seem to be a rather long detour for our undertaking, which is to analyze a text that aims at discovering what it means to be learned in love. Please excuse this detour. We know that the *Symposium* dates back to the time of Greek love and that this love was, so to speak, "schoolish," in other words, love of pupils. For technical reasons – for reasons of simplification, exemplification, and use as a model – this love allows us to understand a connection [*articulation*] that is always elided in what is overly complicated in love involving women. It is in this respect that this love for school[boys] [*amour de l'école*] can legitimately provide us and everyone with schooling in love [*d'école de l'amour*].

45

Which doesn't mean it should be reinstituted. I would like to avoid all possible misunderstandings – soon people will be saying that I am advocating Platonic love. There are many reasons why it can no longer serve as a love school. Were I to tell you which reasons, I would be making great lunging thrusts with a sword into the curtains without being sure what lies behind them. I generally avoid such things, believe me. There are reasons why it should not be reinstituted, and why it would even be impossible to do so. One of the reasons, which will perhaps surprise you if I propose it here, is that for us, at the stage we are at, love – and its phenomenon, culture, and dimension – has for some time now been disconnected from beauty. That may surprise you, but that's the way it is.

Even if you haven't yet noticed, you will if you reflect a bit. Consider it from both sides, from that of beautiful artworks, on the one hand, and from that of love, on the other, and you will realize that it is true. It is, in any case, a condition that makes it difficult to prepare you to see what is at stake, and it is precisely why I have taken this long detour. We now return to beauty, whose tragic function I brought out last year, since it supplies the true meaning of what Plato tells us about love.

Moreover, it is quite clear that, currently, love is no longer situated at the level of tragedy at all, nor at another level I'll talk about later. It is at the level of what is called Polyhymnia in Agathon's speech [187e]. This is the level of what presents itself as the most vivid materialization of what is essential in fiction, which for us is film.

Plato would be overjoyed by this invention. There is no better illustration in the arts of what Plato places at the beginning of his vision of the world. What is expressed in his myth of the cave is illustrated every day for us by the dancing beams that shine on the screen, showing all our feelings in a shadowy state. In contemporary art, the defense and illustration of love most clearly belong to this dimension.

This is why I told you before – a remark that was not without eliciting your reluctance, made as it was as an aside, but which will nevertheless be the linchpin of our progress here – that love is a comical feeling. But an effort is necessary to arrive at the focal point at which one can appropriately appreciate its import.

There are two things that I've noted about love in my prior work, and I will remind you of them here.

The first is that love is a comical feeling. You will see what illustrates it in our investigation, and we will come full circle in this regard, which will allow us to bring up again what is essential – the true nature of comedy. It is so essential and indispensable that it is

why there is in the *Symposium* a presence that, for a long time, commentators were never able to explain, that of Aristophanes, who
was nevertheless, historically speaking, Socrates' sworn enemy.

The second thing I wanted to mention, which we'll come across
constantly and which will serve us as a guide, is that love is giving
what you don't have. You will also see this appear in one of the
essential full spirals of what we will encounter in our commentary.

In any case, to begin the step-by-step examination by which
Socrates' speech will have an enlightening function for us, let us
assume that Greek love allows us to isolate in a love relationship
the two partners in the neuter. It is a question of something pure
that is naturally expressed in the masculine, and that first allows us
to articulate what happens in love at the level of the couple formed
by the lover and the beloved, ἐραστὴς (*erastés*) and ἐρώμενος (*erómenos*), respectively.

Next time I will show you how the process that unfolds in the
Symposium allows us to characterize these two functions, the
lover and the beloved, with all the rigor of which psychoanalysis is
capable.

In other words, at a time at which psychoanalysis did not yet exist,
and the unconscious in its true function in relation to the subject was
assuredly the most unsuspected of dimensions – thus with all the
limitations this implies – something was quite explicitly articulated
that converges with the crowning point of our experience, the same
thing I tried to lay out for you under the twofold heading of *The
Relation to the Object*, one year, and *Desire and Its Interpretation*
two years later. To formulate it in the terms we arrived at, you will
clearly see that the lover appears here as the desiring subject [*le sujet
du désir*], with all the weight that the term "desire" has for us, and
the beloved as the only one in the couple who has something.

The question is to figure out whether or not what he has bears a
relation, I would even go so far as to say, any relation whatsoever,
to what the other, the desiring subject, is lacking.

The question of the relations between desire and that upon which
it becomes fixated has already led us to the notion of desire qua
desire for something else. We arrived at this by analyzing the effects
of language on the subject. It is quite strange that a dialectic of love,
that of Socrates, that was established entirely by means of dialectic
and by putting the imperatorial effects of questioning as such to the
test, does not bring us to the same crossroads. It does much more –
it allows us to go beyond, and to grasp the moment at which a shift
or reversal occurs in which, from the conjunction of desire with its
object qua inadequate, the signification called love must arise.

Anyone who has not grasped this shift [*articulation*] and the conditions it implies in the symbolic, imaginary, and real, cannot grasp what is at work in the effect called transference, whose automatic functioning is so strange. Nor can he compare transference and love or gauge the share or dose of illusion or truth that must be attributed to each and both.

In this respect, the investigation to which I have introduced you today will turn out to be of inaugural importance to us.

November 23, 1960

III

THE METAPHOR OF LOVE

Phaedrus

The other's being: an object?
From "Know thyself" to "He doesn't know."
The gods belong to the real.
Orpheus, Alcestis, and Achilles.

Last time we ended with the positions of ἐραστὴς (*erastés*) and ἐρώμενος (*erómenos*), the lover and the beloved, the dialectic in the *Symposium* allowing us to present them as the basis, crux, or essential articulation of the problem of love.

The problem of love interests us insofar as it allows us to understand what happens in transference – and, to a certain extent, because of transference.

To justify such a long detour, which may seem superfluous to those of you who are attending this Seminar for the first time this year, I will try to help you immediately grasp the import of our study here.

1

It seems to me that at some stage of his training, something must occur to the psychoanalyst that can give him pause for thought at more than one turning of the way.

Isn't the simplest point – one that is difficult to avoid, it seems to me, starting at a certain age, and that must already pose for you, very directly and in and of itself, the problem of what love is – the following? Hasn't it ever struck you at some turning of the way that something was missing in what you gave to those closest to you? And not simply that something was missing, but that there was something that left the abovementioned loved ones irremediably missed by you? What could that be?

Being an analyst allows you to understand it – with those close to you, you have merely revolved around the fantasy that you have basically sought to satisfy through them. This fantasy has more or less replaced them with its own images and colors.

The being you can suddenly be reminded of by some accident, of which death is clearly the example that makes us best understand its full resonance, this veritable being – should you so much as call it to mind – flees and is already eternally lost. Yet it is this being that you are attempting to connect up with along the paths of your desire. But this being [*être-là*, which is also the French for *Dasein*] is yours. As analysts, you are well aware that it is, in some sense, because you failed to want it that you also basically missed it. But at least here you are at the level of something that is your own fault, and your failure reflects the precise magnitude of that fault.

Is it because you made mere objects, so to speak, of these other people you have cared for so poorly [*mal*]? Would that you *had* treated them like objects, objects whose weight, taste, and substance we savor! Today you would be less troubled by your memories of them. You would have given them their due, paid them the proper homage and love. You would have at least loved them as thyself, except that thou hardly [*mal*] lovest thyself. But it is not even the fate of the barely [*mal*] loved that we have all known. You wanted to make subjects, so to speak, of them – as if that were the end-all of the respect they deserved, respect, so to speak, for their dignity, the respect owed to your semblables.

I'm afraid that this neutralized use of the expression, "our semblables," is quite different from what is at issue in the question of love. I suspect that the respect you have for these semblables all too quickly tends to come down to chalking everything up to their whimsical resistance, narrow-minded ideas, and inborn stupidity – in short, to their own "beeswax." Let them work it out for themselves. This is, I think, the basic reason why you stop short of infringing on their freedom, one of your common behavioral traits. "Freedom to be indifferent [*Liberté d'indifférence*]," people say. However, it is not their freedom but rather yours.

It is here that a question arises in analysts' minds: "What is our relation to our patient's being?" We are well aware that it is what is at stake in analysis. Is our access to this being the access allowed by love? Does this access bear any relation to what we can know about the nature of love, beginning with the question that I am raising this year? As you will see, this will take us rather far. There is a metaphor in the *Symposium* that I intend to make use of in this regard. It seems, indeed, that there were, at the time, statues representing a satyr or a silenus on the outside, and inside of which something was

51

lodged, as in Russian dolls. We don't really know what was inside, but they were assuredly precious objects. In any case, Alcibiades compares Socrates to these small objects. My question will aim, but only at the end of our exploration, at what, in analysis, there must be, can be, or is supposed to be inside.

I am trying to broach the problem of the relation of the analysand to the analyst, which manifests itself in the odd phenomenon known as transference, in a way that homes in on it as closely as possible and that eludes its forms as little as possible. Every analyst knows it, but people more or less seek to extract its true weight or avoid it altogether. We can do no better, in this regard, than to begin with an investigation of what the phenomenon of transference is supposed to imitate to the greatest extent, even to the point of becoming indistinguishable from it – namely, love.

One of Freud's famous articles sets off in this direction, "Observations on Transference-Love," a text which is part of what are usually called his "Papers on Technique." It situates transference with respect to what it is closely related to. But there has always been an uncertainty in the problem of love, an internal dissension, some kind of duplicity, which is precisely what we must try to focus in on. It can be shed light on by the ambiguity of something else, which is the substitution that takes place in the process – which, after attending this Seminar for a while, you should know is something that happens in analytic action and that I can summarize for you.

He who seeks us out does so on the basis of the assumption that he doesn't know what he has, and the whole unconscious, the fundamental "he doesn't know," is already implied therein. It is in this way that a bridge is erected that can link up our new science with the whole "know thyself" [γνῶθι σαυτόν (gnóthi sautón)] tradition.

There is, of course, a fundamental difference. The emphasis shifts completely due to this "he doesn't know." I believe I've said enough about it already not to have to do anything other than point out the difference in passing.

52   It is a question of what the subject truly has in himself, of what asks to be educated, brought out, and cultured in accordance with all traditional pedagogical methods – which take refuge behind the fundamentally revelatory power of a dialectic, and are the shoots and suckers of Socrates' inaugural method insofar as it is philosophical. Is this where we are going to lead someone who seeks us out as analysts?

In your sole capacity as readers of Freud's work, you should already know something of what, at first glance at least, manifests itself as the paradox of what is considered to be the term, *telos*, end, or termination of analysis. What does Freud tell us if not that, in the final analysis, what is found at the end of this path by those who follow it is essentially nothing other than a lack?

Whether you call this lack "castration" or *Penisneid* ["penis envy"], it is a sign or metaphor. But if this is truly what analysis runs up against in the end, isn't there already some ambiguity here? In short, in recalling the twofold register between the beginning or theoretical starting point of an analysis and its end, it does not escape me that its first appearance may seem deceptive, and quite necessarily so. Its whole unfolding is nevertheless inscribed therein. The course of an analysis involves, strictly speaking, the thorough revelation of something that is called the unconscious Other.

To anyone who is listening to me talk about it for the first time – but I suspect this is not the case for any of you here – all of this can only be taken as an enigma. But that is not why I am presenting it to you – I am doing so in order to assemble the terms in which our action is formulated. It is also in order to immediately sketch out the general trajectory we will follow. It is but a question, for goodness' sake, of immediately apprehending the analogy between this unfolding and these terms, on the one hand, and the fundamental, original situation of love, on the other. The latter, while obvious, has never, to the best of my knowledge, been situated in the terms in which I propose that we articulate it right away, the two terms with which we are beginning: *erastés*, the lover (or ἐρῶν, *erón*, the one who loves [*l'aimant*]), and *erómenos*, the one who is loved (the beloved).

Isn't all of this best laid out right at the outset? There's no point playing hide-and-seek. We can see it right away in such a gathering – isn't it essentially what the *erastés* or lover is lacking that characterizes him for all those who come into contact with him? As analysts, we can immediately add that he knows not in what he is lacking, furnishing the particular accent of inscience that is characteristic of the unconscious.

On the other hand, hasn't the *erómenos* or loved object always been situated as the one who knows not what he has, what he has that is hidden, and which makes him appealing? Isn't what he has something that, in love relationships, is destined not only to be revealed, but to come into being, to be rendered present, whereas up until then it was merely possible? In short, let us state it with an analytic accent, or even without such an accent: the beloved doesn't know either. But it is a matter of something else in his case – he knows not what he has.

Note that the two terms that, in their essence, constitute the lover and the beloved in no way coincide. What the one is missing is not what is hidden in the other. This is the whole problem of love. Whether one knows it or not is of no consequence. In the phenomenon of love, at every step of the way one encounters the wrenching and discordance associated with it. No one needs, for all that, to dialogue [διαλέγεσθαι (*dialégesthai*)] or dialectize, διαλεκτικεύεσθαι (*dialektikeúesthai*) about love to be involved in this gap or discord – it suffices to be in the thick of it, to be in love.

Does that say it all? Is that sufficient? I can't go any further here. I'm already going pretty far in saying this. I am exposing myself to the risk of a certain immediate misunderstanding. But I have no intention here of misleading you, so I'll lay my cards on the table at once.

Of course things go further. We can provide here, in the terms we use, a formulation that takes up anew what is already indicated in the analysis of the creation of meaning in the signifier–signified relation, provided we are prepared to see in what follows how it should be handled and its truth. Love as a signifier – for to us it is a signifier and nothing else – is a metaphor, assuming that we have come to understand metaphor as substitution.

This is where we enter uncharted waters. For the time being I bid you to simply accept it, and to consider what I am saying as what it is: an algebraic formula. It is insofar as the function of *erastés* or the person who loves, as a lacking subject, comes to take the place of, or is substituted for, the function of *erómenos*, the loved object, that the signification of love is produced.

It will perhaps take me some time to explain this formulation. We have the time to do so in the year before us. At least I won't have failed to give you, right from the outset, this reference point which can serve, not as a riddle, but as a landmark that may help you navigate around certain ambiguities in the discussions to come.

54

2

Let us now enter into the *Symposium* whose set I depicted and whose characters I presented last time.

These characters have nothing primitive about them, despite the fact that they present us with a simplification of the problem [of love]. They are highly sophisticated characters – that's the word for it! Let me retrace now one of the staves [*portées*] I spoke with you about last time, for I think it's important that it be stated as provocatively as possible.

It really is quite funny that, in close to 24 centuries of religious thought, there hasn't been a single reflection on love, whether by libertines or clerics, which hasn't referred to this inaugural text. Now, after all, to someone who happens along unawares – to the country bumpkin who leaves his little patch of ground [*lopin*] outside Athens – this symposium, taken in its outer trappings, seems rather like a gathering of aging fairies, as people call them, a meeting of old faggots [*lopes*]. Socrates is 53, Alcibiades, who is apparently still handsome, is 36, and Agathon himself, whose house they are meeting at, is 30 – he has just won the prize for the best tragedy, and this is what allows us to precisely establish the year of the symposium [416 B.C.].

One must not stop at such outward appearances. It is always in sitting rooms – in other words, in places where people are not especially good-looking – at the homes of duchesses, in the course of an evening, that the most refined things are said. They are lost forever, naturally, but not for everyone, in any case not for those who say them. Here, for once, we have a chance to know what these characters, each in his turn, exchanged that particular evening.

A lot has been said of the *Symposium*. You don't need me to tell you that those whose job it is to be philosophers, philologists, and Hellenists have scrutinized it with a magnifying glass. I haven't exhausted the sum total of their remarks, though they are not inexhaustible, as they always revolve around one point. However far from inexhaustible they may be, it is nevertheless out of the question for me to go into all of the little debates that have sprung up over one line or another. First of all, it is not clear that it would prevent me from leaving out something important. And furthermore, it is not easy for me, being neither a philosopher, a philologist, nor a Hellenist, to put myself in their shoes and give you a class on the *Symposium*. All I can hope to do is to give you a first take on it.

I hope you won't imagine that I am relying on a first reading alone. Be so kind as to believe that I am not taking up this text for the first time strictly for the purposes of this Seminar. Be so kind as to also believe that I have taken some pains to refresh my memory of the works that have been devoted to the text, and to familiarize myself with those I had previously neglected.

I am telling you this to beg your pardon for having discussed the last part first. I did so because I think it's the best part. Of course, on the basis of the very method that I am teaching you, what I see in the text must be greeted by you with some reservations. It is here that I run the greatest risks – you should be grateful to me for running them in your stead. Let this serve simply as an introduction to your commentaries, which should not so much target what I am going to tell you about what I've understood, as what is in the text itself. The latter, after what I tell you, will seem to you to be what

55

attracted my attention. Whether my understanding of it be true or false, the signifiers that justify it in the text are impossible for you to ignore, even if you understand them differently than I do.

I will thus skip the first few pages, pages which are always found in Plato's dialogues. This dialogue is not like the others, but one nonetheless encounters here a situation constructed to create what I called the illusion of authenticity – distance, indications of transmission, of who repeated what another told him. This is always the way Plato attempts to create a certain depth at the outset, and it no doubt serves, in his eyes, to amplify what he has his characters say.

56   I will also skip over the rules I mentioned last time, the laws of the symposium. I indicated that the laws were not simply local or improvised, but based on a prototype. A symposium was something that had its laws – although no doubt not exactly the same ones everywhere, in Athens and in Crete, for example.

I will skip over all these references, in order to come to the unfolding of a ceremony that involves something that must have a name – a name which, I might mention in passing, can be debated – a "eulogy" of love. Is it ἐνκώμιον (enkómion) or is it ἐπαίνεσις (epaínesis)? I will skip that discussion – it is of interest, but only of secondary interest. Today I would simply like to situate the progression of events through the succession of speeches.

The first speech is made by Phaedrus. Phaedrus is another rather odd character. His character traits should be traced, although this is not terribly important. For the time being, you should simply know that it is odd that he is the one who proposed the topic, who is the πατὴρ τοῦ λόγου (patér toú lógou) [177d], the father of the topic, for we know him a bit from the beginning of the *Phaedrus* – he's a curious sort of hypochondriac. This may serve us a bit further on.

Now that I think of it, let me take the opportunity to apologize for something. When I spoke to you about darkness last time, I referred, I don't know why, to the *Phaedrus*. It occurred to me later that it is not the *Phaedrus* which begins with nighttime, but the *Protagoras*. That corrected, let us proceed.

Phaedrus, Pausanias, and Eryximachus. Aristophanes was supposed to have spoken before Eryximachus, but he had the hiccoughs and let Eryximachus speak before him. It is a perennial problem to figure out why Aristophanes, the comic poet, was there with Socrates, when everyone knows that he didn't just criticize Socrates, but ridiculed and defamed him in his comedies. Indeed, historians generally hold him partly responsible for Socrates' condemnation and tragic fate. There is no doubt a profound reason for his presence here, as I said, for which I am not offering, no more than anyone else, a final answer. But perhaps we can try to shed a few dim rays of light on the question.

Then comes Agathon, and after Agathon, Socrates. This constitutes what is, strictly speaking, the symposium, that is, everything that happens up until the crucial moment which, as I pointed out last time, should be considered essential: Alcibiades' entrance. The latter is accompanied by the breaking of all the rules of the symposium, if nothing else by the mere fact that Alcibiades shows up drunk, declares himself to be essentially drunk, and is thereby immersed in drunkenness as such.

Suppose you were to claim that the *Symposium* is of interest primarily because it shows how difficult it is to say something about love that holds water. If that were all that were at issue, we would be purely and simply mired in full-blown cacophony. But what Plato shows – at least this is what I maintain, and it is not especially audacious to do so – in a way that is never revealed or brought to light, is that the contour traced out by this difficulty indicates to us the point at which lies the fundamental topology which stops us from saying anything about love that holds water.

What I am saying here is not very new. No one dreams of disputing it, certainly none of the people who have studied this so-called "dialogue" – in quotes, because it is barely a text that deserves such a title, as it is a series of eulogies, a series of ditties or drinking songs in honor of love. Since, of course, the speakers at the symposium are a bit smarter than others, it takes on more importance. Moreover, we are informed that it is a topic that is not often selected, which might surprise us at first.

We are told that each person transposes the topic into his own key. But we don't really know why, for example, Phaedrus is given the task of introducing it from the standpoint, we are told, of religion, myth, or even ethnography. And, in effect, there is some truth in all of that. Our Phaedrus introduces love by telling us that it is μέγας θεὸς (*mégas theós*), a great god. That's not all he says, but he refers to two theologians, Hesiod and Parmenides, who, for different reasons, spoke of the genealogy of the gods, which is of great significance. I don't feel obliged to go into Hesiod's *Theogony* and Parmenides' *Poem* just because a verse of each is quoted by Phaedrus. I will nevertheless mention that two or three years ago, maybe four, a very important study of Parmenides' *Poem* came out, by a contemporary of ours by the name of Jean Beaufret. But let us leave that aside and try to figure out what there is in Phaedrus' discourse.

There is thus a reference to the gods in it. Why to the gods in the plural? I don't know what meaning the gods may have for you, especially the gods of Antiquity, but they are spoken about enough in this dialogue for it to be rather useful, if not necessary, that I answer as if you had asked me, "What do you really think of the gods? Where are they situated in relation to the symbolic, imaginary, and real?" It is not a pointless question by any means. Right up to the end of the *Symposium*, the question at issue is whether or not love is a god, and we make at least some progress by the end of the dialogue inasmuch as we know with certainty that it is not.

I am not going to give you a class in this context on the sacred. It will suffice if I make a few formulaic statements about the topic. The gods – insofar as they exist for us in the register that allows us to make headway in our practice, if it is true that my three categories are of any use to us whatsoever – quite certainly belong to the real. The gods are a mode by which the real is revealed.

This is why all philosophical progress tends, by its own inherent necessity, to eliminate them. And it is why Christian revelation, as Hegel so astutely remarked, is also situated along the path of their elimination – it is a bit more advanced, it goes a little further down the road that leads from polytheism to atheism. Compared to the notion of god as the height of revelation, of *numen*, as real shining and appearance – this is fundamental – the mechanism of Christian revelation is indisputably situated along the path that leads to the reduction and, in the final analysis, abolition of the notion. Indeed, it tends to displace the God of Christian revelation – and the same is true of dogma – onto the Word, Logos. Stated differently, it is situated on a path parallel to that trodden by the philosopher, insofar as he is destined to deny the gods.

Man will thus seek in Logos, in other words, at the level of signifying articulation, the revelations he encountered up until then in the real – in the real in which what revealed itself was, moreover, real – through the real that displaces [the God of Christian revelation].

This is what any investigation does which, at the outset of the philosophical approach, tends to articulate itself as science, and Plato teaches us, rightly or wrongly, faithfully or unfaithfully [*au vrai ou au pas vrai*], that this was what Socrates was doing. Socrates demanded that we not be content with that to which we have this innocent relation known as δόξα (*dóxa*) [opinion], and which is – why not, for God's sake? – sometimes right [*vrai*], but rather that we ask why, that we be satisfied only by the assured truth [*vrai assuré*] which he calls ἐπιστήμη (*epistéme*): science, knowledge that provides its reasons. This, Plato tells us, was the point of Socrates' φιλοσοφεῖν (*philosopheín*) [philosophizing].

I have already mentioned what I called Plato's *Schwärmerei*. One must indeed believe that something of his enterprise remained

59

stymied in the end, since the rigor and talent deployed in demonstrating such a method didn't stop so many things in Plato's work from being used by all the mystagogies. I am speaking above all of gnosis and of everything in Christianity itself which has always remained gnostic. The fact remains that it is clear that what Plato liked was science. How could we hold it against him for not having followed this path all the way, right from its very first step?

Whatever the case may thus be, to introduce the problem of love, Phaedrus refers to the notion that love is a great god, almost the oldest of the gods, born right after Chaos, Hesiod says. Love is also the first god thought of by the mysterious goddess, the primordial Goddess of Parmenides' poem.

We cannot now determine – and the enterprise is perhaps impossible to carry out in any case – everything these terms might have meant in Plato's day. But try, nevertheless, to entertain the idea that the first times people said these things, they could not possibly have had the appearance of stupefying provincialism they had, for example, in the seventeenth century in which, when one spoke of Eros, everyone played at it. In the 1600s, it was situated in a wholly different context, that of courtly culture, with echoes of *L'Astrée*, and all that followed – namely, words with no import. Here words have their full import, and the discussion is truly theological.

To convey this import, I have found nothing better than to tell you – if you really want to grasp it – to get a hold of Plotinus' second *Ennead*, where you will see that what he is talking about is situated at approximately the same level. Eros is at issue there too; in fact, it is the only thing at issue there. You cannot, if you have at least cursorily read a theological text on the Trinity, fail to notice that Plotinus' discourse – written at the end of the third century A.D. – is, if we change but three words in it, quite simply a discourse on the Trinity. Zeus, Aphrodite, and Eros are the Father, the Son, and the Holy Spirit. I say that simply to allow you to imagine what is at stake when Phaedrus speaks of Eros.

60

For Phaedrus, to speak of love is, in short, to speak of theology. It is very important to realize that his speech begins with such an introduction, as for many people even today, and especially in the Christian tradition, for example, to speak of love is to speak of theology.

But his speech does not stop there. It continues with an illustration of these ideas. The type of illustration employed is also quite interesting in its own right.

For it speaks to us of divine love, and specifically of its effects.

3

The eminence of love's effects depend on the degree of dignity they involve.

We encounter here a theme which has since worn a bit thin in the rhetoric that has grown up around love – namely, that love is a bond against which no human effort can prevail. An army made up of beloveds and lovers – the implicit classic illustration is the famous Theban legion – would be invincible, inasmuch as the beloved for his lover, and the lover for his beloved, are eminently able to represent the highest moral authority, that before which one does not yield, that before which one cannot bring dishonor upon oneself. This notion leads, at its most extreme, to love as at the heart of the ultimate sacrifice.

I find it noteworthy that Euripides' version of Alcestis surfaces here, illustrating once again what I formulated for you last year as what delimits the zone of tragedy – namely, the between-two-deaths. I will summarize it: King Admetus is a happy man, but a man to whom death has suddenly signaled its imminence. Alcestis [the king's wife], the incarnation of love, is the only one who is willing to take the king's place to satisfy death's due – the only one among all the relatives, including the king's elderly parents who in all probability have very little time left to live, and the king's friends and children.

In a speech in which it is essentially male love that is discussed, this may seem remarkable, and it is worth keeping in mind. Alcestis is thus offered up to us as an example. This lends import to what is to come. Indeed, two examples follow on that of Alcestis, both of which, in the words of the orator, were also situated in the field of the between-two-deaths.

The first, Orpheus, managed to descend into hell to seek out his wife Eurydice. As you know, he came back up empty-handed because of a mistake he made, that of looking back before he was allowed to. This mythic theme is reproduced in many legends of other civilizations than Greece, one of which is a famous Japanese legend. The other example Phaedrus provides is that of Achilles.

Showing you what results from a comparison of these three heroes is as far as I can take things today. It is a first step which will already put you on the scent.

Let us consider first Phaedrus' remarks about Orpheus [179d]. What interests us here is Phaedrus' commentary – not whether he gets to the bottom of things, nor whether it's justified – we cannot go that far. What concerns us is what he says. And it is precisely the strangeness of what he says that should attract our attention.

61

He tells us that the gods did not at all appreciate what Orpheus, son of Oeagrus, did. The reason he gives is found in the interpretation he proposes of what the gods did to the guy, who was not so great as all that, who had gone soft [*amolli*] – we don't know why Phaedrus has got it in for him, or why Plato does either. The gods didn't show him a real woman, but rather the wraith of a woman. This echoes what I began my talk with earlier regarding the relation to the other – namely, the difference between the object of our love insofar as our fantasies cover it over, and the other's being, insofar as love wonders whether or not it can reach it.

In death, Alcestis truly takes the place of or substitutes for the other's being, according to Phaedrus. You will find a term in the text, and you won't be able to say that I put it there – ὑπεραποθανεῖν (*hyperapothanein*). The substitution or metaphor I was telling you about earlier is literally realized here. Alcestis authentically takes Admetus' place. Paul Ricoeur, who has the Greek text open before him, can find ὑπεραποθανεῖν at 180a. Orpheus having been eliminated from the contest for merit in love, this expression is provided to signal the difference between Alcestis and Achilles.

62

The case of Achilles is rather different. He is the one who chooses ἐπαποθανεῖν (*epapothanein*). He is *the one who will follow me*. He follows Patroclus in death.

To understand what this interpretation of Achilles' gesture would have meant to an ancient Greek would warrant a great deal of commentary. It is much less clear than the case of Alcestis. We are forced to consult Homer's texts, where it turns out that Achilles in fact had a choice. The question is whether or not to kill Hector merely to avenge Patroclus' death. "If you don't kill Hector," his mother Thetis tells him, "you will return home in peace, and you will live happily to a ripe old age. If you kill him, your fate is sealed – it is death that awaits you." Achilles doesn't doubt what she says, for there is another passage where he himself has the thought, as an aside, "I could leave in peace." But then, it's unthinkable, and he says why. This choice is considered, all by itself, to be as decisive as Alcestis' sacrifice. The choice of *Moira*, fate, has the same value as the substitution of being for being.

There is really no need to add to this, as Mario Meunier, who is otherwise a fine scholar, does in a footnote (why he does so, I don't know) that in what follows Achilles kills himself on Patroclus' tomb. I have looked a great deal into Achilles' death the past few days, as it bothered me, and I can't find a reference anywhere in the legend of Achilles which would allow one to say such a thing. I have, moreover, seen a great many versions of Achilles' death, certain of which attribute to him activities that are rather curious from the vantage point of Greek patriotism, as he is supposed to have betrayed the Greek cause for the love of Polyxena, who is a Trojan woman. This would diminish some of the import of Phaedrus' speech.

Sticking to the speech itself, what is important is that Phaedrus gives detailed consideration to the respective functions of Patroclus and Achilles in their erotic bond. He sets us straight: "Don't imagine for a minute that Patroclus was the beloved, as was generally believed. It turns out," says Phaedrus, "upon careful scrutiny of the characteristics of the characters, that the beloved could only have been Achilles, who was younger and still beardless." I am highlighting this because the question is constantly raised whether one must love them before or after their beards begin to grow. The Greeks talk of nothing else. We encounter this discussion of beards everywhere. We can thank the Romans for having done away with this problem for us. There must be some reason for it. In any case, Achilles didn't have a beard. Therefore he must have been the beloved. Patroclus was ten years older than Achilles. A careful examination of the texts shows that Patroclus must have been the lover.

That's not what interests us – it is simply the first indication of something that bears a relation to what I specified as the target starting from which we are going to make headway. Indeed, what the gods find sublime, more marvelous than anything else, is when the beloved behaves as one would expect a lover to behave. With respect to this point, the example of Alcestis is strictly opposed to that of Achilles.

What does this mean? It is what the text says. One cannot imagine why Phaedrus would tell this whole story that runs on for two pages if it were of no importance. You think I am exploring the *Carte du Tendre* [the Map of the Tender Feelings], but it isn't me, it's Plato. And it is very well articulated. One must deduce therefrom what forces itself upon us. Since Phaedrus explicitly contrasts Achilles with Alcestis, and tips the scales in favor of giving the gods' love prize to Achilles, this means that Alcestis was in the position of the *erastés*, of the lover. It is insofar as Achilles was in the position of the beloved that his sacrifice was so much more admirable than hers.

In other words, the entire theological speech by Phaedrus, the hypochondriac, culminates in pointing out that what I earlier called the signification of love leads to this. Its most sensational, remarkable, sanctioned appearance, crowned by the gods who give Achilles a special place on the Isles of the Blest – as everyone knows it is an island that still exists at the mouth of the Danube, on which they have now stuck an insane asylum or some sort of reform school – is precisely related to the fact that in this case a beloved behaved like a lover.

63

I won't be able to go any further today, but I would like to end with something suggestive, which will perhaps allow us to raise a practical question here. It is the following: in an erotic couple, it is, on the whole, on the side of the lover that one finds activity in the natural position, so to speak.

This remark will be full of consequences for us if, in considering the Alcestis/Admetus couple, you are willing to glimpse something that lies especially within your ken due to what we discover in psychoanalysis about what women can experience regarding their own lack. Why not formulate, at a certain level at least, that in a couple, a heterosexual couple in this case, we find in the woman both lack, as we say, but also, and at the same time, activity?

In any case, Phaedrus never suspects that it could be otherwise. Now what do we find in the other half of the couple? In the beloved, *erómenos*? – or to put it in the neuter, ἐρώμενον (*erómenon*), for what is it that one "eromenoses," one errs or loves, in this whole story of the *Symposium*? It is something that is very often put in the neuter: τὰ παιδικά (*tá paidiká*) [darling]. It is the object. What this designates – namely, a neuter function – is associated with the function of what is loved. It is in the beloved that we find the element of strength.

You will see this in what follows, when we will have to articulate why the problem is situated at a more complex level when heterosexual love is at issue. At that level, it can be plainly seen that the distinction between activity and strength is useful. But it was important to pinpoint it at the moment at which we encounter it so clearly illustrated in the example of Achilles and Patroclus. It is illusory to think that strength is identical to activity, and that Achilles is not the beloved just because he seems to be stronger than Patroclus. This is refuted here in the text, and this is what we should learn from it in passing.

Having arrived at this point in his speech, Phaedrus gives the floor to Pausanias, who for centuries has been taken to express Plato's opinion regarding love for boys.

I will take special pains in dealing with Pausanias. He is a very odd character indeed, and is far from deserving the esteem in which he has been held, having been considered to have Plato's *imprimatur*. He is, in my view, an altogether episodic character, who is never theless important from a certain vantage point – inasmuch as the best comment to jot down in the margin next to his speech is the Christian truth that the kingdom of heaven is off-limits to the rich.

I hope to show you why next time.

November 30, 1960

IV

THE PSYCHOLOGY OF THE RICH

PAUSANIAS

The myth of the beloved's molting.
The rules of Platonic love.
Calvinist love.
Kojève and Aristophanes' hiccoughs.

Today I am going to try to make some headway in my analysis of the *Symposium*, as it is the path I have chosen by which to present you the topic of transference this year.

Last time we proceeded as far as the end of the first speech, that by Phaedrus. You know which speeches follow – those by Pausanias, Eryximachus, Aristophanes, and Agathon, the host of the symposium at which Aristodemus was present. From start to finish it is Apollodorus who narrates, repeating what he heard from Aristodemus. Socrates speaks after Agathon, and you will see how unique the path is that he takes to express what he knows love to be. You know that the last episode is Alcibiades' entrance, an astonishing public confession in its quasi-indecency, which has remained an enigma to all commentators. There is also something after that entrance, but we'll come to that later.

I would like to avoid leading you along this path step by step, speech by speech, in such a way that you will, in the end, be either lost or bored, or lose sight of the goal toward which we are headed. This is why I began class last time with these words about the object, the object's being: we can always tell ourselves, with more or less good reason, but always with some reason, that we have missed it – that we have failed it.

I will come back to the other's being, this being that it was fitting for us to try to reach while there was still time, indicating what is at stake in relation to the two main terms of what is, in this case, called "intersubjectivity."

1

When people invoke intersubjectivity, they are claiming that we must recognize in the other a subject like ourselves. Access to the other's being supposedly lies quintessentially in this direction.

But there is also another direction, one that I indicate when I try to articulate the function of desire in the apprehending of the other as it occurs in the *erastés-erómenos* couple, which has been the organizing principle of all reflection on love from Plato right up until Christian reflection.

I think I have already indicated clearly enough that, in desire, the other as a being [*l'être de l'autre*] is not a subject. *Erómenos* is *erómenon*, in the neuter, and also *tá paidiká*, in the neuter plural – things about the beloved child, one might translate it. The other, insofar as he is aimed at in love, is, as I said, aimed at as a beloved object.

What does this mean? What can we say we have missed in he who is already too far away for us to make good our having failed him? It is clearly his quality as an object. What sparks off the movement involved in the access to the other that love gives us is the desire for the beloved object, which I would compare, if I wished to illustrate it, to a hand that reaches out to pick a fruit when it is ripe, to draw close a rose which has opened, or to stir a fire, the logs of which suddenly burst into flames.

Try to follow me so that you will grasp what I'll say next. With this image, which I won't develop any further, I am sketching out before you what is known as a myth. You will see it in the miraculous character of what follows. Last time I told you that the gods, the starting point in the *Symposium* – *mégas theós*, love is a great god, Phaedrus says right at the outset – are a manifestation of the real. Now any shift from this manifestation to a symbolic order distances us from the revelation of the real.

Phaedrus tells us that Love is the foremost of the gods imagined by the Goddess in Parmenides' *Poem*. Jean Beaufret, in his book, identifies the Goddess with truth – with better reason I think than with any other function – with the radical structure of truth. Recall   69
the way I talked about it in "The Freudian Thing." Truth's first imagining or invention is Love. Hence Love is presented to us here as having no father or mother. There is no genealogy of Love. Yet already in Hesiod's work, in the most mythical forms of the presentation of the gods, a genealogy is sketched out: a system of kinship, a theogony, or a symbolism.

What is the Christian God – who, owing to His internal organization, is at the midpoint about which I spoke to you between theogony and atheism, this trine God, one and yet three – if not the radical articulation of kinship as such, of what is most irreducibly and mysteriously symbolic about it? The most hidden relationship – and, as Freud says, the least natural, the most purely symbolic – is that of father to son. The third term remains present there, going by the name of love.

This was our point of departure: Love is a god, in other words, a reality that manifests and reveals itself in the real. As such, we can only speak of it through myth. This is also what allows me to lay out before you our orientation here, by directing you toward the formula, metaphor, or substitution of *erastés* for *erómenos*. This metaphor generates the signification of love.

To illustrate it for you, I will take the liberty of completing my image and of truly making it into a myth.

The hand that extends toward the fruit, the rose, or the log that suddenly bursts into flames – its gesture of reaching, drawing close, or stirring up is closely related to the ripening of the fruit, the beauty of the flower, and the blazing of the log. If, in the movement of reaching, drawing, or stirring, the hand goes far enough toward the object that another hand comes out of the fruit, flower, or log and extends toward your hand – and at that moment your hand freezes in the closed plenitude of the fruit, in the open plenitude of the flower, or in the explosion of a log which bursts into flames – then what is produced is love.

But we must not stop there. We must say that what we are looking at here is love – in other words, that it's your love when you were first *erómenos*, the beloved object, and suddenly you become *erastés*, he who desires.

70   Consider what I mean to emphasize with this myth. Every myth is related to the inexplicable nature of reality [*réel*], and it is always inexplicable that anything whatsoever responds to desire.

The structure in question is not one of symmetry and reciprocity [*retour*]. For this symmetry is not symmetrical, since insofar as the hand extends, it extends toward an object. The hand that appears on the other side is the miracle. But we are not here to orchestrate miracles. We are here for something quite different – to know. What must be emphasized in this context is not what happens between here and the hereafter, but rather what happens here – in other words, the substitution of *erastés* for *erómenos* (or for *erómenon*).

A few of you thought there was some vagueness in what I articulated last time concerning the metaphorical substitution of *erastés* for *erómenos*, feeling it contradicted the supreme example to which the gods award the crown, before which the gods themselves are astonished, ἀγασθέντες (*agasthéntes*) [179c and 180a]. Namely, that Achilles, the beloved, *epapothaneín*, dies, let's say – to remain imprecise for we will see what this means – for Patroclus, which is why Achilles is superior to Alcestis who offered to die instead of the husband whom she loves. The term used by Phaedrus to describe her, *hyperapothaneín*, is contrasted with *epapothaneín*. She dies in the stead, ὑπέρ (*hypér*), of her husband. The case of Achilles is different, because Patroclus is already dead.

Alcestis changes places with her husband who is called upon by death – she crosses the space I mentioned earlier which is between the one that is here and the hereafter. She does something that serves to wrest from the gods a disarming testimony before this extremity, that wins her the singular prize of being able to come back among human beings from death as what lies beyond [life].

But there is something still more remarkable, as Phaedrus explains. It is even more remarkable that, instead of returning to his land to be with his father amid his fields, Achilles accepted his tragic destiny, his fatal destiny, the certain death that was promised to him, if he avenged Patroclus. Now Patroclus was not his beloved. Achilles was the beloved. Phaedrus claims – rightly or wrongly, and this is of little consequence to us – that Achilles was the beloved of the couple, and that he could have occupied only that position. Through his action, which comes down to accepting his fate as it was written, he places himself, not in the stead of, but rather in the wake of Patroclus. He makes of Patroclus' fate the debt he must pay, the debt with which he must come to terms. And this is what commands, in the eyes of the gods, the most necessary and the greatest admiration, for the level attained by Achilles in the order of love's manifestations is, as Phaedrus tells us, higher. Achilles is more honored by the gods, inasmuch as it is they who judge his action. They are full of admiration, strictly speaking, and simultaneously astonished – for they are overwhelmed by the value of love as they see it manifested by humans. To a certain extent, the gods, being impassive and immortal, are unable to understand what happens at the mortal level. They detect a certain gap between themselves and mortals, and view what happens in the manifestation of love as a miracle.

Emphasis is thus placed in Phaedrus' speech, where *epapothaneín* is contrasted with *hyperapothaneín*, on the fact that Achilles, *erómenos*, turns into *erastés*. The text says so and affirms it – it is as *erastés* that Alcestis sacrifices herself for her husband, and this is a less radical, total, and brilliant manifestation of love than the switching of roles that takes place in Achilles when he changes from *erómenos* into *erastés*.

71

Thus it is not a question, in this *erastés* over *erómenos*, of a relation whose amusing image would be that of the lover over the beloved, "the father over the mother," as Jacques Prévert says somewhere. This is no doubt what led Mario Meunier to make the bizarre error I mentioned to you of claiming that Achilles kills himself on Patroclus' tomb. One cannot say that Achilles, as *erómenos*, replaces Patroclus, since Patroclus is already out of range, already out of reach. The event that is, strictly speaking, miraculous in itself is that Achilles the beloved becomes the lover.

This is how the phenomenon of love is brought into the *Symposium*'s dialectic.

2

We cannot take up Pausanias' speech in all its details, line by line, because of time constraints. We must punctuate [*scander*] it.

You have all read the *Symposium* in enough depth for me to say that this speech begins with the distinction between two orders of love. Love, says Pausanias, is not one. We must determine which kind of love we should praise. *Enkómion* and *épainos*, which for some reason I called *epaínesis* last time, are slightly different in nuance. The praising, *épainos*, of love must thus begin with the fact that love is not one. The distinction is based on its origin. "Love and Aphrodite are inseparable" [180d], he says, but there are two Aphrodites.

One Aphrodite has nothing to do with women – she had no mother, for she was born from the projection onto Earth of the rain engendered by the primal castration of Uranus by Cronus. Urania – that is, Heavenly Aphrodite – was born therefrom, and thus owes nothing to sexual difference.

The other Aphrodite was born somewhat later, from the union of Zeus and Dione. Let me remind you that the whole history of the advent of he who governs the present world, Zeus, is linked – see Hesiod – to his relations with the Titans who are his enemies, and Dione is a Titaness. I will not stress the point any further. The Aphrodite born of man and woman is called Pandemos [or Common Aphrodite]. The deprecatory, scornful tone is explicit in Pausanias' speech – she is the common Venus, altogether plebian, the Venus of those who confuse one form of love with the other, who seek it at base levels, who do not make love into the kind of elevated subjugation that Uranian Aphrodite provides.

Such is the theme around which Pausanias' speech develops. Unlike Phaedrus' speech – which is a myth lover's [*mythomane*]

speech, in the strict sense of the word, a speech about a myth –
Pausanias' speech is a sociologist's discourse, or rather, for that
would be exaggerating, the discourse of an observer of societies.
Everything in it apparently hinges on the diversity of positions in
the Greek world with respect to higher love, the kind of love that
develops between those who are both the strongest and the most vigorous, and who are also the most intelligent, ἀγαθοὶ (agathoí) [181e],
who know how to think – in other words, between people situated
at the same level owing to their capacities: men.

Customs, Pausanias tells us, differ greatly between Ionia and
Persia, on the one hand, where this kind of love – he adduces evidence of this – would be disapproved of, and Elis and Sparta, on
the other, where this love is more than simply approved of, since it
appears to be very unseemly for the beloved to refuse to grant his
favors to his lover: he must χαρίζεσθαι (charízesthaí) [gratify, 182b].
The Athenians seem to Pausanias to have a superior apprehension
of the rite, so to speak, of the social shaping of love relationships.

If Pausanias approves of the fact that the Athenians erect obsta-   73
cles, forms, and prohibitions – at least this is how, in a more or less
idealized form, he presents it to us – it is because these practices
correspond to a certain goal. This love quite deliberately manifests
itself, is borne out, and is established over a certain span of time, and
what's more, over a span which is comparable, he says formally, to
that of marriage. There is a love contest, ἀγωνοθετῶν (agonothetón)
[184a] – love presides over struggle and rivalry among candidates,
by putting to the test those who compete for the position of lover.
May the best man win.

This ambiguity is oddly maintained for a full page. Where do we
situate the virtue or function of he who chooses the winner? For
while Pausanias would like he who is loved to be at least a bit more
than a child, and already capable of some discernment, he is in any
case the one of the two who knows the least, the one who is least
capable of judging the virtue of what one could call the beneficial
relationship between the two. This is left to a kind of test [184a]
between the two. Virtue is also found in the lover – namely, in the
way in which his choice is made, according to what he seeks in the
beloved. What he seeks in the beloved is something to be given to
the beloved. Both are going to meet up at a point that Pausanias
refers to somewhere as the place where "these two principles [of
conduct] coincide absolutely" [184e], at which the conjunction or
combining takes place. What is it really?

It has to do with an exchange. The lover, as Léon Robin translates
it in the text of the Budé edition, shows that he is able to contribute
something whose object is intelligence, φρόνησις (phrónesis), and the

whole of the field of merit or excellence, ἀρετὴ (*areté*). The beloved needs to gain in education, and generally in knowledge, παιδεία (*paideía*) and σοφία (*sophía*). They will meet up here and, according to what Pausanias says, constitute a partnership at the highest level [184e]. It is at the level of κτάομαι (*ktáomai*) – an acquisition, profit, acquiring, or possession – that this couple comes together, and this couple will forever articulate the so-called higher form of love: the love which, even once the partners have changed, will be called "Platonic love" for centuries to come.

Reading this speech, it seems to me very difficult not to realize under what heading such a psychology falls. The whole speech is elaborated in terms of a valuation [*cotation*] of values, a search for listed values [*valeurs cotées*]. The point is clearly to invest one's psychic funds properly. If Pausanias demands somewhere that severe rules – I'm referring back to the earlier part of his speech – be imposed on the blossoming of love and the courting of the beloved, these rules are justified by the fact that too many favors, πολλὴ σπουδὴ (*pollé spoudé*) – here the investment I just mentioned is clearly at stake – should not be expended or wasted on young things who aren't worth it [181d–e].

This is, moreover, why we are requested to wait for them to be further along in their development so that we know what we are dealing with. Later on, Pausanias says that those who muddle the order of candidacy [*postulance*] and merit are savages and barbarians. In this respect, access to the beloved must be limited, he says, by the same kinds of prohibitions and laws by which we strive to impede access to freeborn women, it being through such women that two families of masters are united. These women represent in themselves whatever you like in terms of a name, value, firm, or dowry, as we call it today. This is why they are protected by orders. It is a comparable protection which must prohibit those who are not worthy of it from gaining access to the desired object.

The further you go in this speech, the more you see what I mentioned at the very end of the last class – namely, the psychology of the rich.

Rich people existed before the rise of the bourgeoisie. Even in agricultural or still more primitive economies, the rich exist. The rich have existed and manifested themselves since the beginning of time, if nothing else in their periodic spending on lavish festivities. The first duty of the rich in primitive societies is to spend money on luxuries.

It is quite strange that, as societies evolve, this duty seems to shift to a secondary or at least clandestine level. But the psychology of rich people is entirely based on the fact that what is at stake in their relations with others is value. It is a question of what can be valued according to the available modes of comparison and scale, of what can be compared in open competition, which is, strictly speaking, that of the possession of goods.

What is at issue is possession of the beloved, because he is a good fund of capital – the very word is there, χρηστὸς (chrestós) [183e] – and a lifetime will not be enough to turn it to good account. As we know from Aristophanes' comedies, several years after this symposium Pausanias takes things a bit further with Agathon, who is the beloved here as everyone is well aware, even though he's already had hair on his chin – which is of great importance in this context – for many moons.

75

Agathon is 30 years old [at the time of the symposium], and has just won first prize in the competition for the best tragedy. Pausanias runs away with him years later to what Aristophanes calls the Isles of the Blest, namely, a place far away, not just in the countryside, but in a distant land. It is not Tahiti, but Macedonia, where he remains for as long as his safety is assured. Pausanias' ideal in matters of love is sheltered capitalization, the stocking up of what rightfully belongs to him because he has been able to discern it and put it to good use.

We can, I think, discern the successor of this type of character, as we glimpse him in Plato's dialogue, in another type that I will designate for you rapidly because he's located at the other end of this chain.

He's someone I met, not in analysis – I wouldn't talk to you about him if he were – but I got to know him well enough for him to open up his heart, or what passed for one in his case, to me. He was quite famous and was reputed to have a lively feeling of the limits imposed, in love precisely, by a rich person's position. He was an excessively rich man, and had – and this is no metaphor – safes full of diamonds, because you never know what might happen. It was right after World War II, and the whole planet could have gone up in smoke.

He was a rich Calvinist. I apologize to any of you who are of this faith. I don't believe that it is the privilege of Calvinism to create rich people, but it is not unimportant to mention this detail, for one can nevertheless observe that Calvinist theology has had the effect of bringing to light as one of the elements of moral guidance that it is on Earth that God rewards the people he loves with plentiful goods. Elsewhere as well perhaps, but it starts here on Earth. The idea that observance of the divine commandments brings success here on Earth did not fail to bear fruit in all sorts of enterprises. Be that as it may, the Calvinist in question treated

the order of merits he acquired here on Earth for the afterlife
exactly as he would have treated entries in an account book: "Such
and such an object bought on such and such a day." All of his
actions were directed toward acquiring a well-stocked safe for the
hereafter.

76

Digressing in this way, I don't want to seem to be telling a facile
apologue, but it is impossible not to complete the picture with a
sketch of his matrimonial fate. One day he knocked someone over
on the street with the bumper of his humungous car, despite the fact
that he always drove very carefully. The person who had been run
over shook it off. She was pretty and a concierge's daughter, which
is not altogether incompatible with being pretty. She reacted coldly
to his apologies, even more coldly to his proposal to indemnify her,
and still more coldly to his proposals to go have dinner together. In
short, as his access to this miraculously encountered object became
more and more difficult, his opinion of her grew higher and higher.
"Here is a sure value," he said to himself. All of which led him to
marriage.

We find here the same theme as that laid out in Pausanias'
speech. For Pausanias tells us to what extent love is a value.
Consider for a minute, he tells us, that we forgive everything done
in the name of love. If, in order to obtain a position, a public function, or some social advantage, a man resorted to the least of the
extravagances that we allow when it comes to relations between a
lover and the person he loves, he would be dishonored: he would
be guilty of what one might call moral baseness, ἀνελευθερία
(aneleuthería), for that is what flattery, κολακεία (kolakeía),
entails. Flattery is not a worthy means for a master to use to
obtain what he desires.

Thus the more something goes off the red-alert value charts [cote
d'alerte], the better we can gauge what love is. It is the same basic
register as the one that led my good Calvinist, accumulator of goods
and merits, to in effect have an amiable wife for a while, provide her
of course with jewels – which every evening were taken off her body
and placed in a safe – and then end up in a situation whereby one
day she ran off with an engineer who made 50,000 francs a month.

I don't want to seem to be overdoing it on this score. Pausanias'
speech is curiously presented to us as an example of the fact that
there is, in love in Antiquity, some kind of glorification of the moral
quest. Even before we get to the end of his speech we notice that it

77

clearly shows the error of any ethics that latches only onto what one
might call outward signs of value.

Indeed, Pausanias cannot do otherwise than end his speech by
saying that, if everyone accepted the primacy of these fine rules

by which value is granted only on the basis of merit, what would happen? Let us read a translation of 185a–b:

> Only in this case, we should notice, is it never shameful to be deceived; in every other case it is shameful, both for the deceiver and the person he deceives. Suppose, for example, that someone thinks his lover is rich and accepts him for his money; his action won't be any less shameful if it turns out that he was deceived and his lover was a poor man after all. For the young man has already shown himself to be the sort of person who will do anything for money – and this is far from honorable. By the same token, suppose that someone takes a lover in the mistaken belief that this lover is a good man and likely to make him better himself, while in reality the man is horrible [κακὸς (*kakós*), fundamentally vile], totally lacking in virtue; even so, it is noble for him to have been deceived.

Strangely enough, people generally try to see in this the first manifestation in history of what Kant called righteous intention. It seems to me that it is truly to lapse into a singular error not to see instead the following.

We know from experience that the entire ethics of educational or pedagogical love, in matters of homosexual and even heterosexual love, always involves some sort of illusion. It is this illusion which, in the end, rears its ugly head. You may, at some point, have had someone – and, as we are talking about Greek love, [we'll take a homosexual example] – brought to you [for treatment] by his protector, assuredly with the best of intentions on the latter's part. I doubt you have seen any patently Good effect stem from this more or less enthusiastic protection, concerning the development of he who has been designated to you as the beloved – that is, as the object of a love that presents itself as a love of the Good, love for the acquisition of the best goods. This is what allows me to tell you that this is far from being Plato's opinion.

Indeed, Pausanias' speech concludes rather abruptly, I must say, with lines [185e] that say more or less the following: "Uranian love, that's the good stuff, and those who don't have it, well, let them resort to the other, Pandemos, common Venus, the great scoundrel, who doesn't have it either. They can go fuck off if they want it. It's on that note," he says, "that I will conclude my speech on love. As for the plebs and their common love, I have nothing more to say." If Plato agreed with that, do you think that we would see what occurs immediately afterward?

78

3

Immediately afterward, Apollodorus speaks in his own name, saying "Παυσανίου δὲ παυσαμένου" (*Pausaníou de pausaménou*), "Pausanias having paused" [185c].

The expression is difficult to translate, and there is a short footnote which says that "no French expression corresponds to" it, the "numerical symmetry of the syllables" being important; "there is probably an allusion; see the introduction to the volume." Léon Robin wasn't the first to have raised an eyebrow at this expression. Already in Henri Estienne's edition we find a marginal note. Everyone has raised an eyebrow at this "*Pausaníou de pausaménou*" because they sensed something intentional here. I will show you that people have not realized exactly what it was.

Immediately after having made this clever remark, Apollodorus emphasizes that it is a pun – "You see, I have learned from the masters to ἴσα λέγειν (*ísa légein*), to speak by isology." One can translate this as a play on words, but isology is truly a technique. I will spare you an account of all the efforts that have been made to find out who the master was. Was it Prodicus [of Ceos]? Or was it Isocrates instead? There is *iso* in Isocrates, and it would be particularly *iso* to isologize Isocrates. This leads to problems – you cannot begin to imagine what these problems have generated by way of research! Were Isocrates and Plato buddies?

People reproach me for not always citing my sources – well, starting today, I have decided to do so. Here my source is Ulrich von Wilamowitz-Moellendorff, a sensational character. If you can read German and you come across his books, buy them. I would love to have his book on Simonides [of Ceos]. He was an erudite German from the beginning of the century, an exceptional person whose works on Plato are truly enlightening. He is not the person I'm referring to here concerning "*Pausaníou de pausaménou*," for he didn't pay any particular attention to this bit of banter.

79

I don't think there is any reference here [at 185c], however distant, to the way in which Isocrates handles isology when it comes to demonstrating, for example, the merits of a political system. The whole discussion that you find on this point in the preface to the *Symposium* by Léon Robin is surely interesting, but it has no bearing on the problem. Here's why.

My mind was no doubt already made up concerning the import of Pausanias' speech, and last time I even explained my impression completely in telling you that it is the epitome of the Christian curse that what is most worthwhile is forever refused to the rich. But I think I had a confirmation of that, which you will be the judge of, last Sunday when I was – I am continuing to cite my sources – with Kojève. I would be distressed if I had neglected to tell you of his importance in my own training, and I think certain people here know that I am indebted to him for having introduced me to Hegel's works.

I was thus with Kojève and, of course, since I'm always thinking of you, I spoke with him about Plato. Kojève is doing something that has nothing to do with philosophy now, for he's an eminent man. But he nevertheless writes from time to time a couple of hundred pages on Plato, producing manuscripts that circulate in various places. He shared with me on this occasion a number of things he very recently discovered in Plato, but he could tell me nothing about the *Symposium* because he had not reread it, and because it does not fall within the ambit of his current work.

Thus my efforts were not rewarded, although I was very encouraged by many things he told me about other aspects of Plato's work, namely, about the following, which is quite obvious – that Plato hides from us what he thinks just as much as he reveals it to us. It is thus only as a function of each individual's abilities – in other words, up to a certain limit which assuredly cannot be gone beyond – that we can glimpse it. You shouldn't hold it against me, therefore, if I don't give you the last word on Plato, because Plato has clearly decided not to give it to us.

At this point, when everything I am telling you about Plato has perhaps led you to open up the *Phaedo*, for example, it is important that you realize that the goal of the *Phaedo* is perhaps not entirely to demonstrate, appearances notwithstanding, the immortality of the soul. I would even say that its goal is obviously the contrary. But let us set that aside.

As I was saying goodbye to Kojève, I remarked to him, "We didn't get around to speaking about the *Symposium* very much." And as Kojève is a very, very proper guy, in other words, a snob, he replied, "In any case, you will never be able to interpret the *Symposium* if you do not know why Aristophanes had the hiccoughs."

I had already told you that this was very important. It is obviously very important. Why would he have the hiccoughs if there were no reason for it?

Naturally, I had no idea why he had the hiccoughs. But encouraged by this little prod, I said to myself, "Let's take another look at it." I did so quite reluctantly, as a matter of fact, expecting merely to once again come across boring speculations on the value, perhaps even the psychosomatic value, of hiccoughing and sneezing in Antiquity. I very distractedly opened up my copy again, and looked at the text where "*Pausaniou de pausaménou*" appears, for it is immediately

80

thereafter that Aristophanes is to be given the floor, and I noticed that for 16 lines [185d–e] the only topic of conversation is how to stop his hiccoughs. When will his hiccoughs stop? Will they stop, or won't they? If they don't, you take this kind of thing, and in the end they will. Such that with the παῦσαί (*paúsai*), παύσωμαι (*paúsomai*), παύσῃ (*paúsei*), παύεσθαι (*paúesthai*), παύσεται (*paúsetai*), and the *Pausaníou de pausaménou* at the beginning, we find seven repetitions of *paus* in these lines, making for an average interval of two and a seventh lines between the occurrences of this constantly repeated word. If you add to this the occurrences of "it will" or "it will not help," and the "I will do what you told me to do," where the term ποιήσω (*poiéso*) [to make] is repeated with almost equal insistence, the homophonies and isologies come up every line and a half. Hence it is extremely difficult not to see that, if Aristophanes has the hiccoughs, it's because throughout Pausanias' discourse he's been splitting his sides laughing – and Plato has been doing the same.

In other words, the fact that Plato gives us something like "it's tempting to tempt temptation," and then repeats for 16 lines the word "tempting" and the verb "to tempt," should make our ears prick up. There is no other example in any of Plato's texts of a passage so directly similar to certain passages in the *Vermot Almanac*. Which brings up one of the authors I cut my teeth on – I read for the first time a Platonic dialogue by Courteline in the *Vermot Almanac* that is called "Theodore Looks for Matches," which is truly a kingly portion.

I think my claim is sufficiently clear that, for Plato himself, insofar as he speaks here through Apollodorus, Pausanias' speech is quite ridiculous.

As we don't have much time left, I will not analyze for you the speech that follows, that of Eryximachus, who speaks instead of Aristophanes. We will discuss the meaning of the doctor's speech on the nature of love next time.

We will also see something that I think is much more important – Aristophanes' role. His speech will take us a step further, making it the first step that really enlightens us, even if it didn't enlighten Antiquity's readers, to whom Aristophanes' speech always remained enigmatic, like an enormous mask. It involves a *dioecisme*, διασχισθησόμεθα (*diaschisthisómetha*) [193a], as he puts it, a being separated in two, a *Spaltung* or splitting,* which, while not identical to what I have developed for you with the Graph of Desire, is certainly not totally unrelated.

After Aristophanes' speech, we will look at Agathon's speech. I can already tell you, so that you know where we are going between now and next time – and here I need no scholarly preparation to showcase this feature – that there is but one thing that Socrates articulates when he speaks in his own name and that is that the speech given by Agathon the tragic poet isn't worth a wooden nickel. People say that it is in order to spare Agathon's feelings that Socrates has himself replaced, so to speak, by Diotima and gives us his theory of love from her lips. I absolutely cannot see how one can spare the feelings of someone who has just been executed. And this is precisely what Socrates does to Agathon.

I beg of you, starting now, to broach the crux of the matter, if only to raise objections if there's any reason to do so. After all the fine things that Agathon, in his turn, says of love – not all the good things [biens] about love, all the profit that can be drawn from love, but all its virtues and beauties, for nothing is too good to be chalked up to love's credit – what does Socrates articulate? In one fell swoop, Socrates undercuts all of that, bringing things back to their root, by asking, "Love? Love of what?"

82

From love we thus shift to desire. And the characteristic of desire, insofar as Ἔρως ἐρᾷ (*Éros . . . erá*) [200a], that is, Eros desires, is that what is at stake – in other words, what desire is supposed to bring with it, beauty itself – is lacking in it, ἐνδεής (*endeés*) [and ἐνδεὴς, 200e, 201b], ἔνδεια (*éndeia*). In these two terms, desire is lacking; desire is in itself identical to lack. Therein lies the entire personal contribution Socrates makes in his own name in his speech in the *Symposium*.

Starting from this, something is going to begin, something that is far from attaining the status of anything you can hold in the palm of your hand. And how would that even be conceivable? Up until the end, on the contrary, we get mired ever deeper in the shadows, and we will find here the ever darker night of Antiquity. Everything there is to be said about the conception of love in the *Symposium* begins here.

December 7, 1960

V

MEDICAL HARMONY

ERYXIMACHUS

On the supposed science in love.
From the good to desire.
Medicine and science.
The path of comedy.

It is important to see the nature of the undertaking into which I have
been drawn, in order for you to be able to put up with the detours,
insofar as they may be fastidious. For, after all, you don't come here
to listen to me comment on a Greek text, in the treatment of which
I do not claim to be exhaustive.

I do the majority of the work for you, in other words, in your
stead, in your absence, and the best service I can do you is to incite
you to look at the text. If you have looked at the text at my suggestion, it will perhaps happen that you read to some extent with my
glasses. Which is probably better than not reading at all.

We must not lose sight of what we are destined to arrive at, the
goal that dominates this whole undertaking, and you must grasp in
what respect you can accompany it, providing more or less commentary on it. We are trying to answer the question from which we
began – the simple question of transference.

1

In saying that this question is simple, I mean that it involves terms
that have already been elaborated.

Here is a man, a psychoanalyst, from whom people seek knowledge [*science*] of what is most intimate about them – this is truly
the state of mind with which people commonly approach him –
and thus of what should immediately be assumed to be most
foreign to him. And yet, at the same time, what we encounter

at the beginning of an analysis is that he is assumed to have this knowledge [*science*].

I am defining the situation here in subjective terms, in other words, from the perspective of the person who requests to do an analysis. For the time being we needn't bring in everything this situation objectively implies and that sustains it – namely, the specificity of what is proposed in this science, in other words, the unconscious as such. The subject has no notion of that, whatever his wishes to the contrary may be.

Defined simply in this subjective way, how does this situation generate something – as a first approximation – akin to love? One can, roughly speaking, define transference as something like love.

Let me try to put this better and go a bit further. Transference is something that calls love into question, calling it into question deeply enough, from the vantage point of analytic reflection, to have introduced what is known as "ambivalence" as an essential dimension of it. This is a new notion compared to the philosophical tradition whose very origins we are, not fruitlessly, investigating here. The close connection between love and hate is absent at the beginning of this tradition, if we situate this beginning – one must situate it somewhere – as Socratic.

But today we are going to see that there is something prior to it that serves as its point of departure.

I would not be sticking my neck out so very far by raising this question – which articulates the possibility of the emergence of transference – if, in some way, the tunnel hadn't already been started at the other end. We are going toward something that we know, having already seriously studied the topology of what the subject must find in analysis in the place of what he is seeking. If he sets off in search of what he has, but does not know he has, what he discovers is what he is lacking in. It is precisely because I have articulated this before that I dare raise the question that I first formulated. What he finds in analysis is articulated in the form of what he is lacking – namely, his desire.

Desire is not a good [*un bien*] in any sense of the term. It certainly is not a good in the sense of a κτῆσις (*ktésis*) [180b provides κτῆσιν (*ktésin*)], something one could have in some way. An inversion must be detected in the time – "time" defined in both chronological and topological senses – it takes for transference love to blossom, which turns the search for a possession [*un bien*] into the realization of desire.

You understand, of course, that when I say "realization of desire," I assume that it is clearly not possession of an object. Indeed, it involves the emergence of desire as such in reality. This is what led me to present the *Symposium* to you this year. It was not an accidental encounter. But as I was seeking, in the midst of my memories, where to find the central axis of what I have been able to retain in what I have learned, guided by some compass deriving from experience, it seemed to me that the *Symposium*, regardless of how far it is from us, is the place where the meaning of this question is debated in the most vibrant way, particularly the moment which concludes it at which Alcibiades appears.

Alcibiades breaks in strangely, in all senses of the term, both at the level of the dialogue's composition and in the supposed scene. All of a sudden, the series of ordered speeches, announced in the *Symposium*'s agenda, is manifestly broken by the eruption of the true party – the upheaval this different order introduces. But Alcibiades' words themselves also constitute an avowal of his own discordance. What he says truly reflects his suffering, his having been ripped apart by Socrates' attitude, which still leaves him wounded, almost as much as at the time [they had been seeing each other], bothered by some kind of strange wound.

Why does Alcibiades make this public confession? And why does Socrates make the interpretation that Alcibiades' confession has an immediate aim – namely, to separate Socrates from Agathon – an interpretation that immediately leads to a return to order? All of you who have looked at this text since I began speaking about it have been struck by what this strange scene has in common with all sorts of instantaneous situations and positions that occasionally arise in the transference. This remains impressionistic, and it will require a much closer and more finely honed analysis to see what is delivered up to us by a situation that is manifestly not to be attributed to a sort of "presentiment of *sychanalisse*," as Aragon calls it in his *Traité du Style*. No, it is rather an encounter – the appearance of several outlines that are revealing to us.

I have been taking my time in showing this to you not simply in order to get a running start before the leap which must be, as Freud says, that of a lion – in other words, a single bound. I have been doing so because, in order to understand the full meaning of the scene between Alcibiades and Socrates, we must understand the general design of the work. It is indispensable to map out the terrain. If we do not know what Plato means by presenting this scene, it is impossible to situate its import.

We have now arrived at the speech given by Eryximachus, the medical doctor.

2

Let us hold our breath for a moment. The fact that he is a physician should pique our interest.

Should Eryximachus' speech lead us to do research on the history of medicine? I could not even sketch out such a task for all sorts of reasons. First of all because it's not our concern here, and this detour would be rather excessive. Second, because I don't truly believe it would be possible.

I don't think that Eryximachus is specified, in other words, that in bringing in this character Plato has a particular doctor in mind. But the fundamental features of his position remain to be examined. They are not necessarily historically accurate features, except insofar as they provide a very general dividing line [between positions or schools], but they will perhaps give us pause to reflect for a moment, in passing, on what medicine is.

Others have already noted that Socrates makes frequent references to medicine. When he wishes to bring his interlocutor to the level of dialogue where he intends to direct him toward the perception of a rigorous approach, he often refers to some technician's art. If you want to know the truth about such and such a subject, he often asks, who would you ask? And among the technicians, doctors are far from being excluded. They are even treated with special reverence. They are certainly not situated, in Socrates' eyes, at a lower level than the others. It is nevertheless clear that the rule of the medical approach cannot be reduced to any sort of intellectual hygiene.

The doctor in question here, Eryximachus, speaks as a doctor,   87
and he immediately declares medicine to be the greatest of all the arts. Medicine is the great Art.

I will only briefly mention that we find confirmation here of what I said to you last time about Pausanias' discourse. In beginning, Eryximachus expressly formulates the following: "Since Pausanias, after a fine beginning" – which is not a very good translation for ὁρμήσας (*hormésas*) [185e] – "having given a fine thrust at the beginning of his speech, did not end as brilliantly, as appropriately," etc. It is thus clear to everyone that Pausanias' speech ended badly – this is taken to be obvious. It must be said that our ears are not exactly attuned to that, and that we don't have the impression that Pausanias' speech concluded as badly as all that. We are, after all, used to hearing such idiotic claims about love. It is all the more strange to see to what extent Eryximachus' words meet with everyone's approval, as if everyone found Pausanias' speech woolly-headed, and as if all the crude jokes about *pausaménou* were transparent to Antiquity's readers.

I think it is rather essential that we articulate what we can gather about these matters of tone, to which the mind's ear always pays attention, even if it doesn't openly make a criterion of it. Socrates refers to tone all the time, in Plato's texts. How often, before beginning his own speech, or making an aside in someone else's speech, does he invoke the gods in a formal way, so that the tone will be sustained, maintained, and harmonized. As you will see, this is very close to the heart of my theme today.

Before taking up Eryximachus' speech, I would like to make a few comments whose retrospective nature, although it leads us to some first truths, still is not easily spelled out. I will show you in passing that medicine has always considered itself scientific. It is in your stead, as I was saying earlier, that over the past few days I have tried to make sense of this brief chapter in the history of medicine. In order to do so, I obviously had to leave behind the *Symposium* and look at various other parts of Plato's opus.

88 As neglected as this aspect of your medical training may have been, you have heard of a series of schools in Antiquity. The most famous, the school that no one is unaware of, is that of Hippocrates. Prior to that there had been the Cnidus school in Rhodes, and even before that, a school headed by Alcmaeon centered in Croton, whose speculations are impossible to dissociate from those of a scientific school that flourished at the same time and in the same place – namely, that of the Pythagoreans. But to speculate on the essential role and function of Pythagoreanism in understanding Plato's thought would, as you know, involve a detour in which we would literally get lost. Instead I will try to bring out the themes that are strictly related to our topic – namely, the meaning of the *Symposium* as a work, insofar as it is problematic.

We don't know very much about the character Eryximachus himself, but we know certain things about a number of other characters who appear in Plato's dialogues, and who are directly related to Alcmaeon's medical school, inasmuch as the latter is itself related to the Pythagoreans. For example, Simmias and Cebes, who speak with Socrates in the *Phaedo*, are disciples of Philolaos, one of the masters of the first Pythagorean school. If you look back at the *Phaedo*, you will see that their answers to Socrates' first propositions on what must ensure the immortality of the soul include the exact same terms as Eryximachus' speech – first and foremost, the notion of ἁρμονία (*harmonía*), harmony or concord [*accord*].

Medicine, as you can see here, has always considered itself scientific. It is in this respect, moreover, that it has always showed its weaknesses. Through a sort of internal positional necessity, it has always referred to the science of its era, whether good or bad. Good or bad, how can you know that from the vantage point of medicine?

My sense is that our science – our physics – is good science, but that for many centuries we had very poor physics. This is, in fact, quite clear. But what is not clear is what medicine should do with science. In other words, how, through what opening, from what end, should medicine approach science? For something has not been elucidated in medicine, which can hardly be considered negligible, since it concerns the very idea of health.

89

What is health? You would be wrong to believe that even in modern medicine – which believes itself to be scientific compared to all other forms of medicine – it is completely clear. From time to time, the ideas of normality and pathology are proposed to some student as a dissertation topic, in general by people with training in philosophy. There is, on that subject, an excellent book by Canguilhem, his *Essai sur quelques problèmes concernant le normal et le pathologique* (*The Normal and the Pathological*), but its influence is obviously quite limited in strictly medical circles. Without attempting to speculate at the level of Socratic certitude about the very idea of health, we can say that what show – all by themselves, especially for we psychiatrists and psychoanalysts – how problematic the idea of health is, are the very means we use to achieve a state of health. To put it in more general terms, these means show that, whatever the nature of health and the propitious form that supposedly corresponds to health may be, we are led to postulate, at the crux of this propitious form, paradoxical states, to say the least – states whose manipulation in our therapies is responsible for the return to an equilibrium which, on the whole, remains rather unexamined.

This is what we find at the level of the postulates of the medical position that are least susceptible of demonstration. It is this very position that is maintained here in Eryximachus' speech by the name *harmonia*. We don't know what kind of harmony is involved, but the notion is truly fundamental to any medical position as such. All we have to seek is concord. And we haven't gotten much further than Eryximachus concerning the essence or substance of this idea of concord.

It is a notion that is borrowed from an intuitive domain and, in this respect, is simply closer to its sources. But it is also historically more defined, and more palpable, inasmuch as it is explicitly related to the field of music, which is taken as a model here. Concord is the Pythagorean form par excellence. And everything that is in any way whatsoever related to the concord of tones – even if it is of a more subtle nature, even if it is the tone of speech I mentioned

earlier – brings us back to the same assessment. It was not idly that
I mentioned the ear in passing – the evaluating of consonances is
essential to the notion of harmony.

As soon as you get into the text of this speech – I will spare you
the boring chore of reading it line by line, which is never very easy
with such a large audience – you will see how essential the notion
of concord is to understanding the way the medical position is presented here.

3

Everything articulated here is a function of a medium that we can
neither exhaust, nor in any way reconstruct – namely, the themes
of prior discussions that we can assume to be present in the minds
of the participants.

Let us not forget that we find ourselves at the historic climax of
a particularly active era. The sixth and fifth centuries of Hellenism
are overflowing with intellectual creativity. You can consult on this
subject fine works, for example, for those of you who read English,
a long book the likes of which only English publishers can afford
the luxury of publishing, a book which is part and parcel of the
philosophical legacy, Bertrand Russell having written it for us in his
old age.

This volume makes a fine New Year's present – its wide margins
are illustrated with admirable color illustrations that are extremely
simple and aim at firing a child's imagination – and it contains
everything one must know from the fertile period to which I am
referring today, that of the pre-Socratics and Socrates, up until
our times, in other words up until English positivism. No one truly
important is left out. If your only concern is to be unbeatable at
fashionable dinners, you will know everything once you've read this
tome, except of course the only important things – namely, those
that are not known. But I nevertheless recommend that you read
the book. It is called *Wisdom of the West*. It will fill in for you, as
it would for anyone, a considerable number of almost necessary
lacunae in your store of general knowledge.

Let us try to organize what we see when we set out to understand
what Eryximachus means.

The people of his time find themselves faced with exactly the
same problem as us. And yet they go more directly to the essential antinomy. Is it because they don't have such an abundance of
minute facts with which to fill out their discourse? That hypothesis
is based on deception and illusion. This antinomy is clearly the one

that I began to bring out for you earlier – in any case, we cannot allow ourselves to take any sort of concord at face value. Experience teaches us that concord hides something in its bosom, and the whole question is to know what can be required of the concord's underpinnings – from the point of view of what cannot be decided by experience, it always involving, as it does, something a priori, apart from which it cannot be posited.

Must we require similarity at the heart of concord or can we remain satisfied with dissimilarity? Does every concord assume some principle of concord? Can that which is in tune [*l'accordé*] come out of what is out of tune? Come out of conflict? Don't imagine for a minute that it was Freud who first raised this question. The proof is that it is the first issue Eryximachus' speech raises. The notion of discord and concord – for us, in other words, the notion of the function of anomaly compared to normality – has pride of place in his speech, starting at about the ninth line, 186b:

Dissimilar subjects desire and love objects that are themselves dissimilar. Therefore, the love manifested in health is fundamentally distinct from the love manifested in disease. And now recall that, as Pausanias claimed, it is as honorable to yield to a good man as it is shameful to consort with the debauched . . .

Here we are led to the question of physical health, and of what this virtue [health] and this disorder [*dérèglement*] signify.

We immediately find a formulation that I can but point out on the page. Not that it gives us much, but it should nevertheless be of interest to analysts in passing. For there is some rustling here that should hold our attention. Eryximachus tells us, and this is a word-for-word translation, that "medicine is the science of the erotics of bodies," ἐπιστήμη τῶν τοῦ σώματος ἐρωτικῶν (*epistéme ton tou sómatos erotikón*) [186c]. No better definition, can, it seems to me, be given of psychoanalysis.

He adds, πρὸς πλησμονὴν καὶ κένωσιν (*pros plesmonén kai kénosin*), "in regard to repletion and depletion," to quote the brutal translation. What I wish to underscore here are the two terms "full" and "empty" – whose role we shall see in topology and in intellectual 92 positions – and what is at stake at this meeting point of physics and medical practice. This is not the only text in which "full" and "empty" are mentioned. It is one of the fundamental intuitions that should be highlighted in the course of any study of Socratic discourse.

He who would engage in such an enterprise would not have to go far to find an additional reference. See the beginning of the

Symposium. Socrates is dawdling in the foyer of the neighboring house, where we can imagine him in the position of a gymnosophist, standing on one foot like a stork, totally immobile until he has found the solution to some problem. He shows up at Agathon's later than everyone expected him to. "So, you found your thing! Come sit by me," Agathon says to him. And Socrates replies something like, "Maybe, and then again maybe not, but what you are hoping for is that what I now feel full of will pass over into your emptiness, like what happens between two vases when a bit of wool is strung between them" [175c–d]. This amusing physics experiment must have been, for some unknown reason, conducted quite often, as this allusion was probably telling for everyone present. The movement from the inside of one vase to another, the transformation of the full into the empty, the communication of contents, is one of the main images that regulates what one could call the "fundamental covetousness" of all these philosophical exchanges. It should be kept in mind in trying to understand the meaning of the speech proffered here.

A little further on one finds a reference to music as a principle of concord, which is the basis of what is offered up to us as the essence of the function of love between beings. This brings us, on the next page, in section 187, to the choice which is vivid in Eryximachus' speech and which I told you was primordial concerning the subject of what can be conceived of as at the crux of concord – namely, the similar and the dissimilar, order and conflict.

When it comes to defining harmony, Eryximachus notes the paradox found in the work of an author who preceded them by about a century, Heraclitus of Ephesus [187a]. Indeed, Heraclitus explicitly referred to the opposition of contraries as being the principle of composition for every unit [or One; *unité*]. The One is constituted, Eryximachus tells us, by "being at variance with itself," "like the attunement of a bow or a lyre." This ὥσπερ ἁρμονίαν τόξου τε καὶ λύρας (*hósper harmonían toxou te kai lýras*) is extremely famous, if only for having been cited here in passing. But it is cited in the work of many other authors as well, and has been handed down to us in several scattered fragments that German scholars have collected concerning pre-Socratic thought. Among those that remain by Heraclitus, this one is truly central. In the book by Bertrand Russell that I recommended to you earlier, you will in fact find an illustration of a bow and its cord, showing the vibration that leads to the arrow's flight [p. 24].

What is striking is Eryximachus' evident bias, the reason for which we do not immediately see, against Heraclitus' formulation. He thinks it must be modified. It seems that he must have criteria

93

whose source we cannot easily fathom. We find ourselves here at a crossroads where we are in no position, above all regarding characters so far in the past, so phantomlike, to determine how much should be attributed to prejudice, a priori judgment, choices made in accordance with a certain consistency of themes in a theoretical system, or psychological tendencies. We must confine ourselves to noting that there is, in fact, something here that is echoed in many other places in Plato's discourse. Some aversion is expressed here to the idea of referring to any conjunction of contraries whatsoever, even if one situates it in reality [*réel*], as involved in the creation of a phenomenon which seems to me to have nothing to do with it – namely, that of concord. It seems that when it comes to concerning oneself with the idea of harmony – to speak in medical terms, of diets and doses – the idea of measure and proportion must be maintained at its very core. Heraclitus' vision of conflict as in itself creative can in no way be defended here to certain people's satisfaction – or perhaps to certain schools' satisfaction, a question we shall leave in abeyance.

I do not share Eryximachus' bias. All kinds of models in physics have given us the idea of the fecundity of contraries, contrasts, and oppositions, and the notion of an absolute non-contradiction of a phenomenon with its opposing principle. On the whole, physics supports far more the image of waves than that of forms, Gestalts, "whole forms" [*la bonne forme*], despite what modern psychology has made of them. We cannot fail to be surprised, it seems to me, at finding maintained here, and elsewhere in Plato's work, the idea of some kind of impasse or aporia, some kind of preference one must have for the necessarily fundamental character of concord with concord or of harmony with harmony.

94

4

If you look at the *Phaedo*, a dialogue that constitutes an extremely important backdrop for our understanding of the *Symposium*, you will see that the whole discussion with Simmias and Cebes is based on the notion of harmony.

As I was telling you last time, Socrates' whole argument for the immortality of the soul is presented in the *Phaedo* in a way that clearly takes the form of a sophism, which is no other than that around which my remarks revolve – namely, that the very idea of the soul qua harmony excludes the possibility of its rupture. When his two interlocutors object that this soul, whose nature implies constancy, permanence, and duration, could easily vanish at the same time that the corporeal elements – whose conjunction constitutes the soul's harmony – disperse, Socrates answers by saying nothing more than that the idea of harmony in which the soul participates is in itself impenetrable, and that it would slip away or take flight at the very approach of whatever could call its constancy into question.

The idea that anything whatsoever that exists could participate in the Platonic idea as incorporeal essence proves to be fictional in nature, an illusion. Things go so far in the *Phaedo* that it is impossible not to remark that there is no reason to believe Plato was any less aware of this illusion than we are. Our claim to be more intelligent than the person who wrote Plato's work is quite unbelievable, unimaginable, and truly astounding.

This is why, when Eryximachus sings his little song, without it immediately having any obvious consequences, we can ask ourselves what Plato meant by having this series of sallies take place in this particular order in the *Symposium*. At least we have realized that Pausanias' speech, which immediately precedes this one, is ridiculous. And if we keep in mind the overall tone that characterizes the *Symposium*, we certainly have the right to wonder whether what is at stake isn't consonant with comedy as such. In discussing love, it is clear that Plato chose the path of comedy.

Everything will confirm this in what follows, and I have my reasons for beginning to assert it now, at the moment at which our famous comedian is going to take center stage. People have been trying to figure out for ages why Plato had him come to the *Symposium* in the first place. It is scandalous, because this famous comedian was one of the people responsible for Socrates' death.

The *Phaedo*, namely, the drama of Socrates' death, is presented to us with the lofty character lent it by the tragic tone with which we are familiar. It is not, however, quite so simple, since there are also comic elements in it, but tragedy dominates and it is staged for us. In the *Symposium*, on the contrary, there is not one single aspect of the dialogue that cannot be suspected of comedy, right down to the incredibly short speech Socrates makes in his own name.

So as to leave nothing out, I would like to respond to one of my auditors whose presence honors me most, and with whom I had a short discussion on the subject. Not without reason, motive, or accuracy, my interlocutor thought he had noticed that I was taking Phaedrus' speech at face value, unlike that of Pausanias. Well, in the sense of what I am asserting here, Phaedrus' speech, in referring to the gods' assessment regarding the topic of love, has no less ironic value than that of Pausanias. For, in fact, the gods cannot understand anything about love. The expression "divine stupidity" should, in my book, be more widespread. It is often suggested by the behavior of the beings we address precisely when it comes to love. Asking the gods to take the stand and give testimony about what is at stake in love seems to me, in any case, not to be discordant with what follows in Plato's discourse.

Here we are on the verge of Aristophanes' speech. But we won't turn to it just yet. I would simply like to bid you to complete, with your own means, what remains to be seen in Eryximachus' speech.

It was an enigma to Léon Robin that Eryximachus relied on the opposition of Heavenly and Common love, given what he says about the medical – physical – handling of love. In fact, I think that astonishment is truly the only fitting attitude we can adopt in response to Robin's astonishment, for the question is clarified in Eryximachus' own speech, confirming the context in which I have been trying to situate it for you.

While Eryximachus refers to astronomy in relation to the effects of love in section 188, it is inasmuch as the harmony with which one must try to converge [confluer, s'accorder] concerning the fine order of the health of men is the very same harmony that dictates the order of the seasons. When it is the kind of love in which people get carried away, in which there is hubris or excess, the kind that prevails during certain seasons, then disasters begin, and mayhem ensues, "destruction," as he expresses himself – damage, under which heading fall epidemics, but also frost, hail, blight, and a whole slew of other things [188b].

This brings us back to a context in which we can use the notions that I propose, as the most far-reaching categories to which we are forced to refer if we are to found a valid discourse about analysis – namely, the imaginary, the symbolic, and the real.

People are surprised that a Bororo identifies with a macaw. Doesn't it strike you that it isn't in the least a question of primitive thought, but rather of a primitive position of thought concerning what thought is about for everyone, for you and for me? Questioning not his place, but his identity, man must situate himself, not on the inside of the limited enclosure which is his body, but in the total, crude reality [réel] he deals with. We cannot escape the law whose consequence is that we will always have to situate ourselves at the precise point of this delineation of reality [réel], which constitutes the progress of science.

In Eryximachus' time, no one had the slightest idea what a living tissue as such was, and it is thus out of the question that the doctor could make anything else of humors than humidity, in which natural vegetation can proliferate in the world. The disorder that leads men to excess owing to intemperance and to getting carried away is the same disorder that leads to the disorders of the seasons enumerated here.

Chinese tradition presents us with the Emperor accomplishing with his hand the major rites upon which the balance of the whole Middle Kingdom depends, tracing out the first furrows at the beginning of the year whose direction and straightness are designed to ensure the balance of nature. There is nothing in this position, I dare say, that isn't natural. Eryximachus endorses the notion of man as microcosm, that is, not that man is in himself a synopsis or image of nature, but that man and nature are one and the same – one wouldn't dream of composing man of anything but the order and harmony of cosmic components. Hasn't this position, despite what we think we have reduced biology to, left some traces in our intellectual presuppositions? I wanted to leave you with that question today.

Assuredly, to detect those traces is not as interesting as to notice where, at what more fundamental level, we analysts situate ourselves when, to understand ourselves, we use notions like the "death instinct." As Freud himself did not fail to recognize, it is an Empedoclean notion.

I will show you next time that the formidable gag constituted by Aristophanes' speech, manifestly presented as the entrance of a clown onto the scene of Athenian comedy, explicitly refers – I will provide you with proof thereof – to the cosmological conception of man. And on this basis I will show the surprising opening that results therefrom, an opening left gaping in the idea of love that Plato may have had.

I will go so far as to say that, in and of itself, the discussion of love leads to a radical ridiculing of the incorruptible, immaterial, super-essential, purely ideal, participatory, eternal, and uncreated order, which is the order that all of Plato's work reveals to us – perhaps ironically.

December 14, 1960

VI

DERIDING THE SPHERE

ARISTOPHANES

> From the universe to truth.
> Socrates and his witness.
> The clown [*pitre*].
> Perfect motion.

My talk today will, I hope, pass through its winter solstice before the celestial conjunction.

Led by its orb, you may have felt we were getting further and further afield from the topic of transference. Rest assured, however, that today we will reach the nadir of this ellipse. From the moment we divined that there was something we could learn from the *Symposium*, and inasmuch as that turns out to be valid, it was necessary to take as far as we are going to today the analysis of important parts of the text that might seem to have no direct bearing on our topic.

But no matter, we are now involved in the endeavor, and once one has begun to follow a certain path in discourse, there is a sort of non-physical necessity that makes itself felt when we wish to take it all the way.

Our guide here is a discourse, Plato's discourse in the *Symposium*. Like a musical instrument, or rather a music box, it is full of all the significations to which it has given rise throughout the centuries, and this is why part of our effort here is to home in as closely as possible on its meaning. In order to understand and judge it, one cannot but mention the discursive context – in the sense of a concrete universal discourse – in which it is situated.

Let me try to make sure you are getting my point. It is not my goal, strictly speaking, to situate the *Symposium* historically. You certainly realize that such is not my method of commentary, and that I always examine a discourse with an eye to what it leads us to understand. I do so even with discourses developed at a very distant era in which things we must understand were not clearly visible. But in the case of the *Symposium*, it is impossible for us not to consider the relationship between discourse and history – not how the discourse is situated in history, but how history itself arises from a certain way that discourse enters into reality [*réel*].

I must thus remind you that the *Symposium* is situated in the second century of the birth of concrete discourse about the universe. Let us not forget the philosophical efflorescence, so to speak, in the sixth century B.C. It was all the stranger and odder owing to the echoes or other modes of a sort of terrestrial chorus, heard at the same era in other civilizations, there being no apparent relationship among them. But I don't even want to so much as sketch out the history of the sixth-century philosophers, from Thales to Pythagoras or to Heraclitus and so many others. What I'd like to bring out is that for the first time in the Western tradition – the tradition discussed in the book by Bertrand Russell that I recommended to you last time – a discourse developed that deliberately targeted the universe, aiming to render it discursive.

At the beginning of this first step of science as wisdom, the universe appears as a universe of discourse. In a sense, there will never be any universe other than a universe of discourse. And everything we encounter from that era, right down to the very definition of the elements, whether four or more, bears the mark, seal, or stamp of the requirement or postulate that the universe must give itself over to the signifying order.

The point was not, of course, to find parts of speech [*éléments de discours*] in the universe, but rather parts that were organized the way speech is. All the steps articulated at that time by the advocates and inventors of this vast investigative movement show that, if one cannot discuss one of the universes thus formed in a manner that is coherent with the laws of speech [*discours*], it must be totally rejected. Recall the *modus operandi* of Zeno the dialectician who, when it came to defending his master, Parmenides, provided sophistical arguments designed to cast his adversary into an irremediable quandary.

Thus, as a backdrop to the *Symposium*, and in the rest of Plato's work as well, we see an attempt that is grandiose in its innocence: the hope harbored by the first so-called physical philosophers to find the ultimate handhold on reality [*réel*] thanks to the guarantee provided by discourse. Discourse was, in the end, their only instrument of experimentation.

Please excuse me for not going into this topic at any greater length. I do not intend to give a talk on Greek philosophy. I am

101

simply providing you with the minimal background you must have to interpret this particular text, if you are to judge it accurately.

1

I must first remind you that reality [*réel*] and a hold on reality [*réel*] did not have to be conceptualized at that time as correlated with a subject, even if it was a universal subject. Such a hold is correlated with a term that I will borrow from Plato, who, in the course of a digression in *The Seventh Letter*, names what is sought through the operation of the dialectic, τὸ πρᾶγμα (*to prágma*).

This is the very term I had to bring out last year in my discussion of ethics, and that I called "the Thing." It is not *die Sache*, an affair, [but rather *das Ding*] – you can understand the latter, if you prefer, as the main concern [*la grande affaire*] or ultimate reality. It is what the very thinking that takes it on and disputes it depends on, and such thinking is, so to speak, but one of the ways to put *to prágma*, the Thing, into practice. It is the essential praxis.

You should realize that theory, the word for which – *theoria* – arose at that very time, as contemplative as it may be made out to be, is not merely contemplative, and the praxis out of which it grows, Orphic praxis, demonstrates this rather well. Theory is neither, as our use of the word implies, the abstraction of praxis, nor its general reference, nor the model of its application. Right from its very first appearance, theory is praxis itself. Theory is itself the exercise of power, *to prágma*, the main concern.

One of the masters of that era – and the only one I choose to cite, for, thanks to Freud, he is one of the patron saints of analytic speculation – Empedocles, in his no doubt legendary trappings (and his trappings are what are important, for they are the trappings that have been bequeathed to us), is all powerful. He claims to be master of the elements, able to resuscitate the dead, a magician, and a lord of the royal secret in the same land where charlatans with a similar style appeared later. People ask him for miracles and he performs them. Like Oedipus, he does not die, but rather returns to the center of the world in the fire of a volcano and the abyss.

102

As you will see, this remains quite close to Plato. Thus it is no accident that, at a much more rationalist era, we quite naturally borrow his reference to *to prágma*.

But what about Socrates? It would be quite odd if the whole historical tradition were mistaken in saying that he contributed something original against this backdrop – a break or opposition. Socrates explains his position – insofar as we can trust Plato, who presents him to us in fact, presumably in the context of historical testimony – as involving a need to take a step back, feeling weary and disgusted by the contradictions generated by the first philosophical attempts as I have just characterized them.

It is Socrates who comes up with the new and essential idea that one must first guarantee knowledge. To show everyone that they know nothing is a path that is in itself revealing – it reveals a virtue which, in its finest successes, does not always succeed. In what Socrates calls *epistéme*, science, what he finds, in the end, what he brings out or detaches, is that discourse engenders the dimension of truth. Discourse, which is ensured by a certainty inherent in its very action, ensures truth as such wherever it can. It is nothing but this practice of discourse.

When Socrates says that it is not him but rather truth itself that refutes his interlocutors, he demonstrates something whose most solid feature is its reference to a primitive combinatory, which, as the basis of our discourse, is always the same. The upshot being, for example, that your father is not your mother, and that it is by the same token, and by this token alone, that one can declare that what is mortal must be distinguished from what is immortal. Indeed, Socrates refers the whole ambition of discourse to the domain of pure discourse. He is not, as people say, the one who brings man back to man or measures all things by man. Protagoras is the one who came up with the watchword, "Man is the measure of all things." Socrates brings truth to the level of discourse. He was, so to speak, a supersophist, and therein lies his mystery, for had he merely been a supersophist, he would have given rise to nothing more than the sophists did – namely, what remains of them: their dubious reputation.

103 It is something other than a temporal subject that inspired his action. Here we come to Socrates' *atopía*, to his unsituable side. This is what interests us. We sense here something that can enlighten us concerning the *atopia* that is demanded of us as analysts.

It is certainly on the basis of his *atopia*, of the "nowhereness" of his being, that Socrates sparked off a whole line of research – the facts attest to it. Its fate is linked, in an ambiguous fashion, to a whole history that can be broken down into the history of consciousness, as we say today, the history of religion, the history of morals or politics, and perhaps even the history of art, though certainly to a lesser extent. I could merely designate this whole ambiguous line, which is both widespread and vigorous, by mentioning the question trotted out anew by the most recent imbecile, "*Pourquoi des philosophes?*" ["What are philosophers for?"], if we didn't already sense that this line is part and parcel of the torch handed down, although it is in fact foreign to everything it illuminates – the Good, Beauty, Truth, the Same – even as it prides itself on dealing with them.

If we try to read Socrates' heritage [*descendance*], relying on contemporary or almost contemporary witnesses, as well as distant effects, the idea might come to us that it is a sort of perversion without an object.

In truth, when one tries to focus in on, approach, imagine, or get a fix on who this person could, in fact, have been, believe me, it's tiring. I can formulate the effect of this fatigue no better than with the words that came to me one Sunday evening: "This Socrates character is killing me." Strangely enough, I woke up the next morning in a much better mood.

It seems impossible not to begin by taking what is attested to by Socrates' entourage literally, right up to just before his death, which is that he said that, in short, we can fear nothing of a death about which we know nothing – and in particular, he added, we don't know that it might not be a good thing [*Apology*, 29a].

We are so used to hearing nothing but lofty sentiments in classical texts that, when we read this, we no longer pay any attention to it. But it is striking to bring this out in the context of Socrates' final days, when, surrounded by his remaining faithful students, he casts a last glance askance [*regard en dessous*], a glance Plato fixes on paper, for he was not present, that he calls the bull's look [*Phaedo*, 117b]. Consider his attitude during the trial. If the *Apology* reproduces exactly what he said to his judges, it is difficult to believe, in listening to his defense, that he did not want to die. In any case, he explicitly repudiates any pathos that might be seen in his situation, thereby provoking his judges, who were used to ritual supplications by the accused parties. 104

I am trying, this being a first approximation, to get at the enigmatic nature of a desire to die. It can, no doubt, be considered ambiguous, as we are dealing with a man who spent 70 years trying to satisfy this desire, and it is clear that it cannot be taken in the sense of a tendency toward suicide or failure, or in the sense of any kind of masochism, whether moral or otherwise. But it is difficult not to formulate the tragic minimum related to the deportment of this man in a sort of gratuitous no man's land* or between-two-deaths.

As you know, when Nietzsche discovered Socrates it went to his head. *The Birth of Tragedy* grew out of it, as did all of his subsequent work. The tone I am adopting in speaking to you of it no doubt indicates some impatience with it on my part, but it is nevertheless indisputable, and Nietzsche put his finger on it: it suffices to open almost any one of Plato's dialogues to see Socrates' profound incompetence every time he broaches the topic of tragedy. Look at the *Gorgias* – tragedy is touched on there and executed in three lines among the arts of flattery as one rhetoric among others, and there is nothing more to be said of it [502b–d]. Nothing tragic, no tragic sense of life, as we say nowadays, sustains Socrates' *atopia*, only a daemon. Don't forget this δαίμων (*daímon* or *daemon*), for Socrates talks about it incessantly.

This daemon seems to haunt him [*l'hallucine*] in order to allow him to survive in space, warning him of possible pitfalls: "Don't do that!" And then there is the message of a god, Socrates himself attesting to the role it played in what one might call his vocation. One of his disciples had the idea, a rather ludicrous idea it must be said, to go consult the god at Delphi, Apollo. The god up and answered, "There are several wise men, one of whom isn't bad, that's Euripides; but the wisest of them all, the *crème de la crème*, is Socrates." Following which, Socrates said to himself, "I must carry out the god's oracle. I didn't realize I was the wisest, but since he said so, I must be." Socrates presents the shift in his path toward public life in those terms. He is, in a word, a madman who believes he is in the god's ordained service. He is a messiah and, what's more, finds himself in the company of chatterboxes.

There is no other guarantor of the Other's words than those very words, and no other source of tragedy than this very fate, which may seem to us in a certain sense pretty damn insignificant. All of this leads him to yield to the gods the better part of the ground about which I was speaking to you last time, that of the reconquest of reality [*réel*], the philosophical conquest – in other words, scientific conquest.

In this respect, if I tell you that the gods belong to reality [*les dieux sont du réel*], it is not in order to be paradoxical, like certain people have told me. You had a lot of fun, they said, in surprising us when you asked, "What are the gods?" Everyone expected you to say they are symbolic, and you had a good laugh in telling us they are real. Well, that is not at all the case. I'm not the one who invented this. To Socrates' mind, manifestly, the gods were real and real alone.

And this reality [*réel*], once we've given it its due, is nothing as regards the principle of Socrates' behavior, which aims only at truth. He is prepared to obey the gods on occasion, provided that one defines this obedience to him. Is this to obey them, or rather to ironically fulfill his responsibility to beings who also have their necessity? In fact, we sense no necessity here which does not recognize the supremacy and the necessity inherent in the deployment of truth – in other words, in science.

What might surprise us is the seductive power of such a severe

105

discourse, which is attested to us here and there in one or another of the dialogues. Even when repeated by children or women, Socrates' discourse exercises an amazing [*sidérant*] charm, that's the word for it. Thus spoke Socrates – a force is transmitted that raises up those who approach him at the simple rustling of his words, Plato's texts always say, and certain say upon mere contact with him.

Observe furthermore that he does not have disciples but, rather, close friends. There are curious onlookers as well, not to mention the enthralled – *santons* as they are referred to in Provençal tales – people who are transported. Other people's disciples also occasionally come knocking at his door.

Plato is none of the above. He is a latecomer who is much too young to have been able to see anything but the end of the phenomenon. He was not one of the friends who were there during the last moments. And that ultimately accounts, let it be said in passing, for the style of testimony to which he holds fast every time he speaks of his strange hero: "So and so heard it from so and so who was there, during such and such a visit when they had such and such a debate." In one case, he says he had the recording on the brain at first hand, and in another case, at second hand.

106

Plato is a very unusual kind of witness. One might say that he lies and on the other hand that he is truthful even when he lies, for in his very investigating of Socrates, it is Plato's own question that shows through [*se fraye son chemin*].

Plato is completely different from Socrates. He does not go about barefoot. He is no errant philosopher, nor does any god speak to him or call him. Indeed, it seems to me that the gods don't mean much to him. Plato is a master, a true master, a master from the time when the city was falling apart, carried away by the democratic winds that were a prelude to the great imperial forces – a sort of Marquis de Sade, but funnier.

Naturally, no one can ever imagine the nature of the powers the future holds in store. The great tumblers [*bateleurs*] of the world tribe – Alexander, Seleucus, and Ptolemy – all such mystical military men were still unthinkable. What Plato saw on the horizon was a communitarian city, as thoroughly revolting to his way of thinking as it is to ours. A well-organized stud farm [*haras*] for everyone, that is what he promises us in a pamphlet, which has always been the bad dream of all those who cannot get over the ever greater discord between society and their sense of the good. It is called the *Republic*, and everyone has taken it seriously, believing that it was what Plato truly wanted.

There are several other misunderstandings and mythical lucubrations. The myth of Atlantis, for example, seems to me rather to echo the failure of Plato's political dreams, and it is not unrelated to the venture of the Academy. But perhaps you will think that my paradox should be better corroborated, and this is why I will move on.

What Plato wants, in any case, is the Thing, *to prágma.*

Plato took up at a literary level the torch of the wise men from the century before. The Academy was a city, a refuge reserved for the best and brightest; and what we know of what he dreamt about during his trip to Sicily is situated in the context of that enterprise, whose horizon certainly went quite far. Curiously enough, such a dream came to him in the same places where his adventure echoes Alcibiades' dream, Alcibiades having clearly dreamt of a Mediterranean empire whose center would be Sicily. Plato's dream bore the mark of higher sublimation. It is a sort of utopia of which he thought he could be the leader. In the case of Alcibiades, all of that obviously sinks to a lower level, and perhaps would go no further than the height of masculine elegance. But it would be to disparage this metaphysical dandyism not to see the range of which he was capable.

I think there are good reasons to read Plato's texts from the perspective of what I call his dandyism, and to see his writings as the outer trappings. I would go so far as to say that he tosses us, we dogs, little good and bad scraps of an often rather infernal sense of humor. But it is indisputable that he has been understood otherwise. The fact that Christian desire, which has so little to do with all these adventures, the fact that a desire whose crux or essence is the resurrection of bodies – read Saint Augustine to see the place this occupies – the fact that Christian desire saw itself in Plato, according to whom the body must dissolve in a supra-terrestrial beauty and be reduced to an extraordinarily decorporalized form, is a sign of utter and complete misunderstanding.

The delusional nature of the return of such a discourse in a context that is contradictory to it leads us precisely to the question of transference. What else could this be but Plato's fantasy, already asserting itself as a transference phenomenon? Don't imagine that these are but general considerations, for we are going to home in as closely as possible on them.

How did the Christians – to whom a god, reduced to the symbol of the Son, had given his life as a sign of love – let themselves be fascinated by the speculative inanity (recall the term I used earlier) offered up as fodder by the most disinterested of men, Socrates? Mustn't one recognize therein the effect of the only palpable convergence between the two creeds – the Word presented as an object of adoration?

One cannot deny that love has, in Christian mysticism, produced rather extraordinary fruits and follies, according to the Christian tradition itself. In contrast to that, it is important to delineate the scope of love in the transference produced around this other, Socrates, who was merely a man who claimed to know something about love, but who left only the most simply natural proof thereof.

Which is the fact that his disciples teased him for losing his head now and then for a handsome young man, and as Xenophon tells us, to have once, though it didn't go very far, touched the naked shoulder of the young Critobulus with his shoulder. Xenophon tells us what resulted therefrom: it left Socrates sore – nothing more, but nothing less either. This is not insignificant for such a tried and true cynic – for we can already see in Socrates all the facets of the cynics. The anecdote proves how violent his desire was, but it also shows that love is a somewhat instantaneous function for him. In any case, it allows us to realize that to Plato these love affairs were sheer foolishness.

The mode of ultimate union with *to prágma*, the Thing, is certainly not to be sought in the meaning of effusive outpourings of love, in the Christian sense of the term. The reason why the only person who speaks of love suitably in the *Symposium* is a clown [*pitre*] – you will see what I mean by this term – need be sought nowhere else.

2

To Plato, that's all Aristophanes is: a clown. Comic poets are clowns, to Plato's way of thinking.

Aristophanes, who is, believe me, hardly one of the hoi polloí, is also an obscene character. Need I remind you what you find when you open any one of his comedies? The least of the things shown on the stage is the following, for example, something found in his play entitled *Thesmophoriazusae*: Euripides' relative disguises himself as a woman to expose himself to Orpheus' fate – in other words, to be ripped to shreds by the assembly of women in Euripides' stead. Given that women at that time removed their body hair, as they still do today in the Orient, the hair on his ass is burned before us onstage, and I will spare you the rest of the details.

His plays go beyond anything you can see nowadays except on the stage of a music hall in London, and that is saying a lot. The jokes are better, but are no more distinguished for all that. The term "Bugger" [*cul béant*] is repeated ten times in a row [*The Clouds*, 1080–1100] to designate the group from which it is appropriate to choose the people that today, in our languages, we would

call the candidates most apt to play all the progressive roles, for
Aristophanes has it in for them in particular.

109   In short, shouldn't the fact that, to say the best things about love,
Plato chooses a character of this type – and what's more, one who
played a role of which you are aware in slandering Socrates – get the
old brain in gear?

I am going to immediately illustrate what I mean by emphasizing
that Plato has him say the best things about love. Even as stuffy a
scholar, careful and measured in his judgments, as Léon Robin – the
academic who established the edition that I have before me – can
sometimes be, even he could not fail to be struck by this. So much
so that it made him cry, "Aristophanes is indeed the first to speak
of love like we speak of it, and says things that get us choked up."

Aristophanes makes the following rather sophisticated remark,
the kind of remark one does not expect from a buffoon, but this is
precisely why Plato has him say it. "No one," he says, "would think
it is ἡ τῶν ἀφροδισίων συνουσία (*he ton aphrodisíon sunousía*)" – it
has been translated by "shared enjoyment of love" [*communauté
de la jouissance amoureuse*], a translation that seems abominable to
me, but Léon Robin provided a much better one in his translation
in the Pléiade edition, "the sharing of sexual enjoyment" [*partage
de la jouissance sexuelle*] – "no one would think [. . .] mere sex is
the reason each lover takes so great and deep a joy in being with
the other," in Greek, οὕτως ἐπὶ μεγάλης σπουδῆς (*hoútos epi megáles
spoudés*) [192c]. It is the same σπουδή (*spoudé*) that we saw last year
in Aristotle's definition of tragedy, and it means solicitude, care, and
eagerness, but also seriousness. In fact, people who love each other
have a funny seriousness about them.

But let us leave aside this psychological observation to designate
wherein lies the mystery. Aristophanes tells us that it is something
altogether different that their soul manifestly desires, something
it is unable to express, but that it divines nevertheless, and that it
proposes in the form of an enigma. "Suppose two lovers are lying
together, and Hephaestus," more commonly known as Vulcan, the
character with the anvil and hammer,

stands over them with his mending tools, asking, "What is it
you human beings really want from each other?" And suppose
they're perplexed, and he asks them again: "Is this your heart's
desire, then – for the two of you to become parts of the same
whole, as near as can be, and never to separate, day or night?
110   Because if that's your desire, I'd like to weld you together and
join you into something that is naturally whole, so that the two
of you are made into one. Then the two of you would share one

life, as long as you lived, because you would be one being, and by the same token, when you died, you would be one and not two in Hades, having died a single death. Look at your love, and see if this is what you desire: wouldn't this be all the good fortune you could want?"

Surely you can see that no one who received such an offer would turn it down; no one would find anything else that he wanted. Instead, everyone would think he'd found out at last what he had always wanted: to come together and melt together with the one he loves, so that one person emerged from two. [192d–e]

This is what Plato has Aristophanes say, but that's not all. You know that Aristophanes tells some rather tall tales, which he himself claims to lie somewhere between the laughable and the ridiculous, depending on whether people laugh at what the comedian intended, or at the comedian himself. It is clear that Aristophanes makes people laugh, and that he goes beyond this, into the realm of the ridiculous. Is Plato going to have Aristophanes make us laugh at love? What we see here already attests to the contrary.

Nowhere, not at any moment of the other speeches in the *Symposium*, is love ever taken as seriously or as tragically as it is by Aristophanes. Here we are at the same exact level where we moderns situate love – after courtly love's sublimation which I spoke to you about last year, and after what I might call the romantic confusion concerning this sublimation – namely, the narcissistic overestimation of the subject, of the subject assumed to reside in the beloved object.

At Plato's time we aren't there yet, thank God, apart from this strange Aristophanes, but he is a buffoon. Rather we are at the stage of an in some sense zoological observation of imaginary beings, which derives its value from what it evokes in real beings and from what certainly can be held therein to be derisory.

We are dealing here with beings cut into two, like hard-boiled eggs sometimes are, bizarre beings like the ones we find on the sandy sea floor – plaice, sole, and flounder – which seem to have everything necessary, two eyes and paired organs, but which are so flattened out that they seem to be but half of a complete being.

The first behavior that follows the birth of beings born from such a partition – which is the bedrock of what turns up here all of a sudden, in a light we find so romantic – is a panic-stricken destiny which makes each of these beings seek first and foremost its other half, and then – sticking to that other half tenaciously and, so to speak, hopelessly – perish beside its other half due to its inability to

111

come together with it. This is what Aristophanes depicts in his long,
detailed discussion in an extremely colorful way, projecting it onto
the level of myth. Such is the image of love relationships forged by
the sculptor that the comic poet proves to be here.

Is it here that we must conclude that there is something laughable
in Aristophanes' words and that we have managed to put our finger
on it? Of course not. But this is nevertheless inserted in a piece that
irresistibly brings to mind what we might see even nowadays in a
circus arena, if the clowns entered, as they sometimes do, hugging,
attached two by two, coupled stomach to stomach, and took a few
turns around the arena in a great twirling of four arms, four legs,
and two heads. In and of itself, it is something that would go very
well with the way of fabricating the kind of chorus that produces, in
another genre, *The Wasps*, *The Birds*, and even *The Clouds*, about
which we will never know how far things went when they were
performed.

But here, what kind of ridiculousness is in question? Is it simply
the in itself rather joyful character of this clownish image, as I called
it?

Here I will go off on a bit of a tangent, and I will ask you to
forgive me if it takes us rather far afield, for it is essential.

3

I am not the only one who knows how to read a text, for Léon
Robin was also struck by something, to such an extent that he
extraordinarily emphasized it – namely, the spherical nature of the
people invented by Aristophanes.

It is difficult not to see this, for this sphericalness or circularity,
this σφαῖρα (*sphaíra*), is repeated with such insistence. We are told
that the back and the flanks, πλευρὰς κύκλῳ ἔχον (*pleurás kúklo
échon*) [189e], are "all continuous in a very round way." We must
imagine that, as I said earlier, as two wheels connected to one
another which are nevertheless flat, while here it is round.

It is round, and this bothered Léon Robin, who did not hesitate,
though not without a footnote, to change a comma that no one
has ever challenged, saying, "I did it this way because I don't want
people to emphasize the sphere so much, for the cut is more important." Far be it from me to try to diminish the importance of this
cut, which we will return to later. But it is difficult not to see that we
are faced with something very unusual here, the crux of which I will
immediately reveal: what is derided here, what is cast in this ridiculous form, is the sphere itself.

112

Naturally, that doesn't make you laugh, because spheres don't mean anything to you. But remember that for many centuries it wasn't that way.

You are only familiar with the sphere as a fact of psychological inertia known as the "whole form" [*bonne forme*]. A number of people, Ehrenfels and others, have realized that shapes have a certain tendency toward perfection – a tendency, in other words, to become like spheres when we are not sure what they are. The idea is that spheres are what give the optical nerve the most pleasure. This is very interesting, but only begins to scratch the surface of the problem, for let me point out to you in passing that the notion of *Gestalten*, which is so unthinkingly used as a foundation, merely pushes the problem of perception back a notch. If there are such whole forms, perception must consist in rectifying them in the direction of partial [*mauvaises*] forms – namely, true forms. But enough on the dialectic of whole forms.

Spherical shapes have an entirely different meaning here than in this factual observation [*objectivation*] whose interest is limited to psychology. In Plato's work, and well before him, this shape, *Sphaíros*, in the masculine, as Empedocles also says – there isn't enough time for me to read the verses – is a being who is "self-identical on all sides, without limits, σφαῖρος κυκλοτερής (*sphaíros kukloterés*), which takes the form of a ball, reigns in its royal solitude, full of its own contentment, and of its self-sufficiency." The *sphaíros* that haunted ancient thought was the shape taken, at the center of Empedocles' world, by the phase of unification [*rassemblement*] characteristic of what he calls, in his metaphysics, *Philie* or *Philótes*, love, which he elsewhere calls σχεδύνη Φιλότης (*schedúne Philótes*), love which unites, agglomerates, assimilates, and agglutinates. To agglutinate is κρῆσις (*krésis*), the *krésis* of love.   113

It is quite curious to see Freud write that love is a pure and simple unifying force, with limitless powers of attraction, opposing it to Thanatos – whereas he also gives us, in a discordant way, such a different notion, and one which is so much more fruitful: the love/hate ambivalence.

We find this sphere everywhere. I was talking to you last week about Philolaos. He situates this sphere at the center of a world in which the earth has an eccentric position and, as you know, this was already suspected at Pythagoras' time. Yet it is not the sun that occupies the center but the spherical central fire, to which the face of the inhabited earth always turns its back. In relation to this fire, we are like the moon in relation to our earth, which is why we do not feel it. It seems that it was in order that we not be wiped out by [*rayés par*] the central shining [*rayonnement*] that Philolaos invented this harebrained lucubration of the anti-earth, which already puzzled people in Antiquity, including Aristotle himself. What need could there have been for this strictly invisible body, which was assumed to harbor within itself all powers opposed to those of the earth, and which at the same time played the role of firebreak? It's something to analyze, as they say.

All of this is merely designed to introduce you to the dimension – to which, as you know, I attribute great importance – of the astronomical or Copernican Revolution. And in order to make this as clear as possible, let me repeat that it is not the so-called geocentricism dismantled by the said canon Copernicus that is important, which is why it is, indeed, quite false and pointless to call the astronomical revolution Copernican. In his book *On the Revolutions of the Heavenly Spheres*, he provides a figure of the solar system that resembles ours, that resembles those in our seventh-grade textbooks where we see the sun at the center and all the stars revolving around it in orbits. But this was hardly a new schema. Everybody in Copernicus' time – I'm not the one who discovered this – knew that in Antiquity a man named Heraclides and another known as Aristarchus of Samos had come up with the same diagram. This is perfectly well attested to in the historical record.

Copernicus is merely a fantasy on the part of history. It would have been different if his system had been not closer to the image that we have of the real solar system, but truer – in other words, less encumbered than the Ptolemaic system of imaginary elements that have nothing to do with the modern symbolization of the stars. But the fact is that the Copernican system is nothing of the kind, since it is chock full of epicycles.

What are epicycles? They are an invention that no one could believe in. People didn't believe in the reality of epicycles. Don't imagine that they were dumb enough to think that we find in the sky what you see when you open up your watch: a series of little wheels. But they did have the idea that the only imaginable motion was circular motion. Everything one sees in the sky is very hard to interpret, for the little wandering planets play all sorts of irregular tricks [*entourloupettes*] among themselves and the point was to explain the zigzags. So people were only satisfied when each element of their circuit could be reduced to a circular motion.

What is odd is that they didn't manage to do a better job of it. One might think that, in theory, if we combine enough circles on top of turning circles, we could manage to account for anything. It turned out to be impossible, because the more closely people observed the heavenly bodies, the more things remained to be explained – if

114

nothing else, once the telescope appeared, their variation in size. But in any case, Copernicus' system was just as replete as Ptolemy's with this imaginary superfluity that weighed it down and encumbered it.

Over Christmas vacation you must read, and – you will see that it is possible – for pleasure, how Kepler began with the elements of the same *Timaeus* that I am going to speak to you about, in other words, from a purely imaginary – with the accent that this term has in the vocabulary that I use with you – conception of the universe. His universe was entirely regulated by the properties of the sphere, defined as the shape that bears within itself the virtues of self-sufficiency, such that it can combine in itself the eternity of place and eternal motion.

Kepler's speculations are of this type. They are, moreover, refined, because he stupefies us by bringing in the five perfect solids that can be inscribed within a sphere – as you know there are only five of them. This old Platonic speculation, which had already been superseded 30 times over, came back at this turning point of the Renaissance at which Plato's manuscripts were reintegrated into the Western tradition, and literally went to the head of this character whose personal life, in the context of the revolution of the peasants, and then of the Thirty Years' War, is really quite weird. Well, the said Kepler, who was seeking the celestial harmonies, managed – through prodigious tenacity, in which one can clearly see the game of hide-and-seek characteristic of an unconscious formation – to give the first take on what the birth of modern science really consists of. It was in seeking a harmonic relationship that he arrived at the relationship between the speed of a planet in its orbit and the area of the surface covered by the line that links the planet to the sun. In other words, he perceived simultaneously that the planetary orbits are ellipses.

Alexandre Koyré wrote a beautiful book that is called *From the Closed World to the Infinite Universe*, which was published by Johns Hopkins University Press and was recently translated into French. And I was wondering what Arthur Koestler, who is not always the best inspired author, had done with Kepler. I assure you that *The Sleepwalkers*, which everyone is talking about, is his best book. It is phenomenal, marvelous. You don't even need to know elementary mathematics; you will understand everything through his biographies of Copernicus, Kepler, and Galileo. Koestler manifests some partiality for Galileo – Koestler was a communist, after all. He says so himself.

Be that as it may, it is absolutely true that Galileo never paid the slightest attention to what Kepler had discovered. The brilliant step he made in his invention of modern dynamics is to have found the

115

exact law of gravity. In spite of this essential step, and despite the
fact that it was regarding geocentricism that he ran into all kinds
of trouble, the fact remains that he was just as behind the times as
everybody else, just as reactionary, just as wedded to the idea of
perfect circular motion as the only motion possible for the heavenly
bodies. To put it in a nutshell, Galileo did not even get as far as what
we call the Copernican Revolution, even though we know it was not
started by Copernicus. You see how long it takes truths to clear a
pathway for themselves when faced with a prejudice as solid as the
perfection of circular motion.

116

I could talk to you about this for hours, for it is very amusing
to consider why it is so, and to see what the properties of circular
motion truly are and why the Greeks made the circle into a symbol
of the limit, πεῖραρ (peírar), as opposed to the ἄπειρον (ápeiron).
Curiously enough, it is precisely because it is one of the things that is
most likely to lapse into the apeiron. I should cut this sphere – which,
as you know, served in the usual symbol for infinity [∞] – down to
size, reduce it to a point, and infinitize it for you.

There is a lot to say. Why does this shape have the finest virtues?
To answer this question would take us to the heart of problems
concerning the function and value of intuition in mathematical
construction.

Prior to all of the exercises that allowed us to disexercise the
sphere, it continued to work its charms on dupes because mental
φιλία (philía) stuck to it, and dirtily, like a strange kind of glue. This
was the case for Plato at least, and I refer you to his *Timaeus* and
his long discussion of the sphere there in which he depicts it for us in
great detail. This corresponds curiously, like an alternating strophe,
to what Aristophanes says of his spherical beings.

On the one hand, in the *Symposium*, Aristophanes tells us that
these beings have feet – small members that point and turn. But on
the other hand, in the *Timaeus*, Plato, with a striking accent since
he is discussing geometry, feels the need to observe in passing that
the sphere has everything it needs inside itself. It is round, it is full,
it is content, it loves itself, and above all it needs neither eyes nor
ears since it is by definition the envelope of everything that can be
alive. By virtue of this, it is the living being par excellence, and this
gives us moreover the intellectual dimension in which biology could
develop – we must take the notion that this form is what essentially
constitutes the living being as an extremely strict imaginary spelling
out [*épellement*].

Thus the sphere has neither eyes nor ears, neither feet nor
arms [33b], and it is left with but one motion, the perfect motion:
revolving around itself in a circle. The six [other] forms of [motion] –

toward the top, toward the bottom, to the left, to the right, forward, and backward [– are excluded (34a–b)]. On the basis of a comparison of the *Symposium* and the *Timaeus* – and of the two-step mechanism that consists in having the person who is for Plato the only one worthy of speaking of love clown around – we see that in Aristophanes' discourse, Plato seems to be having a good time by turning his own conception of the world and of the world soul into a comical exercise.

Aristophanes' discourse derides Plato's *sphairos* [sphere] as it is articulated in the *Timaeus*.

We don't have much time left and there would be plenty to add. But to show you that the astronomical reference is sure and certain in this context, I will nevertheless supply proof, for it might seem to you that I'm simply having a good time. The three types of sphere that Aristophanes imagined – the one that is all male, the one that is all female, and the one that is male and female, the androgynes as they're called (beings of each type have a pair of genitals) – have origins. And what are these origins? They are stellar. The males come from the sun, the all-women come from the earth, and the androgynes from the moon – confirming, moreover, in this way the lunar origin, as Aristophanes tells us, of those who have a propensity for adultery, for it is tantamount to having a composite origin [190a–b]. So much for the astronomical element.

Well, doesn't something show its face here that reveals the mainspring of our fascination with the spherical shape?

It is the shape that one is not supposed to mess with or contest. For centuries it left the human mind in error, in the error of refusing to think that, in the absence of any action or foreign impulse, a body is either at rest or in uniform rectilinear motion. A body at rest was supposed to not be able to have, apart from rest, anything other than circular motion, and all of dynamics was ruled out. Now, doesn't the incidental illustration that is furnished by Plato, who one can also call a poet, show us that what is at stake in shapes in which nothing sticks out or can be latched onto, has its foundations in the imaginary structure? But what is our attachment to such shapes due to, insofar as it is affective, if not to the *Verwerfung* [foreclosure] of castration?

This is so true that we find it in Aristophanes' discourse. These beings, split in two like pear halves, die, at a time x that is not specified since it is a mythical time, in a futile attempt to fuse anew. They are doomed to vain efforts to procreate in the earth, and I will skip the whole mythical discussion as it would take us too far afield. How is their problem to be resolved? Aristophanes speaks to us here exactly like little Hans does: their genitalia – which are in

117

118

the wrong place, because they are where they were when the beings were round, that is, they are on the outside – are unscrewed and screwed back onto the stomach, just like the faucet in Hans' dream as reported in Freud's case history.

It is unique and astonishing to see in Plato's work that the possibility of amorous relief is connected to something that is indisputably related, to say the least, to an operation involving the subject's genitalia. Whether we place this under the heading of the castration complex or not, it is clear that the text stresses the shift of the genitalia to the front side [191b]. This does not merely mean that the genital organ now has the possibility of serving as a copula, allowing junction with the beloved object, but that it is literally printed over [en surimpression] this object, almost superimposed on it. This is the only point at which the function of the genitals is betrayed or translated. Since we know that Plato's grasp of tragedy – he gives us a thousand proofs of this – did not go much further than Socrates', how can we fail to be struck by the fact that here, for the first and only time, he brings into play the genital organ as such in a discourse concerning a serious matter, that of love?

This confirms what I told you was essential to the mainspring of comedy, which is always, in the end, a reference to the phallus. And it is no accident that Aristophanes is the one who talks about it. He is the only one who can do so. But Plato does not realize that in having him speak of it, he has delivered to us – to those of us here – the linchpin that shifts the entire discourse that is to follow into another register.

This is where we will pick up the thread next time.

December 21, 1960

THE *ATOPIA* OF EROS

AGATHON

The commandments of the second death.
The signifier and immortality.
The analyst's desire.
The tragedian's macaronic fancy.

Let me pause briefly before leading you into the great enigma of transference love.

I have my reasons for occasionally pausing: it is important that we understand each other and that we not lose our bearings.

1

Since the beginning of this year I have felt a need to remind you that, in everything I have taught you, I have done nothing but point out that Freud's doctrine situates desire in a dialectic.

On this note, I must stop to remark that we are taking the road less traveled by. For I have already stated hereby that desire is not a life function, in the sense in which positivism defines life. Desire is caught up in a dialectic because it hinges – I have already said how it hinges, in the form of metonymy – on a signifying chain. The latter is, as such, both constitutive of the subject and that by which the subject is distinct from individuality taken simply as *hic et nunc* [here and now]. Keep in mind that this *hic et nunc* is what defines individuality.

Let us make an effort to delve into what individuation or the instinct of individuality is, inasmuch as individuation requires each individual, or so we are told in psychology, to conquer anew all of   120 real structure, whether by experience or learning. This is no small task, and one cannot conceptualize it without the presupposition that it is at least already prepared for by an adaptation or a whole set of adaptations. The human individual, as knowledge, is taken to be the flower of consciousness at the end of an evolutionary process.

I profoundly doubt that. Not that I consider it to be a fruitless direction or a dead end. I doubt it insofar as the idea of evolution gets us intellectually used to all sorts of elisions that are highly debilitating for reflection, especially as concerns our ethics as analysts. In any case, it seems essential to me to re-examine these elisions, and to indicate or reopen the gaps left in the theory of evolution insofar as it always tends to cover them over in order to make our practice [*expérience*] easier to conceptualize. If evolutionary theory is true, one thing is nevertheless certain, which is that evolution is not, as Voltaire said in another context, as natural as all that.

As for desire, it is in any case essential that we examine its conditions. The latter are given to us by our practice, which overturns the whole problem of givens. Indeed, what we find is that the subject keeps an articulated chain outside of consciousness, making it inaccessible to consciousness. It is a demand, and not a pressure, malaise, imprinting, or any other term you might try to use to characterize it as primitive – that is, as definable in terms of instincts [*tendanciellement*]. On the contrary, a trace is traced out there, so to speak, that is encircled by a line [*trait*], isolated as such, and raised to an ideographic power, let's say, on the condition that it be emphasized that we are not dealing with an index that can be attributed to anything isolated whatsoever. Rather, it is always linked to a concatenation, on one line, with other ideograms that are themselves encircled by the function that makes them signifiers. This demand constitutes a constant, albeit latent, claim upon the subject that is inaccessible to him. It is a statute or set of specifications that must be met. It is not the modulation that would result from some sort of phonetic inscription of the negative recorded on film or tape but, rather, a trace that goes into effect once and for all. It is a kind of recording, but only if you emphasize the term "record," with its connotation of classification in a file. It is a kind of memory, but only in terms of the meaning this word takes on in the realm of electronic machines.

121

Well, it was Freud's genius to have designated the medium of this chain. I think I have sufficiently shown you – and I will show it to you again, above all in an article I felt I needed to rewrite on the basis of what I said at the conference in Royaumont, and which will be published – that, in speaking of the id, Freud designated the death drive itself as the medium of this chain, insofar as he emphasized the lethal character of repetition compulsion.

Death. What Freud articulated as a tendency [*tendance*] toward death, as the desire of an unthinkable subject who presents himself in the living being in which it speaks [*ça parle*], is responsible for the eccentric position of desire in man, which has always constituted a paradox for ethics. This paradox is altogether unsolvable, it seems to me, from the perspective of evolutionary theory. How could desires – in what one might call their transcendental permanence, namely, the transgressive character that is fundamental to them – be neither the effect nor the source of what they constitute, that is, a permanent disorder in a body assumed to be subject to the statute of adaptation, regardless of the impact its effects are acknowledged to have?

Here, as in the history of physics, people have up until now merely tried to save the appearances. And I think I have helped you realize the import, and have given you ample opportunity to assess the importance, of what is meant by "saving the appearances" when it comes to epicycles in the Ptolemaic system.

Don't imagine that the people who taught this system for centuries – with the proliferation of epicycles it required, from about 30 to about 75 depending on the accuracy demanded of the system – truly believed in epicycles. Not for a minute did they believe that the heavens were made like little armillary spheres. They manufactured them with their epicycles, and I saw some recently in a hallway at the Vatican – quite a nice collection – showing the movements of Mars, Venus, and Mercury. A certain number of epicycles must be placed around each little ball in order for it to mimic a planet's movements, but no one ever seriously believed in them. Saving appearances simply meant accounting for what one saw in accordance with a theoretical requirement: the bias in favor of the perfection of the circle.

Well, it is more or less the same when one tries to explain desires by the system of needs, whether individual or collective. And I submit that no one in psychology – and by that I mean the psychology that runs through the entire moralist tradition – believes that any more, no more than anyone ever believed in epicycles, even at the time when people were working on them. In both cases, saving appearances means nothing but the following: trying to reduce to forms that are assumed to be perfect and necessary to the foundations of deduction, what can in no way – not with any good reason at least – be thus reduced.

I am trying to ground with you the basic topology of desire, its interpretation, and – in short – its rational ethics. The "between-two-deaths" – which is not so difficult to grasp, because it simply means that, for humankind, the two borders related to death do not overlap – grew out of this topology over the course of the last year.

122

The first border – whether linked to the fundamental time period [*échéance*] we call old age, aging, or decline, or to an accident that cuts the thread of life – is that at which life effectively ends and comes undone. Hence it is obvious, and has always been obvious, that man's situation is characterized by the fact that this border does not overlap with the second death, which can be most generally defined by saying that in it man aspires to annihilate himself in order to have his being inscribed [in history]. The hidden contradiction or rub is that man aspires to destroy himself in the very act of becoming immortal.

You will find this point throughout [Agathon's] speech, as well as in the others. You find myriad traces of it in the *Symposium*. I attempted to illustrate it for you last year by showing you the four corners of the space in which tragedy is situated. There is not one tragedy that is not shed light on thereby, precisely because an aspect of tragic space has been stolen [*dérobé*], to use that word, from poets in the course of history – in the seventeenth century, for example.

Consider any of Racine's tragedies and you will see that, in order for there to be any semblance of tragedy, the space of the between-two-deaths must in some way be invoked. If something resembling tragedy subsists in *Andromachus*, *Iphigenia*, or *Bajazet* – need I remind you of the plot? – it is because the two deaths are always there, regardless of how they may be symbolized. What lies between Hector's death and the death that is hanging over Astyanax's head is but the sign of another doubling [*duplicité*]. The hero is always placed in imminent danger of death but faces it in order to be remembered by posterity, which is a derisory form of the problem. This is what is signified by the two terms we continually encounter that refer to the twofold nature [*duplicité*] of the lethal function.

True enough. But while this may be necessary to maintain the framework of tragic space, we must still figure out how it is inhabited. I would simply like to clear away in passing the cobwebs that obstruct a direct view, in order to incite you to look at Racine's tragedies, pinnacles of Christian tragedy, which remain, through all their lyrical vibrations, so rich in poetic resonance.

Take *Iphigenia* for example. Everything that takes place in the play is irresistibly funny, you can see for yourselves. Agamemnon is fundamentally characterized there by his terror of the conjugal scene – "There, those are the cries I was afraid of hearing" [Act IV, Scene 5] – while Achilles appears in an unbelievably superficial position.

Why? I will try to indicate why a little later, in terms of Achilles' relation to death, a traditional relation for which he is always one of the first cases cited by Socrates' most intimate circle when they

123

exhibit their moralism. The history of Achilles, who deliberately prefers a death that will make him immortal to a refusal to fight that would spare his life, is mentioned everywhere, including in the *Apology*, where Socrates talks about it in order to define what his own conduct will be before his judges [28c–d]. We find echoes of it even in Racine's tragedies, cast in another light, which is far more important. It is one of the commonplaces which, in the course of the centuries, ceaselessly sound, echoing ever more loudly with a resonance that is increasingly hollow and bombastic.

What is lacking in tragedy when it is pursued beyond the range of limits that gave it its place in the living, breathing world of Antiquity? There is some kind of shadow, obscurity, or occultation related to the commandments of the second death.

124

There is no trace of these commandments in Racine, because by his time we are no longer in a context in which the Delphic oracle can make itself heard. The playwright gives us mere cruelty, vain contradiction, and absurdity. The characters talk on and on, dialoguing and soliloquizing, saying nothing more, in the end, than that there has surely been some sort of misunderstanding somewhere.

This is not at all the case in ancient tragedy. The commandment of the second death is ever present there. Being present there in a veiled form, it can be formulated and acknowledged as linked to the debt that accumulates without there being a guilty party and that is paid by a victim who does not deserve the punishment. It is, in short, the "he did not know" that I wrote for you at the top of the Graph of Desire, on the enunciation line that is fundamental to the topology of the unconscious. This is what is already achieved in ancient tragedy, or rather prefigured – I would say, were it not an anachronistic word – in relation to Freud, who immediately recognized it as being related to the *raison d'être* he had just discovered in the unconscious.

Freud recognized his discovery and his field in the tragedy of Oedipus, but it was neither because Oedipus killed his father nor because he wanted to sleep with his mother. A very amusing mythologist, Robert Graves – who has compiled a vast collection of myths in a work of no renown, but which is very useful and highly practical, two small volumes that were published by Penguin Books, in which he has gathered all of ancient mythology – thinks he is being clever concerning the Oedipus myth. "Why didn't Freud," he asks, "seek out his myth among the Egyptians, where the hippopotamus is said to sleep with its mother and crush its father? Why didn't he call it the hippopotamus complex?" He thinks he has, thereby, given Freudian mythology a fine punch in the gut.

But this is not why Freud chose Oedipus. Many heroes other

than Oedipus kill their fathers and want to sleep with their mothers.
The reason Freud found his fundamental figure in the tragedy of
Oedipus lies in the fact that "he did not know" he had killed his
father and was sleeping with his mother.

The fundamental terms of our topology have now been recalled
to mind. This reminder was necessary to continue our analysis of the
125   *Symposium*, in order that you perceive why it is of interest that it is
now Agathon, the tragic poet, who gives a speech on love.

But I must prolong this pause a little longer to clarify my remarks
on the subject of what, little by little, through the *Symposium*, I am
proposing concerning the mystery of Socrates.

2

I told you last time that for a while I had the feeling that I was killing
myself over the mystery of Socrates. It does not seem to me to be
unsituable. It is precisely because I believe, on the contrary, that we
can situate it perfectly well that we are justified in beginning with
this mystery in our research this year.

What is the mystery of Socrates? I will remind you of it in the
same annotated terms that I have just rearticulated for you, so you
can compare it with Plato's texts, which are our firsthand docu-
ments. Since I have noticed that, for some time now, it is no longer
in vain that I recommend certain readings to you, I will not hesitate
to invite you to supplement the *Symposium* – which almost all of
you have now read – with the *Phaedo*, which will give you a fine
example of Socratic method and suggest why it is of interest to us.

I would say that the mystery of Socrates – and one must look
at this firsthand document in order to make it shine anew in all its
originality – is the instituting of what he calls science, *epistéme*.

You can verify what it means in the text. It is quite obvious that it
has neither the same meaning nor the same accent in the *Phaedo* as
it has for us, since there was not at the time even the slightest beginning of what has since been articulated for us under the heading of
"science." The best formulation you can give for the instating of this
science – in what? in consciousness – in a position, in an absolute
dignity, or more precisely in a position of absolute dignity, is to
say that it involves nothing other than what we can express in our
vocabulary as the promotion of the signifier itself to a position of
absolute dignity. What Socrates calls science is what is necessarily
imposed on every interlocution as a function of a certain manipula-
126   tion or internal coherence that is linked, or that he believes to be
linked, to the sole, pure, and simple reference to the signifier.

As you will see, in the *Phaedo* Socrates is pushed as far as he can go by the disbelief of his interlocutors who, however constraining his arguments may seem, do not altogether agree, no more than anyone would, with his assertion that the soul is immortal. What he refers to in the final analysis, and in a less and less convincing way, at least to us, are properties such as even and odd. It is on the basis of the fact that the number three cannot in any way be qualified as even and on other such points that he bases his demonstration that the soul cannot be said to be destructible, as it is at the very crux of life [103d–106d]. You will see to what extent what I call the privileged reference to the signifier, which is proposed as a sort of cult or essential rite, accounts for everything that the emergence of Socrates in the midst of the Sophists contributes that is new, original, decisive, fascinating, and seductive – there is historical testimony of this.

The second term I will extract from the testimony that has been handed down to us is as follows: thanks to Socrates, his total presence, his destiny, his death, and what he asserts before dying, it appears that this promotion [of the signifier to a position of absolute dignity] is consistent with the effect I showed you, which is to abolish in a man, totally it seems, what I would call, borrowing Kierkegaard's terms, fear and trembling. Fear and trembling before what? Not the first, but rather the second death.

Socrates does not hesitate on this score. He claims that it is in this second death – embodied in his dialectic by the fact that he raises the coherence of the signifier to an absolute power, to the power of being the sole ground of certainty – that he, Socrates, will indubitably find eternal life.

On the condition that you not read anything more into what I am going say, I will take the liberty of tracing out tangentially, as a sort of parody, the appearance of Cotard's syndrome. Socrates, the indefatigable questioner, seems to me to overlook the fact that his mouth was flesh, and it is in this sense that his assertion is coherent, though not his certainty. Don't we almost find ourselves faced here with an apparition that is foreign to us, with a manifestation that I would qualify – to use our jargon in order to make myself perfectly clear and progress quickly – as akin to the psychotic core? I am thinking of the way, the very exceptional way, I assure you, Socrates implacably unfolds his arguments, which are not really arguments, but also posits before his disciples, the very day of his death, the assertion, perhaps more affirmative than any ever before heard from him, that he, Socrates, is serenely leaving this life for a truer, immortal life. He does not doubt but that he will join those who still exist for him, let us not forget it, the Immortals. The notion of the Immortals cannot be eliminated or removed from his thought. It is in terms of the antinomy between the Immortals and the mortals, which is absolutely fundamental in ancient thought, and no less, believe me, in ours, that his living, real-life testimony takes on its full value.

Let me thus summarize. This indefatigable questioner – who is not a speaker, who keeps his distance from rhetoric, metrics, and poetics, who eliminates metaphor, who lives entirely in the game, not of the finessed [*forcée*] card, but of the forced question, and who derives all of his sustenance from it – generates before our eyes and develops throughout his life what I will call a formidable metonymy. Its result, which is historically attested as well, is a desire that is embodied in an assertion of immortality, an immortality that is, I would say, fixed – sad "immortality, all black and gold" [*immortalité noire et dorée*], wrote Valéry – a desire for infinite discourses.

Indeed, while he is sure he will join the Immortals in the next world, he is also, he says, more or less certain he will be able to continue his little verbal exercises for all eternity with interlocutors worthy of him: those who came before him and all those who will come to join him later [*Apology*, 40d–41c]. Admit it: this conception, as satisfying as it may be for people who like allegorical painting, is nevertheless a fancy which singularly smacks of delusion. To argue about even and odd, the just and the unjust, the mortal and the immortal, hot and cold, and about the fact that hot cannot allow cold within itself without weakening, without retiring in its essence of hot to one side, as is explained at length in the *Phaedo* [103c] as the main reason for the immortality of the soul – to debate about that for all eternity is a very odd conception of happiness.

Let us put things in perspective. One man thus experienced the question of the immortality of the soul. I would go even further: the soul as we still handle it today and are still weighed down by it, the notion or figure of the soul that we have – which is not the conception that developed in the course of all the waves of the traditional legacy – the soul we deal with in the Christian tradition has as its internal brace, frame, or truss the by-product of Socrates' delusion of immortality. We are still living off it.

What I would simply like to conjure up before you is the energy behind Socrates' assertion concerning the immortality of the soul. Why is that? It is obviously not for the import that we can give it now, for it is quite obvious that after several centuries of exercise and even of spiritual exercises, the rate, so to speak, of belief in the immortality of the soul – among all of those here before me, whether believers or nonbelievers – is quite tempered, as one says that a scale is tempered. No, that is not the point. If I ask you to reflect on the postulation of the immortality of the soul at that time, on certain

128

grounds, by a man who, in his wake, astonished his contemporaries by his discourse, it is in order to get you to wonder about the following, which is quite important: for this phenomenon to have occurred, for a man – who has, over Nietzsche's Zarathustra, the advantage of having existed – to have acceded to this same "Thus spoke . . . ," as they say, what must Socrates' desire have been?

This is the crucial question that I think I can raise here, and all the more easily since I have at length described for you the topology that gives it its meaning.

Open any of Plato's dialogues to a passage related directly to Socrates as a person, and you can check the well-founded nature of what I am telling you about the forthright, paradoxical position of his assertion of immortality, and about what it is founded on – namely, his idea of science insofar as I situate it as the pure and simple raising of the function of the signifier in consciousness to an absolute value. To what does the position he introduces correspond? To what *atopia*? As you know, I am not the one who applied this term, *atopia*, to Socrates. To what *atopia* of desire?

Atopos refers to a case that is unclassifiable or unsituable. *Atopia*, you cannot put it anywhere. That's the point. This is what Socrates' contemporaries were whispering about him.

Doesn't this *atopia* of desire about which I am raising a question,   129
coincide to me, to us, in a certain way with what I might call a certain topographical purity? For it designates the central point at which, in our topology, the space of the between-two-deaths is found in a pure state, emptying out the place of desire as such. Desire is no longer anything but its place there, insofar as it is no longer anything for Socrates than a desire for discourse, revealed discourse, discourse that is forever revealing. Hence the *atopia* of the Socratic subject, assuming that such a purified place of desire was never occupied by any man before him.

I will not answer this question, confining myself to raising it. It is plausible and, at the very least, it gives us a first landmark by which to situate the question, one that we cannot eliminate once we have raised it. And, after all, I am not the one who first raised it – it was already posed as soon as we realized that the complexity of the topic of transference could in no way be limited to what takes place in the subject known as the patient, he who is analyzed. Consequently, the question arises of articulating, in a slightly more sophisticated way than has ever been done up until now, what the analyst's desire must be.

It does not suffice to speak of training *catharsis* or of purification, so to speak, of the bulk of the analyst's unconscious. Such a notion remains terribly vague. Analysts must be credited with the fact that, for some time now, they have not been satisfied with it. We must realize, not in order to criticize them, but rather in order to understand the obstacle at hand, that we don't have at our disposal even the slightest sketch of what one could nevertheless articulate so easily, in the form of a question, concerning what must be attained in someone so that he may be an analyst. People say that he must come to know a little bit more about the dialectic in his unconscious. But what exactly does he know about it in the final reckoning? And, above all, how far does what he knows about it have to go concerning the very effects of knowledge? I will simply raise the following question: what must remain of his fantasies? You know that I can go further still and say of his *fantasy*, assuming that there is one fundamental fantasy. If castration is what must be accepted at the end of an analysis, what role must the scar of castration play in the analyst's Eros?

130   These are questions that are more easily raised than answered. Which is why people do not raise them. And, believe me, I would not raise them either in a void, for the simple purpose of sparking your imagination, if I did not think that there must be a method – a method that broaches this from a different angle or even proceeds indirectly or in a roundabout fashion – by which to shed some light on these questions that we obviously cannot for the moment answer utterly and completely. All I can say for the time being is that it does not seem to me that what is called the doctor–patient relationship – with all it brings with it by way of presuppositions, prejudices, and molasses attracting swarms of flies – allows us to make much headway in this direction.

We must thus try to articulate and situate what the analyst's desire should be, and what it is fundamentally. And we must do so in accordance with the markers that can, on the basis of an already sketched out topology, be designated as the coordinates of desire. We cannot find appropriate landmarks by referring to articulations of the situation for the therapist or the observer, nor in any of the phenomenological notions of "situation" being elaborated around us. For the analyst's desire is not such that it can be explained by reference to a dyad. It is not the relationship to the patient that can, through a series of eliminations and debarments, give us the key thereto. Something more intrapersonal is at stake.

Nor is this to say that the analyst must be a Socrates, a virtuous person [*un pur*], or a saint. Explorers like Socrates, the virtuous, and saints can, no doubt, give us several indications concerning our field. But they do not go far enough – upon reflection, all of our science, I mean experimental science, is related to this field. Yet it is precisely because they are the ones who do the exploring that we can perhaps define, in terms of longitude and latitude, the coordinates the analyst must be able to attain simply in order to occupy the place that is his, defined as the place he must offer up as vacant to the patient's desire in order for the latter to be realized as the Other's desire.

It is in this respect that the *Symposium* is of interest to us and that it is useful terrain to explore. This is due to the privileged place that testimony about Socrates occupies in it, inasmuch as this text is supposed to show him grappling with the problem of love right before our very eyes.

I believe I have said enough to justify why we are approaching the problem of transference through a commentary on the *Symposium*. I felt it was necessary to recall these coordinates to mind before we enter into what occupies the central or almost central place in this famous dialogue – namely, Agathon's speech.

131

3

Is it Aristophanes or Agathon who occupies the central place? Why bother to try to decide? The two of them certainly occupy the central place, since everything that was demonstrated before turns out, apparently, to be already remote and devalued when their turns come, and what comes afterward is no other than Socrates' speech.

Concerning the speech by Agathon, the tragic poet, one could say a great many things – not simply for the sake of erudition – that would lead us into details about and even into a history of tragedy, of which I gave you a brief sketch a bit earlier. What is of importance is not that, but rather to get you to see its role in the economy of the *Symposium*.

As you have seen, Agathon's speech takes up five or six pages in the French translation by Robin, published in the Guillaume Budé collection. I will begin with its pinnacle, and you will see why. Let me remind you that I am here less in order to provide you with an elegant commentary, than to lead you to what the *Symposium* can or should provide us.

The least one can say of Agathon's speech is that it has always struck readers for its extraordinary sophistry, in the modern, everyday, pejorative sense of the word. His sophistry here consists in saying that Love "does no wrong to gods or men, nor they to him." Why? Because "if anything has an effect on him, it is never by violence," for everyone knows that "violence never touches Love." Thus "the effects he has on others are not forced, for every service we give to Love," so we are told, "we give willingly. And whatever one person agrees on with another, when both are willing, that is

right and just; so say the laws that are kings of society" [196b–c].
Morality – love is what is at the very core of the laws of the city, and
so on and so forth. As love is the strongest of all desires, irresistible
passion, it is tempered with moderation, for moderation is what
regulates desires and pleasures. Love must thus, by all rights, be
identified with moderation.

Manifestly, a bit of fun is being had here. Who is having fun? Is
it simply we the readers? We would be wrong to think that we are
alone. Agathon certainly does not play a secondary role here, if only
for the fact that, at least according to the givens of the situation, he
is Socrates' beloved. Let us give Plato the benefit of the doubt by
believing that he is having a bit of fun as well with what I will now
call – and I will justify it better a little later – the tragedian's macaronic discourse. But I am sure, and you too will be sure as soon as
you read it, that we would be wrong not to realize that it is neither
simply us nor Plato having a bit of fun here. As opposed to what
commentators have said, it is altogether out of the question that
Agathon not know perfectly well what he is doing.

Things go so far and he gets so carried away that, at the pinnacle
of his speech, Agathon says to us, "I am suddenly struck by a need
to say something in poetic meter" [197c].

He expresses himself in the following terms – εἰρήνην μὲν ἐν
ἀνθρώποις (eirénen men en anthrópois) [peace among people] –
which means that love puts an end to all the ruckus [rififi]. Quite an
unusual conception. It must be admitted that up until this idyllic
modulation, one hardly suspected any such thing.

But to spell it out for you letter by letter, he tops it all off by
saying, πελάγει δὲ γαλήνην (peláge de galénen), which means that
everything has stopped, a flat sea [no waves or wind]. We must keep
in mind what a flat sea meant in Antiquity – it meant that nothing
was going right, that the ships were blocked at Aulis, and when that
happened in the middle of the deep blue sea, people were bothered
by it, almost as bothered as when that happened to them in bed. To
evoke peláge de galénen concerning love makes it quite clear that a
bit of fun is being had here. Love is what makes you break down, it's
what leads to a fiasco.

This is not all – afterward, Agathon says, there is no more wind
among the winds. He goes on – love, there is no more love, νηνεμίαν
(nenemían), ἀνέμων (anémon) [stillness, without wind]. It sounds,
moreover, like the forever comic verses of a certain tradition, like
the following two verses by Paul-Jean Toulet:

Sous le double ornement d'un nom mol ou sonore,
Non, il n'est rien que Nanine et Nonore.

This is the sort of realm we are in here. And we have κοίτην (*koíten*) in addition, which means in bed, beddy-bye, no more wind in the sails, all the winds have gone to sleep. Then we have ὕπνον τ' ἐνὶ κήδει (*húpnon t'ení kédei*). Strangely enough, love brings us "sleep amidst our worries," as one might translate it at first glance, but look closely at the meaning of these cadences and of κῆδος (*kédos*).

This Greek term is quite rich in connotations, which allow us to reassert the value of what Émile Benveniste once – with no doubt a great deal of goodwill toward me, but perhaps nevertheless missing something essential in that he did not follow Freud – articulated concerning the ambivalence of signifiers for our first issue of *La Psychanalyse*. *Kédos* does not simply mean worry, but also kinship. ὕπνον τ' ἐνὶ κήδει (*húpnon t'ení kédei*) [regard for another] sketches it out for us as [in the SiRonga proverb]: "A relative by marriage is an elephant's shank," as one finds it in Lévi-Strauss' work. This *húpnos*, peaceful sleep, *t'ení kédei*, in relation to in-laws, seems to me to be worthy of crowning verses that are indisputably designed to wake us up in case we have not yet understood that Agathon is making fun of something.

Moreover, from this moment on, he literally lets loose, and tells us that love is what liberates us, alleviating us of "the belief that we are strangers to each other." Naturally, when one is possessed by love, one realizes that we are all part of one big happy family, and it is truly from that moment on that one feels all warm inside and at home, and so on and so forth. This goes on line after line [197c–d] – I will leave you the pleasure of spending your evenings savoring it.

Do you agree that love clearly "moves us to mildness" and "removes from us wildness," that it spreads "kindness" and is incapable of "meanness"? Agathon provides here an enumeration on which I would like us to dwell at length. Love is said to be the father of Τρυφή (*Truphé*), Ἁβρότης (*Habrótes*), Χλιδή (*Chlidé*), Χάριτες (*Chárites*), Ἵμερος (*Hímeros*), and Πόθος (*Póthos*). One can, as a first approximation, translate – well-being, delicateness, languidness, graciousness, ardor, and passion. It would take us more time than we have here to carry out the twofold task of finding the French equivalent for the Greek terms, and to compare them with the headings of kind deeds and honesty in courtly love, as we discussed them last year. It would thus be easy for you to see that it is impossible to be satisfied when Léon Robin relates Agathon's list to the *Carte du Tendre*, as one could to the virtues of the knight in the *Minne* that he does not even mention.

Taking text in hand, I could show you that not one of these terms lends itself to such a parallel. *Truphé*, for example, which people willingly translate as "well-being," is, by most authors, and not just the comic authors, used with the most unpleasant connotations. In Aristophanes, for example, the word designates what is suddenly introduced by a woman or wife into the peace enjoyed by a man – her unbearable pretensions. The woman known as τρυφερά (*trupherá*) is an unbearable snob, one who does not for a single second stop telling her husband that her father and her family are better than his. And so on and so forth. Every one of these terms is habitually and for the most part conjoined or juxtaposed by Antiquity's authors – whether tragedians or even poets like Hesiod in this case – with αὐθαδία (*authadía*), which signifies one of the most unbearable forms of hubris and smugness.

I merely wish to point these things out to you in passing. Let us move on. Love "cares well for good men, cares not for bad ones. In pain, in fear, in desire or speech," etc. Such translations signify absolutely nothing, for we have in Greek ἐν πόνῳ, ἐν φόβῳ [. . .], ἐν λόγῳ (*en póno, en phóbo* [. . .], *en lógo*), which means, "in deep trouble, in fear [. . .], in discourse." And κυβερνήτης, ἐπιβάτης (*kubernétes, epibátes*) is the one who is at the helm. It is also the one who is ready to guide. In other words, they're having quite a fine time. *Póno, phóbo, pótho*, and *lógo* are all jumbled up here [197d–e]. The point is always to produce an ironic effect, and even disorientation. This, for a tragic poet, has no other meaning than to stress that love is what is truly unclassifiable, blocking every important situation. Love is what is never in its place and is always inopportune.

Whether or not this conception can be defended is not the issue and, strictly speaking, it is certainly not the acme of what the *Symposium* teaches us about love. What is important is that it is the tragic poet who gives the only speech about love that is openly and completely derisory. To seal the well-foundedness of this interpretation, it suffices to read Agathon's conclusion. "This, Phaedrus, is the speech I have to offer. Let it be dedicated to the god, part of it in fun, part of it moderately serious, as best I could manage."

The speech itself is affected, so to speak, by its connotation as jesting speech, the speech of a jokester. This is all Agathon as such – in other words, as he who is being celebrated here, let us not forget, for his triumph at the tragedy competition, the day after his victory – has the right to say about love.

There is nothing here that should throw us off. In every tragedy situated in its full context, in other words in the context of Antiquity, love always figures as a marginal incident and drags behind, so to speak. Rather than being what directs and runs on ahead, love merely lags behind in tragedy. This is the exact term that you will find in Agathon's speech – love lags behind what he compares it to, strangely enough, in one passage: *Áte*.

I pointed out the function of Ἄτη (*Áte*) in tragedy last year. *Áte* means mischief [195d], the thing that has arisen as an obstacle and can never be exhausted. It is the calamity that lies behind every tragic adventure and that – as the poet tells us, for it is to Homer that people refer here – "gets around only by running on the heads of men with its feet which are too tender to touch the ground" [*Iliad*, XIX, 91–4]. Thus *Áte* moves rapidly and indifferently, striking and forever dominating, making heads bow down and driving men crazy. Oddly enough, Agathon mentions *Áte* in order to tell us that Love must, like *Áte*, have very delicate feet since it can only walk on the heads of men. Confirming yet again the fanciful nature of Agathon's speech, he makes a number of jokes on this score about the fact that, after all, skulls are perhaps not as soft as all that [195e].

Our entire experience of tragedy confirms the analysis we are making of the style of this speech. Owing to the Christian context, [the idea that one has an] ultimate destiny is purged [*vidé*], as are the closed and incomprehensible nature of the fatal oracle and the inexpressibility of the commandment as regards the second death. It is inasmuch as this commandment can no longer be sustained – since we find ourselves faced with a god who is unable to give senseless orders and who removes death's cruel sting – that love appears. Love takes their place, filling up this emptiness [*vide*].

136

Racine's *Iphigenia* offers us the finest illustration of this, embodying this change in some sense. We had to reach a Christian context for Iphigenia to no longer suffice as a tragic figure, and for it to be necessary to double her with Eriphilia. And rightly so, not simply so that Eriphilia could be sacrificed in Iphigenia's stead, but because Eriphilia is the only one who is truly in love. Her love is depicted as terrible, horrible, evil, and tragic in order to restore a certain depth to tragic space. It is also because every time this love – with which the play is quite concerned, with Achilles primarily – manifests itself as love pure and simple, and not as dark love [*amour noir*] or jealous love, it is irresistibly comic.

In short, we find ourselves at a crossroads at which, as will be recalled in the final conclusions of the *Symposium*, it is not enough, in speaking of love, to be a tragic poet. One must also be a comic poet.

It is at this point that Socrates responds to Agathon's speech. To appraise how he does so, it was necessary, as you will see in what follows, to articulate it with all the stress that I felt I needed to give it today.

January 11, 1961

VIII

FROM *EPISTÉME* TO *MÝTHOUS*

From love to desire.
The limits of Socratic knowledge.
Socrates "diocesed."
Masculine desirable, feminine desiring.
Love as *metaxú*.

We have now reached the point in the *Symposium* at which Socrates is going to take the floor and give an *épainos* or *enkómion*. The two terms are not exactly equivalent, as I mentioned in passing some time ago, but I didn't want to dwell on their difference as it would have taken me off on quite a tangent.

In praising love, we are told by Socrates himself, and his word cannot be disputed in Plato's work, that if he knows anything, if there is anything about which he is not ignorant, it is about matters of love. Let us not lose sight of this in all that takes place.

1

Last time I emphasized, in a way which I believe was convincing enough, the strangely derisory character of Agathon's discourse.

Agathon the tragedian speaks of love in a way that gives you the feeling he is playing the fool in his macaronic speech. The impression he gives us at every instant is that he's pulling our leg a bit. I stressed – both in the content and body of his arguments, on the one hand, and in his detailed elocutionary style itself – the exceedingly provocative nature of the short verses he comes up with at one point, and how disconcerting it is to see the theme of the *Symposium* culminate in such a speech. My reading of his speech is not new, although the function I give it in the unfolding of the *Symposium* perhaps is. The derisory character of his speech has always given pause to those who have read it and commented upon it. So much so that the German scholar from the beginning of the century – whose name, Wilamowitz-Moellendorff, the day I mentioned it, made you laugh, though I don't know why – says, following thereby in the footsteps of almost all those who came before him, that Agathon's speech is characterized by its *Nichtigkeit*, its vacuousness.

It is thus quite odd that Plato put this speech in the mouth of the person who immediately precedes Socrates, and who is, let us not forget, Socrates' beloved at the moment of the symposium.

There is a sort of interlude even before Agathon takes the floor. Socrates says something like, "After all we have just heard, and if now Agathon is going to add his speech to the others, how am I going to be able to speak?" [194a]. Agathon, for his part, apologizes, and announces some hesitation, fear, and intimidation too, about speaking before an audience that is, let us say, so enlightened, so intelligent, so ἔμφρονες (*émphrones*) [sensible, 194b]. And here a debate begins with Socrates, who questions Agathon in more or less the following terms: "Are you, then, embarrassed to show yourself to be possibly inferior only in front of us? Would you be serene about putting forward less well-assured ideas in front of others, in front of a crowd or throng?" [194b–d]. Here, by goodness, we don't know very well what we're getting into. The direction could be rather risqué. Is he trying to get at some sort of aristocratism of dialogue? Or, as seems more likely, for all of Socrates' practice attests to it, is the point, rather, to show that even an ignoramus or slave is capable of revealing in himself the seeds of sure judgment and truth when appropriately questioned?

As they proceed in this direction, Phaedrus interrupts: "Agathon, don't let Socrates get you going. He knows nothing more pleasurable," he says expressly, "than to speak with the one he loves, and once we get started in such a dialogue, we'll never see the end of it" [194d]. On that note, Agathon commences his speech, after which Socrates finds himself in a position to correct him.

It is all too easy for Socrates to do so. His method immediately proves to be brilliantly superior, and effortlessly brings out what has just dialectically exploded in Agathon's speech. The procedure is such that it can only be a refutation or annihilation of Agathon's speech, revealing its ineptitude and vacuousness, which commentators, namely the one I mentioned earlier, think Socrates is loath to take too far for fear of humiliating his interlocutor. This would, in their view, explain why Socrates stops short, and proceeds instead by means of she who will go down in history as but a prestigious figure, Diotima, the stranger from Mantinea. If Socrates has Diotima speak in his stead, if he has himself instructed by her here,

139

it is supposedly so as not to put himself any longer in the position of
grandmaster in relation to Agathon, to whom he has dealt a decisive
blow.

According to this view, Socrates gives the floor to an imaginary
character who instructs him in order to attenuate the distress he has
caused Agathon.

I beg to differ with this view. If we examine the text more closely,
we cannot say that this is its precise meaning. At the very point
where people try to show us that Agathon admits he got off track –
"It turns out, Socrates, I didn't know what I was talking about in
that speech" [201b] – the impression we are left with in listening
to him is rather that of someone who replies something like, "We
are not on the same level, I spoke in a way that had a meaning
and an underside; we might even go so far as to say that I spoke
by enigma" – don't forget αἶνος (aínos) and αἰνίττομαι (ainíttomai),
which take us to the very etymology of the word "enigma" – "I
adopted a certain tone in saying what I said."

Furthermore, we find in Socrates' reply that there is a certain
way of conceptualizing the kind of praise that involves enveloping
the object of praise with all that is best. Socrates denigrates this
approach for a moment, but did Agathon really adopt it? On the
contrary, it seems that in the very excessive quality of his speech,
there was something that was simply asking to be heard. In short, if
we understand Agathon's answer in what I think is the right way, we
may have the impression for an instant that Socrates, by introducing his critique, dialectic, or mode of interrogation here, ultimately
finds himself in a pedantic position.

It is clear that there was something ironic in what Agathon said.
Socrates, who tramples over everything with his hobnailed boots,
changes the rules of the game. And actually, when Agathon retorts,
Ἐγώ, φάναι, ὦ Σώκρατες (Egó, phánai, O Sókrates) and so on – "I'm
not going to argue or debate with you, but I agree; go to it in your
own way, using your own *modus operandi*" [201c] – we have the
impression of someone withdrawing here and saying to Socrates,
"Let us now shift to another register, to another way of speaking."
But we cannot agree with the commentators, even with the one
whose translation I have before me, Léon Robin, that this constitutes a sign of impatience on Agathon's part.

To determine whether or not Agathon's speech can be bracketed
from this truly paradoxical game, from this sophistic *tour de force*,
we need but take seriously – which is the right way to go about it –
what Socrates says about it himself. To avail myself of the French
term that is most apt here, I would say that Agathon's is a speech
that shocks [*sidère*] or dumbfounds [*méduse*] him. This is expressly

140

stated in the text, for Socrates puns on the name Gorgias and the Gorgon's head [198c]. Agathon's speech, which closes the door to the dialectical game, fascinates Socrates and turns him, as he says, to stone. Such an effect should not be neglected.

Socrates, naturally, shifts things to the level of his method, as it is presented to us by Plato. This involves his method of questioning, his way of questioning, and also of articulating and dividing the object – that is, his way of operating in accordance with this *diairesis* thanks to which the object is presented for examination and situated in a certain way whose register we can locate. The Socratic method thus promises at the outset a development of knowledge that will constitute progress. But the import of Agathon's speech is not anni- hilated for all that. It is situated in another register, yet it remains exemplary and plays an essential role in the progress of what is shown to us by way of the succession of eulogies concerning love.

It is probably significant, and rich in instruction, suggestions, and questions for us, that it is Agathon the tragedian who turns love into a comical *romancero*, so to speak, and that it is Aristophanes the comedian who speaks of love in the sense of passion, with an almost modern accent. Socrates' intervention comes as a kind of rupture or break, but one that does not discredit or annihilate what was just stated in Agathon's speech. Can we consider meaningless or as merely antiphrastic the fact that Socrates emphasizes only the fact that it was καλὸν λόγον (*kalón lógon*), a fine speech [198b]? What is ridiculous and can give rise to laughter is often evoked in the text that precedes this, but Socrates in no wise seems to tell us this is the case when he makes his shift in register. At the very moment at which he introduces the wedge that his dialectic rams into the topic to contribute what one expects from the Socratic light, we have the sense of a discordance, and not of a comparison designed to alto- gether annul what was formulated in Agathon's speech.

With Socrates' questioning, with what is articulated as being Socrates' own method – by which, if you will allow me this Greek pun, the *erómeno*s, the beloved, becomes ἐρωτώμενος (*erotómenos*), the questionee – a topic is raised that I have announced several times since the beginning of my commentary: the function of lack.

Everything Agathon says, for example, about the beautiful – that it belongs to love and that it is one of love's attributes – succumbs to Socrates' questioning: "Is the love about which you spoke love of something? Does loving and desiring something mean having it or not having it? Can one desire what one already has?" [199e–200a].

I will skip over the details regarding the way this question is artic- ulated. Socrates casts it and recasts it with an acuity that, as usual, turns his interlocutor into someone he can handle and manipulate.

141

This is precisely the ambiguity of Socrates as a questioner – he is always the master, even when this may in many cases seem to us, his readers, to be an easy way out. It is, moreover, of little import to know what, in this case, must or can be rigorously developed. What concerns us here is the testimony that constitutes the essence of Socrates' questioning, and also what Socrates introduces, wants to produce, and conventionally speaks about.

We are told that his adversary is unable to refute the conclusion that "such a man or anyone else who has a desire, desires what is not at hand and not present, what he does not have, and what he is not, and that of which he is in want; for such are the objects of desire and love" [200e]. The text is certainly weakly translated: ἐπιθυμεῖ (*epithumeî*) means he desires, τοῦ μὴ ἑτοίμου (*tou me hetoímou*) is strictly speaking "what is not ready to wear," τοῦ μὴ παρόντος (*tou me paróntos*), what is not there, ὃ μὴ ἔχει (*ho me échei*), what he does not have, ὃ μὴ ἔστιν αὐτός (*ho me éstin autós*), what he is not himself, and οὖ ἐνδεής ἐστι (*hou endeés estí*), that which he is lacking or essentially lacks.

This is what is articulated by Socrates in what he brings to this dialogue. It concerns something which he says is not situated at the level of word play, by which the subject is captured, captivated, transfixed, and fascinated, and it is in this respect that his method is distinguished from that of the Sophists. He makes the progress of the discourse he develops – with no concern for elegance, so he tells us, using everyday words – reside in the exchange, dialogue, or consent obtained from the person with whom he is speaking. Such consent is presented as the springing forth or necessary emergence of knowledge that his interlocutor already has.

This is, as you know, the linchpin of the whole Platonic theory of the soul, its nature, consistency, and origin. All of this knowledge is already and has forever been there in the soul, and it suffices to pose the right questions to re-evoke and reveal it. This attests to the pre-existence of knowledge, which is why we can but presuppose that the soul partakes of an infinite anteriority. The soul is not merely immortal – it has always been in existence. This is what paves the way for reincarnation and clears the way for metempsychosis. It is, no doubt, what accompanies the development of Platonic thought at the level of myth, which is not that of dialectic.

Something should strike us in this regard. Having introduced what I earlier called the wedge of the function of lack as constitutive of love relations, Socrates goes no further when speaking in his own name. To ask why he substitutes Diotima's authority for his own is to raise a good question.

Yet to say that it is in order to spare Agathon's pride is to answer this question a bit too easily. If things stand as we are told, Plato could simply execute an altogether elementary judo or jiu-jitsu move, since Agathon expressly says, "Please excuse me, I didn't know what I was saying; my concern lies elsewhere." It is not so much Agathon as Socrates who is in a pickle here. Since we cannot in any way assume that Plato intended to show Socrates to be pedantic or heavy-handed, after Agathon's assuredly lighthearted speech, were it only for its amusing style, we must surely conclude that if Socrates hands the floor over to someone else in his speech, it is for some other reason than because he himself cannot continue without offending Agathon.

143

This other reason can be immediately situated – it is due to the nature of the affair or thing, *to prágma*, that is at stake.

2

We can suspect, and what follows confirms it, that Socrates is necessarily led to proceed in this manner because they are speaking of love.

Let us note, indeed, the point on which his question bears. The function of lack, to which he gave its own efficacy, is quite patently a return to the desiring function of love: the substitution of ἐπιθυμεῖ (*epithumeî*), he desires, for ἐρᾷ (*erá*), he loves. We can point in the text to the moment at which, asking Agathon whether he thinks love is or is not the love of something, he substitutes the term "desire" for the term "love" [200a].

One might legitimately object, in the name of the very method which is that of Socratic knowledge, that the way love is related to desire is not, strictly speaking, articulated here as a substitution. We have every right to remark that the substitution is carried out a bit quickly here. Which is not to say, however, that Socrates errs in this context, since it is clearly around the articulation of love-Eros and desire-Eros that the entire dialectic developed in the dialogue as a whole in fact revolves. The thing nevertheless needs to be pointed out in passing.

Let us note again that it is hardly accidental that we find thus isolated what is, strictly speaking, Socrates' presentation. Socrates goes so far that what, last time, I called his method – which is to bring to bear the effect of his questioning on what I call the coherence of the signifier – becomes manifest and visible in the very flow of his speech. Consider the way in which he poses his question to Agathon: εἶναι τινὸς ὁ Ἔρως ἔρως, ἢ οὐδενός (*eînai tinós ho Éros éros, e oudenós*), "Is Love such as to be love of something or of nothing?"

[199d]. As the Greek genitive, like the French genitive, has its ambiguities, "something" can take on two meanings here, and these two meanings are articulated in a heavy-handed, almost caricatural way, in the distinction that Socrates draws – τινὸς (*tinós*) can mean being someone's descendant. "I'm not asking," he says, "if he is born of some mother or father" [199d], referring to the whole theogony that was discussed earlier on in the dialogue. The point is not to know from what Love descends, from whom, from what god, it comes – "my kingdom is not of this world," as it is said. The point is, rather, to know, at the level of the questioning of the signifier, what love as a signifier is correlated with.

To the first way of understanding the question [199d], Socrates opposes an example that we cannot help noticing. It is the same thing, he says, to ask regarding "Father," "When you say father, what does that imply?" It is not a question of a real father – that is, what he has by way of a child – but rather of the fact that, when one speaks of a father, one necessarily talks about a son. The father is, by definition, father of a son insofar as he is a father. "You'd tell me, of course, if you wanted to give me a good answer," as Léon Robin translates the Greek, "that it's of a son or a daughter that a father is the father" [199d]. Here we are in the specific realm of Socrates' dialectic, which consists in questioning the signifier as to its coherence as a signifier. Socrates is very nimble and sure-footed on this turf. This is what allows the rather quick substitution I mentioned earlier between Eros and desire to occur. To his mind, this is a form of marked progress that is made possible, he says, by his method.

If he yields the floor to Diotima, isn't it because, concerning love, the Socratic method itself can go no further? Everything shows this to be true, and Diotima's speech itself does so as well.

Why should we be surprised by this? If the *initium* [beginning] of the Socratic approach constitutes a step forward compared to that of his contemporaries, the Sophists, it is because this knowledge – the only certain knowledge, as Socrates tells us in the *Phaedo* – can be asserted on the sole basis of the coherence of discourse that involves dialogue and that revolves around apprehension of the necessity of the law of the signifier. Need I remind you that what is involved when one speaks of even and odd is a domain entirely enclosed within its own register? I think that I have taken enough pains in my teaching here and given you enough exercises to have shown you that even and odd owe nothing to any other experience than to that of the play of signifiers themselves. There is nothing even or odd, in other words countable, other than what has already been raised to the function of a signifying element or seed of the signifying chain. One can count words or syllables, but one can only count things on the basis of the fact that words and syllables are already counted.

We are clearly at this level when Socrates situates himself outside of the confused world of the debate among the physicists who preceded him, and outside of the discussion of the Sophists who exploit, at various levels, what I might call, in an abbreviated way – and you know that I only resolve to do so with all kinds of reservations – the magical power of words. Socrates, on the contrary, asserts that knowledge resides within the play of the signifier. He posits at the same time that this knowledge, which is entirely transparent to itself, is what constitutes its truth.

Now, haven't we taken a step forward in the same realm that leads us to disagree with Socrates? Socrates' no doubt essential step ensures the autonomy of the law of the signifier, and prepares for us the field of the word that allowed him to criticize all human knowledge as such. But the novelty of psychoanalysis, assuming that what I have been teaching you about the Freudian revolution is correct, is precisely the fact that something can find sustenance in the law of the signifier, not only without involving knowledge but by explicitly excluding it, by constituting itself as unconscious – in other words, as necessitating the eclipse of the subject at the level of knowledge, in order to subsist as an unconscious chain, as constituting what is fundamentally irreducible in the subject's relationship to the signifier.

This is why we are the first, if not the only, people not to be necessarily surprised that the specifically Socratic discourse, that of ἐπιστήμη (*epistéme*), knowledge transparent to itself, cannot be pursued beyond a certain limit concerning a particular object, when this object – assuming that it is the one on which Freud was able to shed new light – is love.

Whatever the case may be, whether you follow me or you do not follow me here, it is clear that in a dialogue like Plato's *Symposium* – which over the ages has, as you know, lost little of its strength, constancy, or interrogative power, retaining all the perplexity that has developed around it – we cannot remain satisfied with an explanation as pitiful as the following, that if Socrates has Diotima speak in his stead, it's simply in order to avoid excessively ruffling Agathon's feathers.

146

If you will allow me an equally ironic comparison, imagine that I have been asked to expound the whole of my doctrine concerning analysis, whether verbally or in writing, it makes little difference, and in doing so, at a particular turning point, I give the floor to Françoise Dolto. You would say, "There must be some reason for it. Why is he doing it?" Assuming, of course, that if I give her the floor it is not in order to have her say something stupid. That would not be my method and, moreover, I would have a hard time putting stupid words in her mouth.

Socrates has far less of a hard time with this, as you will see: Diotima's speech is full of glaring gaps. This allows us to easily understand why Socrates does not take responsibility for it. Moreover, Socrates points out these gaps with a whole series of responses that are – it's quite striking, and it suffices to read the text to see this – increasingly amused. His replies are at first quite respectful, and then more and more of the kind, "You think so?" and then, "So be it, let us go as far as the point to which you are dragging me," and in the end, it becomes clearly, "Knock yourself out, my dear girl, I'm listening, go on" [204c, 206e, 208b].

Here I cannot fail to point something out that seems not to have struck commentators. Aristophanes introduces a term concerning love which is transcribed quite simply in French by the word "*dioecisme*," which qualifies the *Spaltung* or division of the round primitive being, that is, of the derisory sphere in Aristophanes' image, whose value I talked about [two classes back]. He uses this word in comparison with a practice that was common in the context of community relations, relations of the city, the mainspring of all politics in Greek society. This dioecism consisted, when one wanted to finish off an enemy city, and this is still done in our times, in dispersing its inhabitants and placing them in what were called relocation camps. This happened shortly before the moment at which the *Symposium* came out, and it is even one of the landmarks that allows us to date it. For it seems that there is something anachronistic here, as the event to which Plato alludes, namely, an initiative on the part of Sparta, took place *after* the supposed meeting narrated in the *Symposium*.

This dioecism is very telling to us. It wasn't at random that I used the term *Spaltung* earlier, which evokes the subjective split. Isn't it insofar as something about love evades Socrates' knowledge that he himself disappears, "dioecizes," and has a woman speak in his stead? Why not say the woman who is in him?

Be that as it may, no one disputes the idea – and certain people have stressed it, Wilamowitz-Moellendorff for one – that there is a difference in register between what Socrates develops with his dialectical method, and what, in Plato's testimony, he presents us in the form of a myth. This is not the case here alone – these things are always clearly separated in Plato's texts. When one arrives, and in plenty of fields other than love, at a certain terminus regarding what can be obtained at the level of *epistéme* or knowledge, myth is necessary in order to go further.

147

It is quite conceivable to us that there is a limit to knowledge, assuming that the latter is solely what can be accessed by purely and simply bringing the law of the signifier into play. In the absence of far-reaching conquests based on experiments, it is clear that in many domains – and even in domains in which we have no need for such conquests – it is urgent to give myth the floor.

What is remarkable is the rigor of this shifting of gears to the level of myth. Plato always knows perfectly well what he is doing or having Socrates do. Everyone knows that they are speaking in myths, μύθους (*mýthous*). I am not talking about myths in the common meaning of the word, for μύθους λέγειν (*mýthous légein*) does not mean that but, rather, "what people say." And in all of Plato's work, in the *Phaedo*, the *Timaeus*, and the *Republic*, myths arise when Plato needs them in order to fill the gap in what can be assured dialectically.

On this basis, we will be able to see more clearly what might be called the headway made by Diotima's speech.

Someone who is here today once wrote an article entitled, if memory serves me well, "*Un désir d'enfant.*" This article was entirely constructed around the ambiguity of the expression *désir d'enfant*, for it can mean either that the child is the one who desires or that someone desires to have a child. It's no accident that signifiers work in this way, and the proof thereof is that it is around this very ambiguity that Socrates' approach to the problem revolves. Indeed, what was Agathon saying in the final analysis? That Eros is eros – that is, desire – of beauty, in the sense that, I would say, it is the god Beauty who desires. And what does Socrates retort? That a desire for beauty implies that one does not possess beauty.

148

One might be tempted to shy away from such verbal arguments, but they are not useless in nature, nor do they constitute a sort of needling or hand waving. The proof thereof is that it is around these two terms that Diotima's whole speech develops.

3

To clearly highlight the continuity between Diotima and himself, Socrates tells us that Diotima commenced her dialogue with him at the same level and with the same kinds of arguments that he used with Agathon.

The stranger from Mantinea is presented to us as a priestess and magician. Let us not forget that at this turning point in the *Symposium*, the arts of divination are spoken of at length – in particular, the way of having one's wishes fulfilled by the gods and of

influencing natural forces. Diotima is highly knowledgeable in all
such matters of γοητεία (*goeteía*), sorcery, or "mantic," as the Count
of Cabanis would have said. *Goeteía* is a Greek term and is found
in the dialogue. We are thus told something about her to which
surprisingly little attention has been paid, which is that she was suc-
cessful through her artifices in delaying the plague for ten years, in
Athens to boot. It must be admitted that this familiarity with the
powers of the plague should give us pause for thought and help us
situate the stature and approach of the person who is going to speak
to us about love.

Things are thus introduced at this level, and Diotima goes on
by responding to Socrates, who is, on this occasion, pretending
to be naive or feigning that it is all Greek to him. He asks her the
following question, "So, if love is not beautiful, is it ugly?" [201e].
Indeed, this is where his method leads, a method said to be one of
more or less, yes or no, presence or absence. This is what is specific
to the law of the signifier: whatever is not beautiful is ugly. This is,
at least, what is rigorously implied by following Socrates' ordinary
way of questioning. To which the priestess is in a position to answer,
"Watch your tongue! Do you really think that, if a thing is not
beautiful, it has to be ugly?" [201e]. Diotima then recounts for us the
myth of the birth of Love, and it is worth our while to dwell upon it.

This myth is found only in Plato's work. Among the innumerable
mythical narrations of the birth of Love found in the literature of
Antiquity, and I took the time to look through a number of them,
there is no trace of anything that resembles what is enunciated here.
Plato's is nevertheless the myth that has remained the most popular.
It thus seems that someone, who owes nothing to tradition in this
regard, to be explicit, a writer of the era of the *Aufklärung* like Plato,
is altogether capable of forging a myth, a myth that must have been
enthusiastically handed down through the ages for it to function
as such. Can anyone be unaware of the fact that Love is the son of
Πόρος (*Póros*) and Πενία (*Penía*) since Plato first said so?

The translator whose work I have before me, simply because it
is placed opposite the Greek text, translates *Póros* with some relevance as Expedient. If that means Resource, it is certainly a valid
translation. *Astuce* [cunning, ruse] is too, since Poros is the son of
Μῆτις (*Métis*), which means something closer to invention than to
wisdom. Opposite him we find the female character who will be
the mother of Love, *Penía*, namely Poverty, even Abject Poverty.
She is characterized in the text as ἀπορία (*aporía*) – namely, she has
no resources. She herself is aware that she has no resources. The
word "aporia," as you know, is the one that serves us concerning
philosophical argumentation: it refers to an impasse, something that

149

makes us throw in the towel, having exhausted our resources. So we have the female Aporia opposite Poros, the Expedient, which seems rather enlightening.

What is so nice about this myth is the way Aporia engendered Love with Poros. At the moment at which this happened, it was Aporia who was awake, who had her eyes wide open. She had, we are told, come to the festivities in honor of the birth of Aphrodite and, like any self-respecting Aporia in this hierarchical era, she remained on the steps near the door. Being Aporia – in other words, having nothing to offer – she did not enter the banquet hall. But the great thing about parties is precisely that things happen at them that overturn the ordinary order of events. Poros falls asleep. He falls asleep because he is drunk, and this is what allows Aporia to get herself knocked up by him, and to have this kid named Love, whose date of conception thus coincides with Aphrodite's date of birth. This is why, we are told, love always has some obscure relationship with beauty, which is what is in fact at stake in the remainder of Diotima's speech. Love and beauty are connected owing to the fact that Aphrodite is a beautiful goddess.

150

Things are stated quite clearly here: masculinity is desirable, femininity is active. This is, at any rate, how things present themselves at the moment of Love's birth.

If I trot out in this regard the formulation that "love is giving what you don't have," there is nothing artificial about it and it's not simply in order to rehash one of my old stock phrases. It is obvious that this is what is at stake here, as the poor Aporia, by definition and structure, has nothing to give above and beyond her constitutive lack or aporia. The expression "giving what you don't have" is literally written out in section 202a of the text of the *Symposium*: ἄνευ τοῦ ἔχειν λόγον δοῦναι (*áneu tou échein lógon doúnai*). It is the exact same formulation, although it is proffered here as regards discourse – in particular, as regards the fact that [one can have a correct opinion or judgment] without having a reason or worthwhile explanation to give for it.

This is said at the moment at which Diotima is led to say what love belongs to. Well, love belongs to a zone, to a form of affair, thing, *prágma*, or praxis that is at the same level and of the same quality as δόξα (*dóxa*). In other words, there are discourses, behaviors, or opinions – those are the translations we provide for the term *dóxa* – that are true without the subject being able to know it. *Dóxa* might well be true, but it is not *epistéme*; it is one of the stock tenets of Platonic doctrine to distinguish the field of *dóxa* from that of *epistéme*. Love as such is part of the former field. It lies between *epistéme* and ἀμαθία (*amathía*) [ignorance], just as it lies between the beautiful and the ugly. It is neither the one nor the other. This might well remind us of Socrates' objection, an objection which is no doubt trumped up, that if love is lacking in beauty, it must be ugly. Yet it is not ugly. The whole domain exemplified by *dóxa*, to which we constantly return in Plato's work, shows that love is, to use Plato's term, μεταξύ (*metaxú*) – that is, between the two.

But that's not all. We cannot remain satisfied with such an abstract, even negative, definition of what is in-between. It is here that Diotima brings in the notion of the demonic as the intermediary between immortals and mortals, between gods and men. This notion is essential here, in that it confirms what I told you we should think concerning what the gods are – namely, that they belong to the field of the real. The gods exist – their existence is in no wise disputed here. The demonic, daemon, or δαιμόνιον (*daimónion*) – and Love is far from the one example – is that by which the gods convey their message to mortals, whether they are asleep or awake.

Something strange that does not seem to have attracted much attention either is who this "whether they are asleep or awake" concerns? The gods or men? I assure you that in the Greek text there is room for doubt. Everyone translates it commonsensically – as related to men – but it is in the dative, which is precisely the case of the *theoí* in the sentence, such that it is another little enigma upon which we will not dwell for long. Let us simply say that this myth situates the demonic order where our psychology speaks of animism.

This should incite us to rectify our overly cursory idea of the notion a primitive person would have of the animistic world. What we are told in passing is that it is the world of messages that we would call enigmatic, which means – but only to us – messages in which the subject does not recognize his own contribution. If the discovery of the unconscious is essential, it is because it has allowed us to extend the field of messages we can authenticate, in the only proper meaning of the term, insofar as it is grounded in the domain of the symbolic. In other words, many of the messages that we believe to be opaque messages from reality [*réel*] are merely our own. This is what we have reclaimed from the world of the gods. Here, at the point at which we have arrived in the *Symposium*, this has not yet been reclaimed.

Next time, we will continue to examine Diotima's myth from end to end, and having given it a thorough working over, we will see why it is doomed to leave opaque the object of the praises that constitute the rest of the *Symposium*. The only field in which the elucidation of its truth can develop is the one that follows Alcibiades' entrance.

Far from being a mere add-on, a null and void part, or one

which must simply be rejected, Alcibiades' entrance is essential. It is only in the action that develops afterward between Alcibiades, Agathon, and Socrates that we can effectively delineate the structural relationship in which we can recognize what the discovery of the unconscious and the practice of psychoanalysis – namely, the experience of transference – finally allow us as analysts to be able to express dialectically.

152

January 18, 1961

IX

EXIT FROM THE ULTRA-WORLD

The fascination with beauty.
Identification with what is supremely lovable.
Socrates' "he did not know."
It takes three to love.
The object of unique covetousness.

Last time we got as far as the point where, in speaking of love, Socrates has Diotima speak in his stead.

I underscored the astonishing substitution that occurs at the dialogue's acme or point of maximum interest, placing a question mark next to it. Socrates has just provided the decisive turning point by showing lack to be at the heart of the question of what love is. Love can, in effect, only be articulated around lack, owing to the fact that love can but lack what it desires. I showed you that Socrates' questioning, with its ever triumphant and magisterial style, is the crux of his dialectic insofar as he brings it to bear on the coherence of the signifier. It is at the point at which he distinguishes *epistéme*, science, from every other kind of knowledge that, strangely enough, he ambiguously yields the floor to she who, in his stead, expresses herself through myth. I pointed out to you that the Greek term for myth is not as narrow as it is in our language, due to the distance we have placed between myth and science: μύθους λέγειν (*mýthous légein*) is both a precise story and discourse – in a word, it is what people say. This is what Socrates defers to in letting Diotima speak.

I briefly highlighted the relation between this substitution and the dioecism whose form and essence Aristophanes had already outlined as being at the heart of the problem of love. By an odd division, it is perhaps the woman in Socrates, I said, that he allows to speak at this point.

The set or succession of forms, the series of transformations – in the sense the latter term takes on in combinatories – [in Diotima's

speech] is expressed in a geometrical demonstration. And it is in the   154
transformation of figures as her speech proceeds that we will try
to find the structural landmarks which, for us and for Plato who is
our guide here, provide the coordinates of the dialogue's theme –
namely, love.

1

Examining Diotima's speech, we see something develop in it that
makes us slip further and further away from the original notion
Socrates introduced in his dialectic by positing the term "lack."

What Diotima questions us about, what she leads us toward, is
already sketched out in the question she asks at the point at which
she takes up Socrates' speech, "What is he who loves lacking in?"
Here we find ourselves immediately drawn into the dialectic of good
things [biens], concerning which I ask you to recall my Seminar last
year on ethics. "Why does he who loves love these things?" [204d–e].
He loves them, she continues, in order to enjoy them. Then she stops
and a backward movement begins.

Is the dimension of love thus going to be said to arise from all good
things [biens]? Diotima here refers to something as worthy of note as
what I accentuated as being the original function of creation as such:
ποίησις (poíesis). When we speak of poíesis, she says, we are talking
about creation, but don't you see that the use we make of it is more
limited when we are referring to poetry and music? The name for the
whole serves to designate the part [205c]. Similarly, every aspiration
toward good things is a sort of love, but in order for us to speak of
love, strictly speaking, something must be made more specific. This is
how she introduces the theme of the love of beauty. Beauty specifies
the direction in which the call or attraction to possession, to the enjoyment of possessing, to the constitution of a κτῆμα (ktéma) arises. This
is the point to which Diotima leads us in order to define love.

In the course of her speech, a moment of surprise or a jump is
clearly emphasized. In what sense is this good thing [bien] related
to beauty or specified especially as beauty? It is here that Socrates   155
attests, in one of his replies, to the fact that he marvels at sophistic
discourse, that he is shocked by it, as I mentioned last time. Diotima
proves here that she has the same priceless authority as that with
which the Sophists exercised their fascination, and Plato warns us
that in this sense she expresses herself exactly like them [208b].

What she presents is the following: beauty has nothing to do with
having, with anything that can be possessed, but rather with being,
and specifically with mortal being.

What is characteristic of mortal being is that it perpetuates itself through reproduction. Reproduction and destruction, such is the alternation that rules the realm of what is perishable. Such is also the feature that makes it an inferior order of reality – at least this is how it is described in the Socratic view, as much by Socrates as by Plato. It is precisely because the human realm is afflicted with this alternation of generation and corruption that it finds its eminent rule elsewhere, higher up, in the realm of essences – which is afflicted by neither generation nor corruption – that of the eternal forms, participation in which alone assures that what exists is grounded in being.

And beauty? In the movement of generation, which is the mode by which what is mortal reproduces itself, approaching thereby the permanent and the eternal, its fragile mode of participating in the eternal – in this very movement or distant form of participation, it is beauty that helps us, as it were, get over the difficult hurdles. Beauty is the mode of a kind of giving birth – which is not painless, but which involves the least pain possible. It is the painful escape route of all that is mortal toward what it aspires to: immortality. Diotima's whole speech articulates the function of beauty as being first and foremost an illusion, a fundamental mirage, by which perishable and fragile beings are sustained in their quest for permanence, which is their essential aspiration.

One finds therein almost shameless occasion for a whole series of slippages that amount to so many dissimulations. Diotima introduces first, as being of the same order, the constancy whereby the subject recognizes himself as always being the same in his life, his short life as an individual, despite the fact that there is not a single detail of his carnal reality, from his hair right down to his bones, which is not the locus of perpetual renewal. The underlying theme is that nothing is ever the same, everything is in flux, everything changes, and yet something recognizes itself, affirms itself, tells itself that it is always itself. This is what Diotima refers to significantly in order to tell us that the renewal of beings via generation is analogous, and in the final analysis, of the same nature. The fact that beings succeed one another by reproducing the same type – in other words, the mystery of morphogenesis – is the same as what sustains the form in its constancy.

Here we see a prime reference to death, and a pinpointing of the function of the mirage of beauty as that which guides the subject in his relationship to death, insofar as he is both outstripped and directed by immortality. It is impossible, in this respect, for you not to be reminded of what I tried to broach last year concerning the function of beauty as a defense, where beauty intervenes as a barrier at the limit of the zone I defined as lying between-two-deaths. If there are two desires that captivate man, on the one hand in relation to eternity, and on the other in relation to reproduction, complete with the corruption and destruction it involves, beauty is designed to veil his desire for death insofar as it is unapproachable. This is clear even at the beginning of Diotima's speech.

We find anew here the ambiguous phenomenon that I brought out concerning tragedy. Tragedy evokes or approaches the desire for death which, as such, hides behind the evocation of *Áte*, the fundamental calamity around which the tragic hero's fate revolves; and tragedy is also, for us, insofar as we are called upon to participate in it, the culminating moment in which the mirage of tragic beauty appears.

This is the ambiguity around which I told you the slippage in Diotima's whole speech occurs. I will leave you to trace it yourselves through all its developments. The desire *for* beauty [*désir de beau*] – desire insofar as it attaches itself to this mirage and gets caught up in it – is what corresponds to the hidden presence of the desire for death. The desire that comes from beauty [*désir du beau*] is what, reversing this function, makes the subject choose the trace or appeals [*appels*] of what the object offers him, or at least certain objects. It is here that the slippage occurs in Diotima's speech that turns beauty – which was not, strictly speaking, a medium, but rather a transition or passageway – into the very goal that is sought. In remaining, so to speak, the guide, the guide becomes the object(ive) or rather takes the place of the objects that can be its prop. And this transition is explicitly indicated in her speech.

But this transition is distorted [*faussée*]. Diotima goes as far as possible in developing functional beauty, beauty in its relation to the aim of immortality, and does not eschew paradox, since she specifically evokes the tragic reality to which we referred last year. She goes so far as to raise a question, which is not without eliciting some cynical smiles: "Do you actually believe that those who prove themselves capable of the most beautiful acts, like Alcestis" – about whom I spoke last year concerning tragedy's between-two-deaths – "insofar as she accepted to die in Admetus' stead, did not do it so that people would talk about it, so that discourse would forever immortalize her?" [208d]. This is where Diotima stops, saying, "While you have been able to follow me thus far, I don't know if you will be able to go as far as *époptie*," evoking thereby the dimension of the mysteries [209e–210a].

She then resumes her speech in this other register, wherein what was but a transition [or guide] becomes a goal. Developing the theme of what we might call a Platonic Don Juanism, she shows

157

us the ladder that proposes itself at this new phase, which develops in an initiation-like vein – we see objects dissolve, in a progressive climb, into pure beauty, beauty in itself, unadulterated beauty [211d–e]. Diotima abruptly shifts to a theme that certainly seems to no longer have anything to do with that of reproduction, and that moves from love, not only for a handsome young man, but for the beauty in all beautiful young people, to the essence of beauty, and then from the essence of beauty to eternal beauty. She thus takes a very lofty perspective, to the point of grasping the play, in the world order, of the reality that revolves around the fixed plane of the stars, which is, as I have already indicated, that by which [human] knowledge joins up with that of the Immortals in Plato's perspective.

I think I have sufficiently made you sense the dissimulation by which, on the one hand, beauty – at first defined and encountered as a bonus along the path of being – becomes the goal of the pilgrimage, while, on the other hand, the object – at first presented as the prop of beauty – becomes the transition toward beauty.

158   To return here to my own terminology, one might say that the dialectical definition of love, as it is developed by Diotima, intersects with what I have tried to define as the metonymic function in desire. What is at issue in her speech is something beyond all objects that resides in the movement of a certain aim and a certain relation – that of desire – through all objects and toward an unlimited perspective.

On the basis of numerous clues, one might believe that this is the last word of the discussion in the *Symposium*. This is basically what we have long been used to taking as Plato's view of Eros.

Erastés, erón, the lover, is led toward a distant *erómenos*, by all the *erómenoi*, all that is lovable, all that is worthy of being loved. It is a distant *erómenos* or *erómenon*, for his quest can also have a neuter goal. The problem then is what is signified by and what can continue to signify – beyond this outstripping, this marked jump – that which presented itself at the beginning of the dialectic as *ktéma*, the goal of possessing.

The step we have made no doubt adequately indicates that the aim is no longer to be situated at the level of having, but rather at the level of being, and also that this progression or ascesis involves a transformation or becoming of the subject: a final identification with what is supremely lovable. In short, the further the subject goes in his aim, the more he is within his rights to love himself, so to speak, via his ideal ego. The more he desires, the more he himself becomes desirable.

Theologians point at this in order to tell us that Platonic Eros cannot be reduced to what Christian *Agápe* has revealed to us, inasmuch as in Platonic Eros, the loving person aims only at his own perfection – love aims only at its own perfection.

Now, the commentary that I am in the process of offering on the *Symposium* seems to me apt to show that this is not at all the case.

This is not where Plato leaves off, on the condition that we are willing to look beyond the immediate terrain and ask ourselves, first, what is signified by the fact that Socrates has Diotima speak in his stead and, second, what happens once Alcibiades arrives on the scene.

2   159

Let us not forget that Diotima first introduces love as not at all partaking of the nature of the gods, but rather of that of daemons, insofar as their nature lies between that of Immortals and mortals.

Let us not forget that, in order to illustrate it and ensure that its impact is felt, she supplies nothing less than a comparison with what, in Plato's discourse, lies midway between *epistéme*, science in the Socratic sense, and *amathía*, ignorance – namely, *dóxa*, true opinion [202a]. *Dóxa* is no doubt true, but the subject is unable to account for it – he does not know in what way it is true.

I highlighted in this context two statements that are very striking. The first, ἄνευ τοῦ ἔχειν λόγον δοῦναι (*áneu tou échein lógon doúnai*), characterizes *dóxa* as giving an answer without having one, echoing the formulation I myself have proposed here that love is giving what you don't have. The other formulation, which stands opposite the first, and which is no less worthy of being emphasized, is on the courtyard side, so to speak, looking out toward *amathia*. *Dóxa*, indeed, is not ignorance either, for how could what perchance hits the real and encounters what is, τὸ γὰρ τοῦ ὄντος τύγχανον (*to gar tou óntos túngchanon*), be absolute ignorance [202a]?

This is what we must perceive in what I might call the Platonic staging of the dialogue. Even though it is posited at the outset that the only matters about which Socrates knows anything are matters of love, he can only speak of them by remaining in the zone of the "he did not know." Even when knowledgeable, he himself cannot speak of what he knows and must have someone else speak who speaks without knowing.

This is what allows us to situate in its proper context, for example, the intangibility of Agathon's response, when he eludes Socrates' dialectic by saying to him quite simply, "Let's just say that I didn't know what I meant." This is why. This – in the extraordinarily derisory way I have brought out – is what makes for the import of Agathon's speech, the peculiar import it derives from the fact that these words are put in a tragic poet's mouth. The tragic poet, as I showed you, can speak of love only in a clownish way, just as Aristophanes, the comic poet, has been given the job of bringing out the passionate aspects that we associate with the tragic landscape.

"He did not know." The myth Diotima introduces concerning the birth of Love takes on its full meaning here. Love is conceived while Poros is asleep, Poros being the son of Metis, Invention, the all-knowing and all-powerful, the most resourceful. It is while he is sleeping, at a moment at which he longer knows anything, that the encounter takes place through which Love is engendered. She who slips in, owing to her desire to produce this birth, Aporia, the feminine Aporia, is *erastés*, the originally desiring person in the veritably feminine position I have emphasized several times. She is quite precisely defined in her essence or nature, let me stress this, before the birth of Love, by what she is lacking – there is nothing *erómenon* about her. In the myth, Aporia, absolute poverty, is at the doorstep of the banquet of the gods being held the day of Aphrodite's birth. She is in no wise recognized, she has in herself none of the qualities [*biens*] that would give her the right to sit at the table of true beings [*étants*]. It is in this respect that she is *prior* to Love. The metaphor by which we always recognize that love is operating, even when it is hidden in the shadows, the metaphor whereby *erón* or *erastés* is restored to *erómenon*, is missing here due to the absence of *erómenon* at the outset. It is the logical time before the birth of Love that is thus described here.

On the other hand, the "he did not know" is absolutely essential. Allow me to highlight what came to me last night while I was trying to punctuate this structural, connecting moment.

It was the echo of the admirable poem from which I deliberately selected an example in order to try to demonstrate the fundamental nature of metaphor. The poem, "Booz Sleeping," would alone suffice, despite all the objections our snobbery might have against it, to make Victor Hugo a poet worthy of Homer. You will not be surprised at the following two verses which suddenly came to me, having known them forever:

Booz ne savait point qu'une femme était là,
Et Ruth ne savait point ce que Dieu voulait d'elle.

Booz did not know that a woman was there,
and Ruth did not know what God wanted from her.

Reread the poem and you will see that it lacks none of the features that give the fundamental drama of Oedipus its eternal meaning and weight, not even the between-two-deaths evoked several stanzas before these concerning Booz's age and widowhood.

Voilà longtemps que celle avec qui j'ai dormi,
Ô Seigneur ! a quitté ma couche pour la vôtre;
Et nous sommes encor tout mêlés l'un à l'autre,
Elle à demi vivante et moi mort à demi.

She with whom I slept has long since,
O Lord! left my bed for yours;
Yet we are still mingled with one another,
She half-living and I half-dead.

We have here the between-two-deaths and its relation to the tragic dimension evoked in it as constitutive of paternal transmission – nothing is missing in this poem. Which is why the metaphorical function is found throughout the poem. Everything is taken to extremes, right up to the aberrations, so to speak, of the poet, since he goes so far as to say what he has to say by forcing the themes he uses: "*Comme dormait Jacob, comme dormait Judith*" ("As Jacob slept, as Judith slept"). Yet it was never Judith who slept, it was Holofernes. But so what? Hugo is right all the same. What we glimpse in effect at the end of the poem is what is expressed by the wonderful image with which it concludes:

et Ruth se demandait,
Immobile, ouvrant l'oeil à moitié sous ses voiles,
Quel Dieu, quel moissonneur de l'éternel été
Avait, en s'en allant, négligemment jeté
Cette faucille d'or dans le champ des étoiles.

and Ruth wondered,
Lying motionless and half-opening her eye beneath her veils,
What God, what harvester of eternal summer,
Had, in departing, negligently thrown
This golden sickle into the field of stars.

The billhook [with which Cronus castrated Uranus] could not fail to be included at the end of this complete constellation that constitutes the paternity complex.

This digression, for which I beg your pardon, concerning the "he did not know," seems to me essential to make you understand what is at stake in Diotima's speech. Socrates can only locate himself in his knowledge here by showing that there can be no discourse on love but from the point at which he did not know. This is the mainspring of what is signified by Socrates' choice of this way of teaching at this precise moment in the dialogue.

162   But at the same time, we have proof that this is not what allows us to grasp what takes place in love relations either. What allows us to is precisely what will follow – namely, Alcibiades' entrance.

3

The marvelous, splendid, oceanic unfolding of Diotima's speech ends without Socrates having, in sum, made any attempt to resist.

Significantly, right after her speech, Aristophanes raises his index finger to say, "Let me get a word in edgewise all the same." An allusion has been made to a certain theory, indeed to Aristophanes' theory, which the good Diotima has just nonchalantly kicked out of the way [205d–e]. This is significantly anachronistic, for while Socrates says that Diotima told him all of this some time before, it doesn't stop him from having her talk about the speech Aristophanes just made. Aristophanes has a thing or two to say in response, and for good reason. Plato indexes this point, showing that there is someone who is not content. Let us see, using my method, which is to stick to the text, whether what develops afterward does not bear some relation to this index, even if this raised index finger, which says it all, gets cut off. And by what? By Alcibiades' entrance.

Here, a change of scene takes place before our very eyes.

We must clearly indicate first of all into what world it suddenly casts us anew, after the great fascinating mirage. I say "anew," for this world is not the ultra-world, it is the world *tout court*, in which we know, after all, how love is experienced. Despite all these fine stories, as fascinating as they may seem, a bit of tumultuous ruckus – the entrance of a few drunkards – suffices to bring us back to reality [*réel*].

We are now going to see incarnated the transcendence by which we have seen played out, in a ghost-like way, the substitution of one for another. And if, as I teach you, it takes three to love, not just two, well, we are going to witness it here.

Alcibiades enters, and it is not unfitting that you see him emerge in the shape in which he appears, with his formidable countenance due not only to his officially drunk state, but also to the large quantity of garlands he is wearing that manifestly have an eminently exhibitionistic meaning in the divine position he assumes as a leader of men [*chef humain*] [212d–e].

163   Never forget what we are missing out on by no longer wearing wigs. Try to imagine what the learned as well as the frivolous agitations of seventeenth-century conversations might have been like when each of the speakers shook, with each of his words, his lionlike

mane, which was moreover a magnet for filth and vermin. Picture to yourself the wig of the seventeenth century. From the perspective of its mantic effect, we are missing out on quite a bit.

Not Alcibiades, however, and he goes right to the only person whose identity he is able to discern given his inebriated condition. Thank God it is the man of the house, Agathon. He goes to lie down next to him, without realizing where that places him, namely, in the *metaxú* position, in-between, between Socrates and Agathon – in other words, precisely at the point at which we have arrived, where the debate swings between the game of he who knows and, knowing, shows that he must speak without knowing, and he who, not knowing, spoke no doubt like a birdbrain, but very well nevertheless, as Socrates himself emphasizes when he comments, "You said some very fine things." This is where Alcibiades seats himself, not without jumping up when he perceives that that damned Socrates is there too.

I will not take our analysis of what is contributed by the whole scene which begins with Alcibiades' entrance all the way today, although not for personal reasons. I will nevertheless sketch out the first outlines of what the scene introduces.

Well, let's say that there is a stage-like atmosphere to it. I will not accentuate the caricatural aspect of things. I spoke offhandedly of this symposium as an assembly of old faggots, given that they are not all characterized by the first flush of youth, yet they are not without being based on a certain model. Alcibiades is a real piece of work. And when Socrates asks to be protected from Alcibiades who does not allow him to look at anyone else, it is not because commentaries on the *Symposium* have been provided over the centuries by university professors, with all that implies both by way of nobility and universal missing the point – we are not going to let this make us overlook the fact that what is happening here is, strictly speaking, as I have already mentioned, scandalous in nature.

We must recognize that the dimension of love is in the process of showing itself to us in a way in which one of its characteristics certainly must be sketched out. First of all, it is clear that when this dimension manifests itself in reality [*réel*], it does not tend toward harmony. The beauty toward which the procession of desiring souls seemed to climb certainly does not seem to structure everything into a kind of convergence.

164

Oddly enough, it is not clear, in love's manifestations, that you call on everyone else to love what you love, to join with you in the ascension toward *erómenon*. The first thing we see is that Alcibiades wants to keep Socrates – this eminently lovable man, since he is depicted as a divine personage right from the very first words of the dialogue – for himself.

You will tell me that you don't believe it, basing yourselves on all sorts of things that prove it. That's not the point. We are following the text, and this is what is presented in it. And not only is this what is presented in it, but it is this very dimension that is, strictly speaking, introduced here.

Is it a question of competition? If the word is taken in the sense and function I gave it when I articulated the transitivisms by which the object is constituted, insofar as it institutes communication between two subjects, no. Something of a different order is introduced here. The object of unique covetousness, so to speak, is introduced and constituted as such at the heart of love's action. One wants to shove aside the competition for this object that one is averse to even having shown.

Recall that this is how I introduced it in my discourse three years ago [Seminar V]. Remember that, in order to define object *a* in fantasy, I took the example, in *La Grande Illusion* by Renoir, of Dalio showing his little automaton, and the woman-like blushing with which he effaces himself after having set it in motion. Alcibiades' public confession is played out in this same dimension, accompanied by some kind of uneasiness of which Alcibiades himself is so well aware that he even mentions it in his speech [214d].

We are no doubt in the truth of wine – this is explicitly stated – *in vino veritas*. Kierkegaard takes up this point when he writes his own *Symposium* ["In Vino Veritas" in *Works of Love*] – but one must truly have gone beyond all the bounds of propriety to speak of love as Alcibiades does when he exposes what transpired between himself and Socrates.

165 What kind of object is there behind all of this that leads to such a vacillation in the subject himself?

I will leave you today with the function of the object, insofar as it is specifically indicated in the whole of this text, in order to present it to you next time.

What I will tell you will revolve around a word that is found in the text, and whose use in Greek allows us to glimpse the history and function, which I believe I have refound, of the object at stake here. This word is ἄγαλμα (*ágalma*), which, we are told, is what is hidden within the disheveled silenus known as Socrates.

I leave you today with the unexplored enigma of this word in the dialogue itself.

January 25, 1961

X

ÁGALMA

Ágalma and the master.
The fetish function.
The god trap.
From the partial object to the other.
A subject is an other.

I ended last time – at a sort of way-station along our path – on a word about which I said I would leave it with its full enigmatic value until this time: *ágalma*.

I didn't realize I had put it so well. For many of you the enigma was so complete that people asked, "What? What did he say? Do you know?" Anyway, to those who manifested this worry, someone in my household was able to provide the following response – which proves that in my home secondary school serves at least some purpose – that it means "ornament" or "jewelry."

Be that as it may, this response was but a first take on what everyone should know: ἀγάλλω (*agállo*) means to "bejewel" or "adorn," and *ágalma* does in fact signify "ornament" or "jewelry" at first glance. But the notion of jewelry is not as simple as it may seem and one realizes right away that it can take us quite far. Why bejewel oneself? And with what?

If we are at the crux of something now, many different avenues must lead us here. The fact remains that I selected the word *ágalma* as the pivotal point of my explanation. Rather than take it as an attempt on my part to find something extremely unusual, assume that in a text like the *Symposium*, to which we attribute the utmost rigor, something leads us to this crucial point.

1

The word *ágalma* appears at the very moment at which I told you the scene changes completely. After the eulogistic games regulated up until then by the topic of love, Alcibiades, the actor who changes everything, enters.

The proof that he changes everything is that he himself modifies the rules of the game, assigning himself the place of he who presides over the symposium. From now on, he says, we are no longer going to provide eulogies of love, but of the other, and namely, of the person to our right. That's already going very far. If love is to be involved here, it's love in action, and it is the relation of the one to the other that will have to manifest itself here.

I have already pointed out to you a remarkable fact that is manifested as soon as things take off in this direction, led by the experienced director whom we assume to be behind this dialogue. I must say that this assumption is confirmed by the incredible intellectual genealogy that stems from the *Symposium*, the second to last echo of which I mentioned last time, Kierkegaard's "In Vino Veritas" [in *Works of Love*], and the last, which I have already mentioned as well, *Agape and Eros*, by Anders Nygren, it too being dependent upon the structure of the *Symposium*. As soon as this experienced director brings into play the other, there has to be more than one – there are two others here. In other words, there have to be at least three in all. This remarkable fact does not escape Socrates in his response to Alcibiades. After Alcibiades' extraordinary avowal, public confession, or outburst that lies somewhere between a declaration of love and almost, as it were, a defamation of Socrates, the latter responds: "It is not for my benefit that you have spoken, but for Agathon's."

This allows us to realize that we are shifting to another register than the one I pointed out in Diotima's speech. What was at stake there was a dyadic relation. He who begins to climb toward love proceeds by the path of identification and of production, as it were, aided by the marvel of beauty. He finds in beauty his terminus and identifies it with the perfection of the labor of love. We see there a twofold relationship whose goal is identification with the Sovereign Good – something that I called into question last year. Something else is suddenly substituted here for the theme of the supreme Good – the complexity or, more precisely, the triplicity that proposes to provide us with what I consider essential in the psychoanalytic discovery: the topology from which the subject's relation to the symbolic results at its core, insofar as the symbolic is essentially distinct from the imaginary and its capture.

This is our terminus, and I will articulate it next time in concluding what I want to say about the *Symposium*, which will allow me to bring out old models that I gave you of intrasubjective topology, insofar as Freud's second topography must be understood accordingly. What I am pointing out today is essential if we are to intersect that topology, in the sense that we have to intersect it regarding the topic of love. In question here is the nature of love and a position, an essential but forgotten or elided connection, of which we analysts have nevertheless provided the linchpin that allows us to bring out its problematic. What I have to say regarding *ágalma* today will revolve around this.

It is all the more extraordinary and almost scandalous that the fact that we have here a specifically psychoanalytic notion has not been better highlighted before. I hope to help you put your finger on it later and obtain your consent on this point.

Here is how *ágalma* presents itself in the text. Alcibiades speaks of Socrates and says that he is going to unmask him. As you know, Alcibiades goes into considerable detail regarding his affair with Socrates. What did Alcibiades try to do? I would say that he tried to get Socrates to manifest his desire to him. He knows that Socrates has some desire for him, but what he wanted was a sign thereof.

Let us leave that in abeyance for a moment. It is too soon to ask why. We are merely at the beginning of Alcibiades' speech, and at first glance, it doesn't seem essentially different from what has been said thus far by the others. Early on, in Pausanias' speech, the question was what we look for in love, and it was said that what everyone looks for in the other – an exchange of courtesies – is what he contains that is *erómenon*, desirable. The very same thing seems to be at stake now.

Alcibiades tells us, as a sort of preamble, that Socrates is someone whose amorous inclinations draw him to pretty boys [216d]. He is ignorant of everything, he knows nothing – at least apparently. On this subject, Alcibiades repeats the famous comparison with the silenus that he mentioned when beginning his eulogy, and which is twofold in scope. First of all, there is Socrates' appearance, which is anything but beautiful. But, on the other hand, this silenus is not simply the image designated by that name. It is also a wrapper that looks like a silenus usually looks: like a container or way of presenting something. There must have been some small items in the industry of the time – little silenuses that served as jewelry boxes or packaging in which to offer gifts.

This is precisely what is involved. This topological indication is essential. What is important is what is inside. *Ágalma* may well mean ornamentation or ornament, but here it means above all gem

170

or precious object – something that is inside. And it is with this that
Alcibiades rips us away from the dialectic of beauty that had, up
until then, served as the pathway, guide, or mode of capture along
the pathway of the desirable. He makes the scales fall from our eyes
regarding Socrates himself.

Let it be known, he says, that Socrates supposedly loves pretty
boys; οὔτε εἴ τις καλός ἐστι (*oúte ei tis kalós estí*), but he couldn't
care less whether one or the other of them is pretty, μέλει αὐτῷ
οὐδέν (*mélei autó oudén*), he despises it on the contrary, καταφρονεῖ
(*kataphroneí*), to an unbelievable extent, τοσοῦτον ὅσον οὐδ' ἂν εἷς
οἰηθείη (*tosoúton hóson oud an heis oietheíe*), you can't even imagine
how much [216d–e]. And in truth the goal he pursues – what is it
exactly? I am underscoring it because it is in the text. It is expressly
articulated at this point that it is not outward good things that he
pursues, wealth, for example, about which everyone up until then –
these are refined people, after all – has said this is not what we
look for in others. It is not any of the other advantages either that
may seem in some way to bring μακαρία (*makaría*), happiness, ὑπὸ
πλήθους (*hupó pléthous*), to one and all [216e]. We would be completely mistaken to interpret this as if the point were to disdain the
things that are considered good by the masses. What are dismissed
here are precisely what was talked about up until this point: good
things in general.

On the other hand, Alcibiades tells us, don't be fooled by Socrates'
strange appearance – he pretends to be naive, εἰρωνευόμενος
(*eironeuómenos*), questions, acts dumb to find out more, truly acts
like a child, and spends his time bantering. But σπουδάσαντος δὲ
αὐτοῦ (*spoudásantos de autoú*) – which is not "when he decides to be
serious," as it is translated, but rather, "let's be serious, pay close
attention" – open this silenus up; ἀνοιχθέντος (*anoichthéntos*), partly
open, I don't know if anyone has ever seen the ἀγάλματα (*agálmata*)
that are inside [216e].

Alcibiades thus immediately calls into question whether anyone
has ever been able to see what is at stake. We know that this is not
merely an impassioned speech. It is the discourse of passion at its
peak of trembling – namely, at a peak that is entirely contained in
his preamble [*origine*], even before he explains himself. It is here,
weighed down by everything he has to tell us, that he is about to
let loose with a back kick. It is thus clearly the language of passion.

We immediately sense this unique, personal relationship. "No
one has ever seen what is in question as I managed to. I saw it. I saw
them, the *agálmata* that are already divine – χρυσᾶ (*chrusá*), they're
wonderful, they're golden – totally beautiful, so utterly amazing
that there was only one thing to do, ἐν βραχεῖ (*en bracheí*), and right

away, as directly as possible: to do everything Socrates ordered" [216e–217a]; ποιητέον (*poietéon*) – what must be done, what becomes one's duty – is to do everything it pleases Socrates to command.

I don't think that it is pointless to articulate such a text step by step. You don't read Plato the way you read *France-Soir* or the *International Journal of Psychoanalysis*.

At stake here is something whose effects are surprising. On the one hand, no one tells us here what the *agálmata*, in the plural, are. On the other hand, they immediately lead to a subversion or falling under the spell of the commandments of he who possesses them. Doesn't this smack of the magic that I already pointed out to you regarding *Che vuoi*? It is truly this key, this essential razor's edge of the topology of the subject that begins with the question, "What do you want?" In other words, "Is there a desire that is truly your will?"

Alcibiades then goes on to say, since I thought Socrates was serious when he spoke of ἐμῇ ὥρᾳ (*emé hóra*) – it's translated as "the flower of my beauty" [or "my youthful bloom," 217a] – and the [account of the] whole seduction scene begins.

We won't go any further into it today. I will try to convey what makes the passage from the first moment to the next necessary – namely, why it is absolutely necessary that Socrates be unmasked. For the time being, I am simply going to dwell on these *agálmata*.

2 172

Give me enough credit to believe that this is not the sole text that made me curious about the meaning of *ágalma*. Not that there would be anything wrong with that, for the *Symposium* suffices to justify my interest in it, but I am going to tell you how it was.

Although I can't exactly date it, my first encounter with *ágalma* was one that, like all encounters, was unforeseen. The word struck me several years ago in a verse of Euripides' *Hecuba*, and you will easily understand why. It was shortly before I situated, here in this seminar, the function of the phallus in the essential place that analytic experience and Freud's doctrine show us it has in the connection between demand and desire, such that I did not fail to be struck in passing by the use of the term by Hecuba.

Hecuba says, "Where are they taking me, where are they deporting me to?" The tragedy of Hecuba is set at the moment of the capture of Troy, and Delos figures among the places that she envisions. Might she be deported to Delos, which is at once sacred and plague-stricken? As you may know, you didn't have the right to give birth there or to die there. And here, in her description of Delos, Hecuba alludes to an object there that was famous. The way she speaks about it indicates that it was a palm tree. This palm tree, she says, is ὠδίνος ἄγαλμα δίας (*odínos ágalma días*); ὠδῖνος (*odínos*) means from pain, and Dias designates Leto here [verse 461]. Hecuba is referring to the birth of Apollo and the *ágalma* of the divinity's [Leto's] pain.

We encounter anew here the theme of giving birth, but it is somewhat different in this case, for here there is a trunk or tree, a magic object erected and preserved as a landmark throughout the ages. This cannot fail to remind us, at least we analysts, of the register or theme of the phallus, insofar as the fantasy of the phallus is here, as we know, on the horizon, situating this infantile object. And the fetish that it remains cannot but echo this signification for us.

It is clear that *ágalma* cannot be translated in any way, shape, or form by "ornament" or "jewelry" here, or even, as we often see in published texts, by "statue." In many instances, when θεῶν ἀγάλματα (*theón agálmata*) is translated quickly, it seems that the latter works and that it is a question in the text of statues of the gods.

173

You see why I think it's a term whose signification should be pointed out. There is a hidden accent here that reminds us not to let ourselves be led down the path of banalization that tends to ever more completely efface the true meaning of texts. Whenever you encounter the word *ágalma*, pay close attention. Even if it seems to have to do with statues of the gods, look closely and you will see that it always has to do with something else.

I am not talking in riddles here. I am giving you the key to the question by saying that this term always emphasizes the fetishistic function of the object.

I am not giving a course on ethnology or even linguistics here and, on this subject, I am not going to take up the fetishistic function of round rocks at the center of a temple, the temple of Apollo, for example, for that is very well known. You very often see the god himself represented. What is the fetish of such and such a tribe, for example, from a bend in the Niger? It is something unspeakable and shapeless, on which enormous quantities of liquids of various origins can at times be poured, liquids that are more or less sticky and disgusting – the accumulated superimposition of which, running from blood to shit, constitutes the sign that there is something around which all sorts of effects revolve. Fetishes are in themselves very different from images or icons, insofar as the latter are intended to be copies.

The special power of the object remains at the root of the usage whose accent, even for us, is still preserved in the terms idol and icon. The term idol, in the use made of it by Saint Polyeuctus, for example, means, "It's nothing at all, it's something you smash on the ground." But all the same, if you say about someone, "That person is my idol," it doesn't simply mean that you turn him into a copy of yourself or himself, but that you make something else of him, around which something happens.

My goal here thus isn't to elaborate on the phenomenology of fetishes, but to show you the function this serves in its place. To do so, I can indicate to you that I tried, as far as I was able, to quickly look over the passages bequeathed to us by Greek literature where the word *ágalma* is used. If I don't read all of them to you, it's merely in order to go more quickly. You should simply realize that it is from the multiple significations deployed that I am isolating the central function, the one that must be seen at the fringe of these uses. For in the type of teaching I provide here, we naturally don't believe that etymology consists in finding the meaning of a word in its root.

174

The root of *ágalma* is not easy to handle. Writers relate it to ἀγαυός (*agauós*), based on the ambiguous word ἄγαμαι (*ágamai*), "I admire," but also "I am envious" or "I am jealous of," which becomes ἀγάζω (*agázo*), "to bear with pain," which goes toward ἀγαίομαι (*agaíomai*), meaning "to be indignant." Writers looking for roots, I mean roots that bear meaning, which is absolutely opposed to the principle of linguistics, isolate γαλ (*gal*) or γελ (*gel*), the *gel* of γελάω (*geláo*), the *gal* which is the same as in γλήνη (*gléne*), pupil [as of the eye], and in γαλήνην (*galénen*), which I cited in passing the other day, the sea that shines because it is perfectly still. In short, the idea of sparkle [*éclat*] is hidden in the root. And Ἀγλαός (*aglaós*) [related to Ἀγλαΐα (*Aglaía*), the youngest of the three Graces or Charites], which means "shining" or "splendor," is there to provide us with a familiar echo. It doesn't run counter to what I have to say about it. I am mentioning it merely as an aside here, because it is simply an occasion to show you the ambiguities inherent in the idea that etymology takes us, not toward a signifier, but toward a central signification. For one could also take an interest, not in *gal*, but in the first part of the phonemic articulation, namely *aga*, which is truly the reason why *ágalma* interests us in its relation to ἀγαθός (*agathós*).

In such an etymological vein, you know that I don't balk at the import of Agathon's speech, but I prefer to go directly to the great fantasy in the *Cratylus*. You will see there that the etymology of Agathon is ἀγαστός (*agastós*), what is admirable. Lord knows why they need to go looking for *agaston*, what is admirable, in θοόν (*thoón*), what is quick. But that's the way everything is interpreted in the *Cratylus* [412c and 422a]. One finds some very nice things in the etymology of ἄνθρωπος (*ánthropos*), where there is articulated language [399a–c]. Plato truly was a very fine guy.

In truth, it is not in this direction that we must turn to establish the value of *ágalma*. *Ágalma* is always related to images, provided that you see that, as in every context, it is always related to a very specific type of image. I must select among the references. There are some in Empedocles, in Heraclitus, and in Democritus. I'm going to take the most common ones, the poetic ones, the ones that everyone knew by heart in Antiquity. I found them in a line-by-line Greek/French edition of the *Iliad* and the *Odyssey*. There are, for example, two occurrences in the *Odyssey*.

175

The first is in Book III of the Telemachy. The context concerns sacrifices that are being made for the arrival of Telemachus. The suitors, as usual, go out of their way, and sacrifice a βοῦς (*bous*), which is translated by "heifer" – it is a member of the ox family – to the god. And they expressly call on a certain Laerceus, who is a jeweler, like Hephaestus, and he is given the job of making an ornament, *ágalma*, for the horns of the beast. I'll skip the practical details concerning the ceremony. What is important is not what happens afterward – whether it is a voodoo-type sacrifice or not – but what they are said to be expecting from *ágalma*. *Ágalma*, in effect, is involved here. It is said expressly. *Ágalma* is the golden ornament itself and it is sacrificed to the hunger of the goddess Athena. The goal here is that, having seen it, κεχάροιτο (*kechároito*) [verse 438], she be gratified – let's use this latter word since it is part of our vocabulary. In other words, *ágalma* appears as a kind of god trap. There are things that attract the eyes of those real beings known as the gods.

Another example can be found in Book VIII of the *Odyssey*. We are told what happened at the capture of Troy, the famous story of the big horse that contained the enemies and all the misfortunes to come in its belly, the horse that bore within itself the destruction of the city. The Trojans, who pulled it inside their city walls, question each other and wonder what to do with it. They hesitate. It seems quite clear that this hesitation was fatal to them, for there were two things they could have done. Assuming the wooden horse was hollow, they could have opened up the stomach to see what was inside. Or, having dragged it to the top of the citadel, they could have let it sit there to be what? Μέγα ἄγαλμα (*Méga ágalma*) [verse 509]. It's the same idea as earlier: it's a charm. It is also something that is as cumbersome [*embarrassant*] to the Trojans as to the Greeks. It is an uncanny object. In short, it is this well-known extraordinary object that is still at the center of a whole series of contemporary preoccupations – I needn't mention here the surrealist horizon.

For the ancients, *ágalma* is also something with which you can, in short, attract divine attention. I could give you a thousand examples of this.

In another spot in Euripides' *Hecuba*, the story is told of the sacri- 176
fice of Polyxena to appease the ghost of Achilles. It's very pretty, and
we have here an exception that gives us the opportunity to awaken
the erotic mirages in ourselves. It is the moment at which the heroine
herself offers a bosom that is akin, we are told, to *ágalma* [verse 561].
Nothing says we have to confine ourselves to what that evokes –
namely, the perfection of the breasts in Greek statuary. Given that
they were not museum pieces at the time, I believe that it has to do
rather with what we see indications of everywhere, in the use made
of the word *ágalma* when it is said that, in the course of ceremonies
in sanctuaries and temples, one hangs up, ἀνάπτω (*anápto*), *agálmata*.
The magical value of the objects mentioned here is related, instead,
to that of something we know very well, what we call "ex-votos." In
short, for people who were much closer than we are to the original
differentiation of objects, Polyxena's breasts were as beautiful as
those found on votive offerings [*ex-votos*]. Indeed, the breasts of
votive figures are made on a lathe or in a mold and are always perfect.

There are plenty of other examples, but we can stop here. It is
enough to indicate that *ágalma* has to do with the meanings *brillant*
[sheen] and *galant* [gallant], the latter coming from *gal*, meaning
éclat [sparkle or gleam] in Old French. In a word, what is at stake
here if not the function we analysts have discovered that is designated by the term "partial object"?

3

The function of the partial object is one of the great discoveries of
psychoanalysis. And what we analysts must be most surprised by
in this case is that, having discovered such remarkable things, our
efforts are always designed to efface their originality.

Somewhere in Pausanias' work [*Guide to Greece*], it is said that
the *agálmata* that are related in such and such a sanctuary to witches
and were placed there expressly to stop Alcmene from giving birth,
were ἀμυδρότερα (*amudrótera*), a tad effaced. Well, that's it, we too
have effaced as much as we could the meaning of the partial object.
We had a real find there, that of the fundamentally partial nature of
the object insofar as it is the pivotal point, crux, or key of human 177
desire. It was certainly worth dwelling on for a moment. But no,
nay, our first effort was to interpret it as pointing toward a dialectic
of totalization, to turn it into a flat, round, total object, the only one
worthy of us – the spherical object without feet or paws, the other
as a whole person, in whom, as everyone knows, our love irresistibly
finds its terminus and its completion.

Even though we took things in this way, we didn't tell ourselves that this other, as an object of desire, is perhaps the summation of a pile of partial objects, which is not at all the same as a total object. We didn't tell ourselves that what we elaborate on, what we have to deal with on the basis of the bedrock [*fond*] we call the id, is perhaps but a vast trophy of all these objects. No, on the horizon of our own ascesis or model of love, we placed something other [*de l'autre*]. And we weren't completely wrong to do so. But we have made that other into another to whom the bizarre function we call oblativity is addressed. We love the other for himself. At least, we do so once we arrive at our goal, at perfection. The genital stage sanctions all of this.

We analysts have clearly gained something by developing a certain topology of the relationship to the other, and we are not the only ones to have done so since there is a great deal of contemporary and variously personalist speculation about it as well. But it is still quite funny that there is something that we have left altogether by the wayside here. And we are certainly obliged to leave it by the wayside when we consider things from the particularly simplified perspective that assumes the problem to be resolved with the idea of a pre-established harmony – namely, that in short it suffices to love genitally in order to love the other for himself.

I didn't bring with me today an incredible passage regarding genital characterology found in a volume entitled *La Psychanalyse d'aujourd'hui* [Contemporary Psychoanalysis] because I have mentioned it elsewhere, in an article that will come out soon ["The Direction of the Treatment"]. I have been pointing out to you for a long time now the ridiculous nature of the kind of preaching we hear around this ultimate idealness. We need not dwell on it today, but, when we look at the textual sources, there is at least one question to raise on this point. If so-called oblative love is merely the homologue, development, or blossoming of the genital act itself – which would suffice, I would say, to reveal its secret, key, or measure – an ambiguity nevertheless persists about whether we seek, regarding this other (to whom we devote our oblativity in this love which is all love, all for the other), to bring him jouissance, as seems to be self-evident in the fact that it has to do with genital union, or rather to perfect him.

178

As soon as a writer, who is even the slightest bit concerned with writing in a style that is accessible to a contemporary audience, wants to discuss ideas as highly moral and topics as old as that of oblativity, the first thing he does to rouse us is bring out a latent binary opposition. For, in the final analysis, terms like "oblativity" cannot be sustained in such a simplified or even abraded form except owing to what underlies them – namely, the altogether modern opposition between the subject and the object. And thus, it is around this opposition that such a writer is led to comment on this analytic theme: we take the other as a subject and not purely and simply as our object.

The object at stake here is situated as being valued for the pleasure, enjoyment [*fruition*], or jouissance it brings. It is taken to boil down what is unique in the other to an all-purpose function, insofar as he must be a subject to us. If we merely turn him into an object, he will be just any old object, an object like all the rest, an object that can be rejected or exchanged – in short, he will be profoundly devalued. This is the theme that underlies the idea of oblativity, as it is articulated when people make of it the necessary ethical correlate of access to true love, which would be adequately termed "genital."

Note that today I am less in the process of criticizing this analytic idiocy – which is why I don't feel the need to remind you of the texts that talk about it – than calling into question what it is based on, namely, the idea that the beloved or love partner would be in some way superior if he were, as we say in our existential-analytic vocabulary, considered as a subject.

I don't think that, after having given such a pejorative connotation to the fact of considering the other as an object, anyone has ever mentioned that to consider him as a subject is no better. Let us admit that one object is just as good as another [*en vaut un autre*], on the condition that we give the word "object" its original meaning, which aims at objects insofar as we distinguish them and can communicate about them. If it is deplorable that the beloved might ever become an object, is it better for him to be a subject? To answer this question it suffices to note that if one object is no better than another [*en vaut un autre*], it's even worse in the case of the subject. For it is not simply another subject that he is equal to in worth [*qu'il vaut*] – a subject, strictly speaking, is an other [*en est un autre*].

Strictly speaking, the subject is someone to whom we can attribute what? Nothing other than the fact of being, like us, a being that is ἔναρθρον ἔχειν ἔπος (*énarthron échein épos*), that expresses itself in articulated language, that possesses the combinatory, and that can respond to our combinatory with its own combinations – someone we can thus bring into our calculation as someone who calculates like us.

I imagine that those of you who are trained in the method that I have inaugurated here are not going to contradict me on this point. It is the only sound definition of the subject, at least the only sound one for us, the only one that allows us to explain how a subject obligatorily enters into the *Spaltung* [splitting] determined by his submission to language.

179

On the basis of these terms, we can see how it is strictly necessary that there be in the subject a part where it [ça] speaks all by itself – in which respect the subject remains in abeyance. And we need to know – how can one ever forget this question? – what function is served by the fact that (in this elective, privileged relationship which is the love relationship) the subject with whom, among all others, we have a bond of love, is also the object of our desire. If one brings out the love relationship while holding in abeyance its anchor, pivotal point, center of gravity, or hook, it is impossible to say anything that is not simply a crock.

We must emphasize the correlative object of desire, for it is this – and not the object that is involved in equivalence, the transitivism of good things, or the transaction of covetous desires – that is the psychoanalytic object. The psychoanalytic object is the something that is the aim of desire as such, the something that emphasizes one object among all the others as incommensurate with the others. The introduction in analysis of the function of the partial object corresponds to this emphasis on the object.

I ask you to note, on this topic, that everything that makes metaphysical discourse seem weighty and noteworthy is always based on some ambiguity. In other words, if all the terms you use when you do metaphysics were strictly defined – each having an unequivocal signification – if the vocabulary of philosophy triumphed, which is the eternal goal of professors, there wouldn't be any point in doing metaphysics any more because there wouldn't be anything left to say. You would notice then that mathematics is much better – there you can use signs with an unequivocal meaning because they don't have any meaning. This implies that when you speak in a more or less impassioned way about the relations between the subject and the object, it is because you are talking about the subject [metaphysically] as if it were something other than the strict subject I was talking about earlier. And you talk about the object, too, as something other than what I just defined – in other words, you talk about it as something that virtually verges on the strict equivalence of an unequivocal communication by a scientific subject. But if this object "impassions" you, it is because hidden inside it is *ágalma*, the object of desire. This is what makes it weighty; this is why it is important to know where this fabulous object is, what its function is, and where it operates in inter- and intrasubjectivity. This privileged object of desire culminates for each of us at the border or liminal point I have taught you to view as the metonymy of unconscious discourse. This object plays a role there that I tried to formalize in fantasy and to which I will return next time.

This object, however you talk about it in psychoanalytic work –

180

whether you call it the breast, the phallus, or shit – is always a partial object. This is what is at stake inasmuch as analysis is a method or technique that has made headway in the field of desire, a field that was left behind, decried, and excluded by philosophy because it wasn't manageable, because it wasn't accessible to philosophy's dialectic.

If we are unable to point out, in a strict topology, the function of what this partial object signifies – which is both so limited and so slippery in its figure – if you don't see the interest of what I am introducing today with the term *ágalma*, which is the main point of analytic practice, well, it would be too bad. I wouldn't believe it for a minute, especially when I note that, regardless of the misunderstanding on which it is based, things are such that all the most modern work in psychoanalysis' dialectic revolves around the fundamental function of the object.

The only proof I need provide of this is that reference to the object as good or bad is considered to be a primordial given in the Kleinian dialectic. I ask you to dwell on that for a moment. 181

In our theoretical work we use a pile of things, and especially a pile of identificatory functions – for example, identification with the person from whom we demand something when we call for love. If our call is rejected, what results is identification with the very person we addressed as the object of our love, with a striking shift from love to identification. This is the third type of identification about which you have to read a bit of Freud, his *Group Psychology and the Analysis of the Ego*, to see the tertiary function taken on by a certain characteristic object: the object insofar as it is the object desired by the other with whom we identify. In short, subjectivity is constructed in the plurality or pluralism of levels of identification that we call the ego-ideal, the ideal ego, and – something that has also been identified – the desiring ego.

But we still must figure out where the partial object is situated and functions in this articulation. Note simply that when we look for this object, *ágalma*, little *a*, the object of desire, in analytic theory as it is currently being developed by Kleinians, it is there right from the outset, before any dialectical development – it is already there as an object of desire. The weight or internal central core of the good or bad object figures in all psychology that relies for its elaboration on Freudian terms. It is this good object or bad object that Melanie Klein situates at the origin, at the beginning of beginnings, even prior to the depressive period. Isn't this sufficiently indicative all by itself?

I think I have done enough today in telling you that it is around this that, inside or outside of analysis, the division between two perspectives regarding love can and must be concretely drawn.

The one drowns, sends off course, masks, elides, and sublimates everything concrete in the experience of love, in an infamous ascension toward a supreme good [*bien*]. It is astonishing that in analysis we can still keep some vague threepenny glints of this with the term "oblativity," this sort of loving-in-God, so to speak, that is supposed to be at the basis of every love relationship. In the other perspective, and analytic work demonstrates this, everything revolves around the privileged or unique point constituted somewhere by something we find in a being only when we truly love. But what is it? *Ágalma* – the object we have learned to discern in analytic practice.

182

I will try next time to situate this object in the threefold topology of the subject, the other with a lowercase *o*, and the Other with a capital *O*, and to reconstruct the point at which it comes into play.

And we shall see that it is only via the other and for the other that Alcibiades, like each and every one of us, wants to make his love known to Socrates.[12]

February 1, 1961

BETWEEN SOCRATES AND ALCIBIADES

Why Socrates does not love.
"I am nothing."
Socrates' interpretation.
The revelation that is ours.

There are thus some *agálmata* in Socrates, and this is what aroused Alcibiades' love.

We are now going to return to the scene that stages Alcibiades addressing a speech to Socrates, to which Socrates responds by providing, strictly speaking, an interpretation of it. We will see in what respect his assessment can be corrected, but one could say that, structurally speaking, Socrates' intervention has, on the face of it, all the features of an interpretation.

Socrates' response is more or less as follows: "Everything you just said that was so extraordinary, so unbelievably impudent, everything you just revealed in speaking of me was in fact said for Agathon's sake" [222c–d].

To understand the meaning of the scene that unfolds between these two points – from Alcibiades' eulogy of Socrates to Socrates' interpretation and what follows thereafter – we must go back to an earlier moment in the text and examine it in detail. What is the meaning of what happens between Alcibiades and Socrates after Alcibiades' entrance?

1

As I told you, after Alcibiades' entrance, there are no more eulogies of Love, but solely of the person seated to one's right. What is important in the change is the following: the point is to make a eulogy, *épainos*, of another person and, in this dialogue, the action

184   [*passage*] of metaphor lies precisely herein. The eulogy of another
person is substituted, not for the eulogy of Love, but for love itself,
and this happens right from the word "go."

"Love for Alcibiades is no trifling matter to me," Socrates says,
addressing Agathon, everyone knowing full well that Alcibiades was
the love of Socrates' life. "Since I became enamored of him" – we
will see the meaning that it is fitting to bestow upon these terms,
Socrates here was the *erastés* – "he hasn't allowed me to say two
words to anyone else – what am I saying, I can't so much as look at
an attractive man but he flies into a fit of jealous rage. He yells; he
threatens; he can hardly keep from slapping me around! Please, try
to keep him under control," he says to Agathon. "The fierceness of
his passion terrifies me!" [213c–d].

A short exchange then takes place between Alcibiades and
Eryximachus and gives rise to a new agenda. Namely, it is agreed
that each person will make a eulogy, each in his turn, of the person
who is seated to his right. *Épainos*, the eulogy in question, has, as
I told you, a symbolic function – more specifically, a metaphorical function. What it expresses has, indeed – from he who speaks
to the person about whom he speaks – a certain function qua
metaphor of love. To praise, *epainein*, has a ritual function here,
which can be translated in the following terms: to speak highly of
someone.

While we cannot exactly refer to Aristotle's *Rhetoric*, as it was
written later than the *Symposium*, in Book 1, Chapter 9, of the
Rhetoric, Aristotle distinguishes between *épainos* and *enkómion*.
Up until now I have told you that I did not want to go into the difference between the two. We have nevertheless been led to it by the
very nature of our endeavor.

What is specific about *épainos* can be seen very precisely in
the way Agathon starts his speech. He begins with the nature of
the object and only elaborates on its qualities afterward. This leads
to a deployment of the object in its essence. *Enkómion* is difficult
to translate into French, and the implied term κῶμος (*kómos*) is
no doubt involved in some way. If we are to find some equivalent
for it in French, it would have to be something like "panegyric." If
we follow Aristotle, it's a question of braiding a wreath from the
object's loftiest deeds – a point of view that goes beyond *épainos'*
aim to get at one's essence, which is eccentric to it.

185   But *épainos* is not something that presents itself unambiguously
at first. When it is decided that it is *épainos* that will be on the
agenda, Alcibiades retorts that the remark Socrates made concerning Alcibiades' ferocious jealousy didn't have a word of truth in it.
"The truth is just the opposite! He's the one who, if I dare praise

anyone else in his presence, even a god, will most surely" – and here he uses the same metaphor we saw earlier – τὼ χεῖρε (*to cheíre*), "beat me up" [214d].

We find in Socrates' reply here a tone, style, malaise, and confusion, an uncomfortable, almost panicked response of the "shut up" kind. "Hold your tongue!" it has been translated quite accurately [214d]. "By Poseidon," Alcibiades responds – which is no small matter – "don't you dare deny it! I would never – *never* – praise anyone else with you around."

"Well, why not do just that, if you want?" says Eryximachus. "Why don't you offer an encomium to Socrates?"

"Should I unleash myself upon him? Should I give him," Alcibiades asks, "his punishment in front of all of you? In making a eulogy of him, must I unmask him?" This is how his speech later unfolds. Indeed, it is not lacking in worry either, as if it were both a necessity of the situation and also an implied facet of the genre that a eulogy might go so far as to make people laugh at the person in question.

Alcibiades thus proposes a gentlemen's agreement*: "Must I speak the truth?" he asks.

Socrates does not refuse this, replying, "By all means, go ahead" [214e].

"Nothing can stop me now," says Alcibiades. "But here's what you can do: if I say anything that's not true, you can just interrupt, if you want, and correct me; at worst, there'll be mistakes in my speech, not lies. But you can't hold it against me if I don't get everything καταριθμῆσαι (*katarithmésai*), in the right order [. . .]. It is no easy task for one in my condition to give a smooth and orderly account of your bizarreness (*atopían*)!" [214e–215a] – here once again we come across the term *atopía*. Then the eulogy begins.

I indicated the eulogy's structure and theme to you last time. Alcibiades' speech is assuredly laughable – γέλως, γελοῖος (*gélos, geloíos*) – beginning as it does by presenting things through a comparison that I already highlighted. This comparison shows up three times in his speech, each time with an almost repetitive insistence. Socrates is compared in it to the satyr's crude and derisory outer crust or envelope. One must in some sense open it up to see inside what Alcibiades calls, the first time, *agálmata theón*, translated as "the statues of the gods" [215b]. The next time he once again calls them godlike and amazing [216e]. The third time, he uses the term ἀγάλματ' ἀρετῆς (*agálmat' aretés*): the marvel of virtue, the marvel of marvels [222a].

During his speech we find a comparison with the satyr Marsyas which, when it is presented, is taken quite far. Despite Socrates'

186

protests, and he is certainly not a flautist [*flûtiste*], Alcibiades returns to the point and takes it still further. He doesn't simply compare Socrates to a box in the form of a satyr, to a more or less derisory object, but to the satyr Marsyas himself – and everyone knows from the legend that when Marsyas began to play, his song was irresistibly charming. The charm was so great that it aroused Apollo's jealousy, who had him skinned alive for having dared rival the supreme, divine music. The only difference, Alcibiades says, between Socrates and Marsyas is that Socrates is not a piper. He does not operate via music and yet the result is of the exact same order [215a–c].

Here we should refer to what Plato explains in the *Phaedrus* concerning the higher states, so to speak, of inspiration, as they are produced beyond the realm of beauty. There are different forms of going beyond that I will not take up here. Among the means used by those who are δεομένους (*deoménous*), who need the gods and initiations, there is the drunkenness brought on by a certain music that produces a state known as possession. Alcibiades refers specifically to this state when he says that it is what Socrates produces with his words. Although his words are unaccompanied, without musical accompaniment, he produces the exact same effect [215c].

When we listen to an orator, he says, even a first-rate orator, it has little effect on us. On the contrary, when it is you that we listen to, or even your words as related by another person, even if he is πάνυ φαῦλος (*pánu phaúlos*), a man of no consequence whatsoever, the listener, whether man, woman, or adolescent, is troubled, as if struck by a blow, and strictly speaking κατεχόμεθα (*katechómetha*) – we become possessed by them [215d].

This situates the experience that makes Alcibiades think that inside Socrates lies a treasure, an indefinable, precious object which will fix his resolve after having unleashed his desire. This object is at the crux of what he says thereafter concerning his resolution and then his schemes designed to seduce Socrates. Let us dwell for a moment on this point.

Alcibiades had an experience with Socrates that was far from ordinary. Having made his decision, he knew he was treading on somewhat sure ground, for he knew that Socrates had long since been paying attention to what he calls his ὥρα (*hóra*) – we translate it as best we can – let's call it "sex appeal."* It seemed to Alcibiades that if Socrates would only deign to declare how he felt, Alcibiades would obtain from him precisely what was at stake – namely, what he himself defines as everything Socrates knows, πάντ᾽ ἀκοῦσαι ὅσαπερ οὗτος ἤδει (*pánt' akoúsai hósaper hoútos édei*) [217a]. He then provides us with the narrative of his seductive maneuvers. But can't we pause here a moment?

As Alcibiades already knows that he has captivated Socrates' desire, why can't he more truly presume that Socrates will comply with his wishes? Alcibiades already knows that he is Socrates' beloved, *erómenos*, so why does he need to have Socrates give him a sign of his desire? Socrates has never made a mystery of his desire in the past. His desire is recognized [*reconnu*] and, by dint of that very fact, known [*connu*], and thus one might think it is already avowed. What then is the meaning of these seductive maneuvers? Alcibiades spins his narrative with artfulness and detail, but at the same time with impudence and a challenge to his audience, which is so clearly felt to go beyond all limits that he introduces it with nothing less than the words that are spoken before the mysteries are revealed: "Cover your ears, you who are here" [218b]. This warning is addressed only to those who have no right to hear, and still less to repeat what is going to be said or how it is going to be said – that is, house slaves, who would be better off not hearing.

Socrates' behavior corresponds, after all, to the mysterious demand that Alcibiades makes. If, indeed, Socrates has always shown himself to be Alcibiades' *erastés*, it may seem in another register, in a post-Socratic perspective, that Socrates is demonstrating a great quality, which the French translator of the *Symposium* indicates in the margin with the term "temperance." But in this context, his temperance is not indicated as necessary. Perhaps Socrates proves that he is virtuous, but what relation could there possibly be between that and the subject in question if it is true that what we are being shown here concerns the mystery of love?

In other words, you see that I am trying to examine every facet of the situation that unfolds before us in the *Symposium*, in order to grasp the structure of this game. Let's immediately say that everything in Socrates' behavior indicates that his refusal to enter into the game of love is closely related to the fact, posited at the outset as the point of departure, that he knows.

188

He knows the score in matters of love – that is even, as he says, the only thing he knows. I will propose that it is because Socrates knows that he does not love.

2

With this key in hand, let us give their full meaning to the words with which Socrates greets Alcibiades' invitation, after three or four scenes in which Alcibiades' attacks are shown to proceed with accelerating rhythm [217–219].

The ambiguities of the situation always verge on the γελοῖος (*geloíos*), the laughable or comic. Indeed, they are buffoonish scenes, these invitations to dinner, which end with a guy who leaves very early, very politely, after having made others wait for him, who returns a second time, and who escapes once again, and with whom the following dialogue takes place under the covers: "Socrates, are you asleep?"

"No, no, not at all," he replies [218c].

It must be said that, in order to arrive at its endpoint, what is at work leads us along paths that are well designed to situate us at a certain level.

Once Alcibiades has truly said his piece, and has gone so far as to tell Socrates, "This is what I desire, and I would certainly be ashamed before people who might not understand; I am explaining to you what I want" [218c–d], Socrates replies, "If you are right in what you say about me, you are already more accomplished than you think. If I really have in me the power to make you a better man, then you can see in me a beauty that is really beyond description and makes your own remarkable good looks pale in comparison. But, then, is this a fair exchange that you propose? You seem to me to want more than your proper share: you offer me the merest appearance of beauty" – what, in the Socratic perspective on science, is illusion, fallacy, and *dóxa*, which does not know its function – "and in return you want" truth. And in fact, for goodness' sake, that means nothing more than "gold in exchange for bronze" [218d–e].

189   But, says Socrates – and we must take things as they are said here – "you should think twice, ἄμεινον σκόπει (*ámeinon skópei*), because you could be wrong, and οὐδὲν ὤν (*oudén on*), I may be of no use to you [219a]. The mind's sight," he continues, "becomes sharp only when the body's eyes go past their prime – and you are still a good long time away from that." But pay attention – where you see something, I am nothing.

What is Socrates refusing here? What is he refusing even though he has already shown himself to be what he has, I would say, almost officially shown himself to be in all of Alcibiades' remarks, to the extent that everyone knows that Alcibiades was his first love? What Socrates refuses to show Alcibiades is something that takes on another meaning. If it is definable in the terms I have given you, it would be the metaphor of love.

It would be the metaphor of love, insofar as Socrates would admit to being the beloved, and I would say even more, would admit to being the beloved unconsciously. Yet it is precisely because Socrates knows that he refuses to be, in whatever sense, whether justified or justifiable, *erómenos*, desirable – what is worthy of being loved.

Why doesn't he love? Why is it that the metaphor of love cannot be produced, that there is no substitution of *erastés* for *erómenos*, that Socrates doesn't manifest himself as *erastés* at the place where *erómenos* was? Socrates can but refuse to do so because, to him, there is nothing in him that is lovable. His essence is οὐδὲν (*oudén*), emptiness or hollowness, and to use a term that was used later in neo-Platonic and Augustinian thought, κένωσις (*kénosis*) – this represents Socrates' central position.

This is so true that the term *kénosis*, emptiness or void – as opposed to the fullness of whom? of Agathon specifically – is present right at the beginning of the dialogue, when Socrates, after his long meditation in the foyer of the neighboring house, finally shows up at the banquet, sits down next to Agathon, and begins to speak. We think he is joking, that this is said in jest, but in a dialogue that is both as rigorous and austere in its unfolding as this one, can we believe that anything here is simply used as filler? Socrates says, "Agathon, you are the one who is full, and just as one makes a liquid move from a full vase to an empty one using a wick along which it flows, similarly I'm going to fill myself up" [175d–e]. This is, no doubt, said ironically, but it expresses something that is precisely what Socrates   190
presents as constitutive of his position, and what I have repeated to you many times. Here we hear the words from Alcibiades' very own lips – namely, that Socrates doesn't know anything except concerning matters of love. Cicero translates *amathía* as *inscientia* by forcing things a bit in Latin. *Inscitia* is brute ignorance, while *inscientia* is non-knowledge constituted as such, as empty [*vide*], as the attraction exercised by the void or vacuum [*vide*] at the center of knowledge.

I think that you get what I mean here, since I exposed to you the structure of substitution or actualized metaphor that constitutes what I call the miracle of the appearance of *erastés* at the very place where *erómenos* was. It is precisely because this is lacking here that Socrates can only refuse to give, so to speak, a simulacrum thereof. If he presents himself to Alcibiades as not being able to show him signs of his desire, it is insofar as he challenges the idea that he himself is, in any way, an object worthy of Alcibiades' desire, or of anyone else's for that matter.

Note thereby that the Socratic message, if it contains something that refers to love, certainly does not fundamentally begin from a center of love. Socrates is represented to us as an *erastés*, someone who desires, but nothing is further from his image than the radiant love which, for example, stems from Christ's message. Neither effusion, nor gift, nor mysticism, nor ecstasy, nor simple commandment flows from it. Nothing is further from Socrates' message than "Love thy neighbor as thyself," a formulation whose dimension is remarkably absent from everything he says.

This has always struck commentators, who, in their objections to the ascesis of Eros, say that what is commanded in this message is, "Love before all else in your soul what is most essential to you." This is only apparently the case, and the Socratic message, such as it is transmitted to us by Plato, does not make a mistake here, since, as you will see, the structure is preserved. It also allows us to more accurately glimpse the mystery hidden behind the Christian commandment precisely because it is preserved.

This is also why it is possible to provide a general theory of love, behind every manifestation that is a manifestation of love. This may, at first glance, seem surprising to you, but keep in mind that once you have the key – I mean what I am calling the metaphor of love – you will see it everywhere.

I illustrated it for you with Victor Hugo's poem, but there is also the original book of the story of Ruth and Booz. If this story stands before us in a way that inspires us – except for those scoffers who see in it only a sordid story of an old letch and a washerwoman – it is because we take this inscience for granted: "Booz did not know that a woman was there." We also take for granted that Ruth is already the object Booz unconsciously loves. We categorically assume as well that "Ruth did not know what God wanted from her" and that the third party – the divine locus of the Other, insofar as the fate of Ruth's desire is inscribed in it – is what gives her nocturnal vigilance at Booz's feet its sacred character.

The whole mystery of the signification of love that the revelation of their desire takes on lies in the underpinning of inscience, in which the dignity of *erómenos* for each of the partners is already situated in a veiled anteriority.

3

Let us return to the *Symposium* to see what transpires.

Alcibiades does not understand. After having heard Socrates out, he says to him, "I really have nothing more to say. I've told you exactly what I think. Now it's your turn to consider what you think best for you and me" [219a]. He calls on him to, as we say, face up to his responsibilities.

To which Socrates replies, "We'll talk about all that. See you tomorrow. We still have a lot to say about it." In short, he situates things at the level of the continuation of a dialogue, leading Alcibiades down his own pathways. He thus makes himself absent to such an extent that Alcibiades' covetousness shows through.

Can we say that this covetousness is covetousness of what is best?

What counts is that it is expressed in terms of objects. Alcibiades does not say, "It's for my own good, or for my own misfortune, that I want what is incomparable, which lies in you – namely, *ágalma*." He says something more like, "I want it because I want it, whether it's for my own good or not." And it is precisely for this reason that Alcibiades reveals the central function of *ágalma* in the articulation of love relations. It is also for this reason that Socrates refuses to respond at the same level.

192

Socrates' commandment is "concern yourself with your own soul, seek your own perfection." Through his attitude of refusal, severity, and austerity, through his *noli me tangere*, Socrates directs Alcibiades along the pathway of his own good. But is it even clear that we mustn't allow some ambiguity to subsist regarding this phrase, "his own good"? Isn't it the equating of the object of desire and "one's own good" that has been called into question since this dialogue by Plato resounded in the world? Shouldn't we translate it by the good such as Socrates, he who brings into the world a new discourse, traces out its path for those who follow him?

Observe that, in Alcibiades' attitude, there is something, I was going to say sublime, in any case absolute and impassioned, that verges on an entirely different character with another message – that of the Gospel, where we are told that he who knows that there is a treasure buried in a field, and we are not told what the treasure is, is capable of selling everything he has in order to buy that field and enjoy the treasure. This is the distance that separates Socrates' position from Alcibiades'. Alcibiades is a man imbued with desire [*l'homme du désir*].

But you will then retort, "Why does he want to be loved?" In truth, he already is and he knows it. The miracle of love has taken place in him insofar as he has become the one who desires. And when Alcibiades shows that he is in love, it is, as they say, no small potatoes. Because he is Alcibiades, he whose desires know no bounds, when he enters into the referential field that is for him the field of love, he shows a highly remarkable absence of fear of castration – in other words, a total lack of the famous *Ablehnung der Weiblichkeit* [repudiation of femininity]. Everyone knows that in Antiquity the most extreme kinds of virility were always accompanied by an utter and complete disdain for the possible risk of being called a woman, even by one's soldiers – which, as you know, happened to Caesar.

Alcibiades here throws a hissy fit in front of Socrates. He nevertheless remains Alcibiades at his own level. And this is why we must still, before moving on from Alcibiades' speech, grant full importance to the complement he provides his eulogy with – namely, the

astonishing portrait designed to complete the impassive figure of
Socrates. Impassivity means that Socrates cannot bear being placed
in the passive [position], as the beloved, *erómenos*. Socrates' attitude – what Alcibiades describes to us as his courage – is constituted
by a profound indifference to everything that happens around him,
even the most dramatic of events [219d–221b].

Once we arrive at the end of this speech, in which the demonstration that Socrates is a being like no other culminates, Socrates
responds to Alcibiades as follows: "You give me the sense of having
all your wits about you" [222c]. Whereas Alcibiades had expressed
himself with the caveat, "I don't know what I'm saying." If
Socrates, who knows, says that Alcibiades gives him the impression
of Νήφειν μοι δοκεῖς (*néphein moi dokeís*), having all his wits about
him, it means, "Although you are drunk, I can read something in
you." What is it? Socrates is the one who knows it, not Alcibiades.

Socrates points out what is at stake when Alcibiades mentions
Agathon.

Indeed, at the end of his speech, Alcibiades turns toward Agathon
to tell him, "I warn you, don't let Socrates fool you! Remember my
torments; be on your guard" [222b]. He says it to Agathon incidentally. And in truth, Socrates' intervention, insofar as I called it
an interpretation, would have no meaning did it not bear on this
"incidentally." "How casually you let it drop," he says, "almost
like an afterthought, at the very end of your speech!" [222c]. What
Socrates tells us is that Agathon was in fact present as an aim in all
of Alcibiades' circumlocutions, and that it was around him that his
whole speech revolved. "As if your speech" – this is how it should be
translated, and not "your language" – "had but the following goal:
to enunciate that I should be in love with you and no one else, and
that for his part, Agathon should let himself be loved by you and by
no one else" [222c–d].

"This," he says, "is κατάδηλον (*katádelon*), entirely transparent, in
Alcibiades' speech." Socrates says quite plainly that he can read this
in Alcibiades' apparent speech. And, more precisely, it is in "this
drama of your invention," as Socrates calls it, this σατυρικόν σου
δρᾶμα (*satyrikón sou dráma*), "that the silenus metaphor is perfectly
transparent and we see things" [222d].

Let us try, in effect, to recognize its structure. Socrates says to
Alcibiades, "What you want, in the final analysis, is to be loved by
me and to have Agathon be your object." No other meaning can be
given to this speech, if not the most superficial psychological meanings, such as the vague awakening of jealousy in the other person,
and there is no question of that here. This indeed is what is at stake,
and Socrates admits it, showing his desire to Agathon and asking

him in sum what Alcibiades had at first asked of him. The proof
thereof is that if we consider all the parts of the *Symposium* as a
long epithalamium [nuptial poem], and if what this whole dialectic
leads to has any meaning, what happens at the end is that Socrates
provides a eulogy of Agathon.

The fact that Socrates eulogizes Agathon is tantamount to responding to Alcibiades' demand. Not his past demand – his present one.
When Socrates eulogizes Agathon, he pays Alcibiades back [*il donne
satisfaction à Alcibiade*]. He pays him back for his just finished public
declaration, his putting at the level of the universal Other what took
place between them behind the veils of modesty. Socrates' response
is as follows, "You can love he who I am going to praise because,
by praising him, I will be able to transmit the image of you loving
[*aimant*], qua image of you loving – that is how you will enter into
the path of superior identifications traced out by the path of beauty."

But we must not misrecognize here that Socrates, precisely
because he knows, replaces one thing with something else. It
is neither beauty, nor ascesis, nor identification with God that
Alcibiades desires, but rather this unique object, this special something he saw in Socrates and which Socrates turns him away from,
because Socrates knows that he does not have it.

But Alcibiades still desires the same thing. What he is looking for
in Agathon, make no mistake about it, is the same supreme point at
which the subject is abolished in fantasy: his *agálmata*.

Socrates substitutes here his lure [*leurre*] for what I will call the
lure of the gods. He does so quite authentically, insofar as he knows
what love is. And it is precisely because he knows this that he is
doomed to be mistaken – namely, to misrecognize the essential function of the targeted object constituted by *ágalma*.

Last night we heard about theoretical models [at a meeting of our
Society]. It is impossible not to mention, in this regard, if only as a
prop for our thought, the intrasubjective dialectic of the ego-ideal,
ideal ego, and partial object, and not to recall the little schema of the
spherical mirror I drew for you in the past.

In front of this mirror, the fantasy is created or arises of the real
image of the vase hidden within the device. If this illusory image can
be propped up and perceived as real, it is insofar as the eye adjusts to
what the vase appears around – namely, the flower we have placed
on top. I taught you to use these three notations – ego-ideal, ideal
ego, and *a*, the *ágalma* of the partial object – to grasp the recipro-
cal relations of the three terms in question every time something is
constituted. What is this something? Precisely what is at stake at the
end of the Socratic dialectic.

It concerns what Freud tells us is essential in falling in love – I introduced this schema in order to give it consistency – namely, the recognition of the basis of the narcissistic image, insofar as this image constitutes the substance of the ideal ego.

The imaginary incarnation of the subject is what is at issue in this threefold reference. Be so kind as to allow me to finally tell you what I've been meaning to say: Socrates' daemon is Alcibiades.

It is Alcibiades, in the sense in which we are told in Diotima's speech that love is not a god, but rather a daemon – namely, a daemon who sends mortals the message that the gods wish to convey to him.

Which is why we couldn't fail, regarding this dialogue, to bring up the nature of the gods.

4

I am going to be away for two weeks and will leave you with a reading assignment: *De Natura Deorum* [*On the Nature of the Gods*] by Cicero.

It's a book that did me a good deal of harm a long time ago: a well-known pedant, seeing me with my nose in it, thought it did not bode well regarding the direction of my professional interests.

Read it in order to get up to speed. You will notice that Cicero is not the lout people try to depict him as by saying that the Romans were people who were simply dragging their feet. He's a guy who articulates things that go right to the quick.

You will also see all sorts of exceedingly funny things in it, as, for example, that in Cicero's time, people went to Athens to look for traces of the great pin-ups of Socrates' day. People went there saying to themselves, "I'm going to meet guys like Charmides on every block." You will see that, compared with the stir created by these Charmides, our Brigitte Bardot wouldn't stand a chance. Even the little street urchins had eyes this big [expansive hand gesture].

196   We find some pretty funny stuff in Cicero's work. There is, in particular, a passage I cannot recite for you, but which is of the following type: when it comes to the pretty boys that philosophers have taught us it is good to love, you can look for them, there's certainly one here and there, but that's all. What does this mean? Did the loss of political independence have, as an irremediable effect, some sort of racial decadence, or simply the disappearance of the mysterious sparkle [*éclat*], the ἵμερος ἐναργής (*himeros enargés*), the shine [*brillant*] of desire Plato speaks about in the *Phaedrus*? We will never know anything about it.

You will learn plenty of other things [from *De Natura Deorum*] as well. You will learn that it is a serious question to know where the gods are situated. The question has not lost its importance for us. If any of what I tell you here can serve you in some way, some day when there is a palpable slippage in your certainties, when you find yourself in a tough position – well, one of those things will be that I have reminded you of the real existence of the gods.

Why not then dwell on the scandalous objects that the gods of ancient mythology were? Without trying to reduce them to piles of files or to sets of themes, let us ask ourselves what it might have meant for the gods to act as you know they did, their most characteristic activities being theft, fraud, and adultery. I won't even mention impiety – that was their specialty.

In other words, the scandalous nature of ancient mythology frankly raises the question of what a god's love is. It reaches its height right at the outset in Homer's work. There is no way to behave more arbitrarily, unjustifiably, incoherently, or derisively than these gods do. Read the *Iliad* – they're always mixed up in men's affairs, intervening constantly. Yet we cannot think these stories were merely tall tales. I don't adopt this perspective, and no one can, not even the thickest Homais. No. They're there and that's all there is to it. What can it possibly mean that the gods only show themselves to men in this manner?

You have to see what happens when they take it into their heads to love a mortal woman, for example. Nothing will stop them until the mortal, out of desperation, turns into a laurel or a frog. Nothing is further from the trembling one feels in one's being when in love than a god's desire, or a goddess' desire for that matter – I don't see why I shouldn't include them as well.

197

It took someone of Giraudoux's stature to represent the dimensions and resonance of the prodigious myth of Amphitryon. Even this great poet couldn't help but let Jupiter shine with something that might resemble a sort of respect for Alcmene's feelings, but that was clearly in order to make it plausible to us. For those who know how to hear, this myth remains the height of blasphemy, one might say, and nevertheless this was not at all how it was understood in Antiquity.

For here things go further than anything. Divine debauchery disguises itself as human virtue. When I say that nothing stops the Greek gods, I mean that they go so far as to make a mockery of even what is best. This is the whole key to the matter: the best ones, the real gods, take impassivity to the very point that I mentioned earlier – namely, to the point of being unable to put up with being called passive.

To be loved is to necessarily enter into the scale of the desirable; as we know, Christian theologians were at great pains to rid themselves of it. For if God is desirable, then He can be more or less desirable. There is thus a whole scale of desire. And what do we desire in God if not what is desirable? But, then, can there be greater degrees of God? The upshot being that it was precisely at the moment at which people tried to give God His most absolute value that people found themselves caught up in a vortex out of which they could only climb with great difficulty to preserve the dignity of the supreme object.

The gods of Antiquity didn't beat around the bush. They knew they could reveal themselves to men only in the guise of something that would cause a ruckus, in the *ágalma* of something that breaks all the rules, as a pure manifestation of an essence that remained completely hidden, whose enigma was entirely below the surface. Hence the daemonic incarnation of their scandalous exploits. It is in this sense that I say that Alcibiades was Socrates' daemon.

Alcibiades provides the true representation, unbeknown to himself, of what is implied by the Socratic ascesis. He shows that the dialectic of love as it was later elaborated in Christianity is there – believe me, it's not absent. For it was around this dialectic that a crisis developed in the sixteenth century, one that called into question the long synthesis – and, I would add, the long equivocation – concerning the nature of love that was sustained and developed throughout the Middle Ages in an oh so very post-Socratic perspective.

I mean, for example, that the god of John the Scot is no different from Aristotle's god, insofar as he acts as *erómenon*. They cohere – it is through his beauty that god makes the world go round. What a gap there is between this perspective and the one that is opposed to it! But what I am trying to express is that it is not really opposed.

People opposed to it the perspective of *agápe*, insofar as it explicitly teaches us that God loves us insofar as we are sinners, loves us as much for our evil doings as for our good deeds. This is, in effect, the meaning of the shift that took place in the history of the amorous sentiments, and curiously enough, at the precise moment at which Plato's message reappeared in its authentic texts [in the West]. Divine *agápe*, insofar as it is addressed to the sinner as such, is the core and crux of Luther's position. But don't believe that this is something that was limited to heresy, to a local insurrection within Catholicism. It suffices to take a look, even a superficial one, at what followed, the Counter-Reformation – namely, the eruption of what was called Baroque art – to realize that it signifies nothing other than the exposing, or erection as such, of the power of the image in all its seductive glory.

After the long misunderstanding that had sustained the Trinitarian relation in divinity, from the knowing to the known, and ascending to the known in the knowing via knowledge, we can see in it the outlines of our own form of revelation – namely, that things go from the unconscious toward the subject who is constituted in his dependence, and ascend toward the core object that I call *ágalma* here.

Such is the structure that regulates the dance between Alcibiades and Socrates.

Alcibiades demonstrates the presence of love, but only insofar as Socrates, who knows, can be mistaken about its presence, and only accompanies him in being mistaken. The deception [*leurre*] is mutual. Socrates is just as caught up in the deception – if it is a deception and if it is true that he is deceived [*leurré*] – as Alcibiades is.

But which of them is the most authentically deceived, if not he who follows closely, and without allowing himself to drift, what is traced out for him by a love that I will call horrible?

Don't believe that she who was placed at the beginning of this dialogue, Aphrodite, is a goddess who smiles.

A pre-Socratic by the name, I believe, of Democritus, says that Aphrodite was there all alone at the beginning. And it was even in this connection that the term *ágalma* appeared for the first time in Greek texts. Venus, as she is more commonly known, is born every day.

The birth of Aphrodite takes place every day, and to borrow a term from Plato himself – an equivocation that is, I believe, a true etymology – I will conclude my talk today with these words, καλημέρα (*kaleméra*), good day [*bonjour*], καλήμερος (*kalémeros*), good day and beautiful desire, based on the reflections I have contributed here about the relation of love to something that has always been called "eternal love." It should not be too burdensome for you to think about it if you recall that Dante [in the *Inferno*] explicitly places the words "eternal love" on the doors of Hell.

February 8, 1961

199

THE OBJECT OF DESIRE
AND THE DIALECTIC
OF CASTRATION

TRANSFERENCE IN THE PRESENT

Decline of the Other.
Dignity of the subject.
Transference is not just repetition.
The true mainspring of love.
Socrates' interpretation.

I think most of you recall that we have arrived at the end of our commentary on the *Symposium*.

As I have, if not explained, at least indicated several times, this dialogue happens to have been historically at the origin, not only of what one might call an explanation of love in our cultural era, but also of the development of a function that is, on the whole, the deepest, most radical, and most mysterious of relations between subjects.

On the horizon of the commentary I proposed was the whole development of ancient philosophy right up until Christianity.

Ancient philosophy, as you know, did not simply promulgate a speculative position. Whole parts of the society were oriented in their practice by the speculation that stemmed from Socrates. It was not at all artificially or fictitiously that Hegel described positions like those of the Stoics and Epicureans as the antecedents of Christianity. Such positions were in fact experienced by a very large set of subjects as something that guided their lives in a way that was equivalent, prior, and preparatory to what the Christian position brought them afterward. The latter also involves a dimension that goes beyond speculation and that the *Symposium* itself has continued to mark deeply.

One cannot in effect say that the fundamental theological positions taught by Christianity were lacking in repercussions. They profoundly influenced each person's problematic, most notably the problematic of those people who found themselves, in the course of history, at the forefront, assuming, as they did, roles as examples in a variety of ways – whether because of what they said or because of their directive action. This is what we call sainthood. This can only be indicated here on the horizon, yet it suffices for our purposes.

It suffices because if it were from this point of departure that I wanted to fuel what I have to say here, I would have broached things from a later point. I chose instead the initial point constituted by the *Symposium* and provided a commentary on it because it harbors within it something altogether radical concerning the mainspring of love – indeed, it is subtitled "On Love" [in Léon Robin's French edition] and it clearly announces that its main topic is love.

1

I don't think it would be exaggerating to say that the point with which I concluded last time has been neglected heretofore by all commentators on the *Symposium*, and that in this respect my commentary marks a milestone in the history of the development of the dialogue's potential.

I believe I was able to perceive the last word of what Plato meant to tell us about the nature of love in the very scenario of what happens between Alcibiades and Socrates. This presupposes that in the presentation of what one might call his thought, Plato deliberately created room for enigma – in other words, his thought is not entirely patent, delivered up, or spelled out in this dialogue.

Now there is nothing excessive in asking you to go along with me on this, for the simple reason that, according to all ancient and especially modern commentators on Plato – it is not the case of just one of them – an attentive scrutiny of the dialogues shows that they quite obviously contain an exoteric as well as a hermetic element. The most peculiar forms of hermeticism, right up to and including the most typical pitfalls bordering on illusion [*leurre*], on difficulty produced for its own sake, have as their aim not to be understandable to those who should not understand. This is truly fundamental in every one of Plato's exposés that has been handed down to us.

205

To admit this is also to admit what can always be risqué in making headway, going further, trying to break through, and guessing the deepest mainspring of what Plato tells us. But concerning the theme of love as it is presented to us in the *Symposium*, to which I have limited my attention here, it is difficult for us as analysts not to recognize the bridge that is standing there and the hand that is extended toward us in the articulation of the last scene in the *Symposium* – namely, the scene that unfolds between Alcibiades and Socrates.

I articulated and emphasized it to you in two stages. I showed you the importance, in Alcibiades' declaration, of the theme of *ágalma*: the object hidden within the subject, Socrates. I showed you that it is very hard not to take it seriously. In the form and articulation in which it is presented to us, Plato does not resort to metaphorical terms or pretty images when he tells us, roughly speaking, that Alcibiades expects a great deal of Socrates. A structure is revealed here, in which we can find anew what we are able to articulate as fundamental in what I will call the position of desire.

Apologizing to those of you who are recent arrivals here, I can assume that most of you are aware of the general outlines of my previous discussions on the position of the subject, outlines that are found in the topological summary we conventionally refer to here as the Graph.

Its general form is supplied by the splitting* or fundamental doubling of two signifying chains by which the subject is constituted. This requires that we admit that it has already been demonstrated that this doubling is, in and of itself, necessitated by the initial, inaugural, logical relationship between the subject and the signifier as such; and that the existence of an unconscious signifying chain stems from the sole position of the term "subject" qua determined as a subject by the fact that he props up the signifier [*il est le support du signifiant*].

Those for whom this is merely an assertion or proposition that remains to be demonstrated, should rest assured – we will come back to it. But for the purposes of our seminar this morning, I ask you to keep in mind that it has already been articulated here.

In relation to the unconscious signifying chain as constitutive of the subject who speaks, desire presents itself in a position that can only be conceptualized on the basis of the metonymy determined by the existence of the signifying chain. Metonymy is the phenomenon that occurs in the subject as a prop for the signifying chain. Due to the fact that the subject undergoes the mark of the signifying chain, something is fundamentally instituted in him that we call metonymy, which is nothing other than the possibility of the infinite sliding of signifiers owing to [*sous*] the continuity of the signifying chain. Everything that at one time finds itself associated with the signifying chain – a circumstantial element, an aspect of activity, an element of the beyond [*l'au-delà*] or of the endpoint [*terme*] to which this activity leads – all of these elements can be taken as equivalent to each other under suitable conditions. A circumstantial element can take on the representative value of the endpoint of subjective enunciation – that is, the object toward which the subject heads or the subject's action itself.

206

Now it is precisely inasmuch as something presents itself as enhancing [*revalorisant*] this infinite sliding – this dissolving element that brings signifying fragmentation into the subject – that it takes on the value of the privileged object that puts a stop to the infinite sliding. An object can thus assume, in relation to the subject, the essential value that constitutes the fundamental fantasy. The subject himself realizes that he is arrested therein, or, to remind you of a more familiar notion, fixated. We call the object that serves this privileged function *a*. It is to the extent that the subject identifies with the fundamental fantasy that desire as such takes on consistency and can be designated – that the desire in question for us as well is rooted, by its very position, in *Hörigkeit* [bondage, sexual dependence]. In other words, to use our terminology, in the subject it stands for the desire of the Other with a capital *O* [abbreviated as A for *Autre*].

A is defined for us as the locus of speech, the locus that is always evoked as soon as there is speech, the tertiary locus that always exists in relations with the other, *a*, as soon as there is signifying articulation. This A is not an absolute other, an other that would be what we call, in our incoherent moral jargon, the other respected as a subject, as our equal, morally speaking. No, this Other, as I teach you to articulate it here, that is both necessitated and necessary as a locus, but at the same time constantly questioned as to what guarantees it, is a perpetually vanishing Other which, due to this very fact, places us in a perpetually vanishing position.

207

Now love itself is related to the questioning of the Other regarding what he can give us and what he can furnish by way of an answer. Not that love is identical to each of the demands with which we assail the Other, for love is situated in what lies beyond this demand, insofar as the Other can or cannot respond to us as an ultimate presence.

The whole problem is to perceive the relationship that links the Other to which the demand for love is addressed, to the appearance of desire. The Other is no longer in any way our equal – this Other to whom we aspire, love's Other – but something that represents, strictly speaking, its deposing [*déchéance*]. I mean that it is something like an object.

What is at stake in desire is not a subject but rather an object. Herein lies what one might call the terrible commandment of the god of love. The commandment is to make of the object it designates to us something that, first of all, is an object, and, second, an object before which we falter, vacillate, and disappear as subjects. For it is we as subjects who suffer from this deposing [*déchéance*] or depreciation.

What happens to the object is precisely the opposite. The terms

I am using here are not the most suitable, but so what? The most important thing is that you get it and that I make myself understood. This object is overvalued. And it is insofar as it is overvalued that it serves the function of saving our dignity as subjects – that is, of making us something other than subjects subjected to the infinite sliding of the signifier. It makes of us something other than subjects of speech, turning us into something unique, inestimable, and irreplaceable in the final analysis, which is the true point at which we can designate what I have called the dignity of the subject.

The equivocal nature of the term "individuality" lies not in the fact that we are something unique, like the body which is specific – this one and not that one. Individuality consists entirely in the privileged relationship in which we culminate as subjects in desire.

Here I am merely repeating once more the merry-go-round of truth on which we have been spinning since the beginning of this Seminar.

My goal this year is to show what the consequences of transference are at the very heart of our practice.

2

"How did it happen that we are coming to transference so late in the game?" you will ask me.

It is, of course, characteristic of truths to never show themselves completely. In short, truths are solids that are perfidiously opaque. They don't even have, it seems, the property we are able to produce in certain solids, that of transparency – they do not show us their front and back edges at the same time. You have to circumnavigate them [*en faire le tour*], and even do a little conjuring [*le tour de passe-passe*].

As for transference as we are broaching it this year – and you have seen how charmingly I have been able to lead you for a while in making you concern yourselves with love along with me – you must, all the same, have noticed that I approached it from a certain direction or angle, which not only is not the classic angle, but is not even the angle from which I had heretofore approached the topic with you.

Hitherto, I always remained reserved in what I asserted regarding transference, by telling you that one has to seriously distrust its appearances – namely, the phenomena that are most often designated with the terms "positive transference" and "negative transference." These terms are situated at the level of a simple collection, at the level of the everyday terms with which not only a more or less informed public, but even we analysts speak of transference.

I have always reminded you that we must begin with the fact that transference, in the final analysis, is repetition compulsion [*automatisme*]. Since the beginning of this year I have done nothing but lead you through the details of the movement in Plato's *Symposium*, where love alone is at work, and this was obviously designed to broach transference by another path. The goal now is to bring these two paths together.

The distinction [between transference and repetition compulsion] is so legitimate that one can find it in the work of other authors.

One reads very odd things in authors' texts, and one realizes that, lacking the proper reference points – that is, the guidelines I provide you with here – they arrive at things that are quite astonishing. I would be more than happy if someone who is a bit incisive would give us a short report here on this topic, which we could truly discuss. I could even say that I wish someone would do so, at this point in my seminar, for precise, local reasons I don't want to dwell on, but that I will come back to. It is certainly necessary that some of you mediate between my rather heterogeneous audience and what I am in the process of trying to articulate for you. It is obviously very difficult for me, without such mediation, to make enough headway regarding subject matter that leads toward nothing less than placing the function of desire – not only in the analysand but essentially in the analyst – at the forefront of what I am articulating this year.

One wonders for whom the risk is greater. Is it for those who, for one reason or another, know something about it? Or is it for those who can still know nothing about it? Whatever the case may be, there must nevertheless be a way of broaching the topic before a sufficiently prepared audience, even if not everyone present has undergone an analysis.

That said, let me draw your attention to an article by Herman Nunberg, published in 1951 in the *International Journal of Psychoanalysis* [32: 1–9], entitled "Transference and Reality." This article, like everything else that has been written on transference, moreover, is exemplary as regards the difficulties that arise and the sleight of hand one encounters when authors lack a sufficiently methodical, situated, and enlightened approach to the phenomenon of transference. In this short article, which is exactly nine pages long, the author goes, in effect, so far as to distinguish transference from repetition compulsion. They are, he says, essentially different. Which is going pretty far, and it is certainly not what I am teaching you. I will thus request that, for next time, someone prepare for us a ten-minute report on what seems to him to result from the structure of the statements made in this article and how we can correct it.

209

For the moment, let us highlight what is involved.

Transference was originally discovered by Freud as a process, let me stress this, that is spontaneous. And, as we are talking about the historical beginning of the appearance of this phenomenon, a spontaneous process that was worrisome enough to scare one of its most eminent pioneers, Breuer, away from the first analytic investigation.

Transference was very quickly noticed and linked to the most essential facet of the presence of the past insofar as it is discovered by analysis. I am weighing my terms very carefully, and I beg you to record what I am retaining in order to establish the main points of the dialectic in question.

It was also very quickly agreed, at the level of an attempt that was confirmed thereafter by experience, that the phenomenon is accessible to interpretation.

Interpretation already existed at that time, showing itself to be one of the tools necessary to induce the subject to remember. People perceived that something other than the tendency to remember was at work. They didn't yet know very well what it was. But, in any case, it was there. Transference was immediately agreed to be accessible to interpretation and thus permeable, so to speak, to the action of speech.

This immediately raised a problem that still remains unsolved for us today, which is the following.

The phenomenon of transference is itself positioned in such a way as to sustain the action of speech. In effect, at the same time at which transference was discovered, it was discovered that if speech hits home [*porte*], as it always had before this was noticed, it is because transference is involved in it. The upshot being that until the present time – and in fact the question has always remained on the agenda, the ambiguity remaining intact – as things stand, nothing can eliminate the fact that transference, no matter how much it is interpreted, retains within itself a kind of irreducible limit.

The topic has been discussed and rehashed at length by the most qualified authors in the field. Let me mention to you in particular an article by Ernest Jones in his *Papers on Psycho-analysis*, "The Action of Suggestion in Psychotherapy," but there are countless others.

What indeed is at issue? Under the normal conditions of analysis – in the case of neurosis, that is – transference is interpreted on the basis of and using the instrument of transference itself. It is thus impossible for the analyst not to analyze, interpret, and intervene in the transference from the position bestowed upon him by transference itself. In effect, there remains an irreducible margin of suggestion, an ever suspect element, which is not related to what

210

happens outside – one cannot know that – but rather to what the theory itself is capable of producing.

But, in fact, it is not such difficulties that thwart our progress in this area. We must nevertheless establish the limits – the theoretical aporia – of the phenomenon. This is perhaps what will later allow us to go beyond it. Let us take careful note of the situation, and perhaps we can already perceive what paths will enable us to go beyond it.

The reality of transference is thus the presence of the past. Isn't there already something that stands out in this, allowing us to provide a more complete formulation? It is a presence that is a bit more than presence – it is a presence in action and, as the German [*Übertragung*] and French [*transfert*] terms indicate, a reproduction.

What is not brought out clearly enough in what is ordinarily said is in what respect this reproduction differs from a simple passivating of the subject. If the reproduction here is a reproduction in action, there is something creative in transference's manifestations. It seems to me essential to articulate this creative element. As always, just because I highlight it doesn't mean it is not already detectable in a more or less obscure way in what other authors have articulated.

If you read Daniel Lagache's landmark paper, you will see that this is the crux of the distinction he introduced between "repetition of need" and "need for repetition" which, in my opinion, remains a bit vacillating and murky as it does not take this last point into account. As didactic as this opposition may be, in reality it is not inclusive – it is not even truly at work for a single instant in what we experience in transference.

Consider first the need for repetition. There is no doubt about it, we can only formulate transference phenomena in the following enigmatic form: why must the subject eternally repeat a signification, in the positive sense of "signification," namely, what he signifies to us through his behavior? To call this a need is already to deflect what is at work. In this regard, to refer to an opaque psychological fact – as Daniel Lagache purely and simply does in his paper, namely, the Zeigarnik effect – better respects in the end what should be preserved that is strictly original in transference.

If, on the other hand, transference is the repetition of a need, a need that can manifest itself at one moment as transference and at another as need, it is clear that we arrive at an impasse, since we also spend our time saying that it is but a shadow of a need, a need that has long since been outgrown, which is why its disappearance is possible.

We also arrive here at the point at which transference, strictly speaking, appears to be a source of fiction. In transference, the subject fabricates or constructs something. Thus it is impossible, it seems to me, not to immediately include the term "fiction" in the function of transference. What is the nature of this fiction? And, second, what is its object(ive)? And if fiction is involved, what is being feigned? And since it is a matter of feigning, feigning for whom?

If we don't immediately answer by saying "for the person one is addressing," it is because we cannot add "knowing full well that one is doing so" [*le sachant*]. It is because we have already distanced ourselves, due to the phenomenon, from any hypothesis of what we might globally [*massivement*] term "simulation."

Thus it is not for the person one is addressing insofar as one knows that one is doing so. But this is not because it is the contrary – namely, that it is insofar as one does not know it that one must believe that the person one is addressing has, for all that, suddenly evaporated or vanished. Everything that we know of the unconscious right from the outset, on the basis of dreams, leads us to the conclusion that there are psychical phenomena which occur, develop, and are constructed in order to be heard [*entendus*, which also means "understood"] – which occur, develop, and are constructed for the Other who is there even if one does not know it. Even if one is not aware that they are there in order to be heard, they are there in order to be heard, and by an Other to boot.

Stated differently, it seems to me impossible to eliminate from the phenomenon of transference the fact that it manifests itself in a relationship with someone to whom one speaks. This fact is constitutive. It constitutes a border, and enjoins us at the same time not to drown the phenomenon of transference in the general possibility of repetition constituted by the very existence of the unconscious.

Outside of analysis, there are of course repetitions that are linked to the constancy of the signifying chain in the subject. These repetitions must be strictly distinguished from what we call transference, even if they can, in certain cases, have analogous effects. It is in this sense that we can justify the distinction into which someone who is nevertheless quite remarkable – Herman Nunberg – allows himself to slip, from an entirely different direction, that of error.

I am now going to slip in here a segment of our exploration of the *Symposium* for a moment, in order to show you its stimulating character.

213

3

Recall the extraordinary scene constituted by Alcibiades' public confession, and let us try to situate it in our terms.

I'm sure you sense the quite remarkable weight that is attached to this action, sensing too that there is something here that goes well beyond a pure and simple account of what happened between Alcibiades and Socrates. It is not neutral. The proof thereof is that before even beginning, Alcibiades takes cover by calling for secrecy, not simply in order to protect himself. He says, "Let those who are neither capable nor worthy of hearing, the slaves who are here, plug up their ears, for there are things that are better not heard when one is unable to understand them."

Before whom is he confessing? The others, all the others, those who, through their assembly, body, or council, seem to give the greatest possible weight to what might be called the Other as tribunal. And what constitutes the value of Alcibiades' confession before this tribunal? It is that he recounts his attempt to make Socrates into something completely submissive and subordinate to a value other than that of a relationship of one subject to another subject. He attempted to seduce Socrates, he wanted to make him, and in the most openly avowed way possible, into someone instrumental and subordinate to what? To the object of Alcibiades' desire – *ágalma*, the good object.

I would go even further. How can we analysts fail to recognize what is involved? He says quite clearly: Socrates has the good object in his stomach. Here Socrates is nothing but the envelope in which the object of desire is found.

It is in order to clearly emphasize that he is nothing but this envelope that Alcibiades tries to show that Socrates is desire's serf in his relations with Alcibiades, that Socrates is enslaved to Alcibiades by his desire. Although Alcibiades was aware that Socrates desired him, he wanted to see Socrates' desire manifest itself in a sign, in order to know that the other – the object, *ágalma* – was at his mercy.

Now, it is precisely because he failed in this undertaking that Alcibiades disgraces himself, and makes of his confession something that is so affectively laden. The daemon of Αἰδώς (*Aidós*), Shame, about which I spoke to you before in this context, is what intervenes here. This is what is violated. The most shocking secret is unveiled before everyone; the ultimate mainspring of desire, which in love relations must always be more or less dissimulated, is revealed – its aim is the fall of the Other, A, into the other, *a*. And on top of all that, it seems in this case that Alcibiades failed in his undertaking, insofar as it was designed to make Socrates fall off his pedestal.

What could more closely resemble what one might call a search for truth? One might believe that this is the endpoint of such a search, not in its function as a sketch, abstraction, or neutralization of all elements, but, quite the contrary, in what it contributes by way of resolution value, or even absolution. It is quite different, as you see, from the simple phenomenon of a so-called unaccomplished task [the Zeigarnik effect].

A public confession made, right up to its very last words, with all the religious overtones we rightly or wrongly attach to confession – this is certainly what seems to be involved. But doesn't it also seem fitting that the homage rendered to the master should end with this brilliant [*éclatant*] testimony to Socrates' superiority? Wouldn't that underscore what some have designated as the apologetic value of the *Symposium*?

You are indeed aware of the accusations with which Socrates, even after his death, remained charged, in particular in a pamphlet by a man named Polycrates. Everyone knows that the *Symposium* was in part written in response to the lampoon – we have several quotes from others who were also involved [in his condemnation] – which still accused Socrates of having corrupted Alcibiades and many others, by having indicated to them that the door to the satisfaction of their desires was wide open.

Now what do we see? A paradox. A truth is brought to light here, which seems in some sense to be self-sufficient, yet everyone senses that a question remains intact: why all of this? To whom is all of this addressed? Who is being instructed at the moment the confession takes place? It is certainly not Socrates' accusers. What desire induces Alcibiades to thus air his dirty laundry in public? Isn't there a paradox here that is worth pointing out? As you will see by looking closely at the text, it's not so simple.

What everyone perceives to be an interpretation by Socrates is, indeed, an interpretation. Socrates retorts to Alcibiades, "Everything you just did, and Lord knows it isn't obvious, was for Agathon's sake. Your desire is more secret still than all the unveiling you have just given yourself over to. It now aims at yet another. And I will designate that other – it is Agathon."

215

Paradoxically, what Socrates' interpretation reveals, what it puts in the place of what is manifested, is not something fantasmatic, arising out of the depths of the past, but which no longer has any existence. If we are to believe Socrates, it is quite clearly reality itself that, in the process of the search for truth, serves as what we could call a transference. So that you will understand me clearly, [I will provide an analogy:] it is as if someone came forward during Oedipus' trial to say, "Oedipus is pursuing his search for truth, which must lead to his own perdition, so breathlessly because he has but one goal and that is to run away with Antigone." Such is the paradoxical situation in which Socrates' interpretation places us.

There are, of course, myriad shimmering details. It is easy to see how pulling off such a brilliant act, showing what one is capable of, could serve to dazzle the ignorant. But nothing in all of that, Socrates tells us, holds up in the final analysis.

One can certainly wonder to what extent Socrates knows what he is doing when he says so. For in responding to Alcibiades, doesn't he seem to deserve Polycrates' accusation? Socrates – who is knowledgeable or learned in matters of love – designates to Alcibiades where his desire lies, and goes much further than simply designating it, as he, in some sense, vicariously plays this desire's game. Indeed, immediately afterward, Socrates is preparing to eulogize Agathon when suddenly, through a freezing of the camera, he is hidden, and we understand nothing due to the effect of the entrance of still more party crashers. Thanks to which the question remains unanswered. The dialogue can indefinitely go back over the same ground – we will never know what Socrates knew about what he was doing.

Or is it rather Plato who replaces him here? No doubt, since Plato wrote the dialogue, knowing a bit more about what Socrates knew, allowing centuries of readers to be misled concerning what he, Plato, designates to us as the true reason for love, believing instead that it lies in leading the subject to ladders which allow him to ascend toward a beauty that is ever more confounded with supreme beauty. That being said, this is not at all what, in following the text, we sense we are obliged to conclude.

Insofar as we are analysts, we can say the following.

If, as seems to be indicated by his words, Socrates' desire is nothing other than to lead his interlocutors to γνῶθι σεαυτόν (*gnóthi seautón*) [know thyself], which is translated in an extreme manner, in another register, by "concern yourself with your soul," then we can imagine that this is to be taken seriously. On the one hand, in effect, and I will explain to you by what mechanism, Socrates is one of those to whom we owe it that we have a soul – I mean, he gave consistency to a certain point designated by Socratic questioning, with what it engenders by way of transference. But if it is true that what Socrates designates thusly is, unbeknown to him, the desire of the subject as I define it, and as Socrates effectively shows us that he makes himself into its accomplice – if this is so, and if he does so unbeknown to himself, we thus see Socrates in a place that we can understand completely, and we can understand at the same time how, in the end, he set Alcibiades ablaze.

For in its root and essence, desire is the Other's desire, and this is

216

strictly speaking the mainspring of the birth of love, if love is what occurs in the object toward which we extend our hand owing to our own desire, and which, when our desire makes it burst into flames, allows a response to appear for a moment: the other hand that reaches toward us as its desire.

This desire always manifests itself inasmuch as we do not know. "And Ruth did not know what God wanted from her." But in order not to know what God wanted of her, it must still have been clear that God wanted *something* of her. If she knows nothing about it, it is not because no one knows what God wants of her, but because, owing to this mystery, God is eclipsed – yet He is always there.

To the extent to which Socrates does not know what he himself desires – it being the Other's desire – Alcibiades is possessed by what? By a love about which one can say that Socrates' only merit is to designate it as transference love, and to redirect him to his true desire.

These are the points that I wanted to establish anew today, in order to continue next time with what I think I can substantiate, namely, how the final articulation of the *Symposium* – this apologue or scenario verging on myth – allows us to structure the situation of the analysand in the presence of the analyst around the position of two desires.

We can thus truly restore it to its veritable sense of a situation involving two people, a real situation with two people. We can at the same time precisely situate the often extremely precocious love phenomena that occur therein – which are so disconcerting for those who broach them – as well as the phenomena that become even more complicated insofar as they come later, in short, all the content of what occurs at the imaginary level. It is at this level that modern theorists thought, not groundlessly, they had to construct the whole theory of object relations, as well as that of projection – a term which is far from adequate – and, in short, the whole theory of what the analyst is to the analysand during analysis.

This cannot be conceptualized without correctly situating the position that the analyst himself occupies in relation to the analysand's constitutive desire, which is that with which the subject engages in the analysis – namely, "What does he want?"

March 1, 1961

XIII

A CRITIQUE OF COUNTERTRANSFERENCE

The unconscious is, at first, the Other's.
Desire in the case of the analyst.
The analytic game of bridge.
Paula Heimann and Money-Kyrle.
The latent effect linked to inscience.

Last time I ended, to your satisfaction so it seems, on a point regarding what constitutes one of the elements, and perhaps the fundamental element, of the subject's position in analysis. It was the question – which intersects for us the definition of desire as the Other's desire, a question that is, in short, marginal, but that thereby signals that it is fundamental to the position of the analysand in relation to the analyst, even if he does not formulate it to himself – "What does he [the analyst] want?"

After having gone that far, we are going to take a step back today, as I announced at the beginning of my talk last time, and start examining the ways other theorists generally manifest, in the evidence they provide of their praxis, the same topology as the one I am trying to ground here, inasmuch as it makes transference possible.

Attesting to it in their own way, they are not, in effect, obliged to formulate it in the same way I do. That seems obvious enough. As I wrote somewhere, one has no need for the blueprints of an apartment to bang one's head on the walls. I would go even further – for this operation, one can normally do perfectly well without the blueprints. But it's not true the other way around. As opposed to a primitive schema of reality testing, it is not enough to bang one's head on the walls to reconstruct the blueprints of an apartment, especially if one has this experience in the dark. An example dear to me is that of *Théodore cherche des allumettes*, a play which illustrates it for you quite amply.

This is perhaps a bit forced as a metaphor, though perhaps not as forced as it may still seem to you. It is what we are going to see put to the test, the test of what occurs in our times when analysts speak of transference.

1

When analysts speak about transference nowadays, what are they talking about? Let us go right to what is foremost in their minds today on this topic. The topic arises at the precise point around which you no doubt sense that I am centering it this year, namely, around the analyst. And to be quite frank, what the most advanced and most lucid theorists articulate best when they discuss it is "countertransference," as they call it.

I would like to remind you of some basic facts about it. It is not because they are basic that they are always expressed, and, while they go without saying, they go even better with saying.

Concerning countertransference, there is first of all the commonly held view. It is the view held by each of us who has at least considered the problem a little bit. It is the first idea that one comes up with about it, the first in the sense of the most common idea, but it is also the oldest approach to the topic, for the notion of countertransference has always been around in psychoanalysis. Since very early on – since the beginning of the development of the notion of transference – everything in an analyst that represents his unconscious insofar as it is, I would say, unanalyzed, has been considered detrimental to his functioning and operating as an analyst.

In the commonly accepted view, it is inasmuch as something has remained in the dark that this something becomes the source of uncontrolled and above all blind responses. This is what leads to an emphasis on the need for a training analysis to be taken quite far – I am using vague terms to begin with – because, as one author wrote somewhere, were one to neglect some corner of the analyst's unconscious, veritable blind spots would result therefrom. This could lead in practice to more or less serious or unfortunate events: nonrecognition, missed opportunities, badly timed interventions, and perhaps even mistakes. Such a view is, in fact, proposed, though I would place it in the conditional tense, in quotes, indicating my reservations – it is a view to which I do not immediately subscribe, but which is widely endorsed.

221

Yet one cannot but relate this view to another, which is that one must, in the end, have faith in the communication of unconsciouses to best provide the analyst with decisive insights.

Thus it would not be owing as much to one's long experience

as an analyst, or to extensive knowledge of what one is likely to encounter in patients' structures, that we could expect the most relevant interventions, the lion's spring that Freud mentions, which only happens once in the best of cases – no, it would be owing to the communication of unconsciouses. This purportedly gives rise to what, in analysis as it is currently practiced, goes furthest and deepest and has the greatest effect. There would be no analysis at all were any of the elements that supposedly attest to it to be lacking. The analyst is, in other words, presumed to be directly informed of what is going on in his patient's unconscious. The pathway by which this transmission occurs remains, nevertheless, quite problematic in the tradition. How can we conceptualize such a communication between unconsciouses?

I am not here to polarize antinomies or fabricate artificial impasses, even from a heuristic or critical standpoint. I am not saying that there is something unthinkable about this, or that it would be antinomical to define the model analyst both as he who, ideally, no longer has anything that is unconscious, but who at the same time has preserved a good deal of it. This would be to postulate an unfounded opposition.

To take things as far as they can go, one might theorize a reserve unconscious. It must be admitted that no one ever undergoes an exhaustive elucidation of the unconscious, regardless of how far his analysis is taken. If we accept the idea of an unconscious reserve, we can quite easily imagine that someone who is alerted to its existence by having undergone training analysis, knows, in some sense, how to play it like an instrument, like the shell of a violin whose strings he also possesses. It is certainly not a raw unconscious we find in him, but rather a supple unconscious, an unconscious plus experience of that unconscious.

After enumerating these reservations, we must still sense the legitimate necessity of elucidating the point of transition by which this qualification is acquired, and by which what psychoanalytic doctrine claims to be fundamentally inaccessible to consciousness can be reached. Indeed, it is this very inaccessibility that we must always posit as the foundation of the unconscious. For it is not the case that it is accessible to men of goodwill – it is not. It is under strictly limited conditions that one can reach it, through a detour, the detour via the Other, and this makes analysis necessary and infrangibly eliminates the possibility of self-analysis. How can we situate the point of transition by which what is thus defined [as inaccessible] can nevertheless be used as a source of information included in a directive praxis?

To raise this question is not to erect a pointless antinomy. What

222

tells us that the problem can be validly raised in this way, I mean in a way that it becomes solvable, is that things really and truly do present themselves like this.

To you who at least have the keys, something immediately makes the point of access recognizable, which is that there is a logical priority in what you hear – namely, that it is first of all in the form of the Other's unconscious that all experience of the unconscious is gained. It was through his patients that Freud first encountered the unconscious. And for each of us, even if this fact is elided, it is first of all as the Other's unconscious that the idea presents itself that such a thing might exist. Every discovery of one's own unconscious presents itself as a stage of ongoing translation of an unconscious that is first of all the Other's. The upshot being that one should not be so surprised that one can admit that, even in the case of an analyst who has gone very far in this stage of translation, translation can always begin anew at the level of the Other. This obviously reduces much of the import of the possible antinomy I mentioned earlier, while simultaneously indicating that the antinomy can only be proposed illegitimately.

What I am telling you about the relation with the Other is designed to exorcize, in part, the fear we may feel of not knowing enough about ourselves. We shall come back to this, for I do not intend to absolve you of all concern on this score – that is quite far from my intent. But once we have accepted the function served by the Other, the fact remains that we encounter here the same obstacle we encounter in ourselves in our own analysis when the unconscious is involved. Namely, the highly essential, not to say historically original, element of my teaching: the positive power of misrecognition in the illusions of the ego, in the widest sense of the term – that is, in imaginary capture.

223

It is important to note here that this domain, which is thoroughly mixed together with the deciphering of the unconscious in our experience of our personal analysis, occupies a position that must be said to be different when it comes to our relation to the Other. Here appears what I would call the Stoic ideal people have of analysis.

People first identified the feelings, roughly speaking, negative or positive, that the analyst may have about his patient, which give rise in him to effects that are due to an incomplete reduction of the themes of his own unconscious. But if this is true for him as concerns his self-regard [amour-propre] in relation to the other with a lowercase o within him, the latter being that by which he sees himself as something other than what he is – and this was glimpsed and discovered well before psychoanalysis came on the scene – it in no wise exhausts the question of what legitimately occurs when he deals with this other with a lowercase *o*, the imaginary other, outside of himself.

Let me spell this out. The path of Stoic apathy demands that we remain unmoved by the attempts at seduction – as well as by the punishments that may be meted out – by this other with a lowercase *o* found outside of us, insofar as he always has some power over us, whether great or small, if nothing else the power to burden us with his sheer presence. If the analyst deviates from the path of Stoic apathy, does this in and of itself mean that it is owing to some inadequacy in his training as an analyst? Absolutely not – at least in theory.

Accept this stage of my argument. That is not to say it is the place I will end up. Let me simply offer the following remark: we have no reason to posit that, in and of itself, the recognition of the unconscious places the analyst out of passion's range. This would be to imply that the total, overall effect, the entire impact of the sexual object – or of another object capable of producing some sort of physical aversion – always and essentially derives from the unconscious.

Why, I ask, would that be necessary to anyone other than those who make the serious mistake of identifying the unconscious as such with the total powers of the *Lebenstriebe* [life drives]? This is what radically distinguishes the import of the doctrine I am trying to articulate before you. There is, of course, a relationship between the two. The point is to elucidate why this relationship can be established, why it is the tendencies of the life instinct that are thus offered up in this relationship to the unconscious. Note that it is not just any of those tendencies, but specifically those that Freud always and tenaciously designated as sexual tendencies. There must certainly be a reason why they are especially privileged, captivated, or captured by the mainspring of the signifying chain, insofar as it is the signifying chain that constitutes the subject of the unconscious.

That being said, at this stage of our investigation it is worth asking why an analyst, just because he is well analyzed, should be unaffected by the appearance of a hostile thought in the other presence there – and one must of course assume, in order for something of this kind to occur, that the presence not be that of a patient, but rather of a being who takes up space. The more we assume him to be imposing, full, and normal, the more legitimately all kinds of possible reactions can occur in his presence. Similarly, when the two are of opposite sexes, for example, why should love or hate reactions be excluded in and of themselves? Why should they disqualify the analyst from serving his function?

Formulating the question in this way, there is no other answer than the following – why indeed? Or better still: the better the analyst is analyzed, the more it will be possible for him to be frankly in love with – or frankly averse to or repulsed by – his partner, according to the most elementary modes of relations between bodies.

What I am saying may seem a bit excessive, in that it bothers us. If we feel that there must, all the same, be something to the requirement of analytic apathy, it must clearly be rooted elsewhere. But in that case it must be stated.

And I am equipped to state it.

2

If I could state it for you right away, if the path we have already traced out allowed me to convey it to you, I would of course do so. But part of the path remains to be traced out before I can give you a strict, precise formulation.

225

Nevertheless, something can already be said about it, which might satisfy you up to a certain point. The only thing I ask of you is not to be too satisfied with it.

It is as follows – if the analyst achieves apathy, as in the general public's conception of him and in accordance with his deontological image, it is to the extent that he is possessed by a desire that is stronger than the other desires that may be involved – for example, the desire to get down to it [en venir au fait] with his patient: to take him in his arms or throw him out the window.

It happens. I dare say that I wouldn't expect much from someone who has never felt such desires. But apart from the very possibility of it happening, it should not become a regular thing.

Why not? Is it for the negative reason that one must avoid a type of total imaginary discharge of the analysis? No – and we need not develop that hypothesis any further, although it would be interesting – it is for the following reason, which I am bringing out here this year: the analyst says, "I am possessed by a stronger desire." He is grounded in saying so as an analyst, insofar as a change has occurred in the economy of his desire. And it is in this regard that Plato's texts can be mentioned.

Every now and then something encouraging comes my way. I have given you this year a long discourse or commentary on the *Symposium*, with which I am not dissatisfied, I must say, and it turns out that someone in my circle surprised me – and you should understand this surprise in the sense the word has in analysis, as something which is basically related to the unconscious – by pointing out that, in one of his footnotes, Freud quotes part of Alcibiades' speech to Socrates [*SE* X, p. 240 n. 2].

Freud could have sought out a thousand other examples to illustrate what he was interested in at that precise moment, which was the death wish involved in love. He had but to bend over to scoop up piles of such examples. Someone once hurled at me an ejaculation, like a heartfelt cry, "Oh, how I would love it if you were dead for two years!" One need not look to the *Symposium* to find such examples. Thus I feel it is not inconsequential that, at an essential moment in his discovery of the ambivalence involved in love, Freud referred to Plato's *Symposium*. It's not a bad sign. It is certainly not a sign that we were barking up the wrong tree.

In Plato's *Philebus*, Socrates says that the strongest of all desires must be the desire for death, since the souls that are in Erebus remain there. The argument is worth whatever it is worth, but it takes on illustrative value here in relation to what I have already indicated to you concerning the direction in which the reorganization or restructuring of the analyst's desire can be conceptualized. It is at least one of the moorings or anchoring points of the question. Surely we cannot confine our attention to that alone.

Nevertheless, we can go further in the same vein, regarding the analyst's detachment from repetition compulsion, which a good personal analysis is supposed to bring about. There is something that must surpass what I will call the particularity of its detour, go a bit beyond, and involve the specific detour Freud articulates when he posits that it is conceivable that the fundamental repetition of the development of life may be nothing other than the long detour of a compact, abyssal drive. He calls the latter the death drive, it being a level at which there is no longer anything but ἀνάγκη (*Anánke*), the necessity of the return to the initial state of inanimate matter.

This is no doubt a metaphor. A metaphor that is expressed only by extrapolation – at which certain people balk – on the basis of what is brought out by our practice, namely, the action of the unconscious signifying chain insofar as it leaves its mark on every manifestation of life in subjects who speak. But it is nevertheless a metaphor or an extrapolation that is not without its why and wherefore. At least it allows us to imagine that it contains a grain of truth, and that there may in fact be some relation between the analyst and Hades – death – as one of my students wrote in the first issue of our journal, adopting a beautifully haughty tone.

Does he or doesn't he play with death? I myself have written that, in the game of analysis, which certainly cannot be understood as involving only two players, the analyst plays with a dummy [*un mort*]. Thus we find again the common requirement that there be in the other with a lowercase *o* something that is capable of playing the part of a dead man [*un mort*].

In his position in the game of bridge, the analyst as S has across from him his own other with a lowercase *o* [*a* for *autre* in French], by which he is in a specular relationship with himself, insofar as he is constituted as an ego. If we locate here the designated place of the other who speaks and that the analyst hears – that is, the patient insofar as he is represented by the barred subject [$], the subject as unknown to him – the patient turns out to occupy $i(a)$, the place of the image of his own little *a*. Let us call the set of them as follows: the image of little *a* squared, $i(a)^2$. We will then have here the image, or rather the position, of the Other with a capital *O* insofar as it is the analyst who occupies it.

In other words, the analysand has a partner. You should not be surprised to discover that the analysand's own ego is attached to the same place. He must discover the truth of this other – the analyst as Other with a capital *O*.

The paradox of the game of analytic bridge is the abnegation which, unlike what happens in an ordinary game of bridge, is such that the analyst must help the subject figure out what is in his partner's hand. In order to direct this bridge game of loser wins, in theory the analyst should not have to make his life more complicated by having a partner. This is why it is said that the analyst as $i(a)$ must act as a dummy. Which means that the analyst must always know which cards were dealt to whom.

I think that you will appreciate the relative simplicity of this solution to the problem. It is a common, exoteric, explanation for the outside world. It is simply a way of talking about what everyone believes, and someone who showed up here for the first time would find plenty of reasons to be satisfied with it and could go back to sleep soundly, reassured about what he had always heard – for example, that the analyst is a superior being.

Unfortunately, it doesn't hold water.

It doesn't hold water, and this is attested to by analysts themselves. Not simply by deploring the situation, tears in their eyes, and saying, "We are never equal to the task." While such declamations still exist, we have, thank God, been spared them for some time now – that's a fact. I am not personally responsible for this. I am simply noting it for the record.

Indeed, for some time now, people have accepted the idea that in analytic practice the analyst must take into account, in his information and his maneuvering, the feelings, not that he inspires, but that he himself feels in the course of an analysis – namely, what is known as his countertransference.

3

It is to the best of analytic circles that I am alluding, and to the Kleinian circle to be specific.

You can easily get a hold of what Melanie Klein wrote on the subject, or what Paula Heimann wrote in an article entitled "On Counter-transference."

But you need not seek out this conception, that everyone currently takes for granted, in any one particular article. People articulate it quite openly, and above all they basically understand what they are articulating. It is nevertheless taken for granted. What is involved?

Countertransference is no longer considered in our time to be in essence an imperfection. Which does not, however, mean that it cannot ever be one. While it is no longer considered to be an imperfection, the fact remains that something makes it warrant the name "countertransference," as you will see.

Apparently, countertransference is exactly of the same nature as the other phase of transference, around which I tried to center the question last time by contrasting it with transference conceptualized as repetition compulsion – namely, transference insofar as it is said to be positive or negative, which everyone takes to imply the analysand's feelings for the analyst. Well, the countertransference in question – concerning which it is agreed that we must take it into account, even if it is a matter of some debate what we must do with it, and you will see at what level – consists of the analyst's feelings in analysis, which are determined at every instant by his relations with the analysand.

Of all the articles that I have read, I am selecting one almost at random, though it is never completely at random that we select anything, and there is probably a reason why I want to tell you the title of this one. It is a good article, whose title contains the very topic we are talking about today, "Normal Counter-transference and Some Deviations," which came out in the *International Journal of Psychoanalysis* in 1956. The author, Roger Money-Kyrle, apparently belongs to the Kleinian circle, and is associated with Melanie Klein through Paula Heimann.

229

Before turning to this article, let me say a word about the article by Paula Heimann, who tells us about certain states of dissatisfaction and worry she felt. According to her, they even involved a certain premonition. She found herself in a situation which one need not be an old experienced analyst to have experienced, for it is only too frequently encountered during the initial stages of an analysis. The fact that a patient may precipitously, in a way patently determined by his analysis, though he may not be aware of it, make premature decisions, enter into a long-term relationship, and perhaps even get married – Heimann is cognizant that this must be analyzed, interpreted, and, to a certain extent, countered. But in this particular case, she mentions an altogether bothersome feeling she has, which she takes to be, in and of itself, a sign that she is right to be especially worried [p. 82]. She shows in her article how it is this feeling that allows her to better understand things and make headway [p. 83].

Many other sorts of feelings can arise. Money-Kyrle's article mentions, for example, feelings of depression, a general decline in interest in things, "listlessness," and even a listlessness the analyst may feel about everything he comes into contact with. Money-Kyrle describes, for example, what resulted from a session in which it seemed to him that he was unable to adequately live up to what he calls a demanding superego.* It is not because the word "demand" is contained therein that you should remain at that level in understanding the particularly English emphasis. "Demand" is more than *demande* in French [which is often no stronger than "request" in English], it is a pressing exigency. The article is a good one to read because the author does not confine himself to description, but calls into question in this regard the role of the analytic superego. He does it in a way that will seem to you to present some kind of gap,* which only truly takes on its full importance if you refer to the Graph of Desire. It is beyond the locus of the Other that the bottom line represents the superego – a dotted line insofar as you dot it.

I am putting the rest of the Graph on the board so that you will realize in this regard how it can serve you, and in particular in understanding that everything should not always be attributed to the superego's severity, which is, in the final analysis, opaque. Such and such a demand can give rise to depressive effects and even more. This occurs in the analyst insofar as there is continuity between the Other's demand and the structure known as the superego. You should understand that we indeed find the strongest effects of what is called the superego's hyperseverity when the subject's demand is introjected, passing as an articulated demand into he who is its recipient in such a way that this demand represents his own demand in an inverted form – for example, when a demand for love coming from the mother encounters in he who must respond to it his own demand for love addressed to his mother.

230

But I am merely indicating this here, as our path does not lead in that direction. It is but a tangential remark.

Let us turn to Money-Kyrle, an analyst who seems particularly agile and clever in recognizing his own experience. He highlights something that happened in his practice and presents it to us as an example. It seems to him to warrant communication, not as an example of an accidental blunder that was more or less well corrected, but as a procedure that can be integrated into analytic technique. He underscores a feeling he detected in himself that he considered to be related to the trouble he was having analyzing one of his patients.

It occurred during the picturesque break in English life known as the weekend, and what he had done with his patient the week prior seemed problematic to him and left him unsatisfied. He tells us that he fell prey, without at first seeing the link at all, to a kind of exhaustion – let us call a spade a spade. During the second half of his weekend, he found himself in a state he could only recognize when he formulated it to himself in the exact same terms his patient had used – a state of disgust bordering on depersonalization.

The patient was, in effect, at times subject to phases verging on depression and paranoid phenomena, which were nothing new to either the patient or the analyst. It was one of those states that had given rise to the whole dialectic of the week, accompanied by a dream that the analyst had lit up in responding to. Rightly or wrongly, he had the feeling that he had not given the right answer, his feeling being based in any case on the fact that his answer had made the patient complain bitterly. Starting at that point, the patient had become exceedingly mean to him. Thus the analyst wound up recognizing in what he himself felt, exactly what, at the outset, his patient had described about the patient's own state.

The analyst in question, like the other members of his circle, which I am referring to on this occasion as the Kleinian circle, immediately conceptualizes what is going on as representative of the effect of projection of the bad object, insofar as the subject, whether in analysis or not, is likely to project it into the other. It is not taken to be problematic, in a certain analytic milieu, to provide such explanations, despite the almost magical degree of belief they presuppose. It must not, nevertheless, be for no reason whatsoever that people slip into them so easily. This projected bad object must be understood as having quite naturally an effect, at least when it is a question of he who is coupled with the subject in a relationship as tight and coherent as that of a longstanding analysis.

Having an effect, to what extent? The article tells you – to the extent that it stems here from the analyst's failure to understand his patient. Thus it constitutes a deviation from "normal countertransference," and the article focuses on the possible utilization of such deviations.

As the beginning of the article tells us, "normal countertransference" occurs through the cyclical rhythm of introjection by the analyst of the analysand's discourse, and projection onto the analy-

231

sand of what is produced by way of imaginary effects in response to this introjection. The author considers these effects to be normal, and you will see just how far he goes. Countertransference is said to be normal when the introjected demand is completely understood. The analyst then has no problem situating himself in what clearly arises in his own introjection. He simply sees its consequences and has no need to even use them. What happens in this case, which is actually situated at the level of $i(a)$, is completely under control. The analyst is not surprised by what occurs in the patient – namely, that the patient projects onto him – and is not affected by it.

It is only when the analyst does not understand the patient that he is affected and that a deviation from normal countertransference occurs. Things can even go so far that the analyst effectively becomes the patient of the bad object that is projected into him by his partner. That is what happens in this case: Money-Kyrle experiences something altogether unexpected, and it is only a thought which comes to him outside of the analytic setting that allows him – and this is perhaps only because the occasion is favorable – to recognize the very state described to him by his patient.

232

I am simply repeating it to you, without taking responsibility for the explanation given. I am not denying it either. I am provisionally bracketing it in order to go step by step, in order to lead you to the precise perspective to which I need to lead you in order to articulate something.

According to this experienced analyst, if the analyst does not understand, he nevertheless becomes the receptacle of the projection in question. He senses these projections like foreign objects in himself, which places him in the odd position of being a garbage dump.

If such things occurred with many patients, you see what this could lead to. When one is unable to situate what gives rise to such events, which are presented in a disconnected manner in Money-Kyrle's description, problems can arise.

This direction in analysis wasn't born yesterday. Ferenczi had already raised the question of knowing to what extent the analyst should reveal to his patient what the analyst really feels. It would be, according to him, in certain cases, a means of giving the patient access to that particular reality. No one dares to go that far today, especially not in the school to which I am referring. Paula Heimann says, for example, that the analyst must be very severe in his log and everyday hygiene, always being ready to analyze what he himself may feel in that register, but that, in the end, it is his own business, his aim being to try to race against the clock – in other words, to catch up for having perhaps gotten behind in understanding* his patient.

Be that as it may, I am taking the following step with our author, Money-Kyrle, who, while not Ferenczi, is not as reserved as Paula Heimann. On the basis of this localized point, the identicalness of the state he felt to that recounted by his patient at the beginning of the [session], he goes so far as to talk about it with his patient. And he notes the effect thereof – an immediate effect, for he tells us nothing of the later effects – which is obvious jubilation on the part of the patient. The latter deduces nothing else therefrom than, "Oh, so you admit it! Well, I'm very happy to hear it, for when you interpreted that state to me the other day" – and indeed, the analyst had interpreted it, in a rather vague and fuzzy way, as the analyst himself realized – "I thought that what you were saying was all about you and not in the least about me."

233

We thus find ourselves in the midst of a complete misunderstanding, and we are content with it. In any case, the author is content with it, for he drops the subject there. The analysis, he tells us, begins anew, providing him, and we can but take his word for it here, every subsequent possibility to interpret. This was the precise point of the talk he gave in 1955 at the Geneva Congress, the text of which is contained in his article.

What is presented to us here as a deviation from [normal] countertransference is simultaneously posited as an instrumental procedure that can be codified. In similar cases, we should at least attempt to correct the situation as quickly as possible by recognizing the effects on the analyst and, by means of qualified statements, offer the patient something which certainly unveils, in some respect, the analytic situation as a whole. People expect a new departure to result therefrom, which will undo what had hitherto seemed to be an impasse in the analysis.

I am not saying that I think this is an appropriate way to proceed. I am simply remarking that if something like a new departure can be brought about in this manner, it is certainly not due to some privileged position. What I would say is that, to the extent that there is any legitimacy to this approach, it is our categories that in every case allow us to understand it.

I am of the opinion that it is not possible to understand it outside of the register of what I have pointed to as the place of *a*, the partial object, *ágalma*, in desire, insofar as desire is itself determined within a broader relationship, that of the demand [*exigence*] for love. It is only through this topology that we can understand such an approach. Indeed, this topology allows us to say that, even if the subject is unaware of it, by the very presupposition – I would even say, the objective presupposition – of the analytic situation, little *a*, *ágalma*, is already functioning in the other. It follows that what is presented to us here as countertransference, whether normal or not, in fact has no reason to be specially qualified as such. What is at work is but an irreducible effect of the transference situation itself.

By the sole fact of transference, the analyst is situated in the position of he who contains *ágalma*, the fundamental object involved in the subject's analysis, as linked and conditioned by the subject's vacillating relationship that I characterize as constituting the fundamental fantasy, inaugurating the locus in which the subject can be fixated as desire.

This is a legitimate effect of transference. There is no need to bring in countertransference, as if some aspect of the analyst himself were involved, and a faulty aspect to boot. But in order to recognize it, the analyst must know certain things. He must, in particular, know that his occupying the correct position is not contingent on the criterion that he understand or not understand.

It is not absolutely essential that he understand. I would even say that, up to a certain point, his lack of comprehension can be preferable to an overly great confidence in his understanding. In other words, he must always call into question what he understands and remind himself that what he is trying to attain is precisely what in theory he does not understand. It is certainly only insofar as he knows what desire is, but does not know what the particular subject with whom he is engaged in the analytic adventure desires, that he is well situated to contain within himself the object of that desire. This alone can explain certain of its effects that are, it seems, still so oddly frightening.

I read an article that I will reference more precisely next time, in which a guy who, despite a great deal of experience, wonders what one should do when, right from the very first dreams, and sometimes even before the analysis begins, the analysand himself clearly takes the analyst to be a love object. The response given by the author in question is a bit more reserved than that given by another who comes right out and says that, when things get off on that foot, there is no point going any further because there are too many reality elements.

Must we formulate things in such a way? If I allow myself to be guided by the categories we have produced, the very crux of the analytic situation is that the subject is introduced as worthy of interest and love, *erómenos*. The analyst is there for him. This is the manifest effect, so to speak. But there is a latent effect, which is related to his non-science or inscience. Inscience regarding what? Regarding the latent – I mean objective or structural – object of his desire. This object is already in the Other, and it is inasmuch as this is the case that, whether he knows it or not, he is virtually constituted as

234

235

erastés. By virtue of this sole fact, he fulfills the condition for the metaphor or substitution of *erastés* for *erómenos,* which in and of itself constitutes the phenomenon of love. It is no surprise that we see its blazing effects right from the beginning of analysis in the form of transference love.

There is not, however, any reason to consider this to be a contraindication against analysis. It is here that the question of the analyst's desire – and to a certain extent, the analyst's responsibility – arises.

In truth, for the situation to be, as lawyers say regarding contracts, "perfect," it is enough to assume that the analyst, unbeknown to himself, places for a moment his own partial object, *ágalma,* in the patient with whom he is dealing. This is, in effect, contraindicated, but it is impossible, as you see, to situate, at least as long as the situation of the analyst's desire has not been precisely spelled out.

It will suffice that you read the paper by the author to whom I am alluding to see that he is forced, by the logic of his own discourse, to raise the question of what interests the analyst. And what does he tell us? That two things are involved in the analyst when he conducts an analysis, two drives.* It is quite strange to see qualified as passive drives the two that I will mention to you – the reparative drive* which, he tells us verbatim, runs counter to the latent destructiveness in each of us, and, second, the parental drive.*

This is how an analyst in a school as well developed as the Kleinian school formulates the position the analyst must adopt. I am not going to avert my gaze or protest loudly. I think that those of you who are regulars at my Seminar can easily see the scandalous nature thereof. But, after all, it is a scandal in which we essentially participate, for we constantly speak as if that is what is at work, even if we are well aware of the fact that we must not act as parents to the analysand. It suffices to hear what we say when we speak of the field of the psychoses.

The reparative drive,* what does that mean? A whole raft of things. It has myriad implications for our practice. But wouldn't it be worthwhile articulating, in this regard, in what sense this reparative drive must be distinguished from the abuses of therapeutic ambition, for example?

In short, what I am challenging is not the absurdity of such a notion, but on the contrary what justifies it. I give the author and the whole school he represents credit for aiming at something that effectively has a place in our topology. But it must for once be articulated, situated, and explained otherwise. How can experienced authors speak of parental and reparative drives in analysis, and at

236

the same time say something which, on the one hand, must have a justification, but which, on the other, imperiously requires a veritable justification?

This is why, next time, I will rapidly summarize what I wound up presenting, in an apologetic manner, since the last time, to a philosophical group concerning the position of desire.

March 8, 1961

XIV

DEMAND AND DESIRE IN THE ORAL AND ANAL STAGES

Psychoanalysts and drives.
The gaping maw of life.
From the pole to the partner.
Bout-de-Zan.
Counterdemand.

For those of you showing up here out of the blue today, I will provide a brief road map.

In this year's Seminar, I first attempted to reformulate, in more rigorous terms than have hitherto been employed, what one might call the theory of love, by commenting on Plato's *Symposium*. It is in the context of what I managed to situate thanks to this commentary that I am now beginning to articulate the nature [*position*] of transference, in the sense in which I announced it this year – in other words, in what I called its "subjective disparity."

By which I mean that the positions of the two subjects present are in no way equivalent. This is why one cannot speak of the "analytic situation," but merely of a pseudo-situation.

In the last two classes, I broached the topic of transference as regards the analyst. This does not mean that I grant the term "countertransference" the meaning it is usually given, which is that of a sort of imperfection in the analyst's purification in relation to the analysand. On the contrary, by "countertransference" I mean the analyst's necessary involvement in the transferential situation, which is precisely why we must distrust this unsuitable term. For, in fact, countertransference simply concerns the necessary consequences of the phenomenon of transference itself, assuming we analyze it correctly.

I introduced the topic by highlighting the fact that countertransference is currently conceptualized rather broadly in analytic practice. Indeed, people think that what we might call a certain

number of affects, insofar as the analyst feels them in analysis, constitute an if not normal, at least normative, way of situating things
in the analytic setting, and constitute part not only of the knowledge
base at the analyst's disposal, but even of his possible interventions,
in that he may communicate his feelings to the analysand.

I never said that I find this method legitimate. I noted that it
has been introduced and promoted in practice, and that it has
been received and accepted by a very broad swath of the analytic
community.

This alone is sufficiently indicative. We shall endeavor for the
time being to analyze how theorists who view the use of countertransference in this way legitimate it.

1

Theorists legitimate the use of countertransference by relating it to
moments when the analyst does not understand [*incompréhension*].
It is as if his failure to understand the patient were in and of itself the
criterion, watershed mark, or aspect that defines what obliges the
analyst to shift to another mode of communication and to another
instrument in order to get his bearings in the analysis.

It is around the term "understanding" [*compréhension*] that what
I intend to show you today revolves, in order to allow you to hone
in on what one might call, in our terms, the relation between the
subject's demand and his desire. Let me remind you that I have
foregrounded the following as the crux of the matter – whose repercussions [*retour*] I have shown to be necessary – namely, that what is
at stake in analysis is nothing other than bringing to light manifestations of the subject's desire.

Where is understanding when we understand, when we think we
understand? I posit that, in its surest and, I daresay, elementary
form, our understanding of anything the subject tells us can be
defined, at the conscious level, by the fact that we know how to
respond to what he [*l'autre*] demands. It is insofar as we think we can   239
respond to his demand that we have the sense that we understand.

Concerning demand, however, we know a bit more than this first
approximation. We know, for example, that demand is not explicit.
It is even far more than implicit – it is hidden from the subject as if
it had to be interpreted. Therein lies the ambiguity.

Indeed, we who interpret it respond to unconscious demand at
the level of a discourse that to us is a concrete discourse. Therein
lies the dodge [*biais*] or trap. We have always tended to slide toward
an assumption that captivates us, which is that the subject should,

in some sense, be content with what we bring to light through our response – he should be satisfied with our response.

We know, nevertheless, that some resistance is always produced at this point. All the stages of the analytic theory of the subject – namely, the theory of the various agencies in him that we deal with – have stemmed from the situation of this resistance, from the way we can qualify it, and from the agencies to which we attribute it. Yet, without denying the role played by the subject's various agencies in resistance, isn't it possible to go further?

The difficulty of the relations between the subject's demand and the response made to him is situated farther along, at an altogether original point to which I tried to bring you by showing you what results in the subject who speaks from the fact – this is how I expressed myself – that his needs must pass through the defiles of demand. At this early point, it turns out that everything that is a natural tendency in the subject who speaks must be situated both in a beyond and shy of demand.

In a beyond that is the demand for love. And in a shy of that we call desire, with what characterizes it as a condition, which we call its absolute condition owing to the specificity of the object it involves: little *a*, the partial object. I tried to show you that the latter is included right from the outset in the fundamental text on the theory of love, the *Symposium*, in the guise of *ágalma*, inasmuch as I also identified *ágalma* with the partial object in psychoanalytic theory.

240

Today we will put our finger on it again by briefly retracing what comes first in analytic theory – namely, *Triebe*, drives and their vicissitudes. We can then deduce what stems from them concerning what is important to us: the drive* involved in the analyst's position.

You recall that it is on this problematic point that I left you last time, insofar as an author [Money-Kyrle], the one who addresses the topic of countertransference, calls the drives involved in the analyst's position the parental drive,* the need to be a parent, and the reparative drive,* the need to go against the natural destructiveness assumed to reside in every subject insofar as he is analyzable.

You immediately grasped the brazenness and audacity of proposing such notions. It suffices to dwell upon them for but a moment to perceive the paradox therein. If the parental drive* must be present in the analytic situation, how can one even dare speak of transference since the analysand truly has a parent sitting across from him? What could be more legitimate than the fact that he falls into the very same position in relation to the analyst as the one he occupied during his whole upbringing in relation to people around whom were constructed the fundamental situations that constitute for him the signifying chain and repetition automatisms?

In other words, how can we fail to perceive that we are heading straight for an obstacle which will allow us to find our bearings? For we have here a direct contradiction, since we also say that the transference situation, as it is established in analysis, is at odds with the reality of the analytic situation? Certain people imprudently qualify the latter as a situation that is exceedingly simple, related to the *hic et nunc* of the relationship to the doctor. How can we fail to see that, if the doctor here is armed with the parental drive* – however evolved we may assume him to be in terms of his educative position – there is absolutely nothing that differentiates the subject's normal response to the situation from what could be considered the repetition of a past situation?

There is no way to even articulate the analytic situation without positing, at least to some extent, the exact opposite requirement. See, for example, the third chapter of *Beyond the Pleasure Principle*. Freud, in taking up anew the kind of articulation at work in analysis, distinguishes there between remembering and reproducing – repetition compulsion, *Wiederholungszwang*. He considers the latter to be a partial failure of the aim of remembering in analysis – indeed, a necessary failure. He even goes so far as to chalk up the function of repetition to the structure of the ego – sensing at this stage of his elaboration a need to characterize the ego as largely unconscious – certainly not the whole of the function of repetition, since the entire work is designed to show that there is something more, but the majority nonetheless. Repetition is chalked up to ego defense, while the remembering of the repressed is considered to be the true or ultimate endpoint of the analytic operation, even though it is perhaps considered to be inaccessible at that precise moment.

Remembering, as the ultimate aim, encounters a resistance situated in the unconscious function of the ego. Following out this line of thinking, Freud tells us that we must tread this path:

> the physician cannot, as a rule, spare the analysand this phase, but must let him relive anew a bit of his forgotten life. He [. . .] must see to it that a certain dose of *Überlegenheit*, superiority, be preserved, thanks to which the apparent reality, *die anscheinende Realität*, can always nevertheless be recognized anew by the subject as a reflection, a mirror effect of a forgotten past.

God knows to what misguided interpretations this indication of *Überlegenheit* has lent itself. The whole theory of the alliance with the so-called healthy part of the ego was built around it. Yet there is nothing of the kind in these pages. I can highlight what must have struck you in passing, namely, the in some sense neutral character of this *Überlegenheit*, which is situated neither on the one side nor the other. Where is this superiority? Is it on the part of the doctor who, let's hope, doesn't lose his head? Or on the part of the patient?

In the French translation, which is just as bad as those that were done in other languages, it is oddly translated: "he must simply ensure that the patient preserve a certain degree of serene superiority" – there is nothing like that in the text – "which nevertheless allows him to note that the reality of what he reproduces is merely apparent."

This *Überlegenheit*, which can no doubt be required, must be situated in an infinitely more precise way than all the elaborations that claim to compare the current abreaction of what is repeated in treatment with a situation that is made out to be perfectly well known.

242

Let us thus begin with an examination of the stages, and the demands or requirements of the subject as we broach them in our interpretations. And let us start, following the diachrony known as the stages of the libido, with the simplest demand, the one to which we refer so frequently: oral demand.

2

What is an oral demand? It is the demand to be fed. To whom or what is it addressed? It is addressed to the Other who hears [*entend*], and who, at this primal level of the enunciation of demand, can truly be designated as what I call the "locus of the Other" – the Other-on [*l'Autre-on*] or "Otron," I would say, to make it rhyme with those designations familiar to us from physics. Thus we see that the demand to be fed is addressed by the subject, more or less unbeknown to himself, to this abstract Otron.

I have stated that every demand, due to the fact that it is [articulated in] speech, tends to be structured in the following way: it calls for an inverted response from the Other. Owing to its very structure, demand evokes its own form transposed according to a certain inversion. Due to its signifying structure, the demand to be fed is thus responded to, in a way that one can state to be logically contemporaneous with that demand, in the locus of the Other – that is, at the level of the Otron – with the demand to let oneself be fed.

We are very familiar with this in our practice. It is not a refined elaboration on a fictitious dialogue. It is what is at work every time the least little conflict breaks out in the relationship between a child and its mother which seems to be designed to form a circle [*se boucler*] in a strictly complementary way. What could, on the face of it, respond better to a demand to be fed than a demand to let oneself be fed? Yet we know that it is in the very way in which these two demands meet that lies the tiny gap* or tear into which discordance – the preformed failure of the meeting – usually creeps. This failure consists in the fact that it is not a meeting up of tendencies, but rather a meeting up of demands.

In the first conflict that breaks out in the nursing relationship, in the encounter between the demand to be fed and the demand to let oneself be fed, the following become clear: [1] a desire goes beyond [*déborde*] this demand; [2] the demand cannot be satisfied without the desire being extinguished; [3] it is so that the desire which goes beyond demand not be extinguished that the subject who is hungry does not let himself be fed – owing to the fact that a demand to let himself be fed responds to his demand to be fed – and refuses in some sense to disappear qua desire by being satisfied qua demand; [4] the extinction or crushing of demand through satisfaction cannot happen without killing desire. All sorts of discordances derive therefrom, the most intriguing of which is the refusal to let oneself be fed in the form of anorexia that is said, with more or less good reason, to be nervosa.

We find here a situation that I cannot better translate than by playing off the equivocations authorized by sounds in French phonemics. One cannot admit to the other what is most primordial, namely, "you are [what I] desire" [*tu es le désir*], without at the same time saying to him, "desire has been killed" [*tué le désir*] – in other words, without conceding to him that he kills desire, without abandoning desire as such to him. The primal ambivalence characteristic of all demand is that it is equally implied in every demand that the subject does not want the demand to be satisfied. The subject aims at safeguarding desire in and of itself, and attests to the presence of unnamed, blind desire.

What is this desire? We know, and can respond in the most classic and elementary way. Oral demand has another meaning beyond that of the satisfaction of hunger. It is a sexual demand. It is cannibalism at its root, as Freud tells us right from the *Three Essays on the Theory of Sexuality*, and cannibalism has a sexual meaning. He reminds us – although this is veiled in his first formulation – that to feed oneself is, for man, linked to the goodwill of the Other, and linked to it by a polar relationship.

The fact, too, is that it is not on the bread alone of the Other's goodwill that the primitive subject must feed, but on the body of the person who feeds him. We must call a spade a spade – a sexual relationship is that by which the relationship with the Other gives

243

rise to a union of bodies. And the most radical union is that of the earliest absorption in which we can glimpse the outlines of cannibalism, which characterizes the oral stage as it is presented in analytic theory.

Let us note what is at stake here. I approached things from the most difficult angle by starting at the beginning, whereas it is always by backing up, by proceeding retroactively, that we must figure out how things are constructed during real development.

There is a theory of the libido that you know I get up in arms about, even though it was proposed by one of my friends, Franz Alexander. Indeed, he makes libido into the surplus energy manifested in a living being once its needs related to self-preservation have been satisfied. It is a convenient theory, but nonetheless false. That is not sexual libido. Sexual libido is indeed a surplus, but a surplus that renders vain any satisfaction of need wherever libido is situated. And if need be – that's the word for it! – libido refuses the satisfaction of need to preserve the function of desire.

All of this is self-evident and confirmed in every quarter, as you will see by backing up and starting anew with the demand to be fed. You can immediately put your finger on it in that, owing to the very fact that the tendency of a hungry mouth is expressed in a signifying chain by the very same mouth, this mouth becomes able to designate the food it desires. Which food? The first thing that results therefrom is that the mouth can say, "Not that kind." Desire's negation or gap, its "I like this and nothing else," already enters into the picture here, the specificity of the dimension of desire bursting onto the scene.

Hence the extreme care we must take in our interpretations at the level of the oral register. For, as I have said, oral demand forms at the same point, at the level of the same organ, at which the tendency arises. This is precisely where the problem lies. It is possible to produce all sorts of equivocations in responding to this demand. Of course, the response made to demand nevertheless leads to the preservation of the field of speech, and thus to the possibility of ever finding anew the place of desire in this field, but it is also the possibility of all subjections – one attempts to force the subject, his need being satisfied, to simply be content with that. And on this basis one turns compensated frustration into the end-all [terme] of analytic intervention.

I am going to go further, and I truly have, as you will see, my reasons for doing so today. I'm going to move on to the so-called "anal libido" stage. For it is concerning the latter that I think I can touch on and refute a certain number of confusions that are very often made in analytic interpretation.

3

What sort of demand is made in the anal stage?

I think you all have enough experience that I need not illustrate any further what I will call the demand to hold it, to hold in excrement, insofar as it no doubt founds something: the desire to evacuate. But it is not as simple as all that, for evacuation is also demanded [*exigée*] at a certain point by the educating parent. The subject is demanded to give something that satisfies the expectation of the educator, in this case, the mother.

What results from the complexity of this demand warrants that we dwell upon it, for it is essential. Let us note that it is no longer a question here of the simple relationship of a need to its demanded form, linked to surplus sexuality [*excédent sexuel*]. Something else is at work. It is a matter of disciplining need, and sexualization is produced only in the movement of a return to need. It is this movement which, so to speak, legitimates need as a gift to the mother, who expects the child to satisfy his functions and make something come out or appear that is worthy of everyone's approval.

The gift-like character excrement takes on has been well known and situated since the beginning of analytic practice. It is so clearly in the gift register that an object is experienced here that the child, in his occasional excesses, naturally uses it, one might say, as a means of expression. The excremental gift is part and parcel of psychoanalysis' oldest theme.

I would like, in this regard, to take as far as possible the extermination I am always trying to carry out of the myth of oblativity, by showing you what it is really related to here. The true field of oblativity is the field of the anal dialectic, and once you have perceived it, you will no longer be able to see it in any other way.

I have long been trying, in many different ways, to show you this road map. In particular, I mentioned to you that the very term "oblativity" is an obsessive fantasy. "Everything for the other person," the obsessive neurotic says, and this is indeed what he does, for being caught up in the perpetual giddiness [*vertige*] of destroying the other, he can never do enough to ensure that the other continue to exist. Here we see its root.

The anal stage is characterized by the fact that the subject satisfies a need only in order to satisfy the other. He has been taught to defer this need, so that it may be founded or instituted solely as an occasion for satisfying the other as educator. The satisfaction of playing the doting parent [*pouponnage*], which involves the wiping of tushies, is first and foremost the other's satisfaction. It is insofar as it is a gift that is demanded of the subject that one can say that oblativity is linked to the sphere of anal-stage relations.

Note the consequence thereof: the room that remains for the subject – in other words, desire – is symbolized in this situation by what is flushed away in the process. Desire, literally, goes down the tubes. The symbolization of the subject as that which disappears into the chamber pot or down the hole is encountered in our practice as related most profoundly to the nature [*position*] of anal desire.

This is what makes for both its attraction and also, in many cases, its avoidance. We are not always able to get the patient to see this. You can nevertheless tell yourself that, insofar as the anal stage is involved, you would be wrong not to distrust the relevance of your analysis if you have not encountered this on every occasion. As long as you have not located at this point the basic, fundamental relationship of the subject as desire with the most disagreeable object, I assure you that you will not have made great strides in the analysis of the conditions of desire.

This precise point is key. It is certainly as important, given the weight it has in analytic practice, as all the primitive oral objects, whether good or bad, that people comment on so much. You cannot deny that we are constantly being reminded of them in the analytic literature. If you have remained deaf [to this key point] for so long, it is because things are not indicated in the literature in their fundamental topology, as I am attempting to do for you here.

But then, you will ask me, what of sexuality and the infamous sadistic drive that, thanks to a dash, is conjugated to the term "anal," as if it were quite simply self-evident?

An effort is necessary here, an effort that we can call "understanding" only insofar as it involves a liminal understanding. Sexuality can only come into the picture violently. This indeed is what happens, since it is sadistic violence that is involved. Yet it harbors within itself more than one enigma, and it makes sense for us to dwell on it.

It is in the anal relationship that the other as such becomes truly dominant. This is precisely why sexuality is manifested in the register characteristic of this stage. We can catch a glimpse of it by recalling its antecedent, which is qualified as oral-sadistic.

In effect, to speak of the oral-sadistic stage is, on the whole, to recall that, at its very foundations, life is devouring assimilation as such. In the oral stage, it is the theme of devouring that is situated in the bit of room [*marge*] occupied by desire; it is the presence of the gaping maw of life.

This fantasy is somehow reflected in the anal stage. The [imaginary] other, being posited as the second term, must appear as an existence offered up to this gap [*béance*]. Will we go so far as to say that suffering is implied therein? [If so] it is a very peculiar kind of suffering. To mention a sort of fundamental schema that will situate for you the structure of sadomasochistic fantasy as well as possible, I will say that what is involved is suffering that is expected [*attendue*] by the other. Suspending the imaginary other over a chasm [*gouffre*] of suffering forms the apex and axis of sadomasochistic eroticization. What is no longer merely the sexual pole, but what is going to be the sexual partner, is instituted at the anal level in this relationship. We can thus say that there is already a sort of reappearance of sexuality here.

What constitutes something like sadistic or sadomasochistic structure in the anal stage marks – starting from a maximal eclipsing of sexuality, from a point of pure anal oblativity – the re-ascension toward what will be achieved at the genital stage. The genital stage – human Eros, desire in its normal fullness, which is situated neither as tendency or need, nor as pure and simple copulation, but as desire – finds its outlines or beginnings and has its point of re-emergence in the relationship to an other who is subject to the expectation of this suspended threat, this virtual attack that characterizes and founds for us what is known as the sadistic theory of sexuality, whose primitive character we are aware of in the vast majority of individual cases.

Moreover, what is at the origin of the sexualization of the other is based on a situational trait: in the first mode of its apperception, the other as such must be delivered over to a third party in order to be constituted as sexual. This is the origin of the ambiguity owing to which, in the original experience discovered by the most recent analytic theorists, sexuality remains indeterminate between this third party and the other. In the first form of libidinal apperception of the other, at the level of the point of re-ascension starting from a certain momentary eclipsing of the libido as such, the subject does not know what he desires most, the other or the intervening third party [i.e., the Other].

This is essential to the structure of any sadomasochistic fantasy. Indeed, if I have provided here a correct analysis of the anal stage, the stage that constitutes this fantasy, let us not forget that the witness who is subject to this pivotal point of the anal stage is what he is – as I just said, he is a piece of shit. And, moreover, he is a demand – he is a piece of shit that demands nothing more than to be evacuated.

This is the true foundation of the whole of a radical structure that you will encounter in the fundamental fantasy of the obsessive neurotic in particular. He devalues himself, and locates the whole game of the erotic dialectic outside of himself – he pretends, as the man said, to be its orchestrator. He bases the entirety of his fantasy on his own evacuation.

Things here are rooted in something which, once recognized, allows you to elucidate even the most banal points. Indeed, if things are truly fixated at the point of the subject's identification with little excremental *a*, what are we going to see? Let us not forget here, nevertheless, that the job of articulating this demand is no longer assigned, at least in theory, to the organ that is involved in the dramatic knotting of need with demand. In other words, one does not speak with one's *derrière* – except in Hieronymus Bosch's paintings. And yet we observe the curious phenomena of cuts followed by explosions, which allow us to glimpse the symbolic function of the excremental flow in the very articulation of people's speech.

A long time ago, and I think no one present today can remember it, there was a little character beloved by children, as there always have been – significant little characters in an infantile mythology that is, in reality, of parental origin. In our times, people talk a lot about Pinocchio, but at a time that I am old enough to remember there was Bout-de-Zan. The phenomenology of the child as a precious excremental object is altogether contained in this name, in which the child is identified with the sweetish element of licorice, *glukurriza*, meaning "sweet root," which seems to be its Greek origin.

It is probably not insignificant that the word "licorice" provides us with one of the sweetest examples – that's the word for it! – of the utter ambiguity of signifying transcriptions.

Allow me this brief parenthetical remark. I came across this gem – which I found for you along the roadside of my trajectory – not just recently, by the way, as I have been saving this one for you for a long time. But since I came across it concerning Bout-de-Zan, I will give it to you now. "*Réglisse*" ["Licorice"] was originally "*glukurriza*." Naturally, it does not come directly from the Greek, but when Latin people heard it they turned it into "*liquiritia*," basing it on the word "*liquor*." This gave rise in old French to "*licorice*," and then "*ricolice*" by metathesis. "*Ricolice*" collided with "*règle*" [rule or ruler], *regula*, and that led to *rygalisse*. You have to admit that the encounter between "*licorice*" and "*règle*" is superb.

But that's not all, for the conscious etymology at which all of that ends up, and to which the most recent generations have confined their attention, is that "*réglisse*" should be written "*rai de Galice*" because licorice is made with a sweet root that is found only in Galicia. The *rai de Galice* is where we wind up after having started with the Greek root – in more ways than one!

249

I think that this little demonstration of signifying ambiguities will have convinced you that we're barking up the right tree.

In the final analysis, as we have seen, we must be reserved about understanding the other at the anal level even more so than elsewhere. Every understanding of his demand, in effect, implicates him so profoundly that we must look twice before broaching it [*aller à sa rencontre*]. What am I telling you, if not something that coincides with what you all know, at least those of you who have done a little bit of therapeutic work – namely, that one must not give the obsessive neurotic the slightest encouragement or absolution of guilt, or even give him any interpretive commentary that goes a bit too far. If you do, then you will have to go much further, and will wind up acceding – and yielding, much to your own detriment – to the precise mechanism by which he wants to make you eat, so to speak, his own being in the form of a piece of shit.

Your practice teaches you that this is not a process by which you render him a signal service – quite the contrary.   250

It is elsewhere that symbolic introjection must be situated, insofar as it must restore in him the place of desire. Since – to get ahead of ourselves regarding the following stage – what the neurotic most commonly wants to be is the phallus, it is certainly to unduly short-circuit the satisfactions to be given him by offering him this phallic communion against which I have already formulated the most precise objections in my seminar on *Desire and Its Interpretation* [1958–9]. The phallic object as an imaginary object cannot, in any case, help completely reveal the fundamental fantasy. In fact it cannot help but respond to the neurotic's demand with what we might refer to approximately as an obliteration. Stated otherwise, it paves the way for the subject to forget a number of the most essential elements that played a part in his bumpy accession to the field of desire.

To pause for a moment at this point in the trajectory I have traced out today, I will say that if the neurotic is [constituted by] unconscious desire – in other words, repressed desire – it is above all insofar as his desire is eclipsed by a counterdemand; that the locus of the counterdemand is strictly speaking the same as the locus in which everything the outside world can add by way of a supplement to the construction of the superego – a certain way of satisfying this counterdemand – is placed and built up afterward; and that any premature mode of interpretation can be criticized inasmuch as it understands too quickly, and does not perceive that what it is most important to understand in the analysand's demand is what is beyond that demand. The space occupied by not understanding [*la marge de l'incompréhension*] is the space occupied by desire [*la marge du désir*]. It is to the extent that this is not perceived that an analysis ends prematurely and is, quite frankly, botched.

The catch is, of course, that by interpreting, you give the subject something speech can feed on, even the very book that is behind it. Speech nevertheless remains the locus of desire, even if you provide it in such a way that this locus is unrecognizable, I mean even if it still cannot be inhabited by the subject's desire.

Responding to the demand for food or to frustrated demand with a nourishing signifier, leaves elided the fact that, beyond all nourishing speech, what the subject truly needs is to signify metonymically, and this is situated at no point in such nourishing speech. Thus, every time you introduce metaphor – and you are probably obliged to do so – you remain on the very path that gives the symptom consistency. It is no doubt a more simplified symptom, but it is still a symptom, in relation, in any case, to the desire that must be brought out [*dégager*].

If the subject has this singular relationship to the object of desire, it is because he himself was initially an object of desire that became incarnate. Speech as the locus of desire is the *Poros* in which all resources reside. And desire, as Socrates originally taught us to articulate it, is above all lack of resources: aporia. This absolute aporia approaches sleeping speech, and gets herself knocked up with its object. What does this mean, if not that the object was [already] there, and that it was the object that was demanding to be brought to light?

Plato's metaphor of the metempsychosis of the wandering soul that hesitates before knowing where it is going to live, finds its medium, truth, and substance in the object of desire, which is there prior to its birth.

And when Socrates delivers a eulogy, *épainei*, of Agathon, he unwittingly does what he wants to do – namely, brings Alcibiades back to his soul – by bringing to life the object that is the object of his desire.

This object – which is the aim and end for each person, and undoubtedly limited because the whole lies beyond it – can only be conceptualized as beyond the end of each person.

March 15, 1961

ORAL, ANAL, AND GENITAL

The jouissance of the praying mantis.
The Other, depository of desire.
Desire's dependence on demand.
The privilege of the phallus as an object.

We are going to wander, I have the urge to say, yet again through the labyrinth constituted by the nature [*position*] of desire. A certain returning to or rehashing of the topic – a certain working through,* as it's called – seems to me to be necessary for an exact positioning of the function of transference. I already indicated this last time and said why.

This is why I will return to it today in order to emphasize the meaning of what I said to you in re-examining the so-called stages of the migration of the libido to the erogenous zones. It is important to see to what extent the naturalist view implied by this definition can be articulated and resolved in our way of enunciating it, which centers it on the relationship between demand and desire.

1

Right at the outset of my discussion of them, I pointed out that there is a place for desire in the margins of demand as such; that it is these margins of demand that constitute desire's locus in a beyond and shy of, a twofold hollow that is already sketched out as soon as the cry of hunger gets articulated; and that, at the other extreme, the object known in English as the "nipple," the tip of the breast, ends up taking on its value as *ágalma*, marvel, and precious object in human eroticism, becoming the medium [*support*] of the pleasure and sensual delight of nibbling, in which what we might call a sublimated voracity is perpetuated, insofar as it takes this *Lust*, this pleasure.

Moreover, these *Lüste*, these desires – you are aware of the equivocation contained within the German term, the slippage of signification produced by the shift from the singular to the plural – the pleasure and covetousness the oral object brings with it stems from something else. It is in this respect, through a reversal in the use of the term "sublimation," that I am justified in saying that we see here a deviation in aim occurring in a way that does not happen when it comes to the object of need.

Indeed, the erotic value of this privileged object does not draw its substance here from primal hunger. The Eros that inhabits it comes *Nachträglich*, retroactively, only after the fact [*après coup*]. The place for this desire is prepared [*creusée*] in oral demand. Were there no demand, with love as the beyond [*l'au-delà d'amour*] it projects, there would be no place for desire shy of it, which is constituted around a privileged object. The oral stage of sexual libido requires the existence of a place that is hollowed out [*creusée*] by demand.

It is important to examine whether or not this presentation of things does not involve, through my own doing, some specification that one might consider overly biased. Mustn't we take Freud literally when he presents us, in one of his statements, with the pure and simple migration of an organic – or, might I say, mucosa-based – erogeneity? Couldn't one say that I am neglecting natural facts? Namely, for example, the instinctive devouring motions we find in nature that are related to the sexual cycle.

It is a fact that female cats [sometimes] eat their kittens, and if the great fantasmatic figure of the praying mantis haunts the analytic classroom, it is precisely because it presents a sort of main [*mère*] image or model of the function attributed to what people so brazenly, and perhaps so incorrectly, call the castrating mother. Yes, of course, in my own initiation to analysis, I willingly relied on this rich image, which echoes in the natural realm what presents itself in unconscious phenomena. By presenting this objection, you could suggest to me the need for an adjustment in the theoretical line with which I think I can satisfy you along with me.

I have spent some time dwelling on this image and what it represents. A simple glance at the diversity of animal ethology shows us, in effect, a rich variety of perversions. My friend Henri Ey looked at it closely, and even devoted an issue of *L'Evolution psychiatrique* to the topic of animal perversions, which go further than anything human imagination has been able to invent. Taken in this sense, aren't we simply brought back to the Aristotelian view that situates the foundation of perverse desire in a realm lying outside of the human realm?

I will ask you to dwell on this for a moment and to consider what we do when we go no further than the fantasy of natural perversion. In asking you to follow me on this ground, I am not underestimating the extent to which such reflection may seem persnickety and speculative, but I think that it is necessary to isolate both what is founded and what is unfounded in this reference [to animals]. As you will immediately see, we will thereby meet up with what I designate as fundamental in subjectivization, as an essential moment of every instating of the dialectic of desire.

To subjectivize the praying mantis in this case is to make an assumption which is not excessive – that it has sexual jouissance. We, of course, know nothing about it. The praying mantis is perhaps, as Descartes would not have hesitated to say, a pure and simple machine, in the sense that machines take on in his terminology, which presupposes the elimination of all subjectivity. But we ourselves have no need to remain at the stage of minimalist positions. We can grant her this jouissance.

Is this jouissance – here is the following step – jouissance of something insofar as this jouissance [*elle*] destroys it? For it can indicate nature's intentions to us only on this basis.

To immediately point out what is essential, so that it may serve us as some kind of model of what is at issue – namely, our oral cannibalism and our primordial eroticism – we must imagine here that this jouissance is correlated with the decapitation of the partner that the praying mantis is supposed to know [*connaître*] to some degree as such.

I have no aversion to going this far. For, in fact, animal ethology is our major reference insofar as it maintains the dimension of knowing [*connaître*] that all progress in knowledge [*connaissance*] renders so vacillating for us in the human world because it is identified with the dimension of misrecognition [*méconnaître*] or *Verkennung*, as Freud says. It is the field of living beings that allows one to observe imaginary *Erkennung* [recognition], and the privileged status of a species' fellow beings [*semblable*] which goes so far, in certain cases, as to lead to organogenic effects. I won't go back over the old examples around which my exploration of the imaginary revolved at the time at which I began to articulate something, my doctrine of analysis, which has been coming to fruition over the years before your eyes – namely, the female pigeon that does not fully develop into a female pigeon until she sees a pigeon-like image, a small mirror placed in her cage sufficing to produce this effect, and also the migratory locust that does not go beyond a certain stage [i.e., solitary] unless it encounters another migratory locust.

256

There is no doubt but that what fascinates not only us, but also the male praying mantis, is her standing-erect posture, a posture that looks to us like that of prayer, from which the praying mantis derives its name, not without finding some kind of vacillating echo [*retour*] in us. We observe that it is when the male is face-to-face with this fantasy – this incarnated fantasy – that he yields and is taken, called, aspirated, and captivated in an embrace that will be fatal to him.

It is clear that an image of the imaginary other as such is present in this phenomenon, and it is not excessive to assume that something is revealed therein. But does this mean that it already somehow prefigures an inverted replica of what presents itself in man as a sort of remainder and repercussion of a definite possibility, of the variations or play of natural tendencies?

While we may value this monstrous example, we must nevertheless note its divergence from what presents itself in human fantasy. In the latter, we can with certainty start with the subject, the only thing we are sure of, insofar as he is the prop [*support*] of the signifying chain. We thus cannot fail to remark that in what nature presents us with here, there is – from the [sexual] act to its excess, to what overflows it, to what leads it to a devouring surplus – something that signals to us that another structure, an instinctual structure, is being exemplified. The signal is that synchrony is involved. It is at the very moment of the [sexual] act that this complement [i.e., devouring] comes into play, exemplifying for us the paradoxical nature [*forme*] of instinct.

Isn't a limit thus sketched out here that allows us to strictly define in what sense the example of the praying mantis can be useful to us? This example serves only to provide the form of what we mean when we speak of a desire.

257   If we speak of the jouissance of the praying mantis as an other, if the praying mantis interests us in this case, it is because she either gets off [*jouit*] where the male's organ is, or she gets off elsewhere as well. But wherever she gets off – something we'll never know anything about, but so what? – the fact that she may get off elsewhere only takes on meaning on the basis of the fact that she gets off (or does not get off, it makes no difference) there. The fact that she may get off wherever she likes has no meaning – for the value taken on by this image – except in relation to a *there* of a virtual getting off. Whatever is at work, synchrony implies that it will never be anything but copulatory jouissance, even if it is indirect.

We can easily find, in the infinite natural variety of instinctual mechanisms, evocative forms, including, for example, those in which the copulatory organ is lost *in loco*, during consummation itself. We can just as easily consider devouring to be one of the many forms of the primacy given to the individual female partner in copulation – as organized in accordance with its specific end – to constrain her to engage in an act that must be allowed to occur. The exemplary character of the image we are presented with thus only begins at the exact point to which we have no right to go.

Let me explain this. The female praying mantis devours the cephalic extremity of her male partner with her mandibles. Now, this part of her anatomy shares as such the property that constitutes, in living nature, the cephalic extremity – namely, a certain uniting of the individual tendency, and the possibility, in whatever register it is exercised, of discernment and choice. Otherwise stated, this leads us to believe that the praying mantis prefers *it* [*ça*], her partner's head, to anything else. We see here an absolute preference. *That* [*ça*] is what she loves.

It is insofar as she loves *that* [*ça*] – which looks to us like jouissance at the other's expense – that we begin to read into natural functions what is at stake: namely, moral meaning. In other words, we enter into the Sadean dialectic.

To prefer jouissance to the other turns out to be the essential dimension of nature, but it is only too plain to see that we are the ones who supply this moral meaning. We only supply it to the extent that we discover the meaning of desire as a relation to the partial object in the other, and as a choice of that object.

258

Let us pay closer attention here. Can this example altogether validly illustrate for us the preference for the part over the whole, a judgment that can be illustrated by the erotic value given to the nipple I mentioned earlier? I'm not so sure. In the case of the praying mantis, it is less the part that is preferred to the whole – in the most horrible way, and in a way that would already allow us to short-circuit the function of metonymy – than the whole that is preferred to the part.

Indeed, let us not overlook the fact that, even in an animal structure as apparently far removed from us as that of the insect, the value of concentration, reflection, and totality somehow represented by the cephalic extremity assuredly functions. In any case, in fantasy, in the image that captivates us, the partner's acephalization appears with a particular emphasis. To go as far as we can, let us not overlook the fable [*fabulatoire*] value of the praying mantis, underlying what it represents in a certain mythology, or more simply in a kind of folklore, in everything Roger Caillois has highlighted in the register of *Myth and Man*. It was his first book, and it seems that he did not sufficiently indicate that, at this level, it is a matter of poetry. This image does not simply derive its savor from a reference to the relation with the oral object such as it is traced out in the *koine* or common language of the unconscious. It involves a more accentuated feature, which designates for us a certain link between acephalia and the telos of the transmission of life, between acephalia and the handing of the torch from one individual to another in a signified eternity of the species – namely, that *Gelüst* [sexual desire or craving] does not involve the head [*ne passe pas par la tête*].

This is what gives tragic meaning to the image of the praying mantis, which has nothing to do with preference for the so-called oral object, which in human fantasy is never, on any occasion, related to the head.

Something altogether different is at work in the link between human desire and the oral stage.

259   **2**

What can be glimpsed by way of a mutual identification between the subject and the object of oral desire goes toward a constitutive fragmentation [*morcellement*], as psychoanalytic practice immediately shows us.

During our recent convention in the provinces, these fragmenting images were said to be related to some kind of primitive terror that seemed, though I don't know why, to take on some kind of value as a worrisome designation for certain speakers, whereas it is clearly the most fundamental, widespread, and common fantasy, at the origin of all of man's relations with his soma. The panoply of anatomical morsels that fill Carpaccio's famous *Saint George and the Dragon* – hanging in the little church known as Saint Mary of the Angels in Venice – have appeared in everyone's dreams, whether they've been in analysis or not. And in the same register, the head that goes about all by itself, as in Cazotte's work, has no trouble telling its little stories.

But that is not what is important.

The discovery made by psychoanalysis is that the subject does not merely encounter images of his own fragmentation in the Other's field, but already, and right from the outset, encounters objects of the Other's desire – namely, the mother's objects, not simply in a state of fragmentation, but with the privileged status granted them by the mother's desire. In particular, as Melanie Klein tells us, one of these objects, the paternal phallus, is encountered right from the subject's first fantasies, and it is at the origin of the *fandum*, "it is going to speak, it must speak." The paternal phallus is perceived – in the internal realm of the mother's body, into which the first imaginary formations are projected – as something that is distinguished as very highly accentuated or even dangerous.

In the field of the Other's desire, the subjective object already encounters identifiable occupants, against whose yardstick he must already be measured, against whom he must already be weighed. I am thinking of the little weights of various shapes that are used by primitive African tribes, where you see little twisted-up animals, or even clearly phalloform objects.

At the fantasmatic level, the privilege of the image of the praying mantis derives solely from the fact – which is not, after all, all that well assured – that the praying mantis is supposed to eat a whole series of males, one after another. The shift to the plural is the essential dimension in which the praying mantis takes on fantasmatic value for us.

We have thus defined the oral stage. It is only within demand that the Other is constituted as a reflection of the subject's hunger. The Other is thus not merely hunger, but articulated hunger – hunger that demands. And the subject is thereby open to becoming an object, but the object of a hunger that he chooses, as it were.

The transition from hunger to eroticism is made by means of what I was earlier calling a preference. She likes something especially – *that* – out of gluttony for special treats [*d'une gourmandise*], so to speak. Thus we find ourselves back in the register of original sins. The subject places himself on the à la carte menu of cannibalism, which everyone knows is never absent from any communional fantasy.

Read on this score a treatise by an author I have spoken to you about over the years with a sort of periodic insistence, Baltasar Gracián. Obviously, only those of you who know Spanish can find it fully satisfying, unless you have it translated for you. For, although Gracián was translated very early on, as works were translated almost instantaneously in all of Europe at that time, several of his books have remained untranslated. I am referring here to his treatise on communion, *El Comulgatorio*, which is a fine text in the sense that something rarely avowed is revealed therein: the delights of consuming Christ's body are detailed in it and we are asked to dwell upon this exquisite cheek, this delicious arm – I will spare you all the other tidbits on which spiritual concupiscence dwells, thus revealing to us what is always implied in even the most elaborate forms of oral identification. You see here the earliest tendency being deployed by virtue of the signifier, in a whole field that is already created in order to be secondarily inhabited.

In opposition to this, I tried to show you last time a meaning of anal demand that is hardly ever or only poorly articulated.

260

Anal demand is characterized by a complete reversal of initiative, to the Other's advantage. It is there (in other words, at a stage which, in our normative ideology, is neither very advanced nor mature) that lies the source of the discipline – I did not say "duty," but "discipline" – of toilet training [*proprêté*], a word whose association with propriety the French language so prettily indicates, with what is proper to it: education and good manners. Here the demand is external, it comes from the Other, and it is posited as articulated as such.

The strange thing is that we must see here – and recognize in what has always been said and whose import no one seems to have truly grasped – the point at which the object as a gift is born. In this metaphor, what the subject can give is precisely correlated with what he can withhold – namely, his own scrap, his excrement. It is impossible not to see something exemplary here, which must indispensably be designated as the radical point at which the projection of the subject's desire onto the Other occurs.

There is a point in this stage at which desire is articulated and constituted, at which the Other is, strictly speaking, its depository. Furthermore, we are not surprised to see that idealists, enamored of the theme of a hominization of the cosmos or, as they are forced to express themselves in our times, of the planet, neglect that one of the manifest stages, since the beginning of time, of the hominization of the planet is that the human animal turns the planet into a garbage dump. The oldest evidence that we have of human agglomerations are enormous piles of shell debris which go by a Scandinavian name [*Kjökkenmödding*].

This is no accident. Moreover, if we are to some day reconstruct how man entered into the field of signifiers, we would have to designate it in those first piles.

The subject designates himself here in the evacuated object. It is, so to speak, the starting point of an *aphanisis* of desire. It is entirely based upon the effect of the Other's demand – the Other makes the decision. The root of the neurotic's dependence clearly lies here. This is the tangible note by which the neurotic's desire is characterized as pregenital. It depends so much on the Other's demand that what the neurotic demands of the Other in his neurotic demand for love, is that he be allowed to do something.

The place of desire manifestly remains, up until a certain degree, dependent upon the Other's demand.

3

What meaning can we, in effect, give to the genital stage? The only meaning that we can give it is the following.

Desire should someday reappear as something that could rightfully be called natural desire, but, given its noble antecedents, it can never be such. In other words, desire should appear as what is not demanded, as aiming at what one does not demand.

Don't rush ahead and conclude, for example, that desire is what one takes. Whatever you say will never do anything more than make you fall back into the petty mechanics of demand.

Natural desire has the characteristic of not being able to be spoken in any way whatsoever, which is why you will never have any natural desire. The Other with a capital O – that is, the Other in which signs are situated – is already instated in that spot [*place*]. And signs suffice to institute the question "*Che vuoi?*" to which the subject has at first no response.

A sign represents something to someone and, as the subject does not know what the sign represents, faced with this question when sexual desire appears, he loses the someone to whom desire is addressed – in other words, himself. Thus is born little Hans' anxiety.

Here we glimpse what, prepared by the subject's fracturing owing to demand, is instated in the mother/child relationship, which we are going to keep – as it often remains – separate for a moment.

Little Hans' mother, and every other mother as well – "I call upon all mothers," as someone once said – defines her position by proffering the words, "That's terribly dirty," concerning what begins to arise in Hans by way of a little quivering or unambiguous stirring during the first awakenings of genital sexuality. That desire – he cannot even say what it is – is disgusting. But her words are strictly correlated with a no less recognizable interest in the object to which we have learned to give its full import – namely, the phallus.

In an undoubtedly allusive, but not ambiguous way, how many mothers, [if not] all mothers, faced with little Hans' or some other boy's little faucet, or whatever they call it, come out with remarks like, "My little boy is very well endowed" or "You will have
many children"? In short, the appraisal of the object – the object clearly remaining partial at this stage – still contrasts here with the refusal of desire, at the very moment of the encounter with what solicits the subject in the mystery of desire. The division is instituted between, on the one hand, the object that becomes the mark of special interest – which becomes *ágalma*, the pearl at the heart of the individual that trembles here around the pivotal point of his accession to living plenitude – and, on the other hand, a

debasement of the subject. He is esteemed as an object, but disparaged as desire.

It is around this that tallies will be made [*vont jouer les comptes*] and that the instating of the register of having revolves. It is worth our while dwelling upon this and I will go into greater detail here.

I have been announcing the theme of having to you for a long time with formulations such as, "Love is giving what you don't have." Of course, when a child gives what he has, it's at the preceding stage [i.e., the anal stage]. What doesn't he have, and in what sense? One can, certainly, make the dialectic of being and having revolve around the phallus. But it is not from that angle that you must look in order to understand things correctly.

What is the new dimension that is introduced by entry into the phallic drama? What he doesn't have at his disposal at the moment of the birth and revelation of genital desire is nothing other than the (sexual) act [*son acte*]. He has nothing but a promissory note. He institutes this act at the level of a project.

I beg you to notice here the power of linguistic determinations. Just as desire has, in many Romance languages, taken on the connotation of *desiderium* – of mourning and regret [for something lost] – it is not inconsequential that the early forms of the future tense were abandoned in favor of a reference to having. *Je chanterai* (I will sing) is exactly what you see written here: *Je chanter-ai* (I have to sing). This in fact comes from *cantare habeo*. The decadent Roman tongue found the surest path to rediscovering the true meaning of the future: *Je baiser__ai plus tard, J'ai le baiser à l'état de traite sur l'avenir, Je désirer__ai* [I'll fuck later, I have fucking in the form of an IOU, I will desire]. And this *habeo* introduces us to the *debeo* of the symbolic debt, to a revoked [*destitué*] *habeo*. This debt is conjugated in the future tense, when it takes the form of a commandment: *Tes père et mère honorer__as* [Thou shalt honor thy father and thy mother], and so on.

Today I want to detain you to make a final point, at the mere threshold of what results from this articulation, which is no doubt slow, but which is precisely designed so that you do not get ahead of yourselves.

The object in question – the phallic object – separated from desire, is not the simple specification, homologue, or homonym of the little imaginary *a* to which the full Other is debased. It is not the specifying, which finally comes to light, of what had earlier been the oral object and then the anal object. As I mentioned earlier today, when I pointed out to you the subject's first encounter with the phallus, the phallus is a privileged object in the field of the Other, an object that is subtracted from the status of the Other with a capital *O* as such.

In other words, at the level of genital desire in the castration stage – to the precise articulation of which all of this is designed to introduce you – little *a* is the Other minus *phi* [$a = A - \varphi$]. In this sense, *phi* comes to symbolize what the Other is missing because it is the noetic A, the full-fledged A, the Other insofar as one can have faith in its response to demand. The desire of this noetic Other is an enigma. This enigma is knotted to the structural foundation of its castration.

It is here that the whole dialectic of castration begins.

Be careful now not to confuse this phallic object with the sign of the Other's lack of response [*manque de réponse*]. The lack at stake here [i.e., the lack related to the phallic object] is the lack constituted by the Other's desire [*le manque du désir de l'Autre*]. The function taken on by the phallus – insofar as it is encountered in the field of the imaginary – is not that of being identical to the Other as designated by the lack of a signifier, it is that of being the root of this lack. For it is the Other who is constituted in a relation to this object *phi*, which is certainly a privileged relation, but a complex one.

It is here that we will find the crux of what constitutes the dead end and problem of love – namely, that the subject can only satisfy the Other's demand by demeaning the Other, turning this Other into the object of his desire.

March 22, 1961

XVI

PSYCHE AND THE CASTRATION COMPLEX

Zucchi and Apuleius.
The tribulations of the soul.
The castration complex as a paradox.
The signifierness of the phallus.
The analyst's desire.

It is not because we are apparently fooling around with respect to your central concern that we do not find it anew at the extreme periphery. I happened to find it at the Borghese Gallery in Rome, almost without realizing it, in the most unexpected of places.

Experience has taught me to always look at what is near an elevator, as it is often significant and people never look there. This experience is altogether applicable to a museum and, applied to the museum in the Borghese Gallery, made me turn at the moment I left the elevator, thanks to which I saw something people never really pause to look at, and about which I have never heard anyone speak – a canvas by a painter by the name of Zucchi.

He is not a very well-known artist, although he has not entirely escaped the critics' notice. He is what is referred to as a Mannerist, from the first period of Mannerism, and he lived from approximately 1547 to 1590.

The painting I saw is called *Psiche sorprende Amore*, the latter being no other than Cupid [*Eros*]. It is the classic scene of Psyche casting light from her little lamp onto Cupid, who has for some time been her nocturnal lover and whom she has never seen.

You probably know a little something about this drama. Psyche, who is favored by an extraordinary love, for she is loved by Cupid himself, experiences happiness that could be perfect if she didn't become curious to see who Cupid is. It's not as if Psyche had never been warned by her lover not to try to cast light upon him, though he is unable to tell her what sanction would result therefrom, but his insistence on remaining invisible is extreme. Nevertheless, Psyche cannot do otherwise than succumb [to her curiosity], and it is at this moment that her misfortunes begin.

I can't recount all of them to you. First I want to show you what is involved, as this is what is important in my discovery. I was able to secure two reproductions of this canvas, and I am going to pass them around the room. I am adding to them a sketch made by a painter whose style will be recognized, I hope, even by those who do not know my family connections. Given his desire to oblige me, he was willing to prepare this little sketch for you this very morning, which will allow me to indicate what is at stake in my demonstration.

You see that the sketch by André Masson corresponds, in its main outlines at least, to what I am now passing around the room.

Let me mention that the tone of my voice today can be explained by the fact that I felt a need to go to the place on the Palatine Hill that, about 50 years ago, Commander Boni thought he could identify with what Latin authors call *mundus*. I managed to go down into it, but I'm afraid it's nothing but a cistern, and I managed to catch a sore throat down there.

1

I don't know if you have ever seen the story of Cupid and Psyche portrayed in this way, even though it has been treated in countless ways in both sculpture and painting. I personally had never seen Psyche appear in a work of art armed as she is in this painting, with what is represented here very clearly as a small blade: a scimitar.

Moreover, you will notice what is significantly projected here in the form of a flower, the bouquet of which it is a part, and the vase in which it is inserted. You will see that, in a very intense and accentuated way, this flower is, strictly speaking, the visual, intellectual center of the painting. This bouquet and this flower are, in effect, in the foreground, and they are backlit, in other words, they form a black mass, which is treated in a way that gives the painting its Mannerist flavor.   267
The whole scene is drawn in an extremely refined way.

There are certainly things we could say about the specific flowers that are included in the bouquet. But around this bouquet, coming from behind it, shines an intense light cast on the extended thighs and stomach of the figure who symbolizes Cupid. It is truly impossible not to see designated here – in the most precise way and as if it were being directly pointed to – the organ that, anatomically speaking, must be dissimulated behind this mass of flowers: Cupid's phallus.

This can be seen in the very manner of the painting, accentuated in such a way that there is nothing in what I am telling you that is in any sense an analytic interpretation. The thread that links the threat of the blade with what is designated to us here cannot fail to come to mind.

This is worth emphasizing, as it is not frequent in art. Many representations of Judith and Holofernes have been made, but that is not what is involved here, since they concern beheading. Nevertheless, the position of Psyche's other arm, which is extended and holds the lamp, is designed to remind us of the paintings of Judith and Holofernes, for the lamp is suspended here above Cupid's head.

You know that in the story it is a drop of oil – spilt owing to an abrupt movement on Psyche's part, as she is quite startled – which wakes up Cupid, inflicting, moreover, so the story tells us, a wound from which he suffers for a long time. If you look closely, you will notice that in the reproduction you have before you, there is something like a shaft of light which runs from the lamp and goes straight toward Cupid's shoulder. Nevertheless, the angle of this shaft does not allow us to believe that it is a drop of oil, but rather a ray of light.

Certain people will think that there is something quite remarkable here, which represents an innovation on the part of the artist, and thus an intention that we can unambiguously attribute to him – that of representing the threat of castration in an amorous context. Were we to try to interpret things in this direction, I think that we would quickly have to retrace our steps.

We would quickly have to retrace our steps because – I haven't yet indicated this fact to you, but I hope it already occurred to some of you – this story, despite the success it has had in the history of art, is told to us by but a single text, which is *The Golden Ass* by Apuleius.

I hope, for the sake of your own pleasure, that you have read *The Golden Ass*. It is an inspiring text, I must say. If certain truths or esoteric secrets are, as has always been said, included in the book, in a mythical and colorful form, they are packaged in the most shimmering – not to say tickling and titillating – of ways. At first glance, it is truly something that has not yet been superseded, not even by the most recent productions which have, over the last few years in France, been a treat for us in the most blatant erotic genre, with all the nuances of sadomasochism that are the most common fodder of erotic novels.

The Golden Ass tells the horrible story of a young girl's abduction, accompanied by the most terrifying threats to which the girl is exposed in the company of the ass, he who speaks in the first person in this novel. It is during an intermezzo included in this rather racy adventure that an old lady, in order to entertain the kidnapped girl for a moment, tells her at length the story of Cupid and Psyche.

Now it is due to the perfidious influence of Psyche's sisters – who constantly prod her to fall into the trap, to break the promises she has made to her divine lover – that she succumbs. The final means employed by her sisters are to suggest to her that Cupid must be a horrible monster or the most hideous of serpents, and that she must certainly be exposing herself to some serious danger by being with him. Following this, the mental short circuit occurs: she recalls the extremely insistent prohibitions imposed upon her by her nocturnal interlocutor in recommending that she in no case contravene his very severe prohibition not to try to see him, and she perceives only too clearly how his words intersect with what is suggested by her sisters. It is at this point that she takes the fatal step.

Prior to doing so, given what her sisters have suggested to her – in other words, what she thinks she will find – she arms herself. Which is why, despite the fact that the history of art gives us no other evidence of this, to the best of my knowledge – I would appreciate it if someone, incited by my remarks here, could provide me with proof to the contrary – Psyche is represented as armed at this significant moment. It is clearly from Apuleius' text that the Mannerist in question, Zucchi, borrowed what constitutes the originality of the scene. 269

What does this imply? At the era at which Zucchi depicted this scene, the tale of Psyche and Cupid was widely known, and for all sorts of reasons. While it is attested to in but one literary text, it is attested to in many works in the plastic and figurative arts. I have heard, for example, that the sculpture group which is at the Uffizi in Florence represents a Cupid with a Psyche, but there both have wings. You will observe that in Zucchi's canvas, while Cupid has wings, Psyche does not.

Psyche is depicted with the wings of a butterfly [when she is depicted with wings]. I possess some Alexandrine objects in which Psyche is represented in several forms, frequently endowed with butterfly wings, which are, in this case, a sign of the immortality of the soul. You are aware of the stages of metamorphosis that the butterfly undergoes: it is born at first as a caterpillar or larva, then wraps itself in a sort of tomb or sarcophagus, in a way that reminds us of mummies, and stays in there until such time as it reappears in a glorified form. The theme of the butterfly as signifying the immortality of the soul had already appeared in Antiquity, and not simply in variously peripheral religions. It was even utilized in the Christian religion to symbolize the immortality of the soul, and it still is. It is very difficult to deny that what is at stake in the story is what one might call the trials and tribulations of the soul.

Only one mythological text transmitted this tale in Antiquity, that by Apuleius. Authors variously emphasize its religious and spiritual meanings, and willingly opine that we have in Apuleius' work but a degraded, Romanesque form, which does not allow us to grasp the original import of the myth. Despite their allegations, I, on the contrary, believe that Apuleius' text is extremely rich.

What is represented here by the painter is merely the beginning of the story. At a still earlier stage, we have what one might call Psyche's happiness, but also a first trial: Psyche is considered at the outset to be as beautiful as Venus, and it is owing to a first persecution by the gods that she finds herself exposed on the peak of a rocky crag – another form of the myth of Andromeda – to a monster who was supposed to seize her. The monster turns out in fact to be Cupid, to whom Venus gave the task of delivering Psyche into the hands of he whose victim she was supposed to be. Cupid, who is slated to execute his mother's [Venus'] cruel orders, is seduced by Psyche, kidnaps her, and hides her in a deeply secluded place, in which she experiences, in short, the happiness of the gods.

The story would end there were poor Psyche not of a different nature than the divine nature, and did not prove to have the most deplorable weaknesses, among them family feeling: she spares no pains and never tires until she has obtained from Cupid, her unknown husband, permission to see her sisters again, and the entire remainder of the story stems from that. There is thus, before the moment represented in this little masterpiece, a brief earlier moment, but the whole tale unfolds afterward. I am not going to tell you the whole story, as that would get us off on a tangent.

This story is recounted, moreover, on the ceiling and walls of the charming Palazzo Farnese, having been painted by the brush of none other than Raphael himself. The scenes there are pleasant, almost too pleasant. We are no longer equal to the task of bearing such prettiness. It seems that what must have appeared as surprising beauty the first time the style sprang from Raphael's wonderful brush, has since become degraded for us. In truth, one must always keep in mind that a certain prototype or form must make, at the moment of its first appearance, an impression that is completely different from what it makes after having been, not simply reproduced thousands of times, but imitated thousands of times. In short, Raphael's paintings at Farnese sketch out for us the further development, scrupulously based on Apuleius' text, of Psyche's tribulations.

So that you will have no doubt that Psyche is not a woman, but rather the soul, suffice it to say that she appeals to Demeter, complete [as depicted in the Palazzo Farnese] with all the instruments and weapons of her mysteries, for it is clearly initiation into the Eleusinian Mysteries that is involved here. She is rebuffed by Demeter because the latter wants above all not to anger her sister-in-law, Venus. What happens is as follows: having fallen – having made at the outset a faux pas of which she is not even guilty, for Venus' jealousy derives merely from the fact that she considers Psyche as a rival – the unfortunate soul finds herself buffeted about, rebuffed by all sources of succor, even religious succor. One could thus establish a whole detailed phenomenology of the unhappy soul, compared with the consciousness qualified by the same adjective.

271

Let us make no mistake about it: couples are not the theme of this very pretty story of Psyche. The tale is not about relations between men and women – it suffices to be able to read to see what is truly hidden merely by being presented in the foreground and as overly obvious, as in [Edgar Allan Poe's] "The Purloined Letter" – it is about nothing other than the relations between the soul and desire.

It is in this respect that we can say, without forcing things, that to us the extremely detailed composition of this canvas gives – in an exemplary fashion, through the intensity of the isolated image produced here – a tangible character to what a structural analysis of the myth of Apuleius could be, an analysis that remains to be carried out.

I have said enough to you about what the structural analysis of a myth is, for you to at least know that it exists. Since Claude Lévi-Strauss analyzes a certain number of North American myths, I don't see why one would not devote oneself to the same kind of analysis concerning Apuleius' fable. We are, strangely enough, not as well-served in matters closer to us than in others, which seem to us further removed as to their sources.

We have but one version of this myth, Apuleius' version. But it does not seem impossible to work in a way that allows us to bring out a certain number of significant pairs of oppositions. Yet without Zucchi's help, we would perhaps run the risk of overlooking the truly primordial and primal nature of this moment in the tale of Psyche.

It is, nevertheless, the best-known moment: everyone knows that Cupid flees and disappears because little Psyche was too curious and, on top of that, disobedient. This is what, in our collective memory, has remained of the meaning of the myth. But something is hidden behind that and, if we are to believe what is revealed to us here by the painter's intuition, it is no other than the decisive moment that he painted.

This is certainly not the first time that such a moment appears in an ancient myth. But its emphasis, crucial character, and pivotal function had to wait many long centuries before being situated at the center of the psyche by Freud.

272

2

Having made this find, it didn't seem to me to be useless to talk with you about it, because the tiny image that will remain engraved in your minds – due to the very fact that I am spending time on it this morning – turns out to illustrate what I can designate today only as the point at which the whole instinctual dynamic converges, insofar as I have taught you to consider its register to be marked by the workings of the signifier.

This is what allows me to highlight how the castration complex must be articulated at this level. It can only be fully articulated if we consider the instinctual dynamic that is going to be structured by the mark of the signifier. At the same time, the image's value lies in showing us that there is a superimposing or superimposition, a common center, in the vertical sense, between the soul and the point of production of the castration complex with which I left you last time. We are now going to pursue this topic further.

I took up the theme of desire and demand in chronological order, but I underscored for you at every moment the divergence, splitting,* or difference between desire and demand that marks all of the initial stages of libidinal evolution. I showed you that it is determined by *Nachträglich* – retroactive – action, starting at a certain point where the paradox of desire and demand appears with minimal clatter [*éclat*], which is the genital stage – insofar as we should, it seems, be able to distinguish between desire and demand at that point at least.

Demand and desire bear the mark there of division and shattering [*éclatement*], which still poses a problem for analysts, if you read their work – a question or enigma that is more often avoided than resolved and that goes by the name of the castration complex.

Thanks to this painting, you must see that the castration complex is, in its structure and instinctual dynamic, centered in such a way that it coincides exactly with what we might call the point at which the soul is born.

273   If this myth has any meaning, it is indeed that Psyche only truly becomes Psyche – in other words, not simply someone endowed with an extraordinary initial gift which makes her the equal of Venus, or with a veiled and unknown favor which offers her infinite and unfathomable happiness, but the subject of a pathos which is, strictly speaking, that of the soul – at the moment at which the desire that fulfilled her slips away and takes flight. Psyche's adventures begin at that very moment.

Venus, as I once told you, is born every day, and as Plato's myth tells us, owing to this very fact Cupid is thus also conceived every day. But the birth of the soul is, in both the universal and the particular, for all of us and for each of us, an historic moment. It is from this moment on that the dramatic story with which we are faced unfolds in all its consequences.

One could, in the end, say that Freud went straight to this point. In closing, he stated that there is a final endpoint – this is articulated in "Analysis, Terminable and Interminable" – at which we arrive when we manage to eliminate in the subject every avenue for the resurgence or reviving of unconscious repetition, when we manage to make the latter converge with the bedrock – the term is in Freud's text – of the castration complex [*SE* XXIII, p. 252].

The castration complex is at work in men and in women – the term *Penisneid* [penis envy] is, in his text, one of the names of the castration complex. It is around this castration complex, and, so to speak, in starting anew on the basis of it, that we must put to the test once more everything that has, in a certain way, been discovered on the basis of this brick wall. Whether it is a matter of emphasizing the decisive and primordial effect of what pertains to knowledge's entreaties [*instances du savoir*], or a matter of operationalizing [*mise en fonction*] what is called the aggressiveness of primordial sadism or what has been articulated in the different possible views concerning the object – running the gamut from its decomposition [into partial objects] and its deepening, to the development of the notion of good and bad primordial objects – all of this can be resituated in an appropriate perspective only if we grasp where the divergence began. It began with this to some extent unsustainably paradoxical point: the castration complex.

The image that I am taking the time to show you today has the benefit of incarnating what I mean by speaking of the castration complex as a paradox. Indeed, up until now, in the different stages we have studied, a divergence was present that was motivated by the distinction and discordance between what constitutes the object of demand – whether it be the subject's demand at the oral stage, or the Other's demand at the anal stage – and what, in the Other, is situated in the place of desire. This is what is masked and veiled to a certain degree in Psyche's case, although it is secretly perceived by the archaic, infantile subject. Now, would it not seem that, in what one might sweepingly call the third stage, and which is commonly known as the genital stage, the conjunction of desire – insofar as it can be involved in any of the subject's demands – must find its surety or carbon copy in the Other's desire?

If there is a point at which desire presents itself as desire, it is certainly at the point at which Freud's first accentuation was precisely made to situate it for us – in other words, at the level of sexual

274

desire, revealed in its real consistency, and no longer in a contami-
nated, displaced, condensed, or metaphorical fashion. Here we are
no longer dealing with the sexualization of some other function, but
with the sexual function itself.

To help you gauge the paradox in question, I was looking for
something to point to this morning with which to exemplify the
awkwardness of analysts when it comes to the phenomenology
of the genital stage, and I stumbled upon an article by René de
Monchy devoted to the castration complex in the *International
Journal of Psychoanalysis*.

What is an analyst who takes a renewed interest in our times in
the castration complex – and there aren't many of them – led to in
order to explain it? You'll never guess. I will summarize it for you
very quickly.

There is a paradox which cannot fail to strike you, in the fact that
the revelation of the genital drive is necessarily marked by the splitting* consisting in the castration complex.

The author, who has a certain knowledge base, mentions at
the beginning of his article what are called "congenital reaction
schemes."* They consist in the fact that, in small birds which have
never had any experience of predators, it suffices to move a piece
of paper in the approximate shape of a hawk over their cage to
provoke all the fright reflexes. In short, the piece of paper serves
here as a decoy [*leurre*] or – as the author of this article expresses
himself in French even though writing in English – *attrape*.

According to him, things are exceedingly simple. The primitive
attrape in man must be sought out in the oral stage. It is the biting
reflex – correlated with the well-known sadistic fantasies that the
child may have, and which involve the sectioning of the object that
is the most precious of all, the mother's nipple – that is the origin of
what, in the later, genital stage, will be manifested (transformed into
fellatio fantasies) as the possibility of depriving the sexual partner
of his organ, of wounding or mutilating his genitalia. And this
explains, not why your daughter is mute, but why the genital stage
is marked by the possible sign of castration.

Such an explanation is telling as regards the present orientation
of analytic thought, and of the reversal that has taken place in it
that progressively places under the heading of primal drives, drives
that become more and more hypothetical the more they approach
the earliest moments of life. Which leads to the accentuation of the
importance of constitution, of that *je ne sais quoi* that is innate in
primordial aggressiveness.

Aren't *we* spelling things out correctly by dwelling instead on the
problems that our practice commonly raises for us? I have already

275

mentioned here the notion found in one of Ernest Jones' articles, in which he is stirred by a certain need to explain the castration complex. I am referring to *aphanisis*, a common Greek term that was put on the agenda in the articulation of analytic discourse by Freud, which means disappearance. According to Jones, what is at work in the castration complex is the fear aroused in the subject by the disappearance of desire.

Those of you who have been following my teaching for some time cannot, I hope, fail to recall – and those who do not remember can have a look at the excellent summaries made by Lefèvre-Pontalis – that I have already made headway on this topic in my Seminar by saying that, while this is one way of articulating the problem, there is also a singular reversal that clinical practice allows us to point to. This is why I commented at length for you on the well-known dream of Ella Sharpe's patient in my Seminar *Desire and Its Interpretation*, a dream that revolves entirely around the theme of the phallus. I will ask you to look at that summary, because I cannot repeat myself and the things said then were essential.

276

The meaning of what is at issue here is, as I indicated, the following: far from it being the case that the fear of *aphanisis* is projected, so to speak, onto the image of the castration complex, it is on the contrary the necessity or determination of the signifying mechanism that, in the castration complex, makes the subject not fear *aphanisis* at all in the majority of cases, but, rather, take refuge in it, tucking his desire away in his vest pocket. What analytic practice reveals to us is that it is more precious to hold onto desire's symbol – the phallus – than to hold onto desire itself. This is the problem with which we are presented.

I hope that you have carefully observed the flowers that are located in front of Cupid's genitals in Zucchi's painting. They are characterized by such abundance only so that one cannot see that there is nothing behind them. There is literally no room for even the smallest genitalia. What Psyche is about to cut off has already disappeared.

Moreover, if something strikes us as being juxtaposed here to the fine, beautiful human form of this woman, who is in fact divine, it is the extraordinarily composite character of the image of Cupid. His face is a child's face, but his body is Michelangelo-like in nature. It is a muscle-bound body, which has almost begun to shows signs of aging, not to say sagging. In addition to that, there are his wings.

You are all aware that the sex of angels was a subject of endless discussion. If people debated about it for so long, it was probably because no one knew very well where to stop. In any case, the Apostle tells us that whatever joys there may be in the resurrection of the body, once the celestial feast has come, there will no longer be any sexual activity, whether active or passive.

The upshot being that what is at stake, and is concentrated in this image, is clearly the center of the paradox of the castration complex. It is that the Other's desire, insofar as it is approached at the level of the genital stage, can never in fact be accepted in what I will call its rhythm, which is at the same time its dissonance [*fuyance*].

This concerns first of all the paradoxes of the child's situation – namely, that we find in him a desire which is still fragile, uncertain, premature, and anticipated. But this observation hides from us what is, in the final analysis, at stake: his psychical organization quite simply does not adapt, so to speak, insofar as it is psychical, to the reality of sexual desire, and this is true at every level. For the organ is brought in and approached only insofar as it is transformed into a signifier, and, in order to be transformed into a signifier, it is cut off.

277

Reread all that I taught you to read regarding little Hans. You will see that it is a question of nothing but this: does it have roots? Is it removable? In the end, Hans works it out – it can be unscrewed. It can be unscrewed and others can be put in its place. That is thus what is at stake.

What is shown to us here is this very elision, thanks to which it [the organ] is no longer anything but the very sign that I mentioned: the sign of absence. For what I taught you is the following – if *Phi*, the phallus as a signifier, has a place, it is precisely that of supplementing the Other at the point at which signifierness disappears – at the point at which the Other is constituted by the fact that a signifier is lacking somewhere. Hence the privileged value of this signifier, which can no doubt be written, but which can only be written in parentheses, by saying that it is the signifier of the point at which the signifying system [*le signifiant*] is lacking [S($\bar{\text{A}}$)].

This is why it can become identical to the subject himself, at the point at which we can designate him as a barred subject [$] – in other words, at the sole point at which we analysts can situate a subject as such. I say, "we analysts," insofar as we are linked to the effects that result from the coherence of the signifier when a living being makes himself into its agent and its prop. If we accept this determination, this overdetermination as we call it, the subject then no longer has any other possible efficacy than on the basis of the signifier that makes him disappear. Which is why the subject is unconscious.

If people – even non-analysts – can speak of double symbolization, it is in the sense that the nature of the symbol is such that two registers necessarily stem therefrom: the one that is linked to the symbolic chain and the one that is linked to the problem or mess that the subject was able to bring to it. For it is there that, in the final analysis, he situates himself in the most certain way.

In other words, the subject asserts that the dimension of truth is original only at the moment at which he uses the signifier to lie.

3   278

I wanted to draw your attention this morning to the relation between the phallus and the effect of the signifying system [*le signifiant*], and to the fact that the phallus as a signifier – which means as given over to an entirely different function than its organic function – is the center of all coherent apprehension of what is at work in the castration complex.

But now I would like to introduce, not in a way that is already articulated and rational, but in a colorful way, what I will discuss next time.

It is, so to speak, beautifully represented thanks to Zucchi's Mannerism. Didn't it occur to you that by placing this vase of flowers in front of the phallus as lacking – and as such raised to major signifierness – the artist managed to anticipate by three and a half centuries (and unbeknown to me, I assure you, up until a few days ago) the very image I used to articulate the dialectic of the relations between the ideal ego and the ego-ideal?

I discussed it a very long time ago, but I completely reworked it in an article that will come out soon. I tried to fit the different pieces of the relation to the object as an object of desire – as a partial object with all the necessary focusing [*accommodation*] – into a system, in an amusing physics experiment that I called the inverted vase illusion.

What I hope to get you to realize is that the problem of castration, the center of the whole economy of desire such as analysis has developed it, is closely related to another problem, which is the following. How is it that the Other – which is the locus of speech, the legitimate subject, and the one with whom we have relations of good and bad faith – can and must become something precisely analogous to what can be encountered in the most inert object: namely, *a*, the object of desire? It is this tension, difference in altitude, or fundamental drop in level that becomes the essential regulation of everything that is problematic about desire in man. This is what must be analyzed, and I think that I can articulate it for you next time quite clearly.

I ended what I taught you about Ella Sharpe's dream with the fol-   279
lowing: "This phallus" – I said, speaking of a subject caught up in the most exemplary neurotic situation, insofar as it was that of *aphani-*

sis brought on by the castration complex – "he is it and he is not it. Language allows us to perceive the interval between to be it and not to be it in a formulation into which the verb 'to be' slips: 'he is not without having it.' It is around the subjective assumption between being and having that the reality of castration is played out. And the phallus," I wrote at that time, "serves as an equivalent in the relation to the object. It is to the extent that he gives up the phallus that the subject is able to possess the plethora of objects that characterize the human world." In an analogous formulation, one might say that "a woman is without having it." Which can be experienced very painfully in the form of *Penisneid*, but which is – I am now adding this to what I said before – also a great strength. This is what Ella Sharpe's patient is not willing to perceive. He shelters the phallus as a signifier. And, I concluded, "there is undoubtedly something more neurosis-inducing than the fear of losing the phallus, which is not to want the Other to be castrated."

But today, now that we have examined the dialectic of transference in the *Symposium*, I am going to propose another formulation. If the Other's desire is essentially separated from us by the mark of the signifier, don't you now understand why Alcibiades, having perceived that the secret of desire lies in Socrates, demands in an almost impulsive way – with an impulsivity that is at the origin of all the false pathways of neurosis and perversion – to see Socrates' desire, which he knows exists since he acts on its basis, to see it in the form of a sign?

This is also why Socrates refuses. For this is but a short circuit. To see desire in the form of a sign is not, for all that, to accede to the course by which desire is taken up in a certain dependency, which is what one wishes to know.

You see here the beginning of the path that I am attempting to open up toward what the analyst's desire must be. In order for the analyst to have what the analysand lacks, he must have nescience qua nescience. He must be in the mode of having it; he too must be not without having it; he must be but one short step away from being as ignorant as his analysand.

280

In fact, he too is not without having an unconscious. He is no doubt always beyond everything the analysand knows, without being able to tell him. He can only give him a sign. Being that which represents something to someone is the definition of the sign. Having on the whole nothing else that stops him from being the subject's desire, than the very fact of having it, the analyst is doomed to false surprise. But get it into your heads that he is only effective when he gives himself over to true surprise, which is untransmittable, and of which he can give only a sign.

*

Representing something to someone is precisely what must be disrupted. For the sign that is to be given is the sign of the lack of a signifier. It is, as you know, the only sign that cannot be borne, because it is the one that induces the most unspeakable anxiety. It is nevertheless the only one that can make the analysand accede to the unconscious – to the "science without consciousness [*science sans conscience*]" concerning which you perhaps understand today, being presented with this painting, in what non-negative, but positive sense Rabelais says that it is "the demise of the soul."

April 12, 1961

XVII

THE SYMBOL Φ

Arcimboldo and persona.
The lack of a signifier and questioning.
The signifier that is always veiled.
The phallus in hysteria and obsession.

I am recommencing my difficult discourse for you, which is ever more difficult owing to its aim.

It would, nevertheless, be inappropriate to say that I am leading you into unknown territory today. If I begin to lead you into a certain territory today, it is clear that I already began doing so right from the outset.

To speak, moreover, of unknown territory as concerns our territory, which is called the unconscious, is still more inappropriate. For what makes for the difficulty of this discourse is that I can tell you nothing about it which does not take on all its importance from what I don't say about it.

The idea is not that one mustn't say everything and that in order to speak accurately we cannot say all that we could formulate. There is something in this formulation that, as we realize at every moment, immediately casts the matter into the imaginary, which is essentially what happens due to the fact that human subjects are, as such, prey to the symbol.

But let's be careful here – at the point we have reached, should we put "to the symbol" in the singular or the plural? In the singular, assuredly, insofar as the one that I introduced last time is, strictly speaking, an unnamable symbol – we will see why and in what respect – the symbol uppercase *Phi* [Φ].

It is here that I must recommence my discourse today, to show you in what respect this symbol is indispensable to us if we are to understand the impact of the castration complex on the mainspring of transference.

1

There is, in effect, a fundamental ambiguity between Φ and φ, between uppercase *Phi* as a symbol, and lowercase *phi*.

Lowercase *phi* designates the imaginary phallus insofar as it is concretely involved in the psychical economy at the level of the castration complex where we first truly encountered it, where the neurotic experiences it in a way that represents his particular mode of operating and maneuvering, with the radical difficulty that I am trying to articulate for you through the use I make of the symbol capital *Phi*.

Last time, and already many times before that, I designated this symbol, Φ, briefly, I mean in a quick and abbreviated manner, as a symbol [that arises or responds] in the place where the lack of a signifier occurs.

I once again unveiled, right at the beginning of the last class, the image that served us last time as a prop by which to introduce the paradoxes and antinomies related to various slippages, which are so subtle and difficult to recall in their various stages, and which must nevertheless be maintained if we wish to understand what is involved in the castration complex. They are, namely, the displacements, absences, levels, and substitutions in which the phallus intervenes, in its multiple and virtually ubiquitous formulations. In analytic work, it springs up constantly – at the very least in theoretical writings, that is undeniable – being reinvoked in the most various forms, even in studies of infancy concerning the very first pulsations of the soul. You see it identified, for example, with the force of the earliest aggressiveness, insofar as the phallus is the worst object [that is] eventually encountered in the mother's breast, and as it is also the most noxious [anal] object. Why this ubiquity?

I'm not the one who is suggesting it, for it is manifest in every attempt to formulate analytic technique, whether at an old, new, or revamped level. So let us try to introduce some order into things here, and see why I must emphasize this ambiguity or polarity, as it were. The polarity concerning the function of the phallus as a signifier involves two extremes: the symbolic and the imaginary.

I said "signifier," insofar as it is used as such. But when I presented it earlier, I called it a "symbol," and it is indeed, perhaps, the only signifier that, in our register, absolutely deserves to be called a symbol.

I thus unveiled anew for you this image of Zucchi's canvas, which is not a simple reproduction of the original from which I began as if from an exemplary image, laden in its composition with all the riches that a certain painterly art can produce, and whose Mannerist mainspring I examined. I'm going to quickly pass around the image again, if only for those who were not able to see it last time. I would simply like, as a complement, to clearly stress, for those who were perhaps unable to grasp it precisely, what I intend to emphasize here concerning the importance of what I will call the Mannerist application. The word "application" must be used both literally and figuratively.

You see the bouquet of flowers in the foreground. Its presence is designed to cover over what must be covered over, which, as I told you, is less Cupid's threatened phallus – Cupid who is caught by surprise and discovered here owing to Psyche's question, "Who is this guy?" – than the precise point of an absent presence, an absence rendered present. The history of that era's painting technique requires us to draw a parallel here – not via my path, but via that of [art] critics who begin with premises that are altogether different from those that could guide me here.

Indeed, we have a few indications that the flowers were probably not painted by Jacopo, but by a brother or a cousin, Francesco, who, due to his technical prowess, was asked to come create this brilliant flourish – the flowers in their vase – in the suitable spot. Owing precisely to this probable collaborator, critics have emphasized the parallel between the technique employed here and that employed by someone I hope a certain number of you know, who was brought, several months ago, to the attention of those of you who stay somewhat abreast of various revivals in interest in phases of the history of art that are sometimes overlooked, veiled, or forgotten – namely, Giuseppe Arcimboldo.

Arcimboldo, who worked in part at the court of the infamous Rudolph II, King of Bohemia – who left behind other traces in the tradition of rare objects – is known for a singular technique which sent out its most recent shoot in the work of my old friend Salvador Dalí in what he called paranoiac drawing. Having, for example, to represent the face of Rudolph II's librarian, Arcimboldo did so using an ingenious construction made of the primary tools of the librarian, namely, books, arranged on the canvas in such a way that the image of a face is much more than suggested – it truly forces itself upon the viewer. Similarly, the symbolic theme of a season, incarnated in the guise of a human face, was materialized by the fruits in season then, the assembling of which was carried out in such a way that a face in the form created is also forcibly suggested to the viewer.

In short, this Mannerist procedure consists in creating the essence of a human image through the coalescence, combination, or accumulation of a pile of objects, the sum total of which is given the task of representing what is thus manifested both as substance and illusion. At the same time that the appearance of a human image is sustained, something is suggested that can be imagined in the ungrouping of the objects. These objects, which in some sense serve as a mask, simultaneously demonstrate the problematic [nature] of this very mask.

This is, in short, what we are dealing with every time the highly essential function of the persona comes into play, which is always in the foreground in the economy of human presence. For if there is a need for a persona, it is because, behind it perhaps, all form slips away and vanishes.

Assuredly, a persona results from a complex grouping [of objects]. Here indeed lies the illusion [*leurre*] and the fragility of its subsistence. Behind it, we know nothing of what can be sustained, for it is a twofold appearance that is suggested to us, a redoubling of appearance that leaves unanswered the question of what there is there in the end.

It is clearly in this register that we see, in the composition of this canvas, the way in which the question of what is at stake in what must concern us here – namely, Psyche's act – is sustained.

Psyche, who is fulfilled, wonders whom she is dealing with, and it is this precise special moment that captured the artist's attention, perhaps well beyond anything he himself could have put into words. He did write a discourse on the gods of Antiquity – I took the trouble to look at it, without having any great illusions about it – and, in effect, there is not much to be gleaned from it. But his painting speaks loudly enough for itself.

285

In this image, the artist has grasped what last time I called the moment of the appearance or birth of Psyche – the sort of exchange of powers whose effect is that she becomes embodied. What follows is a whole string of misfortunes that befall her before she comes full circle, and finds anew what, at that instant, will disappear the instant thereafter for her, what she wanted to unveil and grasp: the face of desire.

2

What justifies my introducing the symbol capital Φ, since I designate it as what arises in the place of the missing signifier [*signifiant manquant*]? What does it mean for a signifier to be missing?

How many times have I told you that once the battery of signifiers is given – beyond a certain minimum which remains to be determined, but at the very least four should be able to suffice for all significations, as Jakobson teaches us – nothing is missing. There is no language, however primitive it may be, in which everything cannot in the end be expressed, with the exception that – as the Vaudois proverb has it, "Everything is possible for man; what he cannot do he leaves aside" – what cannot be expressed in that language is, quite simply, neither felt nor subjectified.

For it to be subjectified would be for it to take up a position in a subject as valid for another subject – in other words, to shift to the most radical point where the very idea of communication is possible. Any signifying battery can tell you that what that battery cannot say signifies nothing in the locus of the Other. Now, everything that is signifying to us always occurs in the locus of the Other.

In order for something to signify, it must be translatable in the locus of the Other. Let us assume there is a language that does not have such and such a figure of speech – then it simply does not express it. Yet it signifies it nevertheless, for example, through the use of "shall" or "have." This is in fact what happens: I pointed out to you how, in French and English, the future tense is expressed. In *je chanterai*, it is perfectly well attested that it is originally the verb "to have" [*avoir*] which is declined [*j'ai*]. "I shall sing" also indirectly expresses the future tense that English does not have.

There is no such thing as a missing signifier [*Il n'y a pas de signifiant qui manque*]. At what moment can a lack of a signifier possibly begin to appear? In the dimension that is subjective and that is called questioning.

I brought out, on an earlier occasion, the fundamental character of the appearance in the child of questioning as such. It is an already well-known fact, noted by the most ordinary observation. It is a particularly embarrassing moment [for adults] because of the nature of the child's questions. As soon as he knows how to work with and get around with the signifier, he enters a dimension that leads him to ask his parents the most inopportune questions which, as everyone knows, give rise to the greatest confusion in his parents and to answers by them that are almost necessarily impotent.

"What is running?" "What does 'stamping your foot' mean?" "What is an imbecile?" What makes us so unable to satisfactorily answer such questions? Something obliges us to answer in a way that is so especially inept, as if we did not know that to say, "Running means walking very quickly," is truly to botch it up; that to say, "'Stamping your foot' means that you're angry" is truly to proffer an absurdity; and I won't go into the definition we might provide of an imbecile. What is involved in this moment of questioning, if not that the subject distances himself from his use of the signifier itself, and is unable to grasp what it means for there to be words,

286

what it means to speak, and what it means to designate something so close to him with that enigmatic something known as a word or a phoneme?

The inability experienced at that moment by the child is formulated in questions that attack the signifier as such, at a moment at which the signifier's action is already indelibly etched into everything. Everything that later presents itself as a question in the aftermath of his pseudo-philosophical meditation, can, in the final analysis, but fall short. By the time the subject arrives at the question "What am I?" he will be still less far along – except, of course, if he undergoes an analysis. But if he does not – and it has not been within his power to do so for very long – by calling himself into question in the form "What am I?" he veils from himself that, to ask himself what he is, is to go beyond the stage of doubt concerning whether he is, for merely by formulating his question in this way, he immediately slips into metaphor – he simply does not realize it. The least we analysts can do is remember this ourselves in order to spare him from once again making this age-old error, which threatens his innocence in every form, and to stop him from answering the question, for example – even with our consent – by concluding "I am a child."

287

This is, of course, the new answer given to him by the updated form of indoctrination supplied by psychologizing suppression. And along with that, in the same package, it sells him, without him realizing it, the myth of the adult, who is supposedly no longer a child – spawning once again the kind of ethics that props up a supposed reality in which he, in fact, allows himself to be led around by the nose by all sorts of social claptrap. We didn't have to wait for analysis or Freud in order for the formulation "I am a child" to be introduced as a corset designed to straighten up what finds itself in a somewhat skewed position for whatever reason.

People go so far as to say that behind every artist is a child and that the artist represents the child's rights to people who are considered to be serious, who are not children. As I told you last year in my classes on *The Ethics of Psychoanalysis*, this conception dates back to the beginning of the Romantic period, starting more or less at the time of Coleridge in England, to situate it in a tradition, and I don't see why we would assume the task of taking up the torch.

I would like to get you to see, in this context, what I alluded to during our recent conference in the provinces.

The lower level of the Graph of Desire, with the two intersections of each of its two arrows, is designed to draw attention to the fact that simultaneity is not synchrony. Let us assume that the two tensors or vectors in question, that of intention and that of the signifying chain, unfold simultaneously. You see that what occurs here by way of an inchoation [i.e., origin or beginning] in this succession – the succession, for example, of the different phonemic elements of the signifier – unfolds substantially before encountering the line on which what is called into being (namely, the intention to signify, we might even say need, as it were) assumes its place, a place that is hidden there. Similarly, this intersecting simultaneously takes place a second time. If *Nachträglich* indeed signifies something, it is the fact that meaning crystallizes out at the very instant at which a sentence ends. A choice has no doubt already been made along the way, but meaning is only grasped once the signifiers successively piled up have, each in its turn, assumed their places, and unfolded in an inverted form – "I am a child" appearing on the signifying line in the order in which its elements are articulated.

288

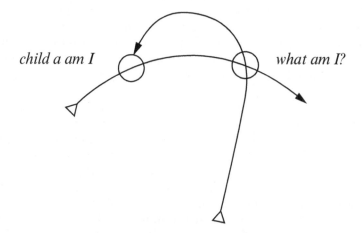

child a am I   *what am I?*

What happens when meaning draws to a close [*s'achève*]? What happens is something that is always metaphorical in any and every attribution. I am nothing other than me who is speaking, and currently I am a child. By saying it, by asserting it, a hold or qualification of meaning is realized, thanks to which I conceptualize myself as having a certain relationship to objects that are infantile objects. I make myself into something other than what I could in any way think of myself as at first. I become incarnate, I crystallize, I make myself into an ideal ego, and I do so very directly in the process of this simple signifying inchoation, in the fact of having produced signs that can refer to the very moment of my speaking. The point of departure is in the "I," and the endpoint is in the "child" ["I am a child"].

What results here – whether I see it or not – is the enigma of questioning itself. This is what must next be taken up anew at the level of capital A. The result of what I am appears in the form in which it remains a question. This result is for me the point aimed at or the correlative point at which I ground myself as an ego-ideal. It is on the basis of this point that the question has importance to me. It is here that the question summons me in the ethical dimension, and supplies the very form that Freud conjugates with the superego.

But what is the status of this noun [*nom*] which directly links up, as far as I know, with my signifying inchoation, and which qualifies the subject in an only partly legitimate way as a child? This answer is hurried and premature. With it, I basically elide the whole central operation that has occurred. What makes me rush headlong toward concluding I am a child is avoidance of the true answer, which must begin much earlier than any endpoint [*terme*] of the sentence. The answer to "What am I?" is nothing other that is articulable – in the same sense in which I told you that no demand can be borne – there is no other answer to "What am I?" at the level of the Other than "Let yourself be." And any hurrying in giving this answer, whatever it may be at the level of dignity, child or adult, is but something whereby I flee the meaning of this "Let yourself be."

What this adventure means, at the degraded point where we grasp it, is that what is at stake in every question formulated is not situated at the level of "What am I?" but at that of the Other, in the form that analytic practice allows us to unveil – namely, "What do you want?" What is involved at this precise point is to figure out what we desire by raising the question. This is how the question must be understood. It is here that the lack of a signifier at stake in the phallus as Φ intervenes.

As we know, psychoanalysis has found that what the subject is faced with is the object of fantasy insofar as it presents itself as alone able to determine a special point in what must be called, alongside the pleasure principle, an economy regulated by the level of jouissance. Analysis also teaches us that by shifting the question to the level of "What does he want?" – of "What does the old coconut want?" – we encounter a world of hallucinated signs, and analysis represents reality testing to us as a way of sampling what? – the reality of the signs that arise in us in a necessary order, which is precisely what constitutes the dominance of the pleasure principle in the unconscious.

What is thus at stake in reality testing, let us observe, is assuredly to verify a real presence, but it is a presence of signs – as Freud emphatically stressed. The goal of reality testing is not to verify whether our representations correspond to something real – we have known for a long time that we don't succeed any better at this than philosophers do – but to verify that our representations are truly

289

represented, in the sense of *Vorstellungsrepräsentanz*. The point is to ensure that the signs are there, but qua signs – since they are signs – of a relation to something else. This is what Freud means when he says the unconscious gravitates around a lost object that can only ever be refound – in other words, never truly refound.

290 The object can never be anything but signified, due to the very fact that the pleasure principle is a chain. The true, authentic object at stake when we speak of objects is in no way grasped, transmittable, or exchangeable. It is at the horizon of that around which our fantasies gravitate. And it is nevertheless with this that we must create objects that are exchangeable.

The problem is very far from working itself out. I sufficiently stressed last year what is at stake in utilitarian ethics. It plays a fundamental role in the recognition of objects constituted in what one might call the market for objects. These are objects that can be of use to everyone, and in this sense so-called utilitarian ethics is more than founded – there is no other. And it is precisely because there is no other that the difficulties that it supposedly entails are in fact perfectly well resolved.

Utilitarians are quite right when they say that whenever we are dealing with something that can be exchanged with our fellow men, the rule of this exchange is utility – not ours, but the possibility of use, utility for all and for the greatest number. This is clearly what creates the gap between the constitution of the extraordinary object that arises in fantasy and every kind of object in the so-called social world – that is, the world of conformity.

Indeed, the world of conformity is already coherent with a universal organization of discourse. There is no utilitarianism without a theory of fictions, and to claim that we can resort to a natural object, that we can even reduce the distances by which the objects of common consent are sustained, is to introduce a confusion or an additional myth into the problematic of reality. On the contrary, the object involved in the analytic relation to the object must be mapped at the most radical point at which the question of the subject's relation to the signifier is raised.

What is the subject's relation to the signifier? We deal, at the level of the unconscious chain, solely with signs. It is a chain of signs. Consequently, there is no end to each sign's deferral to the one that follows it. For the essence of communication with signs is to make a sign of that very other whom I address in order to incite him to aim in the same way as me at the object to which a certain sign refers.

291 The imposition of the signifier on the subject freezes him in the position characteristic of the signifier. The point is to find the guarantor of the chain that, transferring meaning from sign to sign,

must stop somewhere – to find what gives us the sign that we have a right to operate with signs.

It is here that the privilege of Φ among all signifiers arises. Perhaps it will seem overly simple, almost childish, to you if I emphasize what is at stake in this particular signifier.

This signifier is always hidden and veiled – to the extent, good gracious, that one is astonished, that one takes it to be a peculiar and almost exorbitant enterprise, to see its form in some obscure representation or artwork. It is more than rare, though of course it happens, to see it brought into a hieroglyphic chain or into a pre-historic rupestrian painting. We cannot say that it plays no role in human imagination, even prior to analytic exploration, and yet it is, of all our fabricated, signifying representations, the one most often elided or eluded. What does that imply?

Of all possible signs, isn't it the one that brings together in itself the sign and means of action along with the very presence of desire as such? If we allow the phallus to come to light in its real presence, isn't that apt to put a stop to the deferral that takes place in the chain of signs and, furthermore, to push the signs back into some kind of a shadow of nothingness? There is no surer sign of desire, on the condition that there is no longer anything but desire.

An either/or relationship becomes established between this signifier of desire and the entire signifying chain. Psyche was very happy in a relationship with what was not in any way a signifier, but the reality of her love for Cupid. But there you have it – she was Psyche and she wanted to know. She asked herself the question, because language already exists, and one does not spend one's life simply making love, but also chatting with one's sisters. Chatting with her sisters, she wanted to possess her happiness, which is not as simple as all that. Once one has entered into the order of language, to possess one's happiness is to be able to show it, to account for it, arrange its flowers – it is to be as good as her sisters by showing that she has something that is better than what they have, and not simply that she has something different. This is why Psyche showed up in the middle of the night with her lamp, and also with her little chopper.

There was absolutely nothing for her to chop, as I told you, because the deed had already been done. There was nothing for her to cut, although she would have done well to cut the lights at the earliest possible occasion. She saw nothing but a great blinding light, followed, much to her dismay, by a prompt return to the shadows, concerning which she would have done better to take the initiative before her object was definitively lost. Cupid was wounded by this, and for a long time thereafter. He was only refound by Psyche after a long series of trials that she was made to undergo.

292

In the painting, Psyche is the one who is illuminated, and – as I have been teaching you for a long time concerning the slender form of femininity, at the border between puberty and prepubescence – she is the phallic image to us. Because of this, we realize that it is neither the woman nor the man who, in the final analysis, is the medium of the castrating action; it is this [phallic] image itself insofar as it is reflected – reflected onto the narcissistic form of the body.

The unnamed relationship – unnamed because it is unnamable, because it is unspeakable – between the subject and the pure signifier of desire is projected onto the localizable, precise organ, which can be situated somewhere in the whole of the bodily edifice. Hence the specifically imaginary conflict that involves seeing oneself as deprived or not deprived of this appendix.

It is around this imaginary point that the symptomatic effects of the castration complex develop.

3

I can only begin here to analyze the symptomatic effects of the castration complex. But I would like to remind you, by way of a summary, of what I have already said on this subject in a much more developed way when I spoke about something I have very often discussed – in other words, the neuroses.

What does the hysteric do? What, in the final analysis, does Dora do?

I have taught you to follow the pathways and detours of the labyrinth of complex identifications by which Dora finds herself confronted with something – with what? Freud himself stumbles and loses his way here. You know that he is mistaken concerning the object of her desire, precisely because he seeks to situate Dora as an hysteric, first and foremost, with regard to her choice of object, an object that is no doubt little *a*.

It is quite true that, in a certain sense, Mr. K. is her little object *a*, and that, in fact, this is her fantasy, inasmuch as fantasy is what props up desire. But Dora would not be an hysteric were she content with this fantasy. She aims at something else, at something better, at A. She aims at the absolute Other.

I have been explaining to you for a long time that, for Dora, Mrs. K. incarnates the question, "What is a woman?" And because of this, at the level of fantasy, we do not see the relation of the fading* of the subject with respect to little *a*, but, as she is an hysteric, something else.

That something else is an uppercase A as such, in which she believes, unlike a paranoiac. "What am I?" has a meaning for her, which is not the meaning mentioned earlier, deriving from ethical or philosophical blunders, but a full and absolute meaning. And she cannot but encounter here, without knowing it, the sign Φ which corresponds to it, which is perfectly hermetic [*clos*] and always veiled. This is why she resorts to all kinds of substitutes, the closest forms, let it be noted, she can find for this sign, Φ. If you follow Dora's operations, or those of any other hysteric, you will see that what is always involved is an intricate game by which she can, so to speak, complicate the situation by slipping φ, the lowercase *phi* designating the imaginary phallus, where it is needed.

Her father is impotent with Mrs. K? Well, what difference does it make – she will serve as the copula herself. She will pay the price personally. She is the one who will sustain their relationship. And since that is still not enough, she will bring into play the image – which takes her place, as I showed you a long time ago [*Écrits*, pp. 221–2] and demonstrated – of Mr. K. She casts him into the abyss, into the darkest shadows, at the moment at which the beast says to her the only thing that he should not have said, "My wife means nothing to me." Namely, she doesn't excite me. "But if she doesn't get you hard, what good are you to me?"

For the only thing that matters to Dora, or to any other hysteric, is to be the procurer of this sign in an imaginary form. The hysteric's devotion, her passion to identify with all kinds of sentimental dramas, to be there, to sustain in the wings everything that can happen which is exciting and which is nevertheless none of her business – this is the mainspring or resource around which all of her behavior revolves and proliferates.

She always exchanges her desire for this sign – we needn't look elsewhere for the reason for her so-called mythomania. There is one thing that she prefers to her own desire – she prefers to let her own desire go unsatisfied and have the Other hold the key to her mystery.

This is the only thing that is of importance to her, which is why, identifying with love's drama, she endeavors to reanimate, reinsure, recomplete anew, or repair that Other. We clearly must distrust this, with the whole of the reparative ideology of our initiative as therapists, of our analytic vocation. But it is not here that my warning can take on the most importance, for the path that reveals itself to us most easily is certainly not that of the hysteric.

There is another path, that of the obsessive, which is, as you all know, far more intelligent in its way of operating.

The formula for the hysteric's fantasy can be written as follows:

294

$$\frac{a}{(-\varphi)} \; \Diamond \, A$$

Here we have a, the substitutional or metaphorical object, over something that is hidden – namely, minus *phi*, one's own imaginary castration – in one's relation to the Other. Today I will merely introduce the formula of the obsessive's fantasy, which is different. But before writing it on the board, I must provide a certain number of hints and indications that will set you on the right course.

We are aware of the difficulty encountered in handling the symbol Φ in its unveiled form. As I told you earlier, what is unbearable about it is that it is not simply a sign and a signifier but the presence of desire. It is the real presence [of desire].

I am asking you to grab hold of the thread that I am extending to you and that, given the time left us, I can only offer here as an indication to be taken up next time. At the root of fantasies and symptoms, of the points of emergence where we see the [hysteric] labyrinth let its mask slip off in some sense, we encounter something that I will call an insult to real presence. The obsessive, too, deals with the mystery of the phallic signifier, Φ, and it is also of importance to him to make it manageable.

An author about whom I shall have to speak next time has broached – in a way which is certainly instructive and fruitful to us if we know how to critique it – the function of the phallus in obsessive neurosis. He took up the subject for the first time in a report on a case of obsessive neurosis in a woman, in which he stressed certain sacrilegious fantasies – in which the figure of Christ, and even Christ's phallus, were trampled underfoot – from which the patient derived a noticeable and avowed erotic aura. The author then immediately dove into the topic of aggressiveness and penis envy, in spite of the patient's protests.

Don't a thousand other facts that I could enumerate show us that it is appropriate for us to dwell far more on the phenomenology of this fantasizing that is all too quickly termed "sacrilegious"? We might recall here the fantasy of the Rat Man imagining that, in the middle of the night, his dead father is resuscitated and comes knocking at the door, the patient showing himself to his father as the patient is masturbating [*SE* X, pp. 204–5]. This too is an insult to real presence.

What we call aggressiveness always presents itself in obsessive neurosis as aggression toward the form of the Other's appearance that, on another occasion, I called "phallophany," the Other insofar as he can present himself as the phallus. To strike the phallus in the

Other, to strike it at the imaginary level, in order to heal symbolic castration is the pathway chosen by the obsessive neurotic to try to abolish the difficulty that I designate as "the parasitic nature of the signifier in the subject," and to try to restore primacy to desire, at the cost of degrading the Other, which makes the Other essentially a function of the phallus' imaginary elision.

At the precise point in the Other where he is in a state of doubt, suspension, loss, ambivalence, or fundamental ambiguity, the obsessive's relation to the object – to an object that is always metonymic, because for him the object is essentially interchangeable – is essentially governed by something that is related to castration, which takes on a directly aggressive form here: absence, depreciation, rejection, or refusal of the sign of the Other's desire. Not abolition or destruction of the Other's desire, but a rejection of its signs. This is what determines the exceedingly odd impossibility that the obsessive's own desire ever manifest itself.

296

Assuredly, to point out to him – insistently, moreover, as did the analyst to whom I was referring earlier – his relation to the imaginary phallus in order, so to speak, to familiarize him with its impasse – well, we cannot say that the solution to the obsessive's difficulties does not lie along this path. But how can we fail to note in passing that, after a certain stage of the working through* of imaginary castration, the subject was in no way relieved of his obsessions, but simply of the guilt attached to them?

What else is new! Such a therapeutic approach is thereby seen to be flawed. Where does it bring us? To the Φ function of the phallus as a signifier, as a signifier in the transference itself.

How does the analyst situate himself in relation to this signifier? If the question is essential here it is because it is already illustrated for us by the forms and impasses demonstrated to us by a certain therapeutic approach that is oriented as we just saw.

This is what I will try to take up for you next time.

April 19, 1961

XVIII

REAL PRESENCE

The contemporary farce.
The obsessive's phallicism.
The signifier that is excluded from the signifying system.
Phobia and perversion.

On Saturday and Sunday I happened to open, for the first time, notes taken at different points of my Seminar over the last few years, to see whether the mile markers I gave you under the heading *The Relation to the Object*, and then *Desire and Its Interpretation*, converge without too much of a gap with what I am trying to articulate for you this year under the heading of *Transference*.

I realized, in effect, that in everything I discussed with you, and which is there, so it seems, in one of our Society's filing cabinets, there is a lot that you will be able to find anew at a time when people have the leisure to bring it out – at a point at which you will say to yourselves that, in 1961, someone was teaching you something.

It will not be said that I never allude to current events in my teaching – there would be something excessive about saying so. To corroborate this, I will thus read to you a little bit of what I also came across on Sunday, in the work of Jonathan Swift. I had far too little time to speak with you about him when I took up the symbolic function of the phallus, though the question is so ubiquitous in his work that one could say that, if we take his work as a whole, it is articulated in it.

Jonathan Swift and Lewis Carroll are two authors whom, while I don't have the time to make a regular commentary upon them, you would do well to consult in order to find a great deal of material that is very closely related, as closely related as possible, as closely as is possible in literary works, to the topic I am currently broaching the most nearly.

In *Gulliver's Travels*, which I was perusing in a charming little edition dating back to the middle of the nineteenth century, illustrated by Granville, I found a passage in the third part, "A Voyage to Laputa," which is characterized by the fact that it is not limited to the trip to Laputa.

It is thus to Laputa, a formidable anticipation of space stations, that Gulliver heads, crossing several kingdoms about which he shares with us a number of significant viewpoints that have lost none of their savor. In particular, he has a discussion with an academic, and tells him that in the kingdom of Tribnia, known as Langden by its natives, where he had resided,

> The Bulk of the People consisted wholly of Discoverers, Witnesses, Informers, Accusers, Prosecutors, Evidences, Swearers; together with their several subservient and subaltern Instruments; all under the Colours, the Conduct, and pay of Ministers, and their deputies.

But let us not dwell on that theme.

Gulliver explains to us how the informers operate [regarding their enemies].

> Then, effectual Care is taken to secure all their Letters and other Papers, and put the Owners in Chains. These Papers are delivered to a Set of Artists, very dextrous in finding out the mysterious Meanings of Words, Syllables and Letters.

This is where Swift really gets going. And as you will see, it's quite pretty concerning the heart of the matter [*substantifique moëlle*].

> For Instance, they can decypher a Close-stool to signify a Privy-Council; a Flock of Geese, a Senate; a lame Dog, an Invader; the Plague, a standing Army; a Buzzard, a Minister; the Gout, a High Priest; a Gibbet, a Secretary of State; a Chamber pot, a Committee of Grandees; a Sieve, a Court Lady; a Broom, a Revolution; a Mouse-trap, an Employment; a bottomless Pit, the Treasury; a Sink, a C---t; a Cap and Bells, a Favourite; a broken Reed, a Court of Justice; an empty Tun, a General; a running Sore, the Administration.
>
> When this Method fails, they have two others more effectual; which the Learned among them call Acrosticks and Anagrams. First, they can decypher all initial Letters into political Meanings. Thus, N, shall signify a Plot; B, a Regiment of Horse; L, a Fleet at Sea. Or, secondly, by transposing the Letters of the Alphabet,

in any suspected Paper, they can lay open the deepest Designs of a discontented Party. So for Example, if I should say in a Letter to a Friend, Our Brother Tom has just got the Piles; a Man of Skill in this Art would discover how the same Letters which compose that Sentence, may be analysed into the following words: Resist, ----- a Plot is brought home ----- The Tour.

I find it not unfitting to reconstruct, with the help of this text which is not so very old, the paradoxical ground of contemporary events, this paradoxical ground being so blatant in so many respects. For in truth, having been untimely awakened last night by someone who told me something that more or less all of you have heard – incorrect news, as it turns out – my sleep was momentarily troubled as I wondered whether I had failed to recognize the tragic dimension of recent events. This posed a problem for me after what I explained to you last year about tragedy, for nowhere could I see the appearance of what I then called the "reflection of beauty."

This effectively stopped me from falling back asleep for a while. I later fell asleep, leaving the question in abeyance. Upon waking this morning, the question had lost a bit of its hold [*prégnance*] over me. It seemed to me that we are still at the stage of farce. And the problem that I was raising suddenly vanished.

Having said that, we are going to take things up where we left them last time.

1

Last time, I put up on the board the following formula for the obsessive's fantasy:

$$\text{\AA} \Diamond \varphi \, (a, a', a'', a''', \ldots)$$

Thus presented in algebraic form, it is clear that it can but be opaque to those who were not present at my earlier discussions. So I will try, in speaking about it, to fill in the missing dimensions.

You know that this formula is juxtaposed to that of the hysteric, which I wrote for you last time as follows: *a* over minus *phi*, in relation to the Other with a capital *O* [uppercase A]. This relation can be read in several ways. "Desire for A" is one way of putting it.

$$\frac{a}{(-\varphi)} \Diamond A$$

300

It is thus important that I indicate the respective functions attributed in my symbolization to uppercase *Phi* and lowercase *phi* – that is, to Φ and φ.

I'll ask you to try not to run headlong toward the analogies to which it is always easy and tempting to yield, saying to yourselves, for example, that Φ is the symbolic phallus and φ the imaginary phallus. This is perhaps true in a certain sense, but if you content yourselves with it you risk overlooking the interest of these symbolizations, symbolizations that, believe me, I do not take pleasure in uselessly multiplying in order to provide superficial analogies and intellectual aids. This is not the goal of a teaching, strictly speaking.

The point is to see what I intend these two symbols to represent, and all sorts of indications allow you to already foresee their importance and appreciate their usefulness.

For example, the year began with a very interesting lecture by my friend Georges Favez who, speaking to you about what the analyst is, and about his function for the analysand, concluded that, in the final analysis, the analyst takes on a fetishistic function for the patient. This was the formulation – around which he had grouped all sorts of converging facts in a certain way – with which his lecture ended. This is clearly a highly subjective view. Certainly, it does not leave him completely isolated, for this formulation was prepared by all sorts of things found in various articles on transference, but, nevertheless, one cannot deny that it takes a somewhat astonishing and paradoxical form. I told him that the things that I was going to articulate this year would not fail to respond in some way to the question raised by his talk.

Let us turn now to an author who has tried to articulate the unusual function of transference in obsessive neurosis. He has bequeathed us a body of work, which is now finished, which began with a discussion of the therapeutic impact of the recognition of penis envy in obsessive neurosis among women, and arrived at a generalized theory of the function of the distance from the object in the handling of the transference, especially elaborated on the basis of his experience conducting analyses with obsessive neurotics. The main, active, and efficient mainspring of a subject's increased possession of the meaning of his symptom, especially when he is obsessive, is, according to this author, the imaginary introjection of the phallus – specifically insofar as it is incarnated in the imaginary fantasy of the analyst's phallus.

I have already sketched out for you my position regarding and critique of the work of this author, Maurice Bouvet, especially as concerns technique. Having more closely broached the topic of transference, we shall now be able to hone this critique still further. This requires that we enter into a precise articulation of what the function of the phallus is, particularly in the transference.

I will try to articulate this function with the help of the terms that are symbolized here, Φ and φ. I fully realize that we never proceed by deduction, from high to low, so to speak, when we develop analytic theory. Nothing begins more clearly from the particular than analytic work. This is why we can still find something worthwhile in an articulation like that of the author to whom I am referring. This is also why his theory of the function of the phallic image in transference begins from an altogether localized experience, which can, in certain respects, limit its scope, but is also precisely what gives it its importance.

It is because Bouvet based himself, in an acute and accentuated way, on work with obsessives, that we must consider and debate what he concluded. We will also begin today with obsessives, which is why, at the beginning of class, I put up on the board the formula by which I am trying to articulate their fantasy.

I have already said a great deal to you about obsessives, and I don't intend to repeat it all here. The idea is not simply to repeat what is fundamentally substitutional, and perpetually eluded, in a sort of sleight of hand that characterizes the way in which the obsessive proceeds in his way of situating himself in relation to the Other, and more exactly, of never being at the place at which he seems to designate himself at any particular moment.

302   The formulation of the second term of the obsessive's fantasy [the part to the right of the lozenge] alludes precisely to the fact that objects are for him, as objects of desire, situated as a function [*mis en function*] of certain erotic equivalences – something we are used to indicating by speaking of the eroticization of his world, and especially of his mental world. This "situating as a function of" [*mise en function*] can be noted by φ. It suffices in effect to reread an analytic case study, assuming it is well done, in order to perceive that φ is precisely what underlies the equivalence instituted between objects at the erotic level. This φ is, in some sense, the unit of measurement by which the subject accommodates the function of little a – namely, the function of the objects of his desire.

In order to illustrate it, I need but point to the first case study of obsessive neurosis. But you will also find it in all the others, assuming they are worthwhile case studies.

Why does Freud call him *Rattenmann*, the Rat Man or "man with the rats," "rats" being in the plural, whereas in his fantasy – in which Freud broaches for the first time a type of inner view of the structure of his desire in the "horror" seen on his face of "a jouissance of which he himself was unaware" [*SE* X, pp. 166–7] – there are not *several* rats, but only one, the one that figures in the well-known Turkish torture that I will have to come back to later? If Freud talks about the "man with the rats" with "rats" in the plural, it is clearly because the rat follows its path in a multiform manner in the whole economy of the peculiar exchanges, substitutions, and permanent metonymy of which the obsessive's symptomatology is the living example.

His formula concerning the payment of fees in analysis, "So many rats, so many florins" [*SE* X, p. 212], is but a specific illustration of the permanent equation of all the objects that are taken up into what is a sort of market – the metabolism of objects in symptoms. In a more or less latent fashion, it is part and parcel of a kind of common unit or gold standard. The rat symbolizes or occupies the place of what I call φ, insofar as it is a certain reduced form of Φ, even a degraded form of this signifier. We shall see what allows me to say so.

What does Φ in fact represent? The function of the phallus in its generality, for all subjects who speak. And the point is to perceive its status in the unconscious on the basis of the point that is given to us in the symptomatology of obsessive neurosis, where this function emerges in forms that I refer to as degraded.

303

It emerges, you should observe, at the level of consciousness. This is what analytic work shows us very clearly in the structure of obsessive neurotics. Here the situating as a phallic function [*mise en fonction phallique*] is not repressed, in other words, profoundly hidden, as it is in the case of hysterics. The φ that is there in the position of situating all objects as a function of it, in the same position as the lowercase *f* of a mathematical formula, is perceptible and avowed in the symptom – it is conscious and utterly and completely visible. "Conscious," *conscius*, originally designates the possibility of the subject's complicity with himself, and thus also of a complicity with the Other who observes him. The observer has almost no problem being his accomplice. The sign of the phallic function emerges from every direction at the level of the articulation of symptoms.

It is in this context that the question can be raised of what Freud is trying, not without difficulty, to illustrate for us when he articulates the function of *Verneinung*. How can it be that things are both so obviously spoken and yet misrecognized? Were the subject but what is made of him by a certain psychologism, which continues to hold sway even at the very heart of our analytic societies, were the subject nothing other than the fact of seeing the other see you, how could one say that the function of the phallus is positioned in such a way as to be recognized by the obsessive? For this function is absolutely blatant. And nevertheless, one might say that even in this blatant form, it shares in what we call repression. However avowed it may be, it is not avowed by the subject without the analyst's help. Without the help of the Freudian register, it is neither recognized nor even recognizable. It is here that we put our finger on the fact that to be a subject is something other than to be a gaze faced with another gaze, according to the formulation that I called psychologistic, which also goes so far as to include among its characteristics the existing Sartrean theory.

To be a subject is to have one's place in the Other [A], in the locus of speech. Now, a vicissitude can arise here that is designated by the bar that strikes through the A – namely, that the Other's speech is lacking. It is at the precise moment at which the subject – manifesting himself as the *phi* function in relation to the object – vanishes and fails to recognize himself, it is at this precise point that, in the absence of recognition, misrecognition automatically occurs. At this point of absence [*défaut*], at which the function of phallicism to which the subject devotes himself winds up being covered over, the mirage of narcissism – that I would call truly frenetic in the obsessive subject – is produced in its stead.

304

This sort of alienation of phallicism is visibly manifested in the obsessive, for example, in what are called his thought disturbances. These latter can be expressed by the subject in a perfectly clear, articulated, and avowed way, and experienced as such. "It is not so much because what I think," the subject says to you in his discourse – implicitly, but in enough detail that the line can be drawn and the addition carried out on the basis of his declaration – "is culpable that it is difficult for me to sustain myself and to progress thereby; it is because it is absolutely necessary that what I think come from me and never from my neighbor, never from someone else."

How many times have we heard this – not only in the obsessive's typical situations, but in what I will call the "obsessivized" relations that we produce artificially in a relationship that is as specific as that of analytic teaching?

2

In my lecture in Rome ["Function and Field of Speech and Language"], I spoke of what I called the "wall of language" [*Écrits*, p. 282]. Nothing is more difficult than to back the obsessive neurotic up against the wall of his desire.

There is something that I don't think has ever truly been high-lighted before, even though it is rather enlightening. In order to situate it, I will use a term you are aware I have already used for more than one purpose, *aphanisis*, introduced by Ernest Jones, in a way all of whose ambiguities I have indicated, to designate the disappearance – that is the meaning of the word in Greek – of desire.

No one has ever, it seems to me, pointed out a very simple fact that is quite tangible in the stories told by obsessives. When an obsessive is following a certain path of autonomous research, or self-analysis, as it were, [or] when he is proceeding along the path of what is known as "realizing his fantasy," regardless of its form, it is truly appropriate to employ the term *aphanisis*. It is even impossible to avoid this function at that point.

When people use the term, it is generally in order to designate,   305
first of all, a natural and ordinary *aphanisis*, which concerns the limited power a subject has to maintain an erection. Desire has, in effect, a natural rhythm. Even without evoking the extremes of the inability to keep it up or the most worrisome forms of the brevity of the act, one can remark that the subject is dealing here with a sort of obstacle or stumbling block that is fundamental in his relation to his fantasy. What is at stake for him is the end of the line: erection and then the fall of desire. There is a precise moment at which the erection goes down. Nevertheless, on the whole, my goodness, the obsessive is endowed with neither more nor less than what we might call quite ordinary genitality, which is even rather wimpy, it seems to me. Indeed, even if what is at stake in the avatars and torments inflicted upon him by the hidden mainspring of his desire were situated at this level, it would be appropriate for us to bring our efforts to bear elsewhere.

I always counterpunctually mention what we do not concern our-selves with at all, but I am astonished that we never ask ourselves why we do not concern ourselves with it. We do not concern our-selves, in effect, with the perfecting of athletic exercises with which to train for sexual embraces, nor with bringing bodies alive in the dimension of nudity and public displays [*la prise au ventre*]. Apart from a few exceptions – you are aware how thoroughly one of those exceptions was condemned, namely Reich – I don't think it is a field to which analysts have ever devoted much attention.

The obsessive can more or less figure out how to handle his desire. It is, in short, a question of mores, in a situation in which things, with or without analysis, are maintained in the realm of the clan-destine, and in which cultural variations consequently don't mean much. What is at stake is thus situated somewhere else altogether, namely, at the level of the discordance between his fantasy – insofar as it is precisely linked to the function of phallicism – and the act in which he aspires to incarnate it, which always falls short of the fantasy. And naturally, it is owing to the effects of the fantasy, this fantasy which is all about phallicism, that all the symptomatic consequences develop that are designed to contribute to it. The fantasy includes everything that contributes to [the act], in the so very typical and characteristic form of isolation, whose mechanism has been highlighted in the birth of the symptom.

306

If one thus finds in the obsessive the fear of *aphanisis* highlighted by Jones, it is insofar as, and solely inasmuch as, it is the putting to the test – which always turns into defeat – of the Φ function of the phallus. Its result is that the obsessive has no greater fear, in the end, than of what he imagines he aspires to: to act freely and to live in the state of nature, if I may put it thus. Natural tasks are not his thing, nor is anything else that leaves him master of his own ship, so to speak, along with God – namely, functions where he has extreme responsibility, pure responsibility, the responsibility one has toward the Other in which what I am articulating is inscribed.

The point I am designating is nowhere better illustrated, let me say in passing, than in the analyst's function, and specifically at the moment at which he proffers an interpretation. You see that in the course of my talk today, I haven't stopped situating the field uncovered for us by analytic action correlatively with the field of the neurotic's experience. It is necessarily the same, as it is there that one must go for it.

At the root of the obsessive's experience, there is always what I will call a certain fear of deflating related to phallic inflation. In a way, the Φ function of the phallus in obsession can be no better illustrated than by [La Fontaine's] fable of the frog that wanted to become as big as an ox. "The puny ninny," as you know, "swelled so much that it burst."

This is a moment of experience that is constantly renewed in the real dead end to which the obsessive is brought at the limits of his desire. It is, it seems, worth emphasizing, not simply in the sense of stressing a pathetic phenomenology, but also to allow you to articulate what is at stake in the Φ function of the phallus, insofar as it is hidden by having been exchanged for the φ function.

3

I began to articulate the Φ function last time by formulating a term: "real presence." I think your hearing is keen enough to realize that

307

I was putting it in quotes. Thus I did not introduce it alone: I spoke of the insult to real presence, in such a way that no one could be mistaken on this point. It has nothing to do with a neutral reality.

If real presence fulfills the radical function toward which I am trying to steer you here, it would be very odd if it had not already been identified somewhere. And I suspect that you have all already perceived that it is a homonym, identical to what goes by that name in religious dogma, the dogma to which, in our cultural context, we accede from birth, so to speak. We have for a long time been more or less used to hearing this pair of words, "real presence," insofar as it constitutes a signifier, murmured in our ears concerning the Apostolic and Roman Catholic dogma of the Eucharist. Well, I assure you that there is no need to look far to realize that it is right at the surface of the obsessive's phenomenology.

Since I spoke earlier of the work of someone who endeavored to focus research about obsessive structure on the phallus, I am going to take up his first article, whose title I mentioned earlier when I spoke of the "Therapeutic Impact of the Recognition of Penis Envy in Obsessive Neurosis among Women." I will quote a few passages from the introduction, and you will see that right from the very first pages, all sorts of possibilities for a critical commentary present themselves:

> Like the male obsessive, the female needs to identify regressively with a man in order to be able to free herself from anxieties dating back to early childhood; but while the male can prop himself up on this identification, in order to transform the infantile love object into a genital love object, she, basing herself first on the very same identification, tends to abandon the first object [the mother] and to move toward a heterosexual fixation, as if she could proceed to a new feminine identification, this time based on the person of the analyst.

Further along, we read,

> Shortly after the desire to possess the phallus, and correlatively to castrate the analyst, is brought to light, and, because of this the aforementioned loosening up has occurred, the male analyst's personality is associated with that of a well-meaning mother.

308

Three lines further on, we come across the well-known "initial destructive drive that targets the mother" – in other words, we come across the major coordinates of the analysis of the imaginary that characterizes the way treatment is currently conducted.

I have only highlighted this topic in order to convey to you in passing the difficulties that this general interpretation – summarized here in the introduction to the article, which the whole of what follows supposedly illustrates – assumes to have been overcome. Yet I need but go half a page further on to enter into the phenomenology of what is at stake, and into what this author, who was a clinician, this being his first paper, decides to tell us about the fantasies of his patient, who is viewed as an obsessive.

The first thing that jumps out at us is the following: "She imagined to herself that there were male genitalia in the place of the communion wafer."

And then it is indicated, "without there being any hallucinatory phenomena involved." I don't doubt it. Everything that we see and articulate has gotten us used to seeing that what is involved is something else altogether. She superimposed male organs in a signifying form. Onto what, if not onto what to us is, in the most identifiable, symbolic way, real presence? The point is to eliminate this real presence, to break it or mash it up in the mechanism of desire. The sacrilegious fantasies that I borrowed last time from a little further on in the same case study highlight this well enough.

Don't imagine that this case study is unique. I will cite for you – among dozens of others, because the experience of an analyst in a field never goes beyond a hundred – the following fantasy, which an obsessive [I worked with] had at one point in his analysis.

The attempts to incarnate desire can go to an extreme of erotic acuteness in obsessives, at times when they encounter in a partner some willingness, whether deliberate or gratuitous, to go along with the degrading of the Other with a capital O into the other with a lowercase o, in the field in which their desire develops. At the very moment at which the subject in question thought he could maintain a type of relationship – which is always accompanied in obsessive neurotics by everything correlated with extremely threatening guilt, which can be counterbalanced, in some sense, by the intensity of his desire – he formed the following fantasy with a partner who represented for him, at least momentarily, such a satisfying complement: having the communion wafer play a role in coitus, in such a way that, placed in the woman's vagina, the host would wind up serving as a hat atop the subject's penis at the moment of penetration.

Don't think that this is the kind of peculiarity found only in a specialized literary genre. It is very common in the register of fancy [*fantasie*], especially obsessives' fancies.

How can we stop ourselves from casting all of this into a banal register like that of the so-called distance from the object, insofar as the object in question would be defined objectively? This is nev-

309

ertheless what is described to us: the objectivity of the world, as it
is recorded by the enumeration and the more or less harmonious
combination of typical imaginary relationships; the objectivity of
form, as it is specified by human dimensions; and the frontiers of
the apprehension of the outer world, threatened by the difficulty
of delimiting the ego with the objects of everyday communication.
How can we not think, on the contrary, that there is something else,
another dimension?

The point is nevertheless to situate this real presence somewhere,
and in a register other than that of the imaginary. Let us say that
it is inasmuch as I am teaching you to situate the place of desire in
relation to the function of man as a subject who speaks that we can
glimpse the fact that desire comes to inhabit the place of real presence and populates it with its ghosts.

But then what does Φ mean? Do I summarize it by designating the
place of real presence insofar as it can only appear in the intervals
between what the signifier covers (over)? Is it on the basis of these
intervals that real presence threatens the whole signifying system?
Yes, there is some truth to that. The obsessive shows it to you at
every point of what you call his mechanisms of projection and
defense, or more precisely, phenomenologically, of conjuring. The
way he has of filling in everything that can present itself as a gap
in the signifying system [*dans le signifiant*] – the way in which, for
example, Freud's *Rattenmann* makes himself count up to so many
between the flash of lightning and its thunder – is designated here in
its veritable structure. Why this need to fill in the signifying interval?
Because something might be introduced there that would dissolve
all of the phantasmagoria.

Apply this key to 25 or 30 of the symptoms with which the
Rattenmann literally overflows and to all the case studies of obsessives, and you will put your finger on the truth of the matter.
Moreover, you will situate at the same time the function of the phobic
object, which is nothing other than the simplest form of this filling in.

What last time, concerning little Hans, I called the "universal
signifier" realized by the phobic object is precisely that and nothing
else. It is at a distant outpost, well before the hole – that of the gap
brought about in the interval where real presence threatens – that
a single sign stops the subject from approaching. This is why the
mainspring of and the reason for phobia are not, as those who have
but the word "fear" on their lips believe, a genital or even narcissistic danger. Owing to certain exceptional developments in the
position of the subject with respect to the Other, as is the case in
little Hans' relationship to his mother, what the subject is afraid of
encountering is precisely a certain sort of desire that would be such

310

as to immediately make the whole signifying system fall back into the nothingness prior to creation.

But then why is the phallus situated at this place and in this role? It is regarding this point that I would like to proceed far enough today to get you to realize what I might call the suitability of this formulation. I am not saying that it is the product of a deduction, for it is experience – that is, empirical discovery – that assures us of it; but there is also something here that makes us perceive that, qua experience, it is not irrational. Thus it is experience that shows us the phallus. But the suitability of the formulation that I want to point out is determined by the fact that the phallus, as experience reveals it to us, is not simply the organ of copulation, but is taken up in a perverse mechanism.

Try to catch my drift here. I am now stressing that the phallus, Φ, can function in such a way as to signify the structural point that represents a lack in the signifying system [*le défaut du signifiant*]. What does this mean? What defines as a signifier something about which I have just said that, by hypothesis, by definition, from the very outset, it is the signifier that is excluded from the signifying system [*c'est le signifiant exclu du signifiant*]? Is it that it can only enter the signifying system by artifice, contraband, and degradation, which is why we never see it except as a function of imaginary φ? But then what allows us to talk about it, nevertheless, as a signifier, and to isolate Φ as such? It is what I call the perverse mechanism.

Let us schematize the phallus, which is in some sense natural, as follows. What is the phallus? The phallus, as we see it in the organic function of the penis, is not a universal organ in the animal kingdom. Insects have other ways of hooking onto each other, and without going so far afield, the relations between fishes are not phallic relations. The phallus presents itself at the human level, among others, as the sign of desire. It is also the instrument and presence of desire, but I am highlighting here its quality as a sign to ask you to dwell on something we must keep in mind – is it simply because it is a sign that it is a signifier? We would be too quickly crossing a border were we to say that it all comes down to this, for there are nevertheless other signs of desire.

We observe, phenomenologically, the easier projection of the phallus, owing to its imposing form [*sa forme prégnante*], onto the female object, for example; this is what has led me to articulate many times, in the phenomenology of perversion, the famous equivalence "girl=phallus"* in its simplest form: the erect form of the phallus. But this does not suffice, although I consider this profound choice, whose consequences we encounter everywhere, to be sufficiently motivated.

A signifier – is it simply about representing something to someone? Is that even the definition of a sign? It is, but that's not all. I added something else last time when I reminded you of the function of the signifier, which is that the signifier does not simply serve to make a sign to someone but, at the same moment of the signifying mainspring or instance, to make a sign of someone – to make the sign assimilate the someone to whom the sign designates something, such that this someone also becomes this signifier.

It is in the moment that I explicitly designate as perverse that we find the instance of the phallus. The fact that a phallus that is shown also produces an erection in the subject to whom it is shown is not, in any sense whatsoever, a condition that satisfies any sort of natural requirement.

It is here that we see what we call, in a more or less confused way, the homosexual instance. And it is not for no reason that we always situate the etiology [of homosexuality] at the level of the male sexual organ [*sexe*]. It is inasmuch as the result is, in short, that the phallus as a sign of desire is manifested as an object of desire, as an object that attracts desire. In this mainspring lies its signifying function, and it is thus that it is able to operate at this level, in this zone or sector, where we must both identify it as a signifier and understand what it is thus led to designate.

What it designates is nothing that is directly signifiable. It is what is beyond all possible signification, and namely the real presence to which I wanted to draw your attention today, as we will continue to work on it in this year's Seminar.

April 26, 1961

THE OEDIPAL MYTH TODAY

TODAY

A COMMENTARY ON THE COÛFONTAINE
TRILOGY BY PAUL CLAUDEL

XIX

SYGNE'S NO

... where we are supposed to know.
Contemporary tragedy.
Twitching on the part of life.
A breach beyond faith.

I am attempting this year to resituate the fundamental question that transference poses to us in our practice by orienting your thinking toward what the analyst's position must be in order to respond to transference.

I am endeavoring in this context to point out at the most essential level what this position must be when faced with the profoundest call for being that emerges at the moment at which the patient comes to us to request our help and aid. In order to be rigorous, fitting, and impartial, and to be as open as is required by the nature of the question that is posed to us, I formulate this by asking what the analyst's desire must be.

It is certainly inadequate to be content to think that the analyst, by virtue of his experience and science, is the modern equivalent or representative – who is authorized by the strength of research, a doctrine, and a community – of some sort of right of nature, and that it is his job to designate for us anew the way toward a kind of natural harmony that can be accessed through the detours of a revised practice.

If I used Socratic practice as a springboard here this year, it was essentially in order to center your thinking around something that is given right from the outset of the establishment of psychoanalytic practice: we are questioned [by patients] as if we knew, and even as if we were in possession of a secret, but a secret that is not everyone's secret – a secret that is specific to one person and one person alone.

1

Those who seek us out already know, as obscurely as it may be –
and if they don't know it, they will quickly be oriented toward
this notion by analytic practice – that the secret we are presumed
to possess is more precious than everything that is not known and
that will continue not to be known – in the sense that this secret will
answer for the fact that what we do know is only partial.

Is this true? Or isn't it? I need not come down on one side or the
other. I am simply saying that this is the way analytic practice presents itself and is approached, and that this is the way that what it
introduces that is new on the horizon of the men we, along with our
contemporaries, are can be defined, in a certain respect.

Each of us who tries his hand at this experience, regardless of
the side from which he approaches it, whether as an analysand or
analyst, fundamentally has this presupposition. It can be found at a
level that is truly central, nay essential, to our conduct. And when I
say "this presupposition," I can even allow it to remain marked with
a smidgeon of doubt, for this experience can be broached tentatively
and, indeed, it is most often broached in that way by those who seek
us out.

What is this presupposition? It is the presupposition that the
impasses owing to our ignorance are perhaps only determined by the
fact that we are mistaken regarding what we might call the power
relations of our knowledge – that, in short, we create false problems.
This presupposition or hope, as I would put it, and what it brings
with it by way of optimism, is favored by something that is now
widely accepted: desire does not show itself openly and is not where
the secular experience of philosophy, to call a spade a spade, has
designated it in order to contain it and, in a certain sense, rule out
its right to govern us. This is so far from being the case that desires
are everywhere and even at the very heart of our efforts to master
them. This is so far from being the case that even when we attempt
to combat them we do little more than execute them [*y satisfaire*]. I
say "execute them" and not satisfy them [*les satisfaire*], because to
say "satisfy them" would be going too far – it would be to take them
to be localizable and graspable. I am using the expression "execute
them" here like when, conversely, we say, "shirk them" [*y couper*]
or "not shirk them" [*n'y pas couper*] – as in a fundamental plan to
shirk them.

Well, we can't shirk them [*on n'y coupe pas*] – indeed, we can shirk
them so little that it does not suffice to avoid [satisfying] our desires
to not feel more or less guilty. In any case, whatever we can attest
to regarding our project, what analytic practice teaches us first and

foremost is that man is marked and troubled by everything that is called a symptom – inasmuch as symptoms are what bind him to his desires.

We can define neither their limit nor their place by executing them in some way; the latter, moreover, brings no pleasure with it.

It seems that such a bitter doctrine would imply that the analyst has, at some level, the strangest of standards. Indeed, stress is placed here on a huge extension of fundamental misrecognition – not, as had been done prior to analysis, in a speculative form whereby misrecognition was thought to arise in some way with the question of knowing, but in a form which I believe I can do no better than to call, at least for the time being, as it occurs to me now, "textual." It is textual in the sense that it is a misrecognition that is woven out of one's personal construction, in the broadest sense of the term – that by making this presupposition, the analyst should have, and by many people is expected to have, if not overcome the misrecognition itself, at least overcome the mainspring of this misrecognition. He should have gone beyond the stage that I have designated for you with the words "*Che vuoi?*" ["What do you want?"] beyond which knowledge of oneself supposedly cannot go. Or at the very least, the path of what I will call one's own good – insofar as it is harmony of oneself with oneself at the level of authenticity – should be open to the analyst. At least regarding this point of individual experience, something of this nature, of this natural disposition, should be able to be grasped that is supposed to be sustained by its own naïveté.

You are, moreover, aware of the degree to which, elsewhere than in psychoanalysis, skepticism – not to say disgust – or nihilism, to use the word employed by the moralists of our times to describe it, has gripped the whole of our culture regarding what one might call "the measure of man."

There is nothing further from modern, contemporary thought than the natural idea, which was so familiar to us for so many centuries, of striving to aim at the right standard of conduct, however it was understood, and without it even seeming that the notion we formed of it could be critiqued.   318

What we thus presume regarding the analyst should not even be limited to the field of his action, having only a local scope insofar as he practices analysis and is present *hic et nunc* [here and now], as they say, but should be attributed to him as habitual. Let us give the word "habitual" its full meaning, the one that refers more to *habitus* in the Scholastic sense of the term – to the integration of oneself, to the constancy of action and form in one's own life, and to what constitutes the ground of all virtue – than to the meaning whereby "habitual" simply points toward the notion of imprinting and passivity.

Need I critique this ideal before we rule it out? It is not that one cannot find examples of pure-hearted analysts, but is it thinkable that this ideal should be required of the analyst right from the outset? Could it in any way be filled if it were attested to? Let us say that it is not terribly common and that analysts have no such reputation. Moreover, we could easily explain why we are disappointed with such ridiculous formulations that always get away from us, whenever we try to formulate in our magisterium something that rises to the value of an ethics.

When I try to lay bare for you the crux of recent and always worthy efforts that are made to detect the ideals implicit in our doctrine, it is not for the sheer pleasure of it, believe me, that I dwell on such and such a formulation of a supposedly analytic characterology in order to expose its weaknesses, its character as a blind window or childish opposition. We see, for example, people formulating the "genital character" of the end of an analysis, assimilating our goals to the pure and simple removal of impasses that they identify with the pregenital stage, which is supposed to be sufficient to resolve all its antinomies. I ask you to weigh the consequences of such a display of analysts' inability to conceptualize the truth of our practice.

The problem of human desire is situated in an entirely different relativity. And if we must be something other than simple companions to the patient in his search, let us at least not lose sight of this standard: that the subject's desire is essentially, as I have been teaching you, desire of the Other with a capital O. Desire can only be situated, positioned, and thus understood within a fundamental alienation that is not simply tied to conflict among men, but to our relationship with language.

319

Desire of the Other – this genitive is both subjective and objective. Desire in the place where the Other is [i.e., to desire as if one were the Other] in order to be in the Other's place – desire for some alterity. To fulfill the search for the objective – namely, for what this other [the patient] who seeks us out desires – we must lend ourselves here to the function of the subjective, so that in some way we may be able, for a while, to represent, not what people believe – and it would be derisive, good Lord, admit it, and so terribly simplistic too [to believe] that we could be the object aimed at by this desire – but rather the signifier. Which is both far less, but also far more.

We must occupy the empty place where a signifier is summoned that can exist only by canceling out all the others, and that is the signifier Φ whose central position and condition in analytic practice I have been trying to demonstrate for you.

Our function, power, and duty are clear and all our difficulties come down to the following: we must know how to occupy its place inasmuch as the subject must be able to detect the missing signifier there. And thus, through an antinomy or paradox, which is that of our function, we are summoned into being – into being nothing but real presence, and precisely inasmuch as it is unconscious – in the very place where we are supposed to know.

In essence, at the horizon of what our function in analysis is, we are there as that [*ça*] – precisely that [*ça*] which shuts up, and it shuts up in that it fails to come into being [*il manque à être*]. We are, in the final analysis, in our presence, our own subject, at the point at which it [*il*] vanishes or is barred. This is why we can occupy the very place where the patient, as a subject, effaces himself and subordinates himself to all the signifiers of his own demand.

This does not occur solely at the level of regression, the signifying treasure troves of the unconscious, or the vocabulary of *Wunsch*, inasmuch as we decipher it in the course of a psychoanalysis, but, in the final analysis, at the level of fantasy. I said "in the final analysis," insofar as fantasy is the only equivalent of the drive-related discovery by which it is possible for the subject to designate the place of the answer – the S(A) that he expects from transference – and for the S(A) to make sense.

In fantasy, the subject grasps himself as faltering [*défaillant*] when faced with a specific object, which is the imaginary degradation of the Other at this point of faltering. In the transference, in order for us to enter into the fantasy at the level of $ for the passive subject, we must truly be this $ in a certain way; we must, in the final analysis, be the one who sees little *a*, the object in fantasy; we must, in any analysis whatsoever, and even in those that are the most foreign to us, be clairvoyant in the end, being the one who can see the object of the Other's desire, regardless of how far this Other may be from himself.

320

It is precisely because this is the case that, throughout the course of my teaching, and in every respect in which not only practice but also tradition can serve us, you have seen me revolve around what man's desire is. Along the path that we have followed together, you see alternate the scientific definition of what man's desire is – in the broadest sense of the term "scientific," the one that has been proposed since Socrates' time – with something that is diametrically opposed to it: tragedy, inasmuch as tragedy is graspable in the monuments of human memory. Need I recall to mind here that two years ago, I led you through the earliest drama of modern man, *Hamlet*? And that last year I tried to give you a glimpse of what ancient tragedy means to us here?

I am going to turn anew to the topic of tragedy now, owing to an encounter – that's the word for it, an accidental encounter – with one of those formulations, which is neither better nor worse than the kind we see all the time in our circle, of what fantasy is. Indeed, I came across an articulation of the function of fantasy in the latest *Bulletin de Psychologie* and I can tell you that its very mediocrity gave me quite a start. But the author will not be too angry with me, I think, for saying so, since he is the very author who expressed the wish, some time back, to train a large number of mediocre psychoanalysts.

This is clearly what gave me the renewed, I cannot say courage, a bit more is needed for that, but fury necessary to fly off on yet another tangent, whose trajectory I hope you will have the patience to follow with me.

I looked around to see if I could find something in contemporary culture to use as a springboard for what I am trying to show you, which surely must always be there, and I would say, more than ever in the years since psychoanalysis came into being, it being inconceivable that its invention was simply a miracle that arose out of some kind of individual accident called Freud, the Viennese petty bourgeois.

321

We assuredly find in our times – we sense this everywhere – all the elements of a kind of dramatic art that must allow us to situate at its proper level the drama we deal with as regards desire. One must not confine one's attention to the kind of med-student jokes one can hear almost anywhere – the kind one finds identified with fantasy, for example, in the article I mentioned a moment ago. The fact is certainly misleading to boot, because, as we can see clearly in the text, it was not even a case of someone who had been analyzed. It is the story of an itinerant stallkeeper who, from the very day he was told that he had only twelve months to live, was supposedly freed from his fantasy, as it is called in the paper – namely, his fear of venereal disease – and who from that point on treated himself to all he could get [*s'en serait payé*], as the author puts it; we might well wonder where the author got this vocabulary from, as one has a hard time imagining that the merchant in question could have said such a thing.

Such is the level – which is never critically assessed, so that it must be more than a little suspect to us – at which the attempt to broach human desire and its obstacles is currently situated.

Is it something else that led me to decide to lead you anew through an examination of tragedy inasmuch as it impacts us?

2

I will begin by telling you which tragedy I will discuss and how it serendipitously came about that I am turning to it.

It is a modern tragedy, by which I mean that it is contemporary. This time there is not but one extant copy of it. You can't find this tragedy absolutely everywhere nevertheless. Since I intend to lead you through a trilogy by Paul Claudel, I will tell you what made me decide to do so.

It had been a long time since I had reread this trilogy, including *The Hostage*, *Crusts*, and *The Humiliation of the Father*. I was fortuitously led back to it a few weeks ago, in a way that I will mention because it is amusing, at least for the personal use that I make of my own criteria.

And because, as I told you in a pithy formulation [*formule*], the great thing about formulas is that you can take them literally – in other words, as stupidly as possible – and that they must lead you somewhere. This is the operational facet of formulas and it is true of my formulas as well. Now, I don't claim to be operational only with regard to other people's formulas.

322

I was reading the correspondence between André Gide and Paul Claudel, which I would say, just among ourselves, doesn't pull any punches – I recommend you take a look at it. But what I am going to say has no connection with the point of the correspondence, which hardly casts Claudel in a flattering light. That won't stop me from putting him in the spotlight he deserves as one of the greatest poets who ever lived.

In this correspondence, André Gide writes as head of *La Nouvelle Revue Française* – not simply the journal, but the series of books they published prior to 1914. He and Claudel are discussing the publication of *The Hostage* – and make sure you are sitting down for this – not as concerns its content but as concerns the role and function that I have attributed to the letter. For this is clearly the efficient cause of the fact you will hear me talk for a couple of classes about a trilogy that is unlike any other.

Indeed, one of the problems discussed in two or three of the letters is that in order to print *The Hostage*, they are going to have to cast a character that does not exist, not only at the *Nouvelle Revue Française*'s print shop, but at any other print shop: capital *U* with a circumflex over it. Never at any point in the French language has anyone needed a *U* with a circumflex accent. It is Paul Claudel who, in naming his heroine Sygne de Coûfontaine – with, owing to his discretionary poetic power, an accent on the *u* – creates this minor difficulty for his typographers. Lowercase *u* is not a problem but uppercase *U* is, and in French the names of people in a play are, in a proper edition, always written in capital letters.

At the sign of this missing signifier, I thought there must be something fishy going on and that rereading *The Hostage* would take me much further. This is what led me to re-examine a large portion of Claudel's theatrical works and, as you likely expect, my efforts were amply rewarded.

To begin with *The Hostage*, let us note that Claudel wrote this play at a time when he was a civil servant in the Office of Foreign Affairs, representing France in some capacity, something like an advisor, probably something more than an attaché. His exact title isn't important – what is important is that he worked for the Republic at a time when that still had a meaning. Now Claudel writes the following to André Gide: given the overly reactionary tone of the play, it would probably be better that it not be signed Claudel.

Let us not make light of this prudence. Prudence has always been considered a moral virtue. And believe me, we would be wrong to think that, just because prudence is perhaps no longer in season, we should be contemptuous of the last people who manifested it.

The values that play a role in *The Hostage* are what I will call values based on faith. The play involves a sad story supposed to have taken place at the time of Napoleon I, the story of a lady who, let us not forget, is getting to be a bit of an old maid as she has been working on a heroic project for some ten years, the tale being set at the height of Napoleon's power.

The play concerns how the Emperor coerced the Pope, and this is naturally transformed for the needs of the play. This situates us thus a little over ten years after the time at which the trials of Sygne de Coûfontaine first began.

Just by hearing her name, you have already realized that she is part of the former aristocracy, of those who were, among other things, dispossessed of their privileges and possessions during the French Revolution. Since that time, having remained in France whereas her cousin emigrated, she patiently worked to reconstitute the former Coûfontaine estate. This is not simply the result of some kind of tenacity on her part, but is represented as part and parcel of the pact with the land which, for two of the characters in the play, as well as for the author who has them speak, is identical to the constancy and value of nobility itself.

You will see in the text the admirable terms in which this bond with the land as such is expressed, which is not simply a de facto bond but clearly a mystical bond. It is also around this bond that an entire order of allegiances is defined which is, strictly speaking,

323

the feudal order; it ties the bond of kinship to a local bond around which everything that defines lords, vassals, birthrights, and clients revolves. I can only very briefly mention all of these themes, for they are not the true reason for our interest in the play. In any case, I think that you will find all you could desire on these topics in the text itself.

It is in the course of this enterprise [reconstituting the former Coûfontaine estate] – which is thus founded on the dramatic, poetic exaltation of certain values that is recreated before us, values that are organized around a certain form of speech [giving one's word] – that the following event occurs.

Sygne de Coûfontaine's cousin, Georges – who has been absent because he emigrated, and who has, moreover, in the course of the preceding years clandestinely shown up at her home several times – reappears accompanied by someone whose identity is not initially revealed to us. He turns out to be none other than the supreme Father, the Pope, whose entire presence in the play will be literally defined as that of the representative on Earth of the Heavenly Father. The whole plot revolves around this fugitive, because it is owing to this cousin's aid that he is in hiding there, beyond the reach of the oppressor's power.

It is at this point that a third character comes into the picture, the one named Baron Turelure, Toussaint Turelure, whose image dominates the entire trilogy.

His portrait is drawn in such a way as to incline us to hate him. As if it were not already low and nasty enough for him to come and torment such a charming woman, he pays her a visit in order to blackmail her more or less as follows: "Mademoiselle, I have desired and loved you for many a year, but now that you have this old eternal daddy at your house, I will capture him and wring his neck if you do not accept my marriage proposal."

It is not undesignedly that I describe this core of the drama with a farcical note. The old Turelure is presented to us with all the attributes not merely of cynicism but of ugliness. It is not enough for him to be mean; he is also presented to us as lame, a bit twisted, and hideous. Moreover, he is the very same man who had everyone in Sygne de Coûfontaine's family decapitated in the good old days of 1793, and quite openly, such that he must also convince the lady to overlook that. Furthermore, he is the son of a sorcerer and a woman who was Sygne de Coûfontaine's wet-nurse and thus her servant – so when she marries him she will be marrying the son of her servant and the son of a sorcerer.

We might wonder whether there isn't something here that is a bit exaggerated in order to tug at the heartstrings of a public

325   for whom these old stories have nevertheless taken on a rather different import – namely, that the French Revolution proved by its aftermath to be something that cannot be judged solely by the yardstick of the martyrdom suffered by the aristocracy. It is clear that the play as it is written cannot be viewed in this way. It is not that this public is very extensive in our country, but one cannot say either that the spectators who went to see the play – who moreover came rather late in the play's history – were all, not partisans of the Count of Paris, for as everyone knows the Count of Paris is very progressive, but people who were missing the era of the Count of Chambord. It was instead an advanced, cultured, and educated public that, watching *The Hostage*, experienced the shock, let us say, of the tragedy involved in the unfolding of events.

Our goal is to understand what this emotion means – namely, not only the fact that the public gets into it, but also that (I promise that upon reading it, you will have no doubt about this) we have here a work that has, in the tradition of the theater, all the rights and merits owed to what is most grand. How can it be that this story – which appears to be a sort of wager and is taken so far as to be caricatural – moves us?

Let us go further. Don't rest content with the idea that what is at stake here is what is always evoked in us by the suggestion of religious values.

It is precisely this point that we are now going to investigate.

3

What is the mainspring, major scene, or crux of the tragedy?

He who encourages Sygne de Coûfontaine to accept the marriage proposal is not the horrible character – and, as you shall see, he is not simply horrible but of capital importance in the entire trilogy – known as Toussaint Turelure. It is Sygne de Coûfontaine's confessor: the priest Badilon, who is a saintly figure.

Sygne de Coûfontaine – who is not included in the play like her cousin is, but in the capacity of someone who has overcome myriad obstacles in her work to maintain the estate – is there at the moment at which her cousin comes to find her, and she learns from her cousin that he has just experienced in his own life and person

326   the most bitter betrayal [p. 18/14]. Indeed, he has realized that the woman he loved had been making a fool of him for many years, he being the only one who did not know it; in effect, she was the mistress of the person who is referred to in Claudel's text as the Prince

[*Dauphin*]. There never was a French Prince who emigrated at that time, but this is of no consequence here, for the point is to show the major characters, Sygne de Coûfontaine and her cousin, being thoroughly disappointed and truly tragically isolated.

This is not the whole story, however. Some sort of measles or whooping cough then struck not only the cousin's wife, an interesting character, but also her young children, his descendants [pp. 18–19/14–15]. He thus arrives on the scene deprived by fate of everything he had, except for his constancy in supporting the royal cause. And in a dialogue that is, in short, the tragic point of departure of what is going to unfold, Sygne and her cousin commit themselves to each other before God. Nothing, whether in the present or in the future, will ever allow them to make good on this commitment. Yet they make a commitment beyond all that is possible or impossible, they promise themselves to one another. Then Badilon, the priest, comes along to require Sygne, not to do anything specific, but to consider the fact that should she refuse what the awful Turelure has proposed, she will become the key to a historical moment in which the Father of all the faithful is delivered into the hands of his enemies.

Assuredly, Badilon the saint does not, strictly speaking, impose any precise duty on her. He goes further than that. He does not even appeal to her strength, as he says and as Claudel writes, but to her weakness [pp. 99–100/60]. He shows her the abyss that would open up for her should she accept the proposal by which she would become the agent of an act of sublime deliverance. Note that everything is designed here to show us that in doing so she must renounce in herself something that goes well beyond anything agreeable, any possible pleasure, or duty. She must renounce her very being – the pact that has kept her forever faithful to her own family, since what is being proposed is that she marry the very man who exterminated her family – and renounce the sacred commitment she has just made to the man she loves, her cousin. This is something that carries her, not to the limits of her life, for we know that she is a woman who would willingly sacrifice that, as she has shown in the past, but to the sacrifice of what for her, as for every being, is worth more than life itself – not simply her reasons for living but something in which she recognizes her very being.

We thus find ourselves carried, by what I am provisionally calling a contemporary tragedy, to the limits of the "second death," the death that I taught you about last year when we discussed *Antigone*, except that here the heroine is asked to go beyond those limits.

Whereas I showed you last year what tragic fate signifies; managed to get you to locate it in a topology that we called Sadean,

327

namely, in a locus for which those attending the Seminar coined the
phrase "between two deaths"; showed that this locus is outstripped
by going – not as people say in a kind of refrain – beyond good
and evil, which is a fine formulation by which to obscure what is
at stake, but beyond beauty, strictly speaking; indicated that the
limit of this domain, the limit of the second death, is designated
and also veiled by what I called the phenomenon of beauty, the one
that explodes in Sophocles' text at the moment at which – Antigone
having gone beyond the limit of her condemnation by Creon, which
is not simply accepted but provoked – the chorus bursts into song
as follows: Ἔρως ἀνίκατε μάχαν (*Eros anikate machan*), "Eros (or
Love), invincible in battle" [verse 781]; here, after 20 centuries of
the Christian era, it is beyond this limit that Sygne de Coûfontaine's
drama brings us.

Whereas Antiquity's heroine is identical to her destiny, *Até* – to
the law that to her is divine and that sustains her in her trials – for
this other heroine, it is against her will (against everything that
determines it, not in her life but in her being) that, through an act of
freedom, she goes against everything related to her being right down
to its very roots.

Life is left far behind here. For don't forget, there is something
else, something that is forcefully emphasized by the playwright,
which is that given what she is and her relationship of faith with
things of this world, to accept to marry Turelure cannot simply
amount to accepting a constraint. Even the most execrable marriage
is indissoluble. But we haven't seen anything yet. Marriage involves
adherence to the duty of marriage insofar as it is a duty to love.

When I say that life is left far behind here, this is proven by the
play's dénouement.

Sygne has thus given in, she has become the Baroness Turelure.
We come now to the day of the little Turelure's birth – we will
concern ourselves with his destiny next time, for he plays a role in
the climax and end of the drama. In the besieged city of Paris, the
Baron Turelure – who comes to occupy center stage here, being the
historical figure of this huge farce of brigadiers whose faithful and
unfaithful oscillations around the great disaster history teaches us
about – must that very day remit the keys of the great city to King
Louis XVIII under certain conditions.

The ambassador of this negotiation – as you probably expect
and as befits the beauty of the drama – is no other than Sygne's
cousin in person. Whatever could possibly be the most odious in
the circumstances of the encounter is included here by the author.
For example, among the conditions that Turelure stipulates for
his pretty and profitable betrayal – this is the only way in which

what he does is presented to us – is the fact that the Coûfontaine appanage, the little that remains of it, it being a mere shadow of its former self, but nevertheless something essential which is the very name Coûfontaine, will be passed on to the descendants of this misalliance.

Things having gone this far, don't be surprised that they end with a little assassination attempt. For once the conditions have been accepted, the cousin, who has not exactly shown largesse here, decides to bump Turelure off, as they say. The latter, being endowed, naturally, with all manner of cunning and malignancy, foresees this and he too has a little revolver in his pocket. By the time the clock has struck the hour three times, the two revolvers have gone off; and, naturally, it is not the villain who we find lying on the floor. What is crucial here is that Sygne throws herself in front of the bullet that is about to hit her husband and, having spared him, dies a few minutes later.

A suicide, we might say, and that would be accurate enough since everything in her attitude shows us that she has drunk the bitter cup without having found anything in it but what it is: absolute dereliction, being abandoned and sorely tried by the divine powers, and a decision to go all the way in what at this point hardly deserves to be called a sacrifice.

In short, in the final scene, prior to the act that leads to her death, Sygne is presented to us as having a facial tic [p. 105/63], thus signaling in some sense the poet's design to show us that the endpoint that is respected even by Sade, as I indicated last year – that endpoint being beauty that is unaffected by affronts – is gone beyond here.

No doubt this twitching on the part of life [*grimace de la vie*], on the part of a live person who is suffering, is more prejudicial to the status of beauty than the wincing of death [*grimace de la mort*] and the tongue hanging out we see on Antigone's face when she has hung herself and Haemon discovers her.

329

So what happens at the very end? Where does the poet leave us in abeyance at the end of his tragedy? There are two endings, as I'll beg you to keep in mind.

One of the endings involves the entrance of the King. It is a buffoonish entrance, where Toussaint Turelure is justly compensated for his services and where the restored order assumes the appearance of the kind of caricatural bedlam the French public all too easily buys after what history has taught us about the results of the Restoration. In short, we have here a truly derisory Epinal-type image, which moreover leaves us no doubt regarding the poet's opinion about any sort of return to what is known as the *ancien régime*.

The second ending is quite interesting. It is intimately tied to
what the poet is able to leave us with through the image of Sygne de
Coûfontaine. What is involved here is her death – not that her death
is left out of the first ending, naturally.

Just before the King enters the picture, Badilon reappears in order
to exhort Sygne; but right up until the end he is unable to obtain
from her anything other than a "no," an absolute refusal of peace,
an absolute refusal to abandon or offer herself up to God who will
receive her soul. All of the exhortations of this saint – he, too, being
torn apart by the final consequence of what he himself has been the
agent of – fail before this final negation. Sygne can find nothing,
by any avenue whatsoever, that can reconcile her with a fate about
which I would ask you to note that it goes beyond anything one
can find in ancient tragedy related to what Paul Ricoeur – who, as I
discovered, was studying the same things as I was in Antigone more
or less at the same time – calls the function of the evil God [*Dieu
méchant*].

The evil God of ancient tragedy is still something that is connected
to man through the intermediary of *Até*, this named and articulated
aberration that the evil God orchestrates. He is connected to the
other's *Até*, as both Antigone and Creon say in Sophocles' tragedy,
even though neither of them attended my Seminar. The other's *Até*
has a meaning in which Antigone's fate is inscribed.

Here we have gone beyond all meaning. Sygne's sacrifice does
nothing but deride her goals. The old man who had to be saved
from Turelure's clutches is represented to us right up until the end
of the trilogy – despite being the supreme Father of the faithful, as
he is – as an impotent Father who, compared to the ideals that are
on the rise, has nothing to offer his flock except the empty repetition
of traditional words which no longer have any power. The so-called
restored legitimacy is but a decoy, fiction, or caricature, and is in
reality but a continuation of the order that subverted the old regime.

What the poet adds in the second ending is the discovery by which
his wager surfaces anew, in having Sygne exhorted by Turelure
using the same words as are found on her family coat of arms,
the motto that for her is the signification of her life: "*Coûfontaine
adsum*, Coûfontaine, I am present."

Standing before his dying wife, who is incapable of speaking or
is refusing to speak, he tries to at least obtain from her a sign – any
sign whatsoever, were it only consent to have her child brought
before her – of recognition of the fact that her action was designed
to protect him, Turelure. To all of this the martyr merely replies,
right up until her last dying breath, with a no.

What does it mean that the poet brings us to this extreme failure [*défaut*], to this extreme derision of the signifier itself? What does it mean that such a thing is presented to us? It seems to me that I have already guided you sufficiently through the different stages of what I will call this outrageous fortune [*énormité*] for this to be clear to you.

You will say that we are tough cookies, that we've been around the block often enough that nothing impresses us any more – and yet! I realize that the poetry of Claudel has something in common with that of the surrealists. What we cannot doubt, in any case, is that Claudel at least imagined that he knew what he was writing. And whatever the case may be, it is written. Someone was able to imagine such a thing.

We spectators realize that if the point were merely to show us in an imaginative way a theme that has been drummed into us regarding the emotional conflicts of the nineteenth century, it would have no effect on us. We are well aware that this is not the point, that this is not what affects us, holds our attention, keeps us in suspense, hooks us, and propels us from *The Hostage* toward the final sequence of the trilogy. There is something else in this image for which we have no words. You recall Aristotle's terms that I quoted last year: δι' ἐλέου καὶ φόβου τεραίνουσα, in other words, not "by terror and by pity," but "all terror and pity having been gone beyond." What is presented to us here takes us yet further. It is the image of a desire next to which only the reference to Sade still seems to be worth anything. 331

Doesn't it seem to you that the substitution of a woman's image for the sign of the Christian cross is not simply designated here but expressly situated in the text? The image of the crucifix lies at the horizon right from the beginning of the play, and we find it anew in the following play. But aren't you also struck by the following: the coincidence between this theme, insofar as it is truly erotic, with what is here – and without there being another thread or landmark that would allow us to transfix the entire plot or scenario – which is the theme of outstripping or creating a breach beyond all values based on faith?

Isn't this play – which is apparently by a believer, and from which believers, including the most eminent among them, Georges Bernanos [1888–1948] himself, turn away as from blasphemy – for us the index of a new meaning given to human tragedy?

This is what I will try to show you next time using the other two parts of the trilogy.

May 3, 1961

XX

TURELURE'S ABJECTION

The father's (hi)story.
The father duped at dice.
How Freud operated.
The object of desire is its instrument.
Three generations suffice.

Please excuse me if, in this venue, which is open to one and all, I ask those united in shared friendship for Maurice Merleau-Ponty to cast their thoughts back for a moment on this man who was their friend and my friend. He was taken from us in a flash last Wednesday, the evening after our last class, and we learned of his death a few hours later. For me it was a direct blow to the heart.

Maurice Merleau-Ponty followed his own path and conducted his own research, which was not the same as mine. We began from different places, we had different aims, and I would even say that it was based on our different aims that we both ended up teaching. He had always wanted to teach, whereas I can say that it is quite in spite of myself that I occupy this podium.

I can also say that we did not have the time, owing to this untimely fatality, to find more connections between our work. He would have been sympathetic to what I teach you. And, believe me, this past week the profound mourning that I have experienced owing to his disappearance has made me wonder about the level at which I can occupy this position and in such a way that I can call myself into question in my own eyes. At least it seems to me that from him – from his responses, attitude, and amicable comments every time he joined us here – I received aid and confirmation that we shared a common idea of teaching, an idea that steers clear of all infatuation with principles and all pedantry as well.

You will thus excuse me if today, whereas I expected to arrive at the end of our present detour, the reasons for which I explained

to you last week, I am unable to take things any further than I will
manage to. Be so kind as to pardon me for not having been able to
devote the time to preparing that I usually do.

1

When we finished last week, we were discussing the end of *The
Hostage* and the image it presents of Sygne de Coûfontaine who
says no. This no is the very place to which a tragedy, that I will provisionally call Christian, pushes its heroine. It is worth dwelling on
each of these terms.

I have spoken with you often enough about tragedy for you
to know that according to Hegel in *The Phenomenology of Mind*,
Christian tragedy is related to reconciliation – *Versöhnung*. It is
related to the kind of redemption that, in his view, resolves the
fundamental impasse of Greek tragedy, and consequently does not
allow it to establish itself at its own level, but instates at most the
level of what we might call a divine comedy, comedy in which, in the
final analysis, the strings are all held by He in whom all bonds – even
those beyond our ken – are reconciled.

Our experience [of theater] undoubtedly runs counter to this
noetic understanding where Hegel's perspective founders owing
to a certain bias; for a human voice, that of Kierkegaard, emerged
afterward and it contradicted Hegel. And Shakespeare's *Hamlet*, to
which we devoted quite a lot of time two years ago [in Seminar VI],
is there to show us something else, to show us that another dimension subsists, meaning that we cannot say that the Christian era puts
an end to the dimension of tragedy.

Is *Hamlet* a tragedy? It surely is, and I believe I demonstrated
this to you. Is it a Christian tragedy? This is where Hegel's investigation intersects ours, for in truth, we don't find the slightest trace
of reconciliation in *Hamlet*. Despite the presence at the horizon of
Christian dogma, there is no resorting at any point in *Hamlet* to the
mediation of some sort of redemption. In *Hamlet*, the sacrifice of the   335
son remains purely tragic.

Nevertheless, we absolutely cannot eliminate something that is
also quite present in this strange tragedy and that inscribes what, a
few moments ago, I called the dimension of dogma or of Christian
faith: the ghost* – he who, beyond death, reveals to the son that
he was killed, how he was killed, and by whom he was killed – is a
father who has been damned.

I just referred to this tragedy, whose resources I assuredly was
unable to exhaust in my commentary on it, as "strange." I would

repeat the word "strange" when considering a supplemental contradiction that we did not dwell upon, which is that it is never doubted
whether the father attests to the flames of hell and eternal damnation. Nevertheless, it is as a skeptic, as a student of Montaigne, as
someone once put it, that Hamlet wonders, "To be, or not to be . . .
To sleep: perchance to dream." Does the afterlife deliver us from
this accursed life, from the ocean of humiliation and servitude that
life is?

Thus we cannot avoid tracing out the scale that is established
on the basis of the gamut which, running from ancient tragedy to
Claudel's drama, could be formulated as follows.

In the case of Oedipus, the father is killed without the hero even
knowing it. He did not know, not only that it was by his hand that
his father was dead, but even that he was dead. The plot of the
tragedy nevertheless implies that he is already dead.

In *Hamlet*, the father is damned. What can that mean beyond
the fantasy of eternal damnation? Isn't this damnation tied to the
emergence of the fact that in *Hamlet* the father begins to know? He
assuredly does not know everything about the plot against him, but
he knows more than we might think. He knows in any case who
killed him and how he was killed. I left unsolved in my commentary
on the play the mystery that is left unsolved by the playwright – the
mystery of what is signified by the orchard* where death came to
him in "the blossoms of [his] sin," as it says in the text [Act I, Scene
5] – and the further enigma that it is through the ear that the poison
is administered. What enters through the ear if not speech? And
behind this speech, what is the mystery of lust?

Doesn't some hubris – which is found in the form the ideal of
the father takes in Hamlet's eyes – correspond here to the strange
iniquity of his mother's jouissance? Nothing is said about this father
except that he embodied what we might call the ideal of the knight in
courtly love. This man would strew flowers on the ground beneath
his queen's feet. This man would wipe from her face, as the text tells
us, the slightest gust of wind [Act I, Scene 2]. Such is the strange
dimension in which his father's eminent dignity and the ever boiling
source of his heart's indignation remains, and for Hamlet alone.
This father is nowhere mentioned as a king nor is his authority
ever debated, I would say. The father here is a sort of ideal for men
and this, too, deserves to remain a question for us, for at each of
these stages we can only hope the truth will appear in a subsequent
revelation.

In light of what seems natural to us as analysts – namely, to
project through history something like a question regarding the
father that is repeated from age to age – you should thus pause to

336

observe to what degree the crux of the father's function was never investigated before psychoanalysis came on the scene.

The very figure of Antiquity's father, inasmuch as we have called upon it in our imagery, is that of a king. Throughout the Biblical texts, the figure of the divine father raises a question that underpins a whole line of research. Starting when did the God of the Jews become a father? Starting when in history? Starting when in the prophetic tradition? All of these things entail thematic, historic, and exegetical questions that are so profound that to merely mention them in this fashion is still not even to properly raise them. It is simply to comment that at some point the topic of the father – Freud's question, "What is a father?" – must have shrunk considerably for it to have taken on the obscure knot-like form, which is not simply mortal but murderous, in which it has become fixed for us in the form of the Oedipus complex.

God as creator, God as Providence – this is not what concerns us in the question of the father, even if all of these resonances form its backdrop. And it is possible that this backdrop will be retroactively clarified owing to the fact that we have articulated this question. Hence, whatever our tastes and preferences may be, and whatever Claudel's work might represent for each of us, isn't it opportune and indeed necessary for us to wonder what the thematics of the father can be in a tragedy – especially when it is a tragedy that appeared at a point in time at which, owing to Freud, the question of the father had profoundly changed?

337

Thus I cannot believe that the fact that Claudel's tragedy is all about the father is an accident. The last part of his trilogy, which completes the series, is called *The Humiliation of the Father* [*Le Père humilié*]. Before, we had the father who has already been killed [Oedipus] and the father who was damned when he died [*Hamlet*]; now we have the humiliated father. What does this mean? What does Claudel mean by the term "humiliated father"? And first of all, in Claudel's thematics, where is this humiliated father? Where is the humiliated father – as they say in certain mystery postcards, "Where is the thief?" or "Where is the police officer?"

Who is the humiliated father? Is it the Pope? Although he is always called Pius [*Pie*], there are nevertheless two of them in the course of the trilogy. The first is a fugitive, but still less than a fugitive in that he is kidnapped, to the point that – and the ambiguity always relates to the wording of the titles – we can wonder if he is not in fact the Hostage. The other Pope, the Pius who appears at the end, in the third play, is the one who confesses in a highly touching scene that is clearly designed to exploit all the thematics of a certain characteristically Christian and Catholic feeling – that of "a servant unto servants" [p. 361/186], he who makes himself into the smallest of the small. I will read you the scene in *The Humiliation of the Father* where the Pope confesses to a little monk who is himself but someone who tends geese or pigs, it doesn't matter which, and who naturally carries within himself the ministry of the most profound and the simplest wisdom.

Let us not dwell too long upon these all-too-beautiful images, where it seems that Claudel is instead sacrificing to what is taken much further in a whole form of English dandyism, starting some 200 years ago, in which Catholics and Catholicism are the very height of distinction.

The problem lies elsewhere. I do not believe that the humiliated father is the Pope. There are many other father-like figures around. All three plays revolve around nothing but that. Moreover, the father that we see the most often – the father whose stature verges on a kind of obscenity, the father whose stature is strictly speaking impudent, the father in whom we cannot fail to note certain echoes of the ape-like form in which Freud's myth [of the primal horde] makes him appear at the horizon – is clearly Toussaint Turelure. His drama and death by murder not only constitute the pivotal point but, strictly speaking, the object of the trilogy's central play, *Crusts*.

338

Isn't the humiliation of the father shown to us through him? He is not simply impulsive or devalued; he takes on the form of the most extreme derision, a derision that even verges on the abject. Is this what we can expect from an author who professes to be Catholic and to revive and reincarnate traditional values before our very eyes? Isn't it strange that people didn't find this play scandalous, this play which – when it came out all by itself three or four years after *The Hostage* – endeavors to captivate and hold our attention with an episode in which a kind of sordidness, with Balzacian echoes, only recovers through a paroxysm, by going beyond all limits there too.

I don't know if I should ask for a show of hands from those who have not read *Crusts* since our last class. I suspect that it is not enough for me to put you on the scent for all of you to run headlong after it. I believe that I must thus briefly summarize what the play is about.

2

Crusts opens with a dialogue between two women.

Over 20 years have surely passed since Sygne de Coûfontaine's death, she having died the day the son she gave Toussaint Turelure was baptized. Turelure, who wasn't terribly sprightly even at that time, has become a rather sinister old man. We don't see him, for he is hidden in the wings, but what we see are two women, one of whom is his mistress, Sichel, and the other of whom is his son's mistress, Lumîr. The latter has just returned from Algeria – a country that has taken on a certain importance since the time at which the play came out – where she left Louis de Coûfontaine. The son's name is naturally Louis, he having been named in honor of the King whose throne was restored to him.

I must seize the opportunity to slip in here an amusing little observation that I don't know if anyone here has already made. The name Louis comes from Ludovicus, Ludovic, Lodovic, and Clodovic that we find among the Merovingians, and is nothing other than Clovis with the C removed. That's easier to see when it's written. This makes Clovis the first Louis. And we might wonder if everything wouldn't have been different if Louis XIV had known that he was actually Louis XV. Perhaps the style of his reign would have been different and so on indefinitely. Well, that was just an aside designed to provide a little comic relief.

339

While Louis de Coûfontaine is still on Algerian soil, at least people think he is, a woman shows up at Toussaint's house to demand what she rightfully has coming to her. This episode so overjoyed the two authors of a book of famous pastiches that they used the scene involving the old Toussaint as the theme of their imitation "in the style of Claudel." In their pastiche, they concocted for generations to come the famous reply, worthy of Claudel and truer than life, that is imputed to the parodic character when someone demands that he return a sum of which he has despoiled an unfortunate woman: "A penny saved is a penny earned."

The pennies in question are not the savings of the girl [Lumîr] who comes to demand that Toussaint Turelure repay them; they are no less than the fruit of the sacrifices made by Polish émigrés. A total of 10,000 francs, or even more, that was lent by the young woman – whose suitable role and function you will see further on – is what she demands. She asks the old Toussaint for them, even though it was not to him that she gave or lent this sum, but to his son. His son is now insolvent and cannot pay either these 10,000 francs or the other 10,000 francs he owes [p. 181/99]. Her goal is to obtain from the father a total of 20,000 francs dating back to the middle of the nineteenth century – in other words, at a time when a franc was a franc, believe you me, and it wasn't earned in a flash.

This young woman [Lumîr] meets another by the name of Sichel. Sichel is Toussaint's official mistress, and she can be rather prickly.

Some brashness comes with the job, and the woman who occupies it lives up to her role.

In short, these two women very quickly agree to try to figure out how to bump the old man off [*avoir la peau du vieux*]. Had they not wanted to get something else from him before they bumped him off, it seems that things would have been resolved still more quickly. Briefly stated, their approach absolutely does not involve tenderness or the highest form of idealism. These two women can truly be qualified as ideal, each in her own way, as you will see, since I will come back to this. For we spectators, they manage to embody odd forms of seduction.

I must point out to you all the calculations, and even extreme calculations, that are made by these two women when faced with Turelure's avarice. Note that his avarice is equaled only by his dissipation, which is itself outstripped only by his utter and complete unscrupulousness, as Sichel herself says verbatim [p. 163/90]. The Polish character Lumîr – whose name Claudel explicitly tells us should be pronounced Loum-yir [p. 161/88] – is ready to go all the way to reclaim what she considers to be a possession, a sacred legacy for which she is responsible. She has given this legacy away, but absolutely must restore it now to those for whom she feels fealty and a unique allegiance. The latter are all the émigrés, all the martyrs, and even all those who died for the cause that stirs most the passions and is the most energizing: the cause of Poland divided, of Poland split up. The young woman is determined to go as far as one can go, even if she has to offer herself up and yield to what she knows to be the old man's desire.

She knows in advance what to expect from him. She is sure that from the moment a woman is his son's mistress, she is in no way for him a prohibited object – far from it! We find here anew a feature that has only surfaced quite recently in what I might call the ordinary thematics of certain functions of the father.

Her partner in the dialogue, Sichel, as I mentioned earlier, is a smart cookie and is fully aware of the situation. Here too we find something new – by which I mean something that, compared to the odd game we call the Oedipus complex, is added by Claudel. Note carefully that Sichel is not the mother [of Louis, Toussaint Turelure's son]. The mother is dead and thus out of the picture. Claudel's play is thus arranged in a way that is undoubtedly designed to bring out elements that will get us interested in this plot, topology, or fundamental dramatic action, inasmuch as something common to one and the same era connects it from one creator to another, from a reflective thinker [Freud] to a creative one [Claudel].

Sichel is not Louis' mother. She is not even the father's wife. She is

340

the object of the father's tyrannical, ambiguous desire. Sichel clearly points out that if there is something that attaches the father to her, it is a desire that is quite close to the desire to destroy her, since he has also made her into his slave. And he is quite capable of speaking of his attachment to her as having arisen from the charming way she plays the piano and from her pinky as it is about to perfectly strike a note on the keyboard. Now, from the day she first began keeping the old man's accounts, she has never been able to open the piano [p. 179/98, but also p. 175/96].

341

Sichel thus has an idea. We see it come to fruition in the guise of Louis de Coûfontaine's sudden arrival at the point at which the plot thickens. For his arrival gives rise in his old father to a veritable gut-wrenching episode, a true fit of abject fear. "He's a comin' here?" the father suddenly cries [p. 181/98], dropping the fine way of speaking he had been adopting just a minute before to describe to the young woman I just mentioned [Lumîr] his poetic feelings for Sichel. "He's a comin' here?"

Indeed he is, and he is coming owing to a scheme developing in the wings, having received a letter from Sichel containing a warning. He comes to center stage, and the play culminates in a sort of singular game with four players [*partie carrée*], one might say, were it not that a fifth person enters into it: Sichel's father, the old Ali Habenichts, whose name is a play on *haben nichts*, meaning he who has nothing. He is an old loan shark and a sort of a doppelgänger of Toussaint Turelure. Turelure uses him as he orchestrates a complicated operation which consists of taking back the possessions of the Coûfontaines piece by piece from his own son, his son having had the objectionable idea to demand them from him as his inheritance as soon as he became an adult, plenty of legal papers in hand [p. 233/121].

You see how all of this comes together. It was no accident that I mentioned the Balzacian themes here. The circulation, metabolism, and conflict at the level of money is doubled by rivalry in the affective realm. The father sees in his son exactly what Freud brought to our attention: someone just like himself, a repetition of himself, a figure born of himself in whom he can see nothing but a rival. And when his son tenderly attempts to tell him at a certain moment, "Am I not a true Turelure?" the father roughly replies, "No doubt you are, but there's already one Turelure, and that's enough. As far as Turelures go, I fill the bill just fine all by myself" [p. 234/122]. This is another element in which we can recognize what Freud's discovery introduced.

But that's not all. We come next to what culminates after a dialogue in which Louis de Coûfontaine's mistress Lumîr had to

342   whip Louis into a frenzy with a slew of insults targeting his vanity [*amour-propre*] and narcissistic virility, as we say: she reveals to Louis that his father propositioned her – the very father who, through his plotting, wishes to force Louis into bankruptcy, into the corner of which he finds himself backed when the play begins; the very father who wishes to take not only Louis' land from him, planning to buy it back on the cheap thanks to his loan-shark intermediaries, but his woman as well [pp. 226–7/118–19]. In short, Lumîr arms Louis against his father, literally putting guns in his hands. And we witness onstage a murder that is very well prepared for at a woman's instigation. She is not simply a temptress here, but the person who plots and creates the entire artifice of the crime around which Louis himself accedes to the father function.

It turns out that both women collaborated in the murder we see take place onstage, the killing of the father on "the other stage" [*anderer Schauplatz*, "the other scene"]. As Lumîr says somewhere, "Sichel is the one who gave me the idea" [p. 230/120]. And indeed, it was during their first discussion that Sichel planted the seed in Lumîr's imagination – namely, that the old man who desires her, this character that Claudel depicts to us, is a scorned father who has, as it were, been duped [*joué*]. The duped father is certainly the fundamental theme of classical comedy, but here we must understand the word *joué* in a way that goes still further than decoy and derision. He is duped [*joué*], so to speak, at dice and he is duped because he is, in the final analysis, a passive element in the game; this is expressly mentioned at the end of the dialogue between the two women.

After having opened up and revealed all of their thoughts to each other, one says to the other, "Play [*jouez*] your game and I'll play mine – I have my trump cards too – both of us playing against the dead man [*le mort*]" [p. 176/96]. Toussaint Turelure makes his entrance at this exact moment and cries, "Hey, who is talking about death [*mort*]?" One of the women replies, "We were discussing the rules of whist and the game last night: the weaknesses and strengths of the dummy [*le mort*]" [p. 177/96]. At that, the old man, suspecting nothing, replies by making a few jokes about what he was left with in that game – namely, the high cards, naturally. Here we have true French elegance, something that is constantly alluded to in the play. "He is a Frenchman to the core!" Sichel says to Lumîr. "And you can

343   get anything you want from him, for he loves women. Oh! He is a true Frenchman! Anything except money." Money – yuck! [p. 171/94].

Isn't it striking that here again we stumble upon the image of a game with four players – whist in this case – which I have often mentioned in a different sense to designate the structure of the analytic situation?

Before the tragic scene occurs, the father is already dead, or almost. All you have to do is blow on him, and he'll keel over. And, indeed, this is what we are going to see. We find next a dialogue wherein the simultaneous presence of tragic and buffoonish dimensions would make it worth our while to read it together. It is, in fact, a scene that deserves, in the world's literature, to be highlighted as ultimately rather unique in kind, and its various twists and turns would also be worth dwelling on if our sole goal here were to provide a literary analysis. Unfortunately, I must push on a bit more quickly than I would if I were going to get you to savor all the different twists here.

Be that as it may, it is quite nice to see that one of these twists involves the son imploring the father to give him the 20,000 francs which he knows full well – and for good reason, since Louis and Sichel plotted the whole business long before – he has in his pocket, making a serious bulge [p. 239/125]. He implores his father to give them to him in order to allow him, not only to meet his commitments, not only to pay back a sacred debt, not only to avoid losing the little he, the son, possesses, but also so as not to be reduced to being no more than a serf on the very land to which he has devoted all his passion [p. 238/124]. For it is on this land near Algiers that Louis de Coûfontaine went to seek the re-jection [*rejet*] – in the sense of something that has sprung up anew and that spurts out, in the sense of an offshoot – the re-jection of his being, of his solitude, of this dereliction he has always felt, knowing that his mother did not want him and that his father, as he says, never watched him grow up with anything other than worried concern [p. 222/116].

What is involved here is a passion for the soil and the return to what he feels he was chased away from – namely, all recourse to nature. And, in truth, we have here a theme that would be well worth considering in the historical genesis of what we call colonialism, which is the theme of émigrés who did not simply invade colonized countries but who broke new ground. This resource given to all the lost children of Christian culture would certainly be worth isolating as an ethical mainspring that we would be wrong to neglect at the present moment where we are weighing its consequences.

344

It is thus at the moment at which Louis finds himself at the height of this trial of strength between his father and himself that he pulls out the pistols that were put in his hands by Lumîr.

There are two pistols. Let us consider this for a moment. It is, strictly speaking, a theatrical artifice, trick, or nicety. He has been armed with two pistols – two pistols which, I'll tell you right away, will not go off even though they are both loaded.

This is the exact opposite of what happens in a famous passage of the *Sapeur Camember* in which the soldier Pidou is given a letter from the general.

> "Look," Pidou says, "this letter ain't loaded. It's not that the general doesn't have the means necessary, but it ain't loaded. Well that won't stop it from going off all the same."

Here it is the exact opposite. Even though Lumîr has loaded them both, the pistols misfire [p. 247/128]. But that doesn't stop the father from dying. The poor guy dies of fright, and this is precisely what people had been expecting all along, since this is explicitly why Lumîr had given Louis one of the pistols, the little one, telling him,

> "This one is loaded, but with a blank; it will simply make noise and it is possible that that will be enough to make him croak. If it isn't, then you will use the big gun – that one has a bullet in it." [p. 230/120]

Louis got his education in a place where land was being cleared, but where one did not acquire the land – this is clearly indicated in the text – without rather roughly dispossessing other people [p. 216/113]. There is certainly no need to fear that the hand that will pull the trigger of the second gun will tremble any more than it will for the first. As Louis says later, he doesn't like pussyfooting around [p. 250/129]. It is not with a smile on my face that I'll go that far, "but as long as I'm there," he says, I might as well use both pistols at the same time.

Now as I said, whether loaded or not, neither of them goes off. There is nothing but noise, and yet this noise does the trick. As is very prettily described in the stage direction, the old man stops dead in his tracks, his eyes popping out and his jaw slack [p. 247/128]. We spoke last time about the twitching of life [*grimace de la vie*]; here the wincing of death [*grimace de la mort*] is anything but elegant. And there you have it: the job is done.

345

As I told you, and as you see, all the niceties regarding the father's imaginary dimension are very well articulated here. Even when it comes to efficacy, the imaginary can suffice. This is demonstrated to us through an image. But in order for things to be still more lovely, Lumîr returns to the stage at that very moment.

Louis is not absolutely calm, naturally. He hasn't the slightest doubt that he has committed parricide, because, first of all, he clearly wanted to kill his father, and because he in fact succeeded in doing so. The terms and style of the concluding dialogue here are worth dwelling on and I will ask you to have a look at them. You will savor them in all their coarseness. I have noted that certain people, and not the least attuned or worthy, find *Crusts* and *The Hostage* to be rather boring plays. I admit that I do not find all the twists and turns of the plot boring in the least. They are rather dark. What is unsettling to us is that this darkness is operative exactly at the same time as a sort of comedy whose quality may appear to be a bit too acerbic. Nevertheless, these are not its least merits.

The question, all the same, is where is this designed to lead us? What fascinates us in all this? I am quite sure that, in the final analysis, this demolition of the farcical father, who is massacred in this buffoonish way, arouses in us feelings that are not terribly well localized or localizable.

What is quite pretty, nevertheless, is to see how this scene ends, namely, with Louis saying, "Stop." Once the deed has been done, while the girl is slipping the wallet out of the father's pocket, Louis says, "Hold on a minute. Let me check something." He empties the little pistol, rifles through the stuff that was used at the time to load weapons, and sees that the small pistol was also loaded. He comments on this to the captivating woman who loaded his gun. She looks at him and gives no other reply than a gentle laugh [p. 250/129].

Doesn't this pose a problem for us? What does the poet mean by this? We will assuredly come to know this in the third act when Lumîr's true colors are shown. But up until this point we have been shown nothing dark or fanatical in her. We will see what the nature of her desire is. The fact that, for her – a woman who considers herself most certainly doomed to the supreme sacrifice – this desire may go as far as being hanged, and the rest of the story confirms her conviction, does not exclude the fact that her passion for her lover, he who, to her, is truly her lover, Louis de Coûfontaine, may go so far as to wish for him a tragic end, for example, the gallows [p. 263/136].

The theme of love bound to death and, strictly speaking, of the lover who is sacrificed, is literarily shed light on for us by what we find in *The Red and the Black* [by Stendhal], at the horizon of the story of the two La Moles: the La Mole who was decapitated and whose head was supposedly received by a woman, and Julien Sorel whose bodily remains are accompanied by a certain Mademoiselle de la Mole – this one is imaginary – who kisses his decapitated head. We must keep in mind the extreme nature of Lumîr's desire. She summons Louis to follow her in the pathway of this desire, of this love that aims at nothing but consuming itself in an extreme instant. But Louis – who has committed parricide and received his inheritance by doing so, and has nevertheless entered into another

346

dimension than the one he knew hitherto – now turns into another Turelure, another sinister character whose caricature Claudel does not fail to draw for us in what follows.

Note carefully that Louis becomes an ambassador – we would be wrong to think that all these flourishes are included by Claudel without our being able to consider him to be ambivalent in some way deep within himself – and thus refuses to follow Lumîr. And it is because he does not follow her that he marries his father's mistress, Sichel.

I will skip the end of the play – namely, how it comes about that this sort of new start or metamorphosis leads him not only to empty out the pockets of the dead man and even slip on the dead man's boots, but also to get into bed with the same woman as him. We are faced here with gloomy stories of IOUs, all kinds of shady dealings, and an insurance policy that the ever clever father had taken out before his death to ensure that those who might get involved with him, especially Lumîr, would have very little pecuniary interest in wishing him dead [pp. 205–8/109–10]. He arranged things in such a way that his possessions were listed in the account books of his obscure associate, Ali Habenichts, as appearing to be owed to Habenichts. It is insofar as Sichel hands this IOU over to Louis that she acquires a truly abnegating status in his eyes [p. 275/142]. He "abnegates," as Paul Valéry put it, his title by marrying her, and this is where the play ends – Louis de Coûfontaine gets engaged to Sichel Habenichts, the daughter of his father's partner in usury.

After such an ending, we can wonder still more about what the poet means, especially what he himself thinks about all this, having created what one might well call, strictly speaking, now that I have recounted it to you as I have recounted it, "this strange comedy." Just as there is, at the beginning of the trilogy, a tragedy that stares us straight in the face, that goes beyond every possibility or requirement imposed upon the heroine, in the place occupied by her image at the end, there can be nothing, at the end of the second play – that is, at the heart of Claudel's trilogy – but the total obscurity of a radical derision.

This goes as far as something, certain echoes of which can strike us as rather antipathetic, inasmuch, for example, as the position of the Jews is brought in here, without us really knowing why. For emphasis is placed here on Sichel's sentiments. She tells us what her position in life is. We must look, without any further reluctance, into this element of Claudel's thematics; moreover, I don't believe that anyone has ever imputed to Claudel sentiments that we could qualify, in any way whatsoever, as suspect. I mean that the grandeur, which is more than respected and exalted by him, of the

347

ancient Law never ceases in his dramatic work to inhabit even the least important characters who can be associated with it. And for him, all Jews are essentially associated with it, even if they turn out to reject that Law, saying that they aspire to put an end to it. What Jews pursue is the sharing by all of the only thing that is real, which is jouissance.

Indeed, this is truly Sichel's way of putting things, and this is how she is presented to us prior to the murder. And she is presented even more in this way afterward, when she offers to Louis the love that it turns out she has always had for him.

Doesn't this strange arrangement pose yet another problem for us? I can see that, having allowed myself to tell you the central story of *Crusts*, and I truly had to, I can hardly do any more today than propose the following. Doesn't it seem to you that to see this play – which will perhaps be performed again, which has sometimes been performed, and which we can't say is badly constructed or that it does not make us feel a certain fondness for it – to see this play end after this strange event, confronts us with a figure (like when we say, in French, "a ballet figure") or cipher that is essentially presented to us in a form that is truly unheralded owing to its very opacity? We have here a scenario that solicits our interest solely at the level of the most total enigma.

We don't in any way have time to even begin to approach what would allow us to solve the enigma. But keep in mind that if I mention it to you – or if I simply remark that it is impossible not to make something of such a construction that appeared in, I won't say the century, but in the decade in which the Oedipus complex was brought to light – I have my reasons for doing so.

Understand why I am bringing it in here and what – along with the solution that I think I can provide to this enigma – justifies that I am bringing it to your attention at such length and in such detail.

3

The father.

At the beginning of psychoanalytic thought was the father, and in a form whose scandalous traits comedy is well designed to help us bring out. Psychoanalysis had to articulate a drama at the origin of the law; it should suffice for you to see it presented on the contemporary stage to gauge not simply its criminal character but the possibility of its caricatural or even abject decomposition, as I said earlier. If this is so, the problem is one of knowing how that was necessitated by our objective, which is certainly the only thing that justifies us in our research. What made it necessary to bring out this image at the horizon of humanity, if it wasn't that it is part and parcel of the highlighting and implementing of the dimension of desire?

In other words, I am designating something that we tend to push ever further back from our horizon, and even paradoxically negate more and more in our practice as analysts: namely, the place of the father. Why? Quite simply because it disappears to the degree to which we forget the meaning and direction of desire, to the degree to which our actions with those who seek us out tend to put this desire on some sort of gentle leash, to slip it some kind of soporific, and to make use of some form of suggestion that reduces desire to need. And this is why we have begun to see the mother ever more at the root of this Other that we evoke in our patients.

There is, unfortunately, something that resists this tendency, which is that we call this mother "castrating." Why? In what way is she castrating?

We know the answer thanks to analytic practice – it is truly the thread that keeps us in touch with this dimension, a dimension that must not be lost – and it is the following: from our standpoint, from our specialized point of view, the mother is all the more castrating insofar as she is not busy castrating the father.

Consider your clinical experience. Mothers who are busy castrating the father exist, but we would not bother talking about the castrating mother if there was no father, whether we see him or not, or whether there was no father to castrate. We wouldn't bother talking about her if the maintenance of the dimension of the father, drama of the father, or function of the father – around which revolves, as you see, what concerns us for the moment regarding our position in the transference – weren't at least possible, whether it be neglected or absent.

We are also well aware that we cannot operate as analysts the way Freud did either, Freud having adopted the position of the father. This is what stupefies us in his way of intervening. And this is why we no longer know where to situate ourselves – because we have not learned to rearticulate on that basis what our position must be. The result is that we spend our time telling our patients, "You take me to be a bad mother," but that is not the position we must adopt either.

The path to which I am trying to redirect you, with the assistance of Claudel's plays, involves re-situating castration at the heart of the problem. For castration is identical to what I will call the constitution of the desiring subject as such – not the constitution of the subject of need or of the frustrated subject, but of the subject of desire. As I have sufficiently emphasized in this ongoing Seminar, castration is identical to the phenomenon that is such that the object that desire lacks – since desire is [based on] lack – is in our experience identical to the very instrument of desire: the phallus.

The object that desire lacks – whatever it may be, and even at a level other than the genital level – must, in order to be characterized as an object of desire, and not the object of one or another of our frustrated needs, come to occupy the same symbolic place that is occupied by the very instrument of desire, the phallus – in other words, this instrument insofar as it is raised to the function of a signifier.

Next time I will show you that Claudel articulated this, whatever his reservations about it might have been, and even if the poet absolutely did not suspect how his creation could someday come to be formulated. This merely makes it all the more convincing, just as it is altogether convincing to see Freud already enunciate the laws of metaphor and metonymy in *The Interpretation of Dreams*.

Why is this instrument raised to a signifying function? Precisely in order to occupy the place I just spoke about, which is symbolic. What is this place? It is the neutral position [*point mort*] occupied by the father insofar as he is already dead [*mort*]. I mean that solely by virtue of the fact that the father is the one who articulates the law, the voice behind it can but falter. Either he is inadequately present or else, as a presence, he is only too present. [This neutral position] is the point at which everything that is enunciated passes anew through zero, between yes and no. I am not the one who invented the radical ambivalence between good and bad, love and hate, or complicity and alienation. In short, he who props up the law must die before the law can be instated as law.

It is not enough to simply say that desire as a phenomenon is produced at this level. We must also locate the radical gap, which is why I strive to come up with topological schemas for you that allow us to do so. In effect, this gap develops over time, and perfected desire is not simply this point, but rather what one might call a set in the subject whose topology I not only try to illustrate for you in a para-spatial sense, but whose various stages [*temps*] I endeavor to indicate. The explosion at the end of which desire's configuration is realized can be broken down into three stages, and you can see this marked in different generations. This is why there is no need, in order to situate the composition of desire in a subject, to go all the way back, in a perpetual recurrence, to Adam, the father. Three generations are enough.

In the first generation we find the mark of the signifier. This is what is illustrated, in an extreme and tragic manner, in Claudel's composition by the image of Sygne de Coûfontaine, who is carried

351

to the very destruction of her being, because she is totally ripped away from all her attachments based on speech and faith.

We come now to the second stage. Even at a poetic level, poetry is not the endpoint. Even among the characters created by Claudel's imagination, this leads to the appearance of a child. People who speak and are marked by speech engender. Something slips into the interval which is at first *infans* [someone who does not speak], and this is Louis de Coûfontaine. In the second generation, we find an object that is totally rejected, an object that is not desired, an object inasmuch as it is undesired.

In this poetic creation, how is what will result therefrom in the third generation – in other words, in the only true generation – configured before our eyes? It is at the level of all the others, naturally, but I mean that the others are artificial decompositions of it – they are the antecedents of the only one that is of concern.

Between the mark of the signifier and passion for the partial object, how is desire composed?

This is what I hope to articulate for you next time.

May 10, 1961

XXI

PENSÉE'S DESIRE

Saying no.
Tragedy is reborn . . .
. . . as is desire, myth, and innocence.
The Other incarnated in this woman.

Sygne: Coûfontaine, I am yours; take me, and do with me as you will! [Make of me] your wife, if you so wish it, or, if you prefer, beyond the limits of this life, where earthly bodies are no more, our souls shall be joined together, and indissolubly made one. [p. 35/24]

I wanted to point out to you the repetition of an expression by which love is articulated throughout the text of Claudel's trilogy. Georges de Coûfontaine immediately responds to Sygne's words in *The Hostage* as follows:

Oh, Sygne whom I have found at last, do not fail me as the world has failed me! Shall I, then, in the end, have something lasting, other than my own will? [p. 35/24]

Indeed, it's all right there. This man, who has been betrayed and abandoned by everyone, who leads, as he tells us, the life "of a hunted beast [. . .] with no sure refuge wherein to hide," recalls

the saying of the monks of India, who proclaim that all this life is bad, a hollow illusion which remains with us only because we move in step with it, and which would pass from us, if we but sat quietly in one place. An unworthy dream! A sordid temptation! In this collapse of all my life, I, at least, remain unchanged, and my honor and my duty are unchanged. But you, Sygne, weigh carefully your words. Do not fail me; you

too, in this hour of my approaching end, as all else has failed
me! Do not deceive me [. . .]. [p. 36/25]

Such is the point of departure that lends gravitas to the tragedy.
Sygne finds herself betraying the very person to whom she has
committed herself with all her soul. We encounter the theme of the
exchange of souls again later, distilled in a single instant in *Crusts*,
in the course of a dialogue between Louis and Lumîr – Loum-yir,
as Claudel expressly tells us the name of the Polish woman should
be pronounced – when, after the parricide has occurred, she tells
him that she will not follow him, that she will not return to Algeria
with him, but instead invites him to come consummate with her
the mortal adventure that awaits her. Louis has just undergone
the metamorphosis that parricide brought to a head in him, and
he refuses. He nevertheless oscillates one more time: he addresses
Lumîr passionately, telling her that he loves her just the way she is
and that there is only one woman for him. To which Lumîr herself,
who is captivated by the call to death that provides the signification
of her desire, replies:

Is it really true that there is only one woman for you? Yes, I
know that it's true. Say what you want to! There is something
in you now – at this moment – that understands me! Something
that makes you my brother! It's a tearing away, an utter weari-
ness, a void which nothing can fill! You are [like] no one, and
no one is like you. You [stand] alone! And no matter how long
you may live, the time will never come when you could have
done otherwise than as you did! (*very softly*) You parricide!
We're alone; wholly, completely alone in this [awful] desert.
Two human souls knocking about in the void of life! Two souls
which can belong to each other. Two souls which, in the space
of a single second, like the thundering report of time that is
annihilated, can, through each other and to each other, be all
things! How sweet it is to live without looking ahead. If life
were only longer! It might be worth while to be happy. But life
is short; and there are ways of making it shorter yet! Yes, so
355   short that all eternity can be contained therein!
   Louis: Eternity means nothing to me.
   Lumîr: Yes! So short that all eternity can be contained
therein! So short that this world, this life which we scorn and do
not want, could be hidden away in it. This happiness on which
people lay such stress! Ah, life could be so small and tight and
narrow and brief that there would be no room in it for anything
or any one – except you and me. [pp. 266–67/137–8]

And a bit further on she continues:

> I will be your country close held in your arms. To you I will
> be happiness foregone, the land of Ur, the old, old power of
> Consolation. You and I only exist; only you and I live in this
> world, and there will, throughout all time, be only this moment
> when we stood face to face – and saw! And we shall be able to
> understand – then – even that mystery which lies hidden deep
> within us. Come! There are ways of drawing our souls out of
> ourselves, as one can draw a flashing sword – loyal, clean, and
> with honor unbesmirched. Yes, there is a way to break the
> chain, to batter down the prison wall. And there's a way of
> pledging one's oath and of sacrificing oneself, heart and soul, to
> the other – the only other! We can do it like brave men! We can!
> In spite of the horrible night, and the rain, and the awful empti-
> ness which surrounds us. Oh, it can be done! There is a way of
> giving all of oneself, and having faith, true faith, in the other.
> There's a way of so giving oneself that, believing implicitly in
> the flash of inspiration, each shall belong to the other and to
> him alone. [pp. 267–8/138]

Such is the desire that is expressed by she who Louis, after the parricide, casts aside in order to marry "his father's mistress," as it is
put in the play. Herein lies the turning point of Louis' transformation. And it will lead us today to question the meaning of what will
be born from him – namely, the feminine figure who, at the outset
of the third play in the trilogy, is the counterpart of Sygne: Pensée
de Coûfontaine.

By looking at her, we are going to examine what Claudel means
here.

1

356

Although it is easy and quite common in French to dismiss any
speech that falls outside of the ruts of ordinary routine by saying,
c'est du Untel ("That's vintage so-and-so") – and you are aware that
people do not fail to say that about he who is speaking to you right
now – it seems that no one even dreams of being astonished by what
poets say. People are happy to accept poets' singularity. And when
confronted with the strangeness of plays like Claudel's, no one any
longer dreams of wondering about the improbabilities and scandalous traits he presents us or about what, in the final analysis, could
have been his Christian aim and his plan.

What is the meaning of Pensée de Coûfontaine in the third play, *The Humiliation of the Father*? We are going to examine the signification of Pensée de Coûfontaine as we would examine that of a living personage. What is at stake is Pensée de Coûfontaine's desire, Pensée's desire. And in Pensée's desire we are, of course, going to find the very idea [*pensée*] of desire.

Do not take this to be an allegorical interpretation. The characters in Claudel's trilogy are symbols only inasmuch as they are at work at the heart of the impact of the symbolic on a person. And the ambiguity of the names that are attributed to them by the poet indicates that we are justified in interpreting them as instances of the impact of the symbolic on our very flesh.

It would be easy for us to read into the way Claudel spells the odd name, Sygne. The word begins with an S, and it truly invites us to recognize a sign [*signe*] therein. Moreover, there is the imperceptible change, the substitution of *y* for *i*. In this superimposing of the mark, one might recognize something that encounters – through some kind of convergence or Kabbalistic geomancy – my $, by which I demonstrated to you that the imposition of the signifier on man is something that both marks and disfigures him.

At the other end of the trilogy, we have Pensée. Here the word is left intact and in order to see what is meant by this Pensée of desire, we must clearly begin with what is signified by the passion undergone by Sygne in *The Hostage*.

The first play in the trilogy left us overcome by the figure of this sacrificed woman who shakes her head saying no, by the mark of the signifier raised to the highest degree: refusal raised to the position of a radical stance. This is what we must explore.

In exploring this stance, if we know how to examine it, we will find in it another of our terms that grows out of analytic practice, at its pinnacle. If you remember what I have taught you several times, here and elsewhere, in this Seminar and at our Society meetings, I asked you to overhaul the use that is currently made in psychoanalysis of the term "frustration." I did so to incite you to return to what Freud, who never uses the term "frustration," means by the original term *Versagung*, insofar as it goes well beyond and far deeper than any conceivable frustration.

Versagung implies not making good on a promise, on a promise for which one has already given up everything – this is the exemplary value of Sygne's character and drama. What she is asked to give up is what she has put all of her effort into, what she has hitched her entire life to, her life having already been marked by the sign of sacrifice. The dimension of sacrifice, raised to the second power, raised to the most profound refusal owing to the workings of the

Word, is open to endless realization. This is what is posited at the outset of Claudel's tragedy, and we cannot remain indifferent to it or simply consider it to be the extreme, excessive, or paradoxical form of a kind of religious madness [*folie*]. For, on the contrary, as I shall show you, this is precisely where we, as people of our own times, are situated to the very extent that this religious folly is not there for us.

Let us observe carefully what is at stake for Sygne de Coûfontaine. What is imposed upon her is not simply something like force or constraint. She is made to freely commit herself, according to the law of marriage, to someone whom she calls the son of her servant and of the sorcerer Quiriace. Nothing connected to what is imposed on her can be anything but accursed to her. Thus the *Versagung* here, the refusal from which she cannot free herself, becomes what the very structure of the word implies: *versagen* is refusal regarding what is said [*le dit*]; and, were I to equivocate in order to find the best translation, perdition. Everything that is a condition becomes perdition. And this is why not saying becomes saying no here.

We have encountered this extreme point before, but what I would like to show you is that it is gone beyond here. We came across it at the end of the Oedipus tragedy in the με φυναι (*me phunai*) of *Oedipus at Colonus* [verse 1224], in the "would that I were not," which means "not to have been born." Let me remind you in passing that we find here the true place of the subject insofar as he is the subject of the unconscious – namely, the με, that is, the highly unusual "not" [*ne*], only vestiges of which we can still find in French, making paradoxical appearances in expressions like *je crains qu'il ne vienne* ["I'm afraid he may (not) come" or "I cannot but fear he is coming"] or *avant qu'il n'apparaisse* ["before he not but appear"]. It appears to be an expletive in such contexts, according to grammarians, whereas it is precisely there that the tip of desire's iceberg appears – not the subject of the statement who is "I," he who is currently speaking, but the subject in which enunciation finds its origin.

Oedipus leaves us with the Greek words *me phunai*: "would that I were not" – or, to follow the Greek even more closely, "were I not" – "not to be here" [*n'y être*], which sounds in French so curiously like the verb to be born [*naître*]. What is designated thereby if not the fact that owing to the imposition upon man of destiny and owing to prescribed exchange via kinship structures, something has been covered over that makes his entrance into the world an entrance into the implacable play of debt? In the final analysis, man is simply guilty of the responsibility [*charge*] he receives for the debt stemming from the *Até* that precedes him.

Something else has happened since that time. For us, the Word

358

has become incarnate. It has come into the world and, as opposed to what the Gospels say, it is not true that we have not recognized it. We have recognized it and are experiencing the aftermath of this recognition. We are at one of the stages of the consequences of this recognition. This is what I would like to try to articulate to you.

To us, the Word is not simply the law into which we insert ourselves in order that each of us bear responsibility for the debt that constitutes our fate. It opens up for us the possibility or temptation on the basis of which it is possible for us to curse ourselves, not only as a particular destiny or life, but as the very pathway by which the Word commits us, and as an encounter with the truth, as the moment of truth. We are no longer solely subject to feeling guilty owing to symbolic debt. We can, in the most proximate sense that the word indicates, be reproached for bearing responsibility for the debt. In short, it is the very debt that gave us our place that can be stolen from us; and it is in this context that we can feel totally alienated from ourselves. Antiquity's *Até* no doubt made us guilty of this debt, but to give it up – as we can now – makes us responsible for a still greater misfortune owing to the fact that fate is no longer anything [for us].

359

In short, what we learn every day from psychoanalytic practice is that the guilt we still have, the guilt that is palpable to us in our work with neurotics, is the exact price we have to pay for the fact that the God of fate is dead. The fact that this God is dead is at the heart of what Claudel presents us.

The dead God is represented here by the proscribed priest who is no longer presented to us in any form but that of what is called the Hostage, who gives his name to the first play in the trilogy. The figure of Antiquity's faith is henceforth held Hostage by politics, prey to those who wish to use it for the purposes of restoring the old order.

But the flipside of this elimination of the dead God is that it is the faithful soul that is held Hostage, Hostage of a situation in which, beyond the endpoint of Christian truth, tragedy is truly reborn – namely, everything slips away from the soul if the signifier can be taken captive.

Naturally, only she who believes can be held hostage – namely, Sygne. And because she believes she must attest to what she believes. This is precisely why she is caught and captivated in a situation that it suffices to create for it to exist: to be called upon to sacrifice to the very negation of what she believes.

She is held hostage by the very negation she is subjected to of what is best in herself. What is presented to us goes much further than the misfortune of Job and his resignation. Job is weighed down by misfortune that he has not deserved, but the heroine of modern tragedy is asked to assume responsibility for the very injustice she abhors as if it were a jouissance.

This is what is opened up as a possibility, for the being who speaks, by the fact that he props up the Word at the moment at which the Word is asked to guarantee him.

Man becomes a hostage of the Word because he tells himself – or, too, in order that he tell himself – that God is dead. At this moment a gap opens up in which nothing can be articulated except what is merely the very beginning of the expression "were I not," that can no longer be anything but a refusal, a no, a *ne*, a tic or grimace – in short, this giving way of the body or psychosomatic phenomenon, which is the endpoint where we must encounter the mark of the signifier.

360

As it develops through the three stages of the tragedy, the drama is that of knowing how – based on this radical stance – a desire can be reborn and of knowing what desire it is.

It is here that we are transported to the other end of the trilogy, to Pensée de Coûfontaine.

2

Pensée de Coûfontaine is an indisputably seductive figure who is obviously presented to the play's spectators – and I will try to say who these spectators are later on – as the object of desire, strictly speaking.

It suffices to read *The Humiliation of the Father* – and what could be more unpleasant than this story? Could any staler crust of bread be offered to us than the import of this father who is presented to us as an obscene old man, and whose murder alone, which is portrayed to us, allows what was transmitted to Louis de Coûfontaine to be continued, which is merely the most degraded and degenerate figure of the father? It is enough to hear what each of you may well have noticed, the ingratitude represented by the appearance – during a night of festivities in Rome at the beginning of *The ·Humiliation of the Father* – of the figure of Pensée de Coûfontaine, to understand that she is presented here as a seductive object.

Why? And how? What does she balance out? What does she make up for? Is something that Sygne sacrificed going to be given to Pensée [p. 381]? To put it more explicitly, is it in the name of her grandmother's sacrifice that Pensée de Coûfontaine will warrant attention here?

An allusion is made to this at one point, in the dialogue between the Pope and the two men who will represent the arrival of love in her life. This old family tradition is alluded to as if it were an ancient story that is told [p. 370/191]. The Pope himself, speaking to Orian who is the object of this love, uses the word "superstition": "Are you afraid of this poor girl? Empty superstition! Raise up your eyes! Show some courage!" [p. 381]. Are you going to give in, my son, to this superstition? Is Pensée going to represent something like an exemplary figure, a rebirth of faith that was momentarily eclipsed? Far from it.

Pensée is freethinking, if one can put it thus, using a term that is hardly Claudel's here. Yet this is clearly what is involved. Pensée has but one passion, which is, as she tells us, for justice that goes beyond all the exigencies of beauty itself [p. 341/176]. What she wants is justice, and not just any old justice, not Antiquity's form of justice, some natural right to distribution or retribution – the justice she wants is absolute. It is the justice that inspires the rumbling and movement of the revolution that constitutes the background noise of the third play in the trilogy. This justice is the flipside of everything real, everything related to life that, owing to the Word, is felt to be an offense or abomination to justice. What is at work in Pensée's discourse is an absolute justice, with all its power to shake up the world.

As you can see, this is the furthest thing from the kind of preaching we might expect from Claudel as a man of faith. And this is what will allow us to give meaning to the figure on which the entire drama of *The Humiliation of the Father* converges.

In order to understand it, we must dwell a moment on what Claudel makes of Pensée de Coûfontaine, who is depicted here as the fruit of the marriage between Louis de Coûfontaine and the woman his father basically gave him as a wife solely by virtue of the fact that this woman was already his woman. We have here the extreme, paradoxical, and caricatural edge of the Oedipus complex. It is the furthest shore of Freud's myth that is offered up to us here: an obscene old man forces his sons to marry his wives, and he does so to the very extent that he wishes to steal theirs from them. This is a more advanced and expressive way to accentuate what comes to light in Freud's myth. It does not create a better quality father but rather another scoundrel [*canaille*].

And, indeed, this is how Louis de Coûfontaine is depicted to us throughout the play. He marries Sichel, a woman who wants him as the object of her jouissance. He marries this odd figure of a woman who rejects all the burdens of the law – namely hers, the ancient Law – as well as the status of the wife as a saintly figure who is the epitome of patience. She is the one who finally brings to light her will to embrace the world.

What will come of this? What will be born from this is, oddly enough, the rebirth of the very thing that the tragedy in *Crusts* showed us was ruled out – namely, the very desire in its absolute character that was represented by the figure of Lumîr.

Lumîr is a rather odd name. Claudel's footnote regarding how to pronounce it (Loum-yir) should give us pause for thought. We should relate it to what Claudel tells us about the fancies of the old Turelure, who changes everyone's name in a derisory way, calling Rachel Sichel, which in German means, as the text tells us, sickle – and in particular, the sickle that portrays the crescent moon in the sky [pp. 167/91–2]. We have here an odd echo of the figure with which Victor Hugo's *Booz endormi* ends. Claudel constantly engages in the very same game of deforming people's names, as if he himself were taking on the role of the old Turelure. Lumîr is what we will encounter later in the dialogue between the Pope and the two brothers, Orso and Orian, in the form of light [*lumière*]: "cruel light."

This cruel light sheds light for us on what the character Orian represents, for, as faithful as he may be to the Pope, when he says "cruel light," it startles the Pope. The Pope retorts to him that light is not in the least bit cruel [p. 378/195].

Yet Orian is indubitably right when he says it. And the poet is on his side. Now, she who is going to come to incarnate the light that is obscurely sought for, without knowing it, by her own mother, the light sought through a form of patience [p. 393/202] that is ready to serve everyone and to accept everything, is Pensée, Sichel's daughter. Pensée is going to become the incarnate object of the desire for this light. And the poet cannot but imagine and portray this flesh-and-blood thought [*pensée*], this living Pensée, to us as blind.

I feel we should pause here for a moment. What does the poet intend by incarnating the object – the partial object, the object insofar as it is the resurgence and effect of the parental constellation – as a blind woman? This blind woman will be paraded before our eyes throughout the third play and in the most moving of fashions.

She appears at a costume ball which figures the end of a moment of Rome's history just prior to its capture by the Garibaldians. There is also another end that is celebrated in this late-night party, that of a Polish nobleman who, pushed to the extreme limit of solvency, must surely see the bailiffs descend upon his property the next day [p. 315/162]. This Polish aristocrat is there to remind us, like a face on a cameo [p. 319/164], of someone we have heard about so often and who died so sadly. Let us forget about her. Let us not speak of her any more. The spectators all realize that the person in question is Lumîr. This aristocrat, characterized by all the nobility

363

and romanticism of martyred Poland, is nevertheless the type of nobleman who always inexplicably has a villa that he can liquidate.

It is in this context that we see the blind Pensée walking about as if she could see perfectly well. For her surprising sensitivity allows her, in the course of a preliminary visit, to locate – through her acute perception of echoes, approaches, and movements – the entire structure of a place as soon as she has gone up several steps [pp. 312–13/161]. Whereas we spectators know she is blind, the guests who are with her at the party are unaware of it for an entire act – especially he on whom her desire alights, Orian.

This character deserves a word of introduction for those who have not read the play. Orian, like his brother Orso, has the last name Homodarmes, which is truly Claudelian in inspiration, given its resonance owing to the same slightly deformed and accentuated construction as a signifier that we bizarrely encounter in so many characters in Claudel's plays. Recall to mind here Sir Thomas Pollock Nageoire. It makes as pretty a sound as the one we find in the passage on suits of armor in André Breton's "*Introduction au discours sur le peu de réalité.*"

These two characters, Orian and Orso, become involved in the plot. Orso is a nice boy who loves Pensée. Orian, who is not quite Orso's twin brother, since he is a year older, is the one on whom Pensée's desire alights. Why on him, if not for the fact that he is inaccessible? For in truth, Claudel's text or myth indicates to us that this blind girl can barely distinguish between their voices [pp. 423–8/216–9]. Indeed, at the end of the play, Orso is momentarily able to fool her into believing that he is Orian, who is dead. It is clearly because she sees something else that Orian's voice, even when it is Orso who speaks, makes her swoon.

But let us dwell for a moment on this blind girl. What is she trying to tell us? And to consider first what she projects before us, doesn't it seem that she is protected by a sort of sublime figure of modesty, which is based on the fact that, since she is unable to see herself being seen, she seems to be sheltered from the sole gaze that unveils?

I do not believe it overly eccentric to bring in here the dialectic of the so-called exhibitionistic and voyeuristic perversions that I have already discussed with you. I pointed out to you that the latter cannot be grasped merely on the basis of the relationship between he who sees and he who shows himself to a partner who is simply other, whether object or subject. What is involved in the fantasy of both exhibitionists and voyeurs is a third element which implies that a certain complicity can blossom in the partner who receives what is shown to her; that what delights her in her apparently innocent solitude is offered up to a hidden gaze; that it is thus the very desire that

364

sustains its function in fantasy that veils from the subject his role in the exhibitionistic or voyeuristic activity; and that exhibitionists and voyeurs enjoy themselves in some sense qua seeing and showing, but without knowing what they see or show.

In the case of Pensée, she is unable to be caught in the act, as it were, owing to the fact that no one can show her anything that would subject her to the small other. Note, too, that one cannot spy on her without being, like Actaeon, struck with blindness and without beginning to be chewed to pieces by the pack of hounds of one's own desires.

We see here the mysterious power of the dialogue between Pensée and Orian – Orian, whose name is but one letter away from that of one of the hunters who Diana transformed into a constellation, Orion. All by itself, the mysterious avowal with which the dialogue ends, "I am blind" [p. 352/182], has the impact of the words "I love you," insofar as it obviates all consciousness in the other of the fact that "I love you" has been said, situating itself directly in him as speech. Who could say, "I am blind," if not from the place where speech creates night? Who, in hearing it, would not feel the depth of night being born within himself?

This is where I wish to lead you – to the distinction between two relationships: that of *seeing oneself* and that of *hearing oneself*. People have long since pointed out that it is characteristic of phonation to immediately echo in the subject's own ear as he speaks. But this does not imply that the other to whom his speech is addressed has the same place or structure as the other in the case of visual unveiling. This is because speech does not incite sight, precisely inasmuch as it is, in and of itself, blindness.

One can see oneself being seen, which is why one steals away [*on s'y dérobe*]. But one cannot hear oneself being heard. In other words, we are not heard where we hear ourselves [*on ne s'entend pas là où l'on s'entend*] – namely, in our heads. Or, rather, those who do, those who in fact hear themselves being heard, are madmen who are hallucinating. This is the very structure of hallucination. They can only hear themselves being heard in the place of the Other, where we hear the Other send our own message back to us in an inverted form.

What Claudel means by introducing blind Pensée is that it suffices that the soul – because it is the soul that is involved here – close its eyes to the world in order to be what the world is missing and the most desirable object in the world; this is indicated throughout the dialogue in the third play. Psyche, who can no longer light the lamp, sucks in, so to speak, or draws to herself Eros' being, which is lack. The myth of Poros and Penia is reborn here in the guise of spiritual blindness, for we are told that Pensée incarnates here the very figure

365

of the "Synagogue" [p. 341/176], such as it is represented in the portico of the cathedral in Reims, with her eyes blindfolded.

Moreover, Orian, who plays opposite her, is clearly he from whom a gift can be received, precisely because he is overabundance. Orian is another form of refusal. If he does not give Pensée his love, it is, as he says, because he owes his gifts to others, to everyone, to divine works. What he misrecognizes is precisely the fact that what is asked of him in love is not his *poros*, his resources, his spiritual richness, his overabundance, or even, as he puts it, his joy; rather, what is asked of him is precisely what he does not have [p. 393/201]. He is a saint, of course, but it is rather striking that Claudel shows us the limits of his saintliness here.

It is a fact that desire here is stronger than saintliness itself. It is a fact that, in the dialogue with Pensée, Orian the saint weakens and gives in; he loses the game, and, to call a spade a spade, goes ahead and screws little Pensée.

Which is exactly what she wants. Throughout the play, she has not lost a split second, a micro-second, in operating in this direction along pathways that I will not call the shortest, but that are assuredly the straightest and surest. Pensée de Coûfontaine is truly the rebirth of all that is ill-fated, which begins with debauchery, continues with gambling one's honor, with misalliance, and with abjuration – the "Louis-Philippisme" that someone once called the "second *temps-pire*" – in order to be reborn from it as though before sin, as innocence, but not as nature for all that.

This is why it is important for us to see on what stage the drama reaches its climax.

366

3

This stage is found in the last scene.

Pensée shuts herself in with her mother, who takes her under her protective wing, because she became pregnant owing to Orian's handiwork. She suddenly receives a visit from his brother, Orso, who comes to convey Orian's final message to her, Orian now being dead. Both the logic of the play and the situation that was created earlier have paved the way for this scene, since all of Orian's efforts were designed to get Pensée and Orso to accept something outrageous: that they marry.

Orian the saint sees no obstacle to his good little brother finding happiness. That is just fine for Orso. He is a good courageous guy. And, moreover, Orso's declaration leaves no doubt that he is quite capable of marrying a woman who does not love him. He is sure that he can break her down. He is courageous and takes up the challenge [p. 374/193]. He initially fought for those on the left; he was told [by Orian] that he had made a mistake, so he fought for those on the right. At first he was on the side of the Garibaldians and then he joined the Pope's soldiers [p. 337/174]. He is always there, fit as a fiddle – he's a guy you can count on.

We should not laugh too heartily at this stupid bastard, for it is a trap. And we will see later in what respect, for in truth, in his dialogue with Pensée, we are no longer inclined to laugh at him.

Who is Pensée in this scene? She is surely the sublime object – the sublime object insofar as I indicated its position to you last year as a substitute for the Thing. As you realized at the time, the nature of the Thing would not be so different from the nature of Woman, were it not true that, in relation to all the ways we have of approaching the Thing, Woman turns out to be something else altogether. Even the slightest woman, I would say. And in truth Claudel does not prove to us, no more than anyone else, that he has a very advanced idea of what a woman is – far from it.

Claudel's heroine, this woman that he creates before us, is the woman [qua object] of a certain desire. Let us nevertheless give Claudel credit for the fact that elsewhere, in *Partage de midi*, he created a female character for us, Ysé, who is not so bad. She strongly resembles a real woman.

367

Here we are in the presence of an object of desire. And what I wish to show you, and this is inscribed in her image, is that it is a desire that no longer has, at this level of deprivation [*dépouillement*], anything but castration to separate it – I mean to separate it radically – from any natural desire.

If you observe what happens onstage, it is in fact rather beautiful. But in order to situate it exactly, I will ask you to recall to mind the anamorphic cylinder that I discussed with you here, the tube placed on a table, on which [an imitation of] a painting by Rubens was projected, that of *The Elevation (or Raising) of the Cross*, through the artifice of a sort of formless drawing astutely placed at its base. I thereby portrayed for you the mechanism for reflecting the fascinating figure, beauty rising up, such as it is projected at the extreme limit in order to stop us from going any further toward the heart of the Thing.

Assuming that the figure of Pensée, as well as the main lines of the play, are designed to take us to this limit that is a bit further off, what do we see, if not the figure of a woman who is deified in order to be crucified yet again here?

The posture of crucifixion is indicated in the text [pp. 305 and 439], and it insistently returns at many other points in Claudel's work, from the Princess in *Tête d'Or*, to Sygne herself and Ysé, and to the figure of Doña Prouhèze. What does this figure bear within itself? A child, no doubt, but let us not forget what Claudel tells us, which is that the child comes alive and begins to move for the first time at the very moment at which Pensée takes, as she tells us, within herself the soul of he who is dead.

How is this capturing of the soul portrayed to us? It is a true act of vampirism. With the flaps of her shawl, Pensée wraps herself, as it were, around the basket of flowers that the brother, Orso, had sent, flowers that grew in soil that – as we learn from the dialogue, constituting a macabre note – contains the eviscerated heart of her lover, Orian. When she stands up again, she is supposed to have brought its symbolic essence inside herself [p. 439]. It is this soul that she presses, along with her own, she tells us, on the lips of the brother, Orso – who has just committed himself to her in order to provide the child with a father – while telling him that he will never be her husband.

This transmission or odd realization of the fusion of souls is what the first two quotes I cited for you at the beginning of class today – from *The Hostage* on the one hand, and from *Crusts* on the other – indicate as love's supreme aspiration. Orso, who we know is going to join his brother in death, is the designated conveyor, vehicle, or messenger of this fusion of souls.

What does this mean? As I told you earlier, we must not kid ourselves or allow ourselves to be taken in by the ridiculousness of the poor Orso, whose very function as a fake husband, where he ends up, makes us laugh. In the final analysis, the place he occupies is the very place by which we ourselves are called upon to be captivated here. This fantasy is offered up to our desire, as though it revealed the structure of our desire, and it reveals the magnetic power in Woman that attracts us, and not necessarily, as the poet says, toward something lofty – this is a third power and it cannot be ours except by representing our downfall.

In desire there is always some delight in death, but in a death that we cannot inflict upon ourselves. We encounter anew here the four terms that are represented, as it were, in us: the two brothers, *a* and *a′*; we as subjects, inasmuch as we don't understand anything about it; and the figure of the Other incarnated in this woman. These four elements allow for the possibility of all sorts of varieties of inflicted death, among which we can enumerate the most perverse forms of desire.

Here it is solely the most ethical case that is realized, insofar as it is Orian – the true, perfect man who asserts himself and maintains his virility – who pays the price by dying. This reminds us that it is true: he always and in every case pays the price – even when he reduces the price to the level of pleasure, in a way that is more costly for his humanity from a moral vantage point.

Thus ends the poet's plan. At the end of the tragedy of the subjects as pure victims of Logos or language, he shows us what becomes of desire. And regarding this desire, he makes it visible to us in the figure of this woman, this astounding [*terrible*] subject who goes by the name of Pensée de Coûfontaine.

She deserves her name Pensée, for she is thought about desire.

It is through love – the love that she expresses – for the other that she becomes the object of desire by becoming frozen [*en se figeant*].   369

Such is the topology in which the long path of the tragedy culminates.

As in any process or progress of human articulation, it is only retroactively that we can perceive what converges in the lines traced out in the traditional past, and announces what one day comes to light. Throughout Euripides' tragedies, we encounter the relationship to desire, and especially to women's desire, as a sort of sore point or wound that exasperates him. We can fathom what people call Euripides' misogyny, which is a sort of aberration or madness that seems to strike all of his poetry, only on the basis of what it became by being filtered through the sublimation of the Christian tradition.

As for the quartering points [*points d'écartèlement*] of the terms whose intersection necessitates the effects with which we as analysts deal – those of neurosis insofar as in Freud's thought they are asserted to be earlier than those of the golden mean, earlier than those of normality – we must pinpoint them, explore them, and grasp their extremes if we want to be able to situate and orient our actions. We want to situate and orient them in such a way that they are not captive to the mirage of the virtues of mutual aid that it is always so easy for us to succumb to, but in such a way that they correspond to what may be there – even in the most obscure forms that must be revealed – in the other that we accompany in the transference.

Someone once said that "the extremes meet up in me." We must pinpoint them at least momentarily in order to be able – and this is what I will end with today – to locate exactly what our place must be at the moment at which the subject is on the only path to which we needed to lead him, the path where he must articulate his desire.

May 17, 1961

XXII

STRUCTURAL DECOMPOSITION

The analyst: object or subject?
The structural analysis of myth.
So-called normality.
The earliest *Versagung*.
The subject exchanged for [the object of] his desire.

What are we going to do regarding Claudel this year, now that we no longer have enough time to formulate what we have to say about transference?

In certain respects, my Seminar this year might give you this particular feeling. At least it could to people less savvy than you. For everything I have said nevertheless has a common axis, which I believe I have articulated clearly enough for you to have realized that it is the crux of my aim this year. In order to designate it, I will try to describe it to you as follows.

1

People have spoken a great deal about transference since analysis first came into existence. And we are still talking about it today. It is not simply a theoretical hope. We should nevertheless know what we deal with incessantly, which is the means by which we sustain the movement of psychoanalytic practice. What I have been designating this year in order to broach the question has an axis that can be formulated as follows: "In what respect must we consider ourselves to be involved in the transference?"

To reformulate the question in this way does not mean that I believe we now know exactly what transference is. But I consider this way of reformulating the question to be necessary if we wish to grasp what has led to the very tangible divergences that have occurred and to the most profound differences in standpoint that have appeared on this topic in the analytic community, not only most recently, but throughout the different stages of the historical development of psychoanalysis. This will allow us to conceptualize in what sense each of these points of view regarding transference has a grain of truth in it and is utilizable – something that I believe is certain.

The question I am raising is therefore that of our participation in the transference. It is not the question of countertransference. People have turned countertransference into a giant grab-bag category of experiences that seems to comprise just about everything we are likely to feel in our work as analysts. People have, in this way, included all sorts of impurities in the analytic setting – for it is quite clear that we are human, and, as such, affected in a thousand ways by the patient's presence – and have now rendered this notion thoroughly useless. If we situate our participation in the transference under the heading of countertransference, defined thusly – and if we include casuistry in it as well, that is, the way in which we reckon what must be done in each case defined by its specific coordinates – we truly make any and all investigation impossible.

I will thus broach the topic of our participation in transference by asking, "How are we to conceptualize it?" This is the path that will allow us to situate what is at the heart of the phenomenon of transference in the subject – namely, the analyst.

Something is undoubtedly already suggested by this particular way of broaching the topic. Does our need to respond to the transference involve our being, or need we but define a line of conduct, a how to* guide to handling* something that lies outside of ourselves? If you have been following what I have been saying for a number of years, you cannot but guess the answer implied by what I am leading you to – namely, that our involvement in the transference is situated at the level of what I just designated when I said that it involves our being.

This is, after all, so obvious that it is recognized even by those analysts who are most opposed to my approach – I mean, those whose ways of broaching the analytic situation, both at its point of departure and at its destination, are so terribly under-articulated – and whose work I am most averse to; for someone of this ilk nevertheless one day proffered, not regarding transference, but regarding the analyst's action, that "the analyst cures not so much by what he says and does as by what he is."

Make no mistake about it: this kind of sweeping remark runs, it seems to me, absolutely counter to my way of proceeding, in the precise sense that it says something apt, but does so in such a way

372

373

that it immediately shuts the door to any further discussion. It is just the kind of thing that gets my dander up. What the analyst is clearly is precisely what has been at issue since the beginning.

When people define the analytic situation objectively, there is a given that is the following: the analyst plays his transferential role precisely to the degree to which he is, for his patient, what he is not at the level of what one might call "reality." This is what allows us to gauge transference's angle of deviation and to bring the patient to realize how far he is from reality [*le réel*], owing to the fiction he produces with the help of transference.

Nevertheless, there is clearly some truth to the idea that the analyst enters the picture through something like his being. This is quite probable. It is, first and foremost, a fact of experience. Why would there be any need for us to adjust or correct the analyst's subjective position – for us to attempt, as part of his training, to get him to take it up or down a notch – were it not so that something in his position could be called upon to function effectively in a relationship that can in no way be exhaustively formulated as a simple manipulation, even if it were mutual.

Everything that has been said since Freud's time concerning the import of transference thus brings the analyst into play as an actual being [*un existant*]. One could even divide rather clearly in two the different ways of articulating transference, in a way which, without exhausting the question, pretty well covers the whole spectrum. The two "trends," as they are referred to, in psychoanalysis today are associated with Melanie Klein, on the one hand, and Anna Freud, on the other; these names do not exhaustively describe the trends, but give us a shorthand with which to refer to them.

The Kleinian trend emphasizes the analyst's function as an object in the transference relationship. If you wanted to, you could even say that it is Melanie Klein who is more faithful to Freud's thought and tradition than Anna Freud, even if that was not, of course, Klein's point of departure; and that it is to the extent that she is faithful to Freud's thought and tradition that she is led to articulate the transference relationship in this way.

Let me explain what I mean. If Melanie Klein is led to make the analyst – the analytic presence in the analyst or the analyst's intention – function as a good or bad object for the subject, it is to the extent to which she believes the analytic relationship to be dominated by unconscious fantasies right from the very first words and steps. This, for Klein, is what we are dealing with right from the outset, and we can – I am not saying that we should – interpret them right from the get-go.

I am not saying that this [recommendation regarding technique]

374

is a necessary consequence [of her conception of the role played by unconscious fantasies]. In fact I think that it is a consequence that is only necessary owing to the shortcomings of Kleinian thought, insofar as the function of fantasy – even though it is perceived in a very compelling [*prégnante*] way – is inadequately articulated by her; this is the major failing of her work. Even among her best acolytes and disciples, who certainly have tried to develop it on more than one occasion, her theory of fantasy has never been truly worked out.

There are nevertheless many extremely serviceable elements in it. For example, the primordial function of symbolization is articulated and emphasized there in a way that, in certain respects, verges on being highly satisfying. In fact, the entire key to correcting Klein's theory of fantasy can be found in the symbol I have proposed for fantasy: ($ \cancel{S} \lozenge a$), which can be read as follows: "barred $\cancel{S}$, desire for a."

We want to know what $\cancel{S}$ is. It is not simply the noetic correlate of the object. $\cancel{S}$ is found in fantasy. It is not easy to broach the experience of fantasy without taking the path around it that I have been leading you along in a thousand different ways. It is in the detours we are forced to make as we broach the experience of fantasy that you will understand better – if you believe you have already glimpsed something, or you will understand for the first time if this has seemed obscure to you heretofore – what I am trying to propound with this formalization.

But let us continue. The other pole of the theory of transference emphasizes something that is just as irreducible and that is even more obviously true, which is that the analyst is involved in the transference as a subject. In this perspective – which I tagged with the name Anna Freud, and which is not a bad designation for it, in effect, although she is not the only analyst associated with it – emphasis is placed on the therapeutic alliance. This emphasis is internally coherent with its correlate – namely, the emphasis placed on the powers of the ego.*

The goal is not simply to recognize these powers objectively, but to know what place they should be given in therapeutic practice. And what are we told on this score? That in the whole first phase of the treatment there is no question of bringing in the unconscious, since at first we are dealing with nothing but defense, and for quite some time, moreover. That is the least you might be told. Of course, this can be seen more clearly in practice than in what is doctrinally formulated, and it must be glimpsed between the lines of the theory.

Now, it is one thing to bring the importance of the defenses to the fore – this is ever so legitimate – and quite another to go so far in one's theorizing as to make the ego* itself into a kind of inertial mass. It is characteristic of the school of Hartmann and his associates to even conceptualize the ego* as including elements that are, in the final analysis, irreducible and uninterpretable. This is what they quite clearly arrive at. I am not trying to make them say something they do not say – they say it themselves.

The following step is to say that this is, in the end, fine and dandy, and that we should even make the ego* still more irreducible by providing it with additional defenses.

This is a conceivable way of conducting an analysis. I am not rejecting the notion at this very moment. It is what the Anna Freudians do. But what I can nevertheless point out is that, compared to the Kleinian perspective, it does not seem that this one is the more Freudian – that is the least one can say.

But I have other fish to fry, don't I, in our pursuits this year, than to once again qualify this trend, to which I gave so much importance in the first years of my teaching, as eccentric. People thought they saw some sort of polemical intention in it, whereas I assure you that such was far from my mind. What is at stake is to change the level at which the mind itself is broached.

Things are no longer precisely the same today. These deviations came to fascinate the analytic community, and they went so far as to dispel the feeling that there were some questions left to be answered. Since that time we have regained some perspective and revived a certain inspiration, thanks to what is also no more than a return to psychoanalytic language, I mean to its structure, to what served to make it emerge at the outset in Freud's work. The situation is different now. The fact that even those who may feel a bit lost owing to the fact that at a certain moment in my Seminar we dove straight into Claudel's work, nevertheless have the feeling that his work is closely tied to the topic of transference, proves all by itself that something has sufficiently changed for there to no longer be any need to emphasize the negative facet of one trend or another.

376   It is not the negative facets that interest us, but the positive ones – those that can, at the point we are at now, serve as elements upon which to build.

2

I would like to draw your attention now to the function of myth in psychoanalysis.

In what way can Claudel's mythology, as I will call it by way of a shorthand, serve us?

I myself was surprised, which is amusing, when I perused lately a talk I gave that I had never reread, which Jean Wahl published without my correcting it. It dates back to a time when I gave some short lectures at the Collège Philosophique that were open to the general public. It was a lecture on obsessional neurosis whose title I no longer recall – it was something like "The Neurotic's Myth," which, as you see, brings us right to the heart of the question. In it I demonstrated the role of mythical structures in determining the Rat Man's symptoms.

I was supposed to correct the transcribed text of that talk for publication, but I considered the task to be impossible. Bizarrely enough, having let some time go by, I reread it without too much discontent and was surprised to see – I would have sworn that I had not done so – that in it I spoke about Claudel's *The Humiliation of the Father*. There must have been some reason for that. It is obviously not [merely] because I encountered the *U* with a circumflex over it that I have been speaking to you about Claudel's work.

So let us begin anew.

What does the analysand come looking for in analysis? He comes looking for what there is to be found, or, more precisely, if he comes looking, it is because there is something to be found. And the only thing to be found by him is, strictly speaking, the trope par excellence, the trope of tropes: what we call his fate [*destin*].

Were we to forget the relationship that exists between analysis and what we call fate, the sort of thing that is akin to a figure – in the sense in which in French we speak of a "figure of fate" or a "figure of speech" – we would simply forget the origins of psychoanalysis. For psychoanalysis could not have made the slightest step forward without this relationship. Parallel to this, a slippage has occurred in the course of the evolution of psychoanalysis to a form of practice that is ever more insistent, striking, and demanding regarding results that must be produced. This is undoubtedly lucky in certain respects, but it risks making us forget the weight of myth. Fortunately, people in other fields have continued to be interested in myth.

377

There is something that, more legitimately than we perhaps think, comes back to us here in a roundabout way. After all, we are perhaps in some way responsible for their interest in the function of myth.

I alluded to this a long time ago, and more than alluded to it – I already articulated it in my lecture on the Rat Man. My Seminar on the Rat Man had already begun and people had come to work on this with me at my home. I brought in the structural articulation of myth, such as it has since been systematically applied and developed

by Lévi-Strauss in his own seminar. I tried to demonstrate its value
to you in explaining the history of the Rat Man.

For those who may have overlooked something or who are
unaware of this, I will briefly define the structuralist articulation of
myth. Taking a myth as a whole, I mean the *épos* or story, the way
in which it is recounted from end to end, we construct a model that
is constituted solely by a series of oppositional designations of the
functions that are involved – for example, in the Oedipus myth, the
relationship between father and son, incest, and so on. Naturally, I
am speaking schematically and boiling it down in order to indicate
what is involved. We realize that a myth does not stop there, for
there are the generations that follow. Since it is a myth, generations
do not simply correspond to the order in which the actors make
their entrances on stage – that is, to the simple fact that, when the
old people are gone, there are young ones who show up for it to
start again. What interests us is the signifying coherence that obtains
between the first constellation and the one that follows. Something
happens, for example, that you can qualify as you like – say, brothers who become enemies – and then the function of a transcendent
love that runs counter to a law, like incest, appears, whose function
is diametrically opposed to it; this gives rise to relations that can be
defined by a certain number of oppositional terms. In a word, I am
talking about Antigone.

It is a game [*jeu*] whose rules, which give it rigor, we must detect.
And let us observe that there is no other conceivable rigor than the
kind that is found in games. In the function and play [*jeu*] of myth,
transformations occur according to certain rules that, owing to this
very fact, turn out to have a revelatory value that creates higher
configurations or illuminating individual cases. In short, these rules
yield the same kind of fecundity we find in mathematics. This is what
is involved in the elucidation of myths. And this interests us quite
directly, since we cannot possibly broach the subject with whom we
deal in analysis without encountering the function of myth.

This is a fact that is attested to by analytic practice. In any case,
right from psychoanalysis' very first steps, in the *Traumdeutung* [*The
Interpretation of Dreams*] and the letters to Fliess, Freud relies on
myth and specifically on the Oedipal myth. Today, psychoanalysts
gloss over that or bracket it, and try to express everything about
our practice in economic terms, as they are called: for example, the
function of the conflict between primordial tendencies, including
the most radical among them, defenses against the drive, [that is,]
the conflict – designated topographically in the theory of narcissism – between the ego* and the ego-ideal,* on the one hand, and
the id, on the other. To go in this direction, and to jettison the land-

mark of myth, must be qualified in our practice as a forgetting, in the positive sense that this word has for us.

This does not stop people from practicing in a way that continues to be an analytic form of practice. But it is an analytic form of practice that forgets its own terms.

As you see, I come – as I often do, as I almost always do – back to formulating the most basic things. It is not merely for the pleasure of spelling them out, although there is pleasure in doing so, but because it is what allows us to raise the right questions in all their density.

But what are they? Does analysis involve presenting a subject with his fate? Is that the true question? Of course not. That would be to situate ourselves in the position of a demiurge, which has never been that of psychoanalysis. But to remain at the level of an altogether preliminary overview, this is nevertheless a formulation that derives its value from the fact that it frees itself from the received ways of posing the question, which are no better than plenty of others.

This was how things stood before we believed we were strong and clever enough to talk about people who were not neurotic, but normal. Personally, I have never, in fact, believed I was so strong or clever not to feel my pen shake a little whenever I would broach the topic of what a normal person is. But Ernest Jones wrote a whole article about it. He certainly was not lacking in courage. And it must be admitted that he managed to pull it off not too badly. Still, we can see the difficulty involved in the endeavor.

Be that as it may, it is truly only through subterfuge that we can bring into play in psychoanalysis any sort of notion of normalization. It is a theoretical view that considers only part of the picture, like when we talk, for example, about "instinctual maturation," as if that were the only thing involved. In such cases we give ourselves over to the kind of extraordinary vaticinations bordering on moralizing preaching, that are so likely to inspire distrust and make people recoil. To unthinkingly bring in the idea of a normal anything in our praxis – whereas we discover in it precisely to what degree the so-called normal subject is anything but normal – should arouse in us the most radical and the most assured suspicion as to its results. We should first ask ourselves whether we can employ the notion of normal for anything whatsoever connected with our practice.

Let us confine our attention for the moment to the following question: "Can we say that the mastery we have acquired – over the deciphering process by which we locate the figure of fate [*destin*] – allows us to obtain the least drama possible or a change of sign [from negative to positive]?"

If the human configuration we deal with is drama – whether

379

tragic or not – can we confine ourselves to aiming at the least drama possible, thinking that a well-informed subject (one well-informed subject in the hand is worth two in the bush) will find a way to get out while the getting is good? Why not, after all? It is a modest claim. But even this has never in any way corresponded, as you know, to our practice. This is not it.

I claim that the doorway through which we must pass in order to say things that make some sense, the one that gives us the sense we are on the right track, is the one I am going to indicate to you.

As always, what must be seen is closer to us than the point at which we stupidly grasp what is supposedly obvious, what people call "commonsensical" – namely, the point where the crossroads of fate [*destin*] begin, the crossroads of "normality" in this case. On the contrary, if there is something that Freud's discovery has taught us, it is to see in symptoms a figure that is related to the figure of fate. We did not know this before and now we know it. Knowledge makes a difference. It does not allow us to situate ourselves on the outside, nor does it allow the subject to place himself to one side, and for everything to go on in the same old way – that would be a crude, absurd way of conceptualizing things. The fact of knowing or not knowing is thus essential to the figure of fate. This is the right doorway. And myth confirms it.

Myths are fashioned figures that can be related, not to language, but to the involvement of a subject caught up in language – and, to complicate matters still further, in the play of speech. On the basis of the relations between the subject and any signifier whatsoever, figures are fashioned in which we can observe necessary points, irreducible points, major points, or points of intersection that are, for example, the very ones I tried to depict in the Graph of Desire. This was an attempt on my part, and the point here is not to ask whether it is faulty or incomplete, or whether it could not perhaps have been much more harmoniously constructed or reconstructed by someone else – I am simply mentioning its aim here. The aim of a minimal structure including eight points of intersection seems to be necessitated by the very encounter between the subject and the signifier. And it is already quite a lot to be able to maintain, by virtue of this sole fact, the necessity of the subject's *Spaltung* [splitting].

This figure, graph, or set of mapped points, in addition to attention to facts, allows us to reconcile the true function of trauma with our experience of development. A trauma is not simply something that erupted at a particular moment and broke its way into a structure that we imagine to be total – certain people thought this was implied by the notion of narcissism. Trauma is the fact that certain events come to be situated at a certain place in this structure. By

380

occupying this place, these events take on the signifying value that is attached to this place by a specific subject. This is what constitutes the traumatic value of an event. Hence the value of going back to the experience of myth.

It should be clear to you that, as concerns Greek myths, we are not terribly well situated [to interpret them]. We have plenty of different versions, but they are not always the right ones, as it were. We have no guarantee of their origin. These are not contemporary versions nor even local versions; they are more or less allegorical or fictionalized rearrangements that cannot be used in the same way as we can use versions collected in real-time, as when we collect myths in a North or South American [tribal] population. We are unable to do with the Greek material what someone like Boas is able to do with the material he collects. Moreover, when I wanted to present to you the model of what becomes of the Oedipal conflict when knowledge as such comes into the myth at one point or another, I sought it elsewhere – namely, in Shakespeare's creation of *Hamlet*, which I examined for you two years ago. And I had every right to do so since, right from the outset, Freud himself had broached things in this way.

I felt that I could indicate something that, in a particularly captivating way, is modified at a structural point. Indeed, it is quite an unusual, aporetic point in the subject's relationship to desire that *Hamlet* spotlighted for reflection, meditation, interpretation, research, and the structured puzzle it represents. I think I have succeeded well enough in conveying to you its specificity by highlighting the following: unlike the father who is killed in the Oedipal myth, we cannot say of the father who is killed in *Hamlet* that "he did not know," but rather that "he knew." Not only did he know, but this factor intervenes in the subjective impact that interests us here, the impact on the central character, Hamlet.

Hamlet is, in truth, the only character. What we have here is a drama that is contained entirely within Hamlet as a subject. He is told that his father was killed, and he is told enough for him to know a good deal about it, even knowing by whom his father was killed. That said, I have done no more than repeat what Freud said right from the outset.

This suggests a method by which we are required to gauge, regarding the structure itself, the effect of what our knowledge introduces. To make a sweeping claim, to put it in a way that allows us to locate the root of what is at stake, I would say that at the origin of every neurosis – as Freud says right from his earliest writings – there is, not what people later interpreted to be a frustration, an ill-defined but unpaid balance owed to one [*un arriéré laissé*

381

ouvert dans l'informe], but rather a *Versagung*. At the origin of every neurosis, there is, in other words, something that is much closer to refusal than to frustration, that is as internal as it is external, and that is truly placed by Freud in an "existential" position, to qualify it with a term that at least has some resonances popularized in our contemporary language. This position does not establish a sequential order from normal, to the possibility of *Versagung*, and then on to neurosis; it establishes a *Versagung* right at the origin, beyond which a path may lead to neurosis or to normality, neither being worth more than the other in relation to what is, at the outset, the possibility of *Versagung*.

It is obvious that this untranslatable *Versagung* is only possible in the register of *sagen*, insofar as *sagen* is not simply the operation of communicating, but of speaking – that is, the emergence as such of the signifier insofar as it allows the subject to deny himself (something) [*se refuser*].

We cannot get past this earliest, primordial refusal [*refus*], this power of refusal in what it has that is prerequisite [*préjudicielle*] to all our experience. In other words, we analysts operate solely in the register of *Versagung*, and don't we know it! And we do so all the time. It is inasmuch as we try to skirt it – and don't we know it! – that our entire technique becomes structured around an idea that is stammeringly expressed in the term "non-gratification," which is found nowhere in Freud's work.

We must go into what this specific *Versagung* is, for it implies a progressive direction, which is the very one that we bring into play in analytic practice.

3

I consider the terms that I have just introduced to be applicable to Claudel's myth, and I am going to return to it for a moment in order to depict for you, in a spectacular fashion, the fact that we must be the messengers or vehicles of *Versagung*.

I think you no longer doubt at this point that what occurs in *Crusts* is the Oedipal myth. We virtually come upon my own play on words at the very moment at which Louis de Coûfontaine and Turelure find themselves face to face.

I am referring to the moment at which a kind of request for tenderness is formulated. It is the first time that such a thing happens. True, it occurs ten minutes before Louis does his father in. Louis says to him, "*Tu es le père* [You are my father], all the same." And this line is truly doubled by *tuer le père* [kill your father], which the woman's desire, Lumîr, suggested to him, and which superimposes itself here literally in a way which, I assure you, does not simply owe to a lucky linguistic accident.

What does what is represented onstage here mean? It means, and this is explicitly stated, that it is at this very moment and owing to it that the boy becomes a man. Louis de Coûfontaine is told that this parricide will weigh on him his whole life long, but also that from this moment on he is no longer a good-for-nothing who botches up everything and who allows his land to be stolen from him by a bunch of meanies and clever cheats. He is going to become a fine ambassador who is quite capable of performing all kinds of dastardly deeds. This brings a certain correlation to mind. 383

He becomes the father. He not only becomes the father, but when he talks about Turelure later, in *The Humiliation of the Father*, in Rome, he says, "I was probably the only man who really knew and understood him; he never wanted to hear about it; he was not the man people think he was" [p. 325/167] – undoubtedly allowing people to think that treasure troves of sensitivity and experience had accumulated in the old hoodlum's heart of hearts. But Louis de Coûfontaine becomes the father. Moreover, this is the only way he could become the father, for reasons that are tied to things that occurred before the dramatic action begins. Things got off to a very bad start, indeed.

But the construction of the plot makes it quite apparent to us at the same time that, owing to this, Louis is castrated. In other words, there can be no outlet, even if it is easy and quite simple, for the little boy's desire, his desire that is sustained in such an ambiguous way, as he says to Lumîr herself.

He has this outlet within hand's reach; he need but bring Lumîr with him to the Mitidja Plain and all will be well; they will even live happily ever after. But something happens. First of all, we do not really know if this is something he wishes to do or not; but one thing is clear, and this is that she does not want to go. She tells him, "You knock off daddy," and then she heads off toward her own fate, which is that of a desire, the true desire of a Claudelian character.

This drama may, for some, depending on their leanings, be redolent of the sacristy and thus be pleasing or displeasing, but that is not our concern here. My point in presenting it to you is that it is nevertheless a tragedy. It is quite funny that this led Claudel to adopt stances that are not designed to please us, but we have to make do with them and, if need be, try to understand him. From one end to the other of Claudel's work, from *Tête d'Or* to *The Satin Slipper*, we encounter the tragedy of desire.

The character who serves as its prop in this generation, Lumîr, thus jilts her former partner, Louis de Coûfontaine, and heads toward her desire, one that is clearly described to us by Claudel as a desire for death. But – and it is here that I will ask you to pause for a moment to note this particular version of the myth – what is it that she thereby gives Louis?

Not his mother, obviously. His mother is Sygne de Coûfontaine, and she is situated in a place that is obviously not that of the mother when her name is Jocasta. But there is another woman, the father's mistress, the father always lying at the horizon of this story in a clearly marked way. This woman – who has herself been rehabilitated owing to the impact of desire – rehabilitates our excluded son, our unwanted child, our drifting partial object. She reinstates him, recreating with him the father who has been defeated. The result of the operation is thus to give him the father's woman.

Listen carefully to what I am saying here. In Claudel's trilogy, we have an exemplary structural decomposition of the function of what, in Freud's myth, takes the form of a type of hollow or vacuum toward which things are drawn, a vertiginous point of the libido that is represented by the mother.

It is getting late and I will have to stop here. Still, I do not want to leave you without indicating where we are heading.

This is not such an astonishing story to us, after all, for we are already a bit hardened by analytic practice. Castration is, in short, cut from such cloth: we take from someone [the object of] his desire and, in exchange, we give him to someone else – in this case, to the social order.

Sichel is the one who is wealthy and thus it is quite natural for Coûfontaine to marry her. Moreover, Lumîr clearly saw this coming: there is but one thing for you to do now, she says to Louis, and that is to "marry your father's mistress" [p. 268/139].

It is this specific structure that is important. It seems insignificant because we see it all the time, but it is rarely expressed as such.

I think you get the picture: [the object of] a subject's desire is taken from him and, in exchange, he is sold on the open market to the highest bidder. But isn't this precisely what happens at the outset, at the earlier stage, being illustrated in the first play in the trilogy in quite a different manner, designed this time to awaken our slumbering sensibility? Isn't this, I mean, what happens at the level of Sygne de Coûfontaine in a way that is clearly designed to be a bit more moving to us?

Everything is taken from Sygne. I am not saying that this is done for no reason – let us leave that aside. But it is quite clear, too, that this is done in order to give her, in exchange for what is taken from her, to what she most abhors.

I am thus led to end today in an almost overly spectacular fashion by playfully proposing an enigma. What is at stake is, in fact, far richer than the question I am currently raising here. I will articulate it far more profoundly next time. In the meantime, I want to allow you to dream about it.

You will see that in the third generation, it is the same blow that is to be dealt to Pensée. But here it has neither the same point of departure nor the same origin, and this is what will be instructive to us, even allowing us to raise questions about psychoanalysts. It is the same blow, but naturally the characters are kinder in her case, they have hearts of gold; even he who wishes to deal her the same blow – namely, Orian – has one. This is quite clearly not to her own detriment, but it is not for her own good either. He, too, wants to give her to someone whom she does not want, but this time the kid does not go along with it. She grabs her Orian in passing, in secret no doubt, for just as long as he is no longer anything but one of the Pope's defenders, albeit a cold one. As for the other, good Lord, he is a true gentleman and agrees to break off the engagement without balking.

What does this mean? As I already told you, it is a lovely fantasy and has not yet spoken its last word.

This nevertheless suffices for me to leave you with the question of what we are going to be able to do with it in order to better discern certain effects that are based on the fact that, as analysts, we enter into the subject's fate and become involved in it.

There is one more point that I must make before leaving you today.

The effects on man of the fact that he becomes subject to the law cannot be exhaustively summarized by saying that everything dear to his heart is taken from him and that he himself is given in exchange to the daily grind of the plot [*trame*] that knots the generations together. In order for it to be a plot that knots the generations together – once the operation by which you see the curious conjugation of a minus that is not coupled with a plus is complete – man still owes something.

This is where we will take up the question next time.

May 24, 1961

CAPITAL I AND
LITTLE *a*

SLIPPAGE IN THE MEANING
OF THE IDEAL

Effects of the psychoanalytic group.
Action as a response to the unconscious.
There is no such thing as a metalanguage.
Love and guilt.
"Extrojection."

How can we situate what the analyst's place must be in the transference? I told you last time that we must locate this place in two ways: where does the analysand situate the analyst and where must the analyst be in order to suitably respond to him?

The analytic relationship – a relationship that people often refer to as a "situation," as if the initial situation were constitutive – can only begin to develop on the basis of a misunderstanding. There is no overlap between what the analyst is for the analysand at the beginning of the analysis and what the analysis of transference will allow us to reveal as concerns what is implied, not immediately, but truly implied by the fact that a subject becomes involved in this psychoanalytic adventure about which he knows little or nothing at the outset.

In what I talked about last time, you might have grasped that it is the dimension of what is truly implied by the opening up, possibility, richness, and the whole future development of the analysis, that raises a question for us about the analyst. Isn't it at least probable and palpable that he must already place himself at the level of this truly, that he must truly be in the place where he must arrive at the end of the analysis, which is precisely the analysis of the transference?

1   390

I am thus asking whether the analyst can be indifferent to his true position.

Let us clarify things more, for this might almost seem not to raise a question for you. Doesn't the analyst's science, you might say, make up for this? Yet the fact that the analyst may know something about the major and minor pathways of the analysis does not suffice, whether he likes it or not, to locate him in this place, no matter how he formulates it to himself. The divergences regarding the analyst's function in technique, once it has been theorized, bring this out quite clearly.

An analyst is not the only analyst around. He is part of a group, part of a "mass" of analysts, in the strict sense that this term takes on in Freud's work, *Massenpsychologie und Ich-Analyse* [*Group Psychology and the Analysis of the Ego*].

It is no accident that the topic is first broached by Freud at a moment at which a society of analysts already exists. Numerous problems connected with Freud's second topography are linked to what happens at the level of the relationship between the analyst and his own function. We have here a phase which, although it is not at all obvious, nevertheless warrants examination, especially by we analysts. I have referred to this on several occasions in my writings. However internally necessary we consider the emergence of the second topography in Freud's work to be, we certainly cannot, in any case, neglect the historical moment at which it arises. We have evidence of this; it suffices to open up Jones' biography of Freud to realize that at the point in time at which Freud developed this topography – we find it in particular in *Massenpsychologie und Ich-Analyse* – he was thinking about how to organize an analytic society.

I mentioned my writings a few moments ago. In them, I pointed out, in a more acute way perhaps than I am doing right now, the drama that this problematic posed for him. In particular, I indicated what comes out quite clearly in certain passages cited by Jones: Freud's romantic conception of a kind of Comintern, a kind of secret committee functioning as such within psychoanalysis. Freud truly gave himself over to this idea in certain of his letters, and it was clearly in this way that he in fact envisioned the functioning of the "group of seven" analysts in whom he truly trusted.

391

As soon as there is a large number or an organized mass of those who serve as analysts, all the problems that Freud mentions in this text clearly arise. As I have indicated in my writings, these are merely organizational problems of the group with respect to the existence of a certain discourse.

We should re-examine *Massenpsychologie und Ich-Analyse* in order to apply its insights to the modified theory of the analyst's function that post-Freudian analysts developed. This would allow us to see something that is almost immediately and intuitively tangible and comprehensible – the necessity or gravitational pull that made the analyst's function converge with the analyst's own image of it. This image is situated very precisely at a point that Freud teaches us to isolate, a point whose function he develops thoroughly at the time at which he articulates the second topography – namely, the *Ich-Ideal*, translated as the "ego-ideal" [*idéal du moi*].

This term is ambiguous. For example, in an article that is very important to us and to which I will refer later, "*Übertragung und Liebe*" by Jekels and Bergler – which was presented at the Vienna Psychoanalytic Society in 1933, published in *Imago* in 1934, and is easier to find in the *Psychoanalytic Quarterly* where it was translated into English as "Transference and Love" in 1949 – *Ich-Ideal* is translated into English by "ego-ideal."* This play in the order of the words has a role that is hardly accidental.

If you do not know German, you might believe that *Ich-Ideal* means ideal ego [*moi idéal*]. I have pointed out that in the first article in which Freud talks about the *Ich-Ideal*, "On Narcissism: An Introduction," we occasionally come across the term *ideal Ich*. And Lord knows that, for all of us, it is an object of some debate. Some people, such as myself, say that we cannot even for an instant overlook such a variation on Freud's part, he being so precise with his signifiers, while other people say that it is impossible, upon examination of the context, to attribute any significance whatsoever to this variation.

What is clear is that even the latter are the first – as you will see in the very next issue of *La Psychanalyse* – to distinguish the ego-ideal from the ideal ego at the psychological level. I am referring here to my friend Daniel Lagache. In his article on "Psychoanalysis and Personality Structure," he draws a distinction between them that, without diminishing it for all that, I can say is descriptive, extremely refined, elegant, and clear. Phenomenologically speaking, the ego-ideal and the ideal ego absolutely do not serve the same function.

392

In a response that I wrote up expressly for the same issue of *La Psychanalyse* on the topic Lagache wrote about, I simply made a few remarks, the first of which is that one could object that in proposing to provide a formulation that is, as he puts it, at some distance from experience, he himself abandons the method that he had announced he would follow in his metapsychology – that is, in his structural elaboration. Indeed, the clinical and descriptive distinction he draws between these two terms, "ego-ideal" and "ideal ego," is not sufficiently inscribed within the method he himself proposed to use. You will see all of this very shortly in the next issue of the journal.

Today I will perhaps go into the thoroughly concrete metapsychological way in which we can distinguish between their functions in the grand economic perspective introduced by Freud around the notion of narcissism. I will turn to it later; for the time being, I am simply highlighting the term *Ich-Ideal* or *idéal du moi* for you, inasmuch as it comes to be translated into English as "ego-ideal." In English, the respective places of the determinative and the determiner are far more ambiguous in a group of two terms; and we already find in "ego-ideal"* the semantic trace of an evolution or slippage of the function attributed to this term when people wanted to use it to indicate what the analyst becomes for the analysand.

It was said very early on that the analyst takes on the role of the analysand's ego-ideal. This is both true and false. It is true in the sense that this sometimes happens. It happens all too easily. I would even say – and I will provide you with an example of this later – it often happens that a subject attributes both strong and comfortable positions to the analyst that are clearly related to what we call resistance. Far from it being simply an apparent or occasional position, this is perhaps how certain analyses actually get started.

Which is not at all to say that this exhausts the question, or that the analyst can in any way be content with this – in other words, that he can push the analysis to its endpoint without flushing the subject out of the position he adopts, insofar as he places the analyst in the position of his ego-ideal. This thus even raises the question of what this truth turns out to have to be in the future. In other words, if at the end, after the analysis of the transference, the analyst must not [. . .] which is not simply at play. This is something that has never been said before. For, in the final analysis, the article I was talking with you about earlier did not have the appearance, at the moment at which it came out, of actively seeking answers; it came out in 1933, and – compared to the 1920s, at which the turning point in analytic technique occurred, as everyone says – by then they had had time to reflect and to see clearly in this context.

I cannot go through this text with you in detail, but I will ask you to read it and we will talk about it in future classes. We are not going to dwell on it here, all the more so because the version I want to talk to you about is the English text. This is why it is the one I have with me today, even though the German text is more incisive. But rather than talk about the main lines of the original text, I want to indicate the semantic slippage that expresses what is produced, in effect, at a critical point in the analyst.

Insofar as he is an analyst – all by himself and captain of his own ship – he is confronted with his own action. What is at stake for him is the examination, exorcism, and extraction of himself that

393

is indispensable for him to have a clear view of his own personal relationship with the function of the ego-ideal, insofar as for him, as an analyst, and consequently in a particularly necessary way, this function is sustained within what I called the analytic group. If he does not acquire such a clear view, what occurs is what has effectively occurred – namely, a slippage of meaning that can in no way be conceptualized at this level as halfway outside the subject, or, to put it bluntly, as an error. On the contrary, this slippage implicates him profoundly and subjectively.

In 1933, psychoanalysts centered a whole paper on "Transference and Love" around the topic of the ego-ideal. Yet, 20 or 25 years later, theoretically articulated articles clearly state, without any ambiguity whatsoever, that relations between the analysand and the analyst are based on the fact that the analyst has an ego that one can call ideal.

In what sense is the analyst's ego said to be an ideal ego in those articles? In a sense that is quite different both from that of the ego-ideal and from the concrete sense of the ideal ego to which I alluded earlier. I am going to illustrate it for you: it is an ideal ego, so to speak, that has been realized – an ideal ego in the sense in which one says that a car is an ideal car. It is not a car's ideal, nor is it the dream of a car when it is all by itself in the garage – it is a truly good and solid car.

394

Such is the meaning that this term ends up taking on. Were it no more than that – a literary creation, a certain way of saying that the analyst must intervene as someone who knows a bit more than the analysand does – it would be situated merely at the level of a platitude and probably would not have much import. But the fact is that the very slippage in meaning of these two signifiers – "ego" and "ideal" – translates something altogether different: the true subjective involvement of the analyst [in the analysis].

We should not be surprised by an effect of this kind. Something is merely being plastered over here. It is but the endpoint of an adventure whose mainspring is far more essential than the simply localized, almost caricatural point where we deal with it all the time, as if we were here for no other purpose.

Where did this come from? From the 1920 turning point. What did the 1920 turning point revolve around? It revolved around the fact – as the people of that time, the heroes of the first analytic generation, say – that interpretation was no longer functioning the way it had functioned prior to that. Times had changed and interpretation was no longer encountering the same success as it had. Why not? This did not surprise Freud. He had long since anticipated this. We can point to a very early passage in one of his "Papers on Technique" in which he says, let us take advantage of the opening up of the unconscious, because soon it will have found another trick. What does that mean to us, to we who can, based on Freud's experience, and slipping alongside him, nevertheless find our bearings?

I propose that what Freud is saying there refers to the effect of a discourse – to wit, that of the first generation of analysts – that does not realize that it concerns the effect of another discourse: namely, that of the unconscious. It doesn't realize this even though the discourse of the unconscious was present already in *The Interpretation of Dreams*, where I teach you to recognize it and spell it out; for what is constantly involved there, going by the name "unconscious mechanisms," is but the effect of discourse. Freud is thus referring to the effect of a discourse [analytic discourse] that bears on the effect of a discourse [that of the unconscious] without realizing it, and this necessarily leads to a new crystallization of unconscious effects that renders the latter discourse more opaque.

What does "a new crystallization" refer to? It refers to observable effects – the fact, for example, that giving patients certain insights or keys, or using certain signifiers with them, no longer has the same effect as it did before.

395   Let us observe, however, that the subjective structures corresponding to this new crystallization need not be new, I am referring to the registers or degrees of alienation, as it were, that we can specify in the subject and qualify, for example, with the terms "ego," "superego," and "ego-ideal." These are like stable waves. Whatever happens, these effects make the subject beat a retreat; they immunize or inoculate him with respect to a certain discourse. They impede us from leading the subject where we want to lead him – namely, to his desire. This changes nothing as concerns the nodal points where he, as a subject, can recognize and instate himself.

This is what Freud notes at this turning point. If Freud attempts to define what the stable points and fixed waves are in subjective constitution, it is because these are what quite remarkably seem to him to be constants. But it is not in order to consecrate them that he concerns himself with them and articulates them – it is with a view to removing them as obstacles. Even when he speaks of the *Ich* and brings it to the fore, it is not in order to institute the so-called "synthetic function of the ego" as a type of irreducible inertia. This is nevertheless how it was interpreted thereafter.

We must reconsider all of this as an acting out* of the self-instituting of the subject in his relationship to the signifier, on the one hand, and to reality, on the other. It is in this way that we will be able to begin writing a new chapter on analytic action.

2

Regarding what I am endeavoring to do here, one might say – with all the caveats implied by it – that I am attempting to provide an analysis, in the strict sense of the term, of the analytic community insofar as it is a mass organized by the analytic ego-ideal, such as it has in fact developed in the form of a certain number of mirages. First among these mirages is that of the "strong ego" that has been so often pointed to wrongly in places where people think they see it. To reverse the pair of terms that make up the title of Freud's text that I referred to earlier, one of the facets of my Seminar this year could be entitled *Ich-Psychologie und Massenanalyse*.

Indeed, *Ich-Psychologie* [ego psychology], which has come to the fore in analytic theory, has for over a decade now been constituting a barrier to and creating inertia for any recommencing of psychoanalytic efficacy. And it is to the degree to which things have gotten to this point that we should interpellate the analytic community as such, allowing each of us to take a look at it, especially as regards what comes to alter the purity of the analyst's position in relation to his analysand, for whom he serves as a respondent. For the analyst himself is inscribed in and determined by the effects that result from the analytic mass – by which I mean the mass of analysts – given the current state of their constitution and their discourse.

396

One would not be at all mistaken were one to present in this way what I am telling you here.

This has nothing to do with an historical accident, the stress being laid on "accident." We are faced with a difficulty or impasse here that concerns what you heard me bring out pointedly earlier – namely, psychoanalytic action.

If there is a place where the term "action" – which has somewhat recently been called into question by the philosophers of our modern times – can be interrogated anew in a way that is perhaps decisive, it is, as paradoxical as this assertion may seem, at the level of the person whom one might believe abstains the most from it – namely, the analyst.

Over the last few years, I have often emphasized in my Seminar the original perspective that our very unusual experience of action as "acting out"* in the treatment must allow us to introduce into any and all thematic reflection about action. Recall what I told you about the obsessive and the style of his performances and even exploits – you can find it in the article in which I gave definitive shape to the talk I gave in Royaumont.

If there is something that the analyst can stand up and say, it is that action as such – human action, if you prefer – is always

enmeshed in the attempt or temptation to respond to the unconscious. And to anyone who is concerned, for whatever purpose,
with what deserves to be called action – the historian, in particular,
insofar as he does not give up on the meaning of history, many formulations of which make our heads spin – I would propose that he
reconsider, as a function of the articulation I am providing, a question that we cannot eliminate from the text of history all the same:
namely, that its meaning does not purely and simply drag us along
as though we were caught in a riptide, but that actions occur in it.

The action with which we are concerned is psychoanalytic action.
And psychoanalytic action is indisputably an attempt to respond to
the unconscious.

It is also indisputable that, when we call something that occurs
in someone in analysis an "acting out"* – as our practice, this thing
that constitutes a psychoanalyst, has gotten us into the habit of
doing – we know what we are saying even if we do not know very
well how to say it.

What is the most general formulation that we can provide for it?
It is important to give the most general formulation, because if we
provide particular formulations here, we obscure the meaning of
things. If we say, for example, that "it is a relapse on the subject's
part," or that "it is the effect of something stupid we did," we veil
what is involved. This can, of course, be the case, but these are particular instances of the definition of acting out* that I am proposing
to you. Since psychoanalytic action is an attempt (a temptation
too, in its own way) to respond to the unconscious, acting out* is
the type of action by which, at a certain moment of the treatment –
undoubtedly inasmuch as it is especially prompted, perhaps by our
stupidity, perhaps by the analysand's, but that is secondary and of
little importance – the subject demands a more accurate response
from us.

All action – whether it is an acting out* or not, whether it is
psychoanalytic action or not – bears a certain relation to the
opacity of the repressed. And the earliest action is related to the
earliest repressed, that is, to the *Urverdrängt* [that which is primally
repressed].

Freud's notion of *Urverdrängt* might strike you as opaque, which
is why I am attempting to supply you with a meaning for it. The
same thing is involved as what I tried to articulate for you last time
by saying that we cannot but explore the earliest *Versagung*. This,
too, is the same thing that is expressed on the theoretical level in my
formulation that, appearances notwithstanding, there is no such
thing as a metalanguage.

We can speak of metalanguage when, for example, I write little signs like *a*, *b*, *x*, and *kappa* on the blackboard. That works, that functions – that's mathematics. But can there be a metalanguage as concerns what is known as speech – namely, the fact that a subject becomes involved in language? One can speak of speech, naturally, and you see that I am in the process of doing so. But in doing so, all of speech's effects are involved, which is why I am saying that, at the level of speech, there is no such thing as a metalanguage – or, if you prefer, that there is no such thing as a metadiscourse. Or, finally, that there is no action that definitively transcends the effects of the repressed. If perhaps there is, in the end, some such action, it is at most the action by which the subject as such dissolves, is eclipsed, and disappears. It is an action about which nothing can be said. It is, if you will, the horizon of this action that gives fantasy its structure.

This is why my little notation for the structure of fantasy, ($ ◊ *a*), is algebraic and why it can only be written with chalk on the blackboard. It is essential that we not forget this unsayable place insofar as the subject dissolves there and insofar as only algebraic notation can preserve it.

In the article entitled "Transference and Love" by Jekels and Bergler, presented in 1933 when they were still at the Vienna Psychoanalytic Society, there is a brilliant clinical intuition which, as usual, gives the article its weight and value. The depth and tone of this article clearly mark it as stemming from the first generation of analysts; and, even now, what we appreciate in an article is when it brings out something like this. The intuition is that there is a close relationship between love and guilt.

As opposed to the bucolic world of shepherds and shepherdesses where, we are told, love basks in pure beatitude, the authors bid us pay close attention to what we actually see. What we see is that love is not simply guilty in many instances – it is that people love in order to escape from guilt. This is obviously not the kind of thing one can come up with every day. It seems a bit simplistic to people who don't like Claudel – to me, it is of the same ilk.

If one loves, in short, it is because lurking somewhere is the shadow of "*Il vecchio con la barba*" [the old man with the beard] – as an hysterically funny woman I once traveled in Italy with called it – the one we see everywhere among the [Flemish or Italian] Primitives.

The following thesis is argued for quite nicely in the article: love is fundamentally the need to be loved by the very person who could make you feel guilty. If you are loved by that person, you feel much better.

This is one of those psychoanalytic insights that I would say is a top-quality truth [*de bon aloi*], but which is also a low-quality truth because it is an *aloi*, it is alloyed. It is not unalloyed – it is a

398

399

clinical truth. Moreover, it is a collapsed truth, as it were, a truth
that crushes a certain articulation. If I want us to separate these
two metals, love and guilt, it is not because I have a taste for juve-
nile schmaltz. It is because the importance of our discoveries rests
entirely on the fact that in reality, as they say, we constantly deal
with the effects of the tamping down [*tassement*] of the symbolic in
the real. It is by making distinctions that we move forward and that
we demonstrate the efficacious mainsprings with which we deal.

That said, even if guilt is not always and immediately involved in
the triggering of love, in the flash of falling in love, or love at first
sight, it is no less clear that, even in relationships that begin under
such poetic auspices, in time it tends to happen that all the effects of
active censure come to revolve around the beloved object. It is not
simply that the whole system of prohibitions recrystallizes around
that person, but that it is to that person that we come to ask for permission – a function that is ever so constitutive of human behavior.
We would do well not to overlook – in truly authentic, high-quality
love relationships – the impact, not of the ego-ideal, but rather of
the superego as such, in its most opaque and unsettling form.

On the one hand, we find this clinical intuition in the article by our
friends Jekels and Bergler. On the other hand, we see in it a partial
and really brutal use – like that employed by the proverbial bull in a
china shop – of the economic point of view that Freud theorized for
us when he discussed narcissism. I am referring, in particular, to the
idea that the libidinal equation aims, in the final analysis, at restoring an initial integrity, at reintegrating everything that was involved
in what Freud calls, if I recall correctly, an *Abtrennung* [separation,
division, or partitioning] – in other words, everything that experience led the subject to consider, at one time or another, as separate
from himself. This notion, which is theoretical, is among the most
precarious when it is applied in every register and at every level;
and the function it plays in Freud's thought, at the time of his "On
Narcissism: An Introduction," raises a question. We need to know
whether we can use it in good conscience.

As Jekels and Bergler clearly state – for at that point in time,
analysts were not built on an assembly line and they knew how to
outline the aporias of a theoretical position – libidinal investment in
400   objects seems miraculous. And in fact, from their particular vantage
point, it is a miracle. If the subject is truly constituted at the libidinal
level in such a way that his end and goal is to be satisfied with an
entirely narcissistic position, how can it be that, in general and on
the whole, he does not manage to remain there? If something can
make this monad quiver ever so slightly by way of a reaction, one
can, of course, theoretically conceptualize that its goal is to return to

its initial position. But it is not easy to see what could give rise to the enormous detour that constitutes the complex and rich structuring with which we constantly deal in reality.

This is truly what is at stake, and it is what the authors of this article attempt to respond to throughout their article. They adopt this perspective – quite slavishly, I must say, following the trail blazed by Freud – concerning the mainspring of the complexification of the subject's structure: namely, the coming into play of the ego-ideal, which is my main topic today. In effect, Freud indicates, in "On Narcissism: An Introduction," that what is involved is the artifice by which the subject maintains his ideal – allow me to abbreviate it in this way because it is getting late – of omnipotence. In Freud's inaugural text, especially if one takes the trouble to read it, this is introduced and already clarifies enough things at this point that we do not ask for anything further. But given that Freud went on to rethink things quite a bit and rendered this first differentiation still more complex, the authors have to grapple here with yet another definition of the ego-ideal, that of an ego-ideal that restores the benefits of love to the subject. Freud explains that the ego-ideal is something that – having itself originated in the first lesions on one's narcissism – becomes domesticated anew by being introjected. As for the superego, we perceive that we are forced to admit that there must be another mechanism at work, for as introjected as it may be, it nevertheless does not become any more beneficial.

I will stop here today on this topic and come back to it at a later date. Jekels and Bergler are necessarily led to resort to the whole dialectic of Eros and Thanatos which, at that time, is no small matter. It gets pretty complex and is even rather nice. Have a look at the article – you will get your money's worth.

3

Before leaving you today, I would like to propose something lively and amusing to you, designed to give you an idea of what a better presentation of the function of narcissism allows us to articulate more clearly, regarding the ideal ego and the ego-ideal, and in a way that confirms all of psychoanalytic practice since these notions were developed.

The ideal ego and the ego-ideal are, no doubt, closely related to the need to preserve one's narcissism. But we have reason to take into account what, after first broaching the question, I proposed to you by way of a necessary modification to psychoanalytic theory, given the path it followed whereby the ego was used as I indicated earlier – this is what I teach you, or rather taught you, under the heading of the mirror stage. What are its consequences as concerns the economy of the ideal ego and the ego-ideal, and their relationship to the preservation of narcissism?

Well, since it is late, I will illustrate this to you in a way that will, I hope, amuse you. I spoke earlier of cars; using them, let us try to see what the ideal ego is.

The ideal ego is a boy from a good family sitting at the wheel of his little sports car. With it, he's going to take you for a ride. He's going to show off. He's going to take some risks, which is not a bad thing, he's going to be a bit reckless [*goût du sport*], as they say, and the point will be to know what meaning he gives this word and whether recklessness might not also imply defiance of the rules – I don't mean simply the rules of the road, but also of safety.

Be that as it may, this is the arena in which he must show – or not show, that is, show how it is suitable to show – that he is tougher than others, even if it means having people say he is going a bit too far. This is the ideal ego. Which is somewhat tangential, for what I want to talk about is its relationship to the ego-ideal. Indeed, the ego-ideal does not leave the ideal ego all by itself and objectless because, after all, on certain occasions – not on every occasion – if the kid gives himself over to scabrous deeds, why is that? In order to catch a girl's eye.

402   Is it as much about catching her eye as it is about the way in which he wants to catch it? The desire itself is perhaps of less import here than the way of satisfying it. This is why, as we know, the girl can be altogether superfluous and need not even be present.

In short, in this context, which is the one in which the ideal ego has just assumed its place in fantasy, we see more easily than elsewhere what regulates the tonal quality of the fantasy elements. We see that there must be something that slips between the two terms here [$ and *a*], so that one of the two can be elided so easily. We know which term it is that slips in. There is no need to comment on it further – it is lowercase *phi*, the imaginary phallus. And what is at stake here is truly something that is put to the test.

What is the ego-ideal? The ego-ideal, which is closely related to the play and function of the ideal ego, is truly constituted by the fact that at the outset, if he has his little sports car, it is because he is from a fine family, because he is a rich man's son, and because – to change registers – if Marie-Chantal, as you know, joins the Communist Party, it's to piss off her father.

To explore whether she does not in fact misrecognize her own identification here with what she is trying to obtain by pissing her father off is yet another tangent that we will not fly off on. Let us say that both of them – Marie-Chantal and the rich man's son sitting at the wheel of his little car – would be quite simply enveloped in the world organized by the father were it not precisely for the signifier "father." For this signifier allows us, as it were, to extract ourselves from that world in order to imagine that we are pissing him off and to sometimes even succeed in doing so. This is what we analysts express by saying that, in such cases, he or she introjects the paternal image.

Isn't this also to say that the signifier is the instrument thanks to which these two characters, male and female, can "extroject" themselves from the objective situation? Introjection is, in short, the following: to organize oneself subjectively in such a way that the father – indeed, in the form of an ego-ideal that is not as mean as all that – is a signifier on the basis of which the youngster, whether male or female, can come to contemplate him- or herself not too unfavorably at the wheel of his little car or brandishing her Communist Party card.

In short, if, on the basis of this introjected signifier, the subject is judged disapprovingly [*le réprouve*], he thereby takes on the dimension of an outcast [*réprouvé*], which, as everyone knows, is not so terribly disadvantageous, narcissistically speaking. But the upshot, then, is that we cannot so easily say, regarding the function of the ego-ideal,* that it brings together all that is narcissistically beneficial, as if it were purely and simply inherent to a single effect at the same point.

403

This is what I try to articulate for you with my little schema of the inverted vase, which I will not draw on the blackboard again because I do not have time, but which is, I imagine, still fresh in many of your minds. It is only from a specific point that, around the desired flowers, one can see an image arise, that of the vase. Note that this image is real. It is produced by means of the reflection generated by a spherical mirror – in other words, by the particular structure of the human being insofar as the hypertrophy of his ego seems to be tied to his prematurity at birth.

The necessary distinction between the locus where the narcissistic benefit is produced and the locus where the ego-ideal* functions forces us to question the relationship of each of these to the function of love in different ways. We must not present this relationship in a confused way, especially at the level at which we are now examining the analysis of transference.

In concluding today, allow me speak to you about the case of a female patient.

I would say that this patient takes more than just liberties with the rights, if not the duties, stemming from the marital bond. And when she has an affair, Lord knows she is able to take its consequences to the most extreme point of what a certain social limit – that of the respect she derives from her husband's position – commands her to respect. Let us say that she is someone who knows how to sustain and deploy the positions of her desire admirably. And believe you me, she has, over time, figured out how to maintain altogether intact – in her family, I mean with her husband and her amiable kids – a force field of demands that is strictly centered on her own libidinal needs.

When Freud tells us somewhere, if I recall correctly, about women's *Knödelmoral* – which literally means a morality based on dumplings, namely, satisfactions that are demanded – we must not believe that this always backfires. There are women who succeed exceedingly well at it, except for the fact that they need an analysis.

What was I for this patient for quite some time? The authors of the article I mentioned earlier will give us the answer: I was her ego-ideal, inasmuch as I was the ideal point at which order was maintained, and in a way that was all the more necessary since it was on this basis that all disorder was rendered possible. In short, it was essential at that point in time that her analyst not be immoral. Had I been so tactless as to approve of any of her excesses, the result would not, I suspect, have been pretty to behold. Moreover, anything possibly atypical that she could glimpse in my own family structure, or in the principles by which I was raising those under my roof, did not fail to open up for her all the depths of an abyss that she quickly covered over.

Don't go thinking that it is necessary that the analyst effectively demonstrate, thank God, all the ideal qualities that people attribute to him. She simply dropped hints to me on each occasion concerning what she did not want to know about me. The only thing that was truly important was the guarantee she had, believe me, that regarding herself, I would not trip up.

What does such a demand for moral conformity imply? Contemporary moralists have, as you suspect, the answer: in order to lead such a fulfilling life, this person must naturally not have been from the lower classes. And thus political moralists will tell you that what was truly of the essence was to keep a lid on questions that might have been raised concerning the legitimacy of social privilege, all the more so in that, as you may well imagine, she was a bit of a progressive.

But if we consider the true dynamic of the forces at play, it is here that the analyst can put in his own two cents' worth. With the abysses open, I could have acted in such a way as to bring about

404

perfect conformity between the ideals and the reality of the analysis. But I believe that the thing that, in any event, absolutely could not be debated was that she had the most beautiful breasts in town.

Which, as you can imagine, bra saleswomen never contradict.

May 31, 1961

XXIV

IDENTIFICATION VIA
"EIN EINZIGER ZUG"

The primitive monad of jouissance.
Introjection of the imperative object.
The Other in the mirror stage.
The three modes.
On rich people and saints.

I am going to keep talking about my topic in view of arriving at my perhaps daring goal this year, which is to formulate what the analyst must truly be in order to respond to the transference – which also implies knowing what he must be and what he can be later on [in the analysis]. This is why I characterized my goal as daring.

Last time you saw me sketch out – regarding the paper by Jekels and Bergler in *Imago* published in 1934, that is, a year after they presented it at the Vienna Psychoanalytic Society – the idea that we are led to broach this question in terms of the function of narcissism, considered with respect to any and all possible libidinal cathexis.

You are aware of what allows us to view the field of narcissism as having already been extensively explored. We shall see in what respect our specific position, by which I mean the one that I have been teaching you here, broadens or rather generalizes the usually received view. By generalizing it, we can perceive certain traps that are included in the peculiarity of the stance that is ordinarily recommended by analysts.

1

I mentioned last time that one can find in Jekels and Bergler's article, entitled *"Übertragung und Liebe"* ["Transference and Love"], if not all the dead ends to which the theory of narcissism risks leading those who articulate it, at least some of them. All of Balint's work, for example, revolves around the notion of a supposedly primordial autoeroticism and around the way in which the latter is compatible both with the observed facts and with the necessary development of psychoanalytic practice.

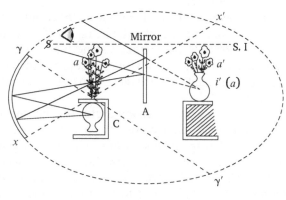

Complete schema

I have just put up on the board, as a visual aid, a little schema that is not new and that you will be able to find in a better-drawn version in the next issue of *La Psychanalyse*. I did not want to include all the details that remind us of its relevance in the optical field in my drawing here today, both because I am not especially inclined to wear myself out and because they would have made this chalk-drawn schema more confused in the end.

Let me remind you of the old story of the illusion – which is one of the amusing experiments of classical physics – of the inverted bouquet: by means of a spherical mirror placed behind a certain device, we can make an image appear that, as I would like to point out, is real – by which I mean that it is not a virtual image, [virtual images being the kind] that are created by [ordinary flat] mirrors. Assuming that we have respected certain ambient lighting conditions carefully enough, the image of a bouquet – the bouquet being in reality hidden under a stand – appears to stand straight up above the stand [see *Écrits*, p. 673].

Such artifices are also used in all sorts of tricks that magicians perform onstage. All kinds of other things can be made to appear above the stand, too, not just a bouquet.

In the present instance, for reasons related to my presentation and to the metaphorical usage of the schema I have in mind, it is the vase itself – the material vase as an authentic piece of pottery – that is hidden under the stand. [Thanks to the spherical mirror,] the vase then appears in the form of a real image [above the stand] on the

407

condition that the observer's eye be, on the one hand, sufficiently far away [from the spherical mirror], and, moreover, situated within the limits of a cone determined by the crossing lines [xx' and yy'] that start at the edges of the spherical mirror, intersect at its focal point, [and continue on from there].

If the observer's eye is sufficiently far away, the result is that small movements of the eye do not make the image itself vacillate much, and allow us to appreciate the image as something whose contours are self-sustaining and that can be visually projected through space. Although this image is flat, it nevertheless gives one the impression of a certain volume.

This is what I use to construct an apparatus that has metaphorical value to us. If we assume, in effect, that the observer's eye is – owing to certain topological or spatial conditions – situated at a point in the spatial field where this illusion can be produced, then it will perceive this illusion even when it is situated at a point that does not allow it to perceive this image directly. In order to make it possible for the eye to perceive it indirectly, one can use an artifice, which involves placing at a certain location a flat mirror – that I will call uppercase A owing to the metaphorical use that I will make of it later – in which the eye will see the same illusion reflected; it will see a virtual image of the real image. In other words, the eye will see the same illusion in the reflected form of a virtual image that would be produced if it were placed in real space – that is, at a point, with respect to the mirror, that is symmetrical to the point it occupies – and if the eye looked at what was happening at the focal point of the spherical mirror, namely, the point at which the illusion formed by the real image of the vase is produced.

In the classical experiment with the bouquet, the vase has its usefulness inasmuch as it allows the eye to focus in such a way that the real image appears to be located in space. As opposed to what is done in the classical experiment, I provide a real bouquet [above the stand] that the real image of the vase comes to surround at its base.

I call this mirror A, the real image of the vase $i(a)$, and the flowers a. As you will see, this will serve us as a visual aid for explanations that I have to give concerning the implications of the function of narcissism inasmuch as the ego-ideal plays the role of the main-spring of narcissism that is introduced in Freud's original text, "On Narcissism: An Introduction" [*SE* XIV, pp. 73–102]. People make an incredibly big deal about its role as a mainspring when they tell us that the ego-ideal is also the pivotal point of the kind of identification whose impact is fundamental in the production of transference.

I truly did not select at random the article that I spoke to you about last time. It is, on the contrary, quite exemplary, significant, and well articulated with respect to the notion of the ego-ideal, as this notion was created and generalized in the psychoanalytic milieu at the time the article was written. How did Jekels and Bergler conceptualize it at the moment at which they began to theorize a notion that was quite new in psychoanalytic theory owing to its topographical function? If you peruse a good cross-section of the clinical papers, case histories, and case presentations from that time, you will get a sense of the idea that authors of the time formed of it and the difficulties they encountered in applying it.

Here is, at least in part, what they came up with. If one reads them attentively enough, it appears that, in order to grasp the efficacy of the ego-ideal insofar as it is involved in the function of transference, they considered the ego-ideal to be a field that is organized in a certain way inside the subject.

The concept of an "inside" serves a major topological function in psychoanalytic thinking, since even introjection refers to it. The organized field was understood quite naïvely, inasmuch as no distinction was made at the time between the imaginary, the symbolic, and the real. In this state of imprecision and indistinctness regarding topological notions, we are truly forced to say that we must, in general, imagine this field in a spatial or quasi-spatial way. We must, in a nutshell, imagine it – this is not indicated, but it is implied in the way these authors spoke about it – as a surface or a volume. In both of these cases, we must imagine it as a form of something that – owing to the fact that it is modeled on the image of something else – presents itself as lending its support and foundation to the idea of identification. In short, it concerns a differentiation that is produced inside a certain topographic field by the specific operation known as identification.

Authors of the time wondered about these identified forms. What could be done with them so that they fulfilled their economic function? It is not my concern today – for it would take us too far afield – to bring out what made Jekels and Bergler adopt the solution they did, a solution that was quite new, or at least not yet altogether popularized, at the time. In the text by Freud to which they referred, one can find certain tangential remarks related to this and a hint at the solution that they went on to propose quite emphatically. This solution involved assuming that the field in question is characterized by the fact that it is cathected with a neutral energy.

What was meant by the term "neutral energy" that was introduced into psychoanalytic dynamics? At the point in the evolution of the theory that we are examining, it meant nothing more than an energy characterized by the fact that it belongs to neither one nor the other – this is what is meant by the term "neutral" – of the two poles of drive energy. Recall that Freud's second topography

409

made him introduce the idea of an energy that is distinct from the libido – that of the *Todestrieb* [death drive], which is the function that henceforth came to be known by analysts as Thanatos, which certainly did not help clarify things – and made him pair up Eros and Thanatos as opposing terms.

It is in such terms that the new dialectic of libidinal cathexis was dealt with by Jekels and Bergler. Eros and Thanatos were employed by them as two primordial destinies behind all psychoanalytic mechanics and dialectic. And the vicissitude – *das Schicksal* [fate or destiny], to use the term Freud himself used regarding the drives – of this neutralized field was explained to us in their article. Their goal was to conceptualize this field and its economic function in a way that rendered it utilizable both in its characteristic function as an ego-ideal, and in the fact that the analyst is called upon to function in the place of this ego-ideal. This is what the authors were led to imagine.

Here we are obviously dealing with the highest, most developed form of metapsychology.

How are we to conceptualize the concrete origins of the ego-ideal? According to Jekels and Bergler – and it is legitimate on their part, our era being no better, given what the developments of Kleinian theory have since wrought – the origins of the ego-ideal are inseparable from those of the superego, even though they are distinct from the latter. In other words, they are paired together. Thus these authors could only conceptualize the origins of the ego-ideal and the superego as involving Thanatos.

410 Now, if one begins with a notion like that of an initially perfect narcissism as regards libidinal cathexis, and if one thinks that the primordial object is originally included in the subject in the narcissistic sphere – which is a primitive monad of jouissance, with which the infant is identified, in a way that is quite iffy – it is difficult to see what could lead to a subjective exit from it. Indeed, the authors themselves did not hesitate to consider such an exit to be impossible. As indeed it is, unless the ravaging power of Thanatos is also included in this monad. Why not consider this power to be the source of what obliges the subject, if I can put it so succinctly, to leave behind his narcissistic self-envelopment?

In short, Jekels and Bergler did not hesitate to attribute all creation of objects to Thanatos itself. Note that I am not in any way trying to argue in favor of their viewpoint, I am merely commenting on it, and I bid you consult their article to see whether I am faithfully reporting what they said. They themselves seemed quite struck by their claim, so much so that, in the final pages of their article, they raised a funny question: have we in fact gone so far as to say

that, in short, we only truly come into contact with any object whatsoever owing to the instinct of destruction?

In truth, although they raised this question in order to temper or
lend a touch of levity to what they themselves proposed, nothing,
after all, contradicts this feature that is necessary if one is led to
follow the path that they follow. For the time being, moreover,
this feature does not pose a problem for us. It seems to me that
what they said is conceivable, at least locally, in a dynamic perspective, under the heading of a significant moment of early childhood
experience. It is, perhaps, at a moment of aggression that the differentiation, if not of every object, at least of a highly significant object,
indeed occurs.

In any case, once the conflict has begun, it is the fact that this
object can be so thoroughly introjected that gives it its import and
value. We thus find anew here Freud's classical, original schema
regarding the introjection of an imperative, prohibiting, and essentially conflictual object.

For Freud told us that it is to the degree to which this object – the
father, for example, in a first rough-and-ready schematization of
the Oedipus complex – is internalized that it comes to constitute the
superego. Overall, this represents progress, it being beneficial from a
libidinal vantage point; for, by dint of being introjected, this object   411
enters – this is one of Freud's first points here – into a sphere that is
sufficiently imbued with narcissism, merely because it is inside, and
can be libidinally cathected by the subject. Note that it is easier to
get oneself loved by one's ego-ideal than by the object on whom the
ego-ideal was at one point modeled.

The fact remains that, even though it is introjected, the ego-ideal
continues to be an unwieldy agency [*instance*]. And it is certainly this
ambiguity that led Jekels and Bergler to theorize a field of neutral
cathexis. The field at stake here is occupied and then evacuated, only
to be reoccupied, by Eros and Thanatos, one after the other – the
Manichaeism of the conceptualization bothering us a bit, we must
say.

In the second stage, the possible function of the ego-ideal in
Verliebtheit [being in love or infatuation] and in hypnosis was introduced – or more precisely, it is in feeling the need to accentuate it
as a second stage that the authors realized that Freud had in fact
introduced it from the outset.

"*Hypnose und Verliebtheit*" ["Being in Love and Hypnosis"] is the
title of one of the chapters in *Massenpsychologie*.

Once it is constituted and introjected, the ego-ideal can be projected onto an object. In truth, the fact that classical psychoanalytic
theory did not distinguish between the symbolic, the imaginary,

and the real means that the stages of introjection and projection
appear to be, not obscure, but rather arbitrary, to be suspended,
to be gratuitous, and to obey a necessity that can only be explained
by the most absolute contingency. It is insofar as the ego-ideal can
be projected anew onto an object that this object – if it happens to
be favorably inclined toward you or to regard you kindly – will be
endowed by you with the highest degree of amorous cathexis. The
description of the phenomenology of *Verliebtheit* was presented
here in a way that allowed it to be almost totally confused with the
effects of hypnosis.

After this second projection, nothing could stop Jekels and
Bergler from proposing a second introjection, a "re-introjection." In
certain more or less extreme states, among which they did not hesitate to include manic states, the ego-ideal itself – caught up, as it is,
in the enthusiasm of the effusive love involved in the second projection – can serve the same function for the subject as that established
in the *Verliebtheit* relationship of total dependency. The ego-ideal
can itself become something equivalent to what, in love, can provide
the full satisfaction of wanting to be loved, of *geliebt werden wollen*.

Although these descriptions, especially when illustrated, brought
with them certain fragments of perspective, flashes of which we find
anew in clinical work, we would not be showing some kind of exaggerated pernicketiness in conceptual matters to feel that, in many
respects, we cannot be completely satisfied with them.

412

2

I am immediately going to highlight what I believe I can contribute
here, and it is something that is articulated more elaborately by
this little montage [i.e., the optical schema at the beginning of the
present class].

Like every other schema of this type – of the topographical type,
like the ones Freud himself provided – it not only does not claim to
represent anything at the organic level, but could not even possibly
do so. It should be quite clear that I am not one of those people who
imagine that with the right surgical operation – a lobotomy, for
example – one can remove the superego with a teaspoon. There are
people who believe that and who have written that by lobotomizing
someone, one removes the superego and sets it aside on a platter.
That has nothing to do with what I am talking about here.

Let us observe what is articulated by the functioning implied by
this little apparatus. It is no accident that it reintroduces a metaphor
of an optical nature. It does so, not for reasons of convenience, but

rather for structural reasons. If mirrors are involved, it is because, as concerns the imaginary mainspring, what is based on mirrors goes much further than the model.

But beware: this schema is a bit more elaborate than is a child's concrete experience in front of a real surface – usually a flat mirror or a polished surface – that serves as a mirror. What is represented here as a flat mirror has a different use. The schema is of interest to us because it introduces the function of the Other with a capital O, whose initial, in the form of the letter A [for *Autre*, meaning Other], designates the flat mirror apparatus here, insofar as this function must be involved in the developments of narcissism that are known as the ego-ideal and the ideal ego, respectively.

413

So as not to give you a dry description of this schema, which would simultaneously risk seeming arbitrary, which it is not, I will first introduce it with the kind of commentary Jekels and Bergler would have called for, inasmuch as they felt the need to broach a thought and mapping problem. My intent is certainly not to bring out the negative aspects of their theory, but rather what is positive about it, which is always more interesting.

Let us note thus that, if we follow them closely, the object is created, strictly speaking, by the destructive instinct, *Destruktionstrieb*, or Thanatos, as they called it. Why not call it "hatred"? Let us follow them step by step. If this is true, is there anything left of the object after the destructive effect? It is not at all unthinkable. Not only is it not unthinkable, but we find anew here what I myself theorize in another way at the level of what I call the imaginary field and its effects. What is left of the object, what survives after the libidinal effect of the destructive *Trieb*, after the action of Thanatos, is precisely what eternalizes the object in the guise of a form – this is what forever freezes it as a fixed type in the imaginary.

There is something in images that transcends the movement and changeability of life, in the sense that images live on after the death of living beings. According to Antiquity's *nous*, this is one of the first steps of art: that which is mortal is immortalized in statuary. This is also the function that is served in a certain way by the subject's image in my theory of the mirror [stage]. When this image is perceived by a child, something is suddenly proposed to him whereby he does not merely receive the sight of an image in which he recognizes himself; this image already presents itself as an ideal *Urbild*, as something that is both ahead of him and behind him, as something that has always existed, as something that subsists by itself, and as something before which he senses his own fissures as a prematurely born being and experiences himself as still insufficiently coordinated to correspond to it in its totality.

It is very striking to see a small child – who is sometimes still being supported by a little device with which he begins to try to make his first attempts to walk [a sort of walker], and for whom even the attempt to take somebody's arm or hand is still characterized by dissymmetry and inadequacy – this being who is still insufficiently stable, even at the cerebellar level, nevertheless move about, lean in, and squirm, accompanying this with expressive gurgling sounds, in front of his own image in the mirror, assuming one has placed a mirror within range, and low enough to the ground for him to see it. He thus shows in a lively way the contrast between the traceable thing that is projected before him there – which attracts him and with which he persistently plays – and the incomplete thing that manifests itself in his own movements.

This is my old topic of the mirror stage, which I take to be an exemplary and highly significant landmark for us. It allows us to point out the key spots or crossroads [in development] and to conceptualize the renewal of the possibility, which is always open to the subject, of a self-fracturing, self-tearing, or self-biting when faced with what is both himself and an other. There is a certain dimension of conflict here that has no other solution than that of an either/or. Either he has to tolerate the other as an unbearable image that steals him from himself, or he must immediately break him, knock him over, or annul the position across from him, in order to preserve what is at that moment the center and drive of his being, which is evoked by the other's image, whether it be specular or incarnate [in another child like himself]. The link between this image and aggressiveness is quite clear here.

Is a development of the individual that leads to a sufficient consistency of the object and to the diversity of the object stage conceivable on this basis? We can say that attempts have been made to conceptualize it. Hegel's dialectic of the conflict [or struggle] of consciousnesses was nothing, after all, but an attempt to expound the whole world of human knowledge on the basis of a pure conflict that is radically imaginary and destructive at its root.

As you know, I have already indicated on various occasions the fissures and gaps in Hegel's conception. Without revisiting that discussion today, I will simply say that it is impossible to deduce, on this radically imaginary basis, everything that Hegel believed he could deduce with his dialectic. The hidden implications of this dialectic that allowed it to function could not in any way be produced on this basis. Even when a child's hand extends toward the face of his semblable and is armed with a stone – and this can be the hand of a very young child, believe me, as the most ordinary, direct observation shows, for a child need not be very old to have, if not the vocation, at least the same impulse as Cain – if that hand is stopped by another hand, that of the person whom the child is threatening, and they lay that stone down together and it comes to constitute an object that is perhaps agreed upon or disputed, then it will become, as it were, the first stone of the world of objects. But it will not go beyond that; nothing can be built upon it.

We hear a sort of echo or overtone here of the apologue of he who must "cast the first stone" [John 8:7]. And indeed, it is quite necessary that, in the first place, this stone not be cast. And once it is not cast, it will not be cast for any other reason. But in order that something be founded that is open to dialectical development, the register of the Other with a capital *O* must come into play beyond this.

This is what is expressed by my optical schema. It is inasmuch as the third party, the Other with a capital *O*, intervenes in the relationship between the ego and the other with a lowercase *o* that something can function that gives rise to the fecundity of the narcissistic relationship itself.

Let me exemplify this with a movement made by children in front of mirrors, a movement that is well known and is not difficult to observe. A child, who is being held in the arms of an adult, is expressly confronted with his image. The adult, whether he understands what is going on or not, is amused by this. We must give full weight to the movement of the child's head when the child – even after having been captivated by the first intimations of the game he plays in front of his own image – turns around toward the adult who is holding him, without our being able to say, naturally, what he expects from the adult, whether it is some sort of agreement or attesting. Referring to the Other nevertheless clearly comes to play an essential role here. I am not exaggerating this role by articulating it in this way, as instituting what will become connected to the ideal ego and the ego-ideal, respectively, in the child's subsequent development.

What can come from this Other, insofar as the child in front of the mirror turns around to look at him? I would say that the only thing that can come from him is the sign "image of *a*" $[i(a)]$ – a specular image that is both desirable and destructive, that is effectively desired or not desired. This is what comes from the person toward whom the child turns, to [*à*] the very place with which he identifies at that moment, inasmuch as he sustains his identification with the specular image.

What I will call the antagonistic nature of the ideal ego is palpable to us from this early moment on. In other words, already in this specular situation, a split occurs – this time at the level of the Other, for the Other, and by the Other – between the desired ego, by which

416

I mean the ego desired by him [the Other], and the authentic ego: the *authent-Ich*, if you will allow me to introduce a term which is not as new as all that in this context. Except that, in this early situation, it is the ideal that is there – I am speaking about the ideal ego, not the ego-ideal – the authentic ego being yet to come.

It is as things evolve – with all the ambiguity the term "evolution" brings with it – that the authentic ego will come to light; and this time it will be loved in spite of everything, in spite of the fact that it is not perfect. This is also how the ideal ego functions in the entire progression. All of its ensuing development, which appears to be progress, goes against the tide, involving risk and defiance.

What is the function of the ego-ideal here? You will tell me that it is the Other, the Other with a capital *O*. But you nevertheless sense that the Other is only involved here as the locus on the basis of which the ego constantly refers – in its emotional [*pathétique*] swings – to the image that is offered up to it and with which it identifies. The ego presents itself and sustains itself qua problematic only on the basis of the Other's gaze. The fact that this gaze may, in turn, be internalized, does not mean that it merges with the place and prop that have already been constituted in the form of an ideal ego. It means something else.

People claim that the ego-ideal is tantamount to the introjection of this Other. This is quite a stretch. It presumes the existence of a relationship of *Einfühlung* [understanding, empathy, or sensitivity] that is as total as what is implied by the reference to an organized being, the real being who holds the child in front of the mirror. This is, as you probably suspect, precisely what is in question.

Although this point must serve as our terminus today, I will tell you right away in what respect my solution differs from the one that is usually given.

It is extraordinarily important to recall that, right from his first steps in articulating *Identifizierung* [identification] – which I will return to later because it cannot be avoided – Freud implied that there is a first possible identification with the father as such, prior to the very first sketching out of the Oedipal situation. Did Freud have fathers on the brain? Whatever the case may be, Freud had the subject identify first with his father, and Freud developed quite a subtle terminology by calling this identification *exquisit männlich*, exquisitely virile [*SE* XVIII, p. 105].[15]

417   This undoubtedly occurs in the course of development. It is not a logical stage, but a developmental stage that is situated prior to the onset of the Oedipal conflict, so much so that Freud went on to write that it is on the basis of this primordial identification that desire

begins to point toward the mother and that the father consequently comes to be considered a rival.

I am not trying to say that this first stage of identification is clinically grounded. I am saying that the fact that it seemed necessary to Freud should not be considered an extravagance on his part or mere drivel. There must be a reason why this earlier stage seemed necessary to him and this is what I will try to show you in what follows.

Freud next spoke about regressive identification [*SE* XVIII, pp. 106–7], the identification that results from a love relationship, inasmuch as the object refuses to love one in return. Here we can already see why there had to be a stage of primordial identification, but this is not the only reason. The subject is thus able, through a regressive process, to identify with the object who disappoints his appeal for love.

After having presented these two modes of identification in Chapter 7, entitled *Die Identifizierung* ["Identification"], Freud introduced a third mode, the good old form of identification that we have known about since the case history of Dora: hysterical identification. This form stems from the fact that the subject recognizes in another person the total or global situation in which he or she lives. Our hysteric has a fit the day that, in the common area where slightly neurotic and nutty girls at a boarding school congregate, one of her friends receives a letter from her lover [*SE* XVIII, p. 107]. In my vocabulary, this is termed identification at the level of desire. Let us leave it aside for the time being.

Freud paused in his text to tell us expressly that, in the first two fundamental modes of identification, identification always occurs via *ein einziger Zug* [a single trait, stroke, or characteristic; *SE* XVIII, p. 107].

This removes many difficulties, in more than one respect – with respect, first of all, to what is conceivable, which we should not disdain. Second, it converges with a notion that we know well, that of the signifier.

This is not to say that this *einziger Zug*, this "single trait," is, for all that, a signifier. Not at all. It is quite probable, if we begin from the dialectic that I am trying to sketch out for you, that it is a sign.   418
To say that it is a signifier, something more is required. It must be used later in, or have a relationship to, a signifying battery. What is defined by this *ein einziger Zug* is the punctual character of the early reference to the Other when it comes to narcissism.

This is what allows us to answer the following question: how can the subject internalize the gaze of an Other who can at any moment change its preference for one or the other of the enemy twin brothers constituted by the ego and the image of the little specular other? We must conceptualize the Other's gaze as being internalized by a sign. *Ein einziger Zug* is enough. There is no need for a whole organized field or for some sort of massive introjection. This point – capital I that stands for the single trait, this sign of the Other's assent, of the choice of love-object on which the subject can operate – is located there somewhere and is fixed in the ensuing mirror play. It suffices that the subject come to coincide with it in his relationship with the Other for this little sign, this *einziger Zug*, to be at his disposal.

We are right to radically distinguish the ego-ideal from the ideal ego. The ego-ideal is a symbolic introjection, whereas the ideal ego is the source of an imaginary projection. The narcissistic satisfaction that develops in the relationship with the ideal ego depends on the possible reference to this primordial symbolic term that can be mono-formal or mono-semantic – that is, *ein einziger Zug*.

This will be of capital importance in all of what I will have to say about this subsequently.

3

If you will grant me a little bit more time, I will begin to recall what I must consider to be clear to everyone here regarding my theory of love.

Love, as I have said, can be conceptualized only within the perspective of demand. Love exists only for beings who can speak. The dimension, perspective, or register of love develops, unfolds, and is inscribed within what one might call the "unconditional" nature of demand.

This is what stems from the very fact of demanding, regardless of what one demands. For in the register or order of demand qua pure – not when one demands this or that, in other words, something specific – demand is merely the demand to be heard [*entendue*, which also means understood].

419

I would go further still. Why does one want to be heard? For what might well be called "no reason." Which is not to say, nevertheless, that this does not take us quite far, for the place of desire is already entailed by this "for no reason."

It is precisely because demand is unconditional that it is not a question of a desire for this or for that, but a question of desire *tout court*. This is why the metaphor of the one who desires [*le désirant, erastés*], which I broached from every angle at the beginning of this year's Seminar, is implied right from the outset.

In love, the metaphor of the one who desires implies what it replaces in the metaphor – in other words, the one who is desired [*erómenos*]. What is desired? It is that which is desiring in the other. This cannot happen unless the subject himself is situated [*colloqué*] qua desirable. Which is precisely what he demands when he demands to be loved.

In this context, I cannot fail to recall to mind, before coming back to it later, that love – as I have always told you and we find it necessitated again and again from every direction – is giving what you don't have. One cannot love without presenting oneself as if one does not have, even if one does. Love as a response implies the domain of not having.

I am not the one who invented this – Plato is. He came up with the idea that only *Penía*, Poverty, can conceive Love, as well as the plan to get herself knocked up at a party one night. Indeed, giving what you have is throwing a party [*c'est la fête*], not love.

Hence – and I am moving along rather quickly, but you will see that we shall land on our feet – for rich people, love exists; yes, even they think about it; but loving always requires refusal.

This is precisely what is annoying. It is not only those to whom something is refused who are annoyed. Those who refuse, rich people, are hardly any more at ease. The *Versagung* of rich people is found everywhere. It is not simply the character trait of avarice, it is far more constitutive of the position of rich people, regardless of what we believe. And the theme in folklore of Grisélidis – with all that she has that is captivating, whereas she is rather revolting all the same – is there to remind us of this.

While I am on the subject, I will go even further: rich people do not have a very good reputation. In other words, we progressives do not like them very much. But we should be suspicious of our dislike   420
for them. Perhaps our hatred of rich people is quite simply, by a secret pathway, part and parcel of a revolt against love. In other words, it is perhaps tied to a negation, a *Verneinung* of the virtues of poverty, which could well be at the origin of a certain misrecognition of what love is.

The sociological result is, moreover, rather curious. We obviously facilitate in this way many of the functions of rich people – we temper our behavior at their homes or, to be more exact, we give them a thousand excuses for avoiding their party-giving function. Which does not make them any happier.

In short, it is quite evident to analysts that rich people have great difficulty loving – which is what a certain preacher from Galilee noted in passing many moons ago. We would perhaps do better to pity rich people for this rather than hating them – unless hating is, after all, merely a mode of loving, which is quite possible.

What is clear is that wealth has a tendency to make you impotent.

Long experience as an analyst allows me to tell you that I consider this a well-attested fact. And this explains quite a few things – for example, the need to do things in a roundabout fashion. Rich people are forced to buy, because they are rich. And in order to make up for this, in order to try to find potency anew, they strive to devalue things by buying them [cheaply]. This [devaluing] comes from them, they do it for their own convenience. To achieve this, the simplest means is, for example, not to pay [for things]. They sometimes hope to provoke thereby what they can never acquire directly – namely, the Other's desire.

But so much for rich people. Léon Bloy once wrote a book entitled *La femme pauvre* [*The Woman Who Was Poor*]. I am annoyed because, for some time now, I have been referring to nothing but Catholic authors, but it is not my fault if I have, for eons, been finding very interesting things in their work. I would like it if, someday, someone would notice and put to good psychoanalytic use the extravagant things that are hidden in Bloy's book, which verges on the unbearable, and that only an analyst can understand. I have yet to see any of them take an interest in it. But Bloy would have done well to also write a book entitled *The Woman Who Was Rich*.

It is clear that only women can incarnate the ferociousness of wealth in a dignified manner. But that is not enough, and it poses for them, and especially for those who wish to win their love, very specific problems. This would, however, require a return to the topic of feminine sexuality, and I apologize for merely indicating it to you as a toothing-stone.

421

Since I cannot go any further today, and since when I speak of love, it is very specifically in order to describe the field where I must say what our place must be in the transference, before leaving you today I would like to indicate something that bears on the topic of wealth, and to say a brief word to you about saints.

This should not seem to come out of the blue, for we have not yet finished with Claudel.

As you know, at the very end of *The Humiliation of the Father*, in the solution given to the problem of desire, we have a saint. He is Orian, about whom it is expressly said that if he does not want to give anything to little Pensée – who, fortunately, is quite capable of taking it from him by force – it is because he has far too much joy, nothing but joy, complete joy. And there is no point debasing such wealth by having a little affair – this is said in the text – one of those affairs that unfolds over the course of a few short nights at a hotel [p. 396/204].

Strange stuff. We would be going a bit too quickly were we to try to discuss the psychology of creation and to simply think that Orian is terribly repressed. Perhaps Claudel was terribly repressed, too. But what is signified by poetic creation, what is signified by the function Orian serves in this tragedy – namely, the fact that it interests us – is something else altogether. And this is what I would like to point out to you by remarking that saints are rich. They do all they can possibly do to seem poor – this is true, at least in varied climes – but it is precisely in this respect that they are rich, and especially filthy compared to other rich people, for theirs is not the kind of wealth that you can get rid of so easily.

Saints exist entirely within the realm of having. They perhaps give up a few trivial things, but they do so in order to possess everything. And if you look closely at the life of the saints, you will see that saints cannot love God except as a name of their own jouissance. And, in the final analysis, their jouissance is always quite monstrous.

In the course of our psychoanalytic discussions here, we have spoken about a number of human types, including heroes. I am merely introducing the difficult topic of saints anecdotally here, rather as a prop, it being one of those that I think is necessary to help us locate our own position.

As you can well imagine, I naturally do not situate us among the saints. Still, it is worth saying so. For by not saying so, it might remain an ideal, as they say, for many people.

There are many things about which one might be tempted to say that they are our ideal. What is ideal is at the heart of problems related to the analyst's position. I will return to this notion in what follows and you will see what it is about this category that we should abandon.

422

June 7, 1961

XXV

THE RELATIONSHIP BETWEEN ANXIETY AND DESIRE

The place of anxiety as a signal.
$a \neq i(a)$.
The unbearable object.
The place of pure desirousness.
Desire as a remedy for anxiety.

[The beginning of the class is missing.]

1

We shall immediately turn to the heart of a problem mentioned by Freud, that of the meaning of anxiety [*angoisse*]. We will go further still, since we will begin with a question that arises from the economic standpoint, which is that of figuring out, as Freud tells us, where the energy for anxiety as a signal comes from.

We find the following sentence on page 120 of the German edition of Freud's *Inhibitions, Symptoms and Anxiety*: "*Das Ich zieht die (vorbewusste) Besetzung von der zu verdrängenden Triebrepräsentanz ab und verwendet sie für die Unlust-(Angst)-Entbindung.*" Translation: "The ego withdraws the preconscious cathexis from the *Triebrepräsentanz*" – that is, from what, in the drive, is a representative – "a representative that must be repressed. It transforms it in order to release unpleasure and *Angst*."

We must not alight upon a single sentence in Freud's work and immediately begin to excogitate about it. It is only after a good deal of reflection that I am asking you to turn to it now. I have carefully chosen it in order to incite you to reread *Inhibitions, Symptoms and Anxiety* as soon as possible.

To return to my own topic, let us turn now to the crux of the matter. I have said enough about it for you to suspect that the

formula ($ ◇ a) must somehow be involved in the stage of the   424
orientation we are at, where fantasy is not simply formulated but
brought up, broached, and tracked down in every possible manner.
In order to grasp the necessity of this formula, you must realize that
in this prop for desire, the respective functions of the two elements
and their functional relationship cannot in any way be verbalized by
any exhaustive attribute, which is why I must abbreviate them with
two algebraic terms and amass their various characteristics around
them.

$ is related to the fading* of the subject, whereas a, the little
other, is related to the object of desire. The effect of this symbolization is already to show you that desire does not involve a simple
subjective relationship to the object. It is not enough to say that,
in the subject's relationship to the object, desire implies a mediation or a reflexive intermediary, if it merely involves, for example,
the subject thinking of himself the way he thinks of himself in his
knowledge relationship to the object. The whole theory of knowledge has been founded on this, which is precisely what the theory of
desire is designed to call into question. This would have us shaking
in our boots if others before us had not already called into question
Descartes' "I am thinking, therefore I am."

Let us consider the sentence by Freud I mentioned earlier and try
to apply this to it. This does not mean that I am immediately conveying you to the endpoint of my thought process; with the following
questioning, I am conveying you halfway there. It is a problematic
question, designed to orient you, to give you the illusion that you
are the ones who are in the process of seeking – an illusion that will,
moreover, be promptly realized, for I will not give you the final
answer. It is not solely my question, but my method, too, that is
heuristic. What does it thus mean to decathect the *Triebrepräsentanz*
if we apply it to my own formulation? It means that anxiety is produced when the cathexis of little a is transferred to $.

$, however, is not something graspable; it can only be con-
ceptualized as a place, since it is not even the subject's point of
reflexivity, [that is, the place where] the subject could grasp himself,
for example, as desiring [*comme désirant*]. The subject does not
grasp himself as desiring. Nevertheless, in fantasy, the place where
the subject could, as it were, grasp himself as such as desiring is
always reserved. It is reserved so thoroughly that it is usually occupied by something homologous that is produced at the lower stage
of the graph: $i(a)$. It is not necessarily occupied by that, but it is   425
ordinarily.

This is expressed by the function of the real image of the vase in
the inverted vase illusion. The image of the vase is produced there

in such a way that it seems to surround the base of the stems of the flowers that elegantly symbolize little *a*. This is what is involved in the narcissistic image or phantom that comes to serve, in fantasy, as the illusion of aligning oneself [*se coapter*] with [the object of] desire, the illusion of having one's object in hand. If $ is thus a place that can, from time to time, be empty – namely, a place where nothing satisfying happens as regards the arising of the image – we can theorize that anxiety as a signal is perhaps produced in response to the call [for something to fill it].

I am going to try to demonstrate this exceedingly important point. One can say that Freud's last work on the subject [*Inhibitions, Symptoms and Anxiety*] gives us almost everything we need to resolve it, without quite giving it the final quarter turn, strictly speaking. In his text, the nut is never completely tightened.

Following Freud, let us say that anxiety as a signal is produced at the level of the ego. However, thanks to my formalizations, we shall perhaps be able to say a bit more about what is meant by "the level of the ego." My notations will allow us to break down the question, to articulate it more precisely, and to thereby go beyond certain points at which the question leads Freud to an impasse.

Here I am immediately going to make a leap.

2

When Freud tells us about the economic transformation necessary for the signal to be produced by saying that it must not require very much energy to produce a signal, he already indicates that there is a relationship between the production of the signal and something like a *Verzicht*, a renunciation – not that different from a *Versagung* – owing to the fact that the subject is barred. The *Verdrängung* of the *Triebrepräsentanz* [the repression of the drive's representative] also connotes the slipping away of the subject, which truly confirms the accuracy of my notation $.

My leap involves designating for you what I have been announcing here for a long time as the place where the analyst is truly situated. Which does not mean that he occupies this place all the time, but it is the place where he waits. The word "waits" takes on its full import here, given what we will find anew here related to the function of waiting or *Erwartung* [anticipation or expectation] in order to structure the place of $ in fantasy.

I said that I was making a leap, in other words, that I would not immediately prove what I am asserting. Let us now take the steps necessary to understand what is involved.

One thing is given, which is that anxiety as a signal is produced somewhere, in a place that can be occupied by $i(a)$ – the ego insofar as it is the image of the other, the ego insofar as it is, fundamentally, the function of misrecognition. It occupies this place not inasmuch as this image occupies it but qua place – in other words, inasmuch as this image can, on occasion, be dissolved there.

Note carefully that I am not saying that it is the absence of the image that provokes anxiety. I am saying what I have been saying forever – namely, that the specular relationship, the subject's earliest relationship to the specular image, arises in the so-called reaction of aggressiveness.

As I already indicated in my article on the topic, the mirror stage is not unrelated to anxiety. I even indicated that we can acquire a cross-sectional handle, as it were, on aggressiveness by orienting ourselves via the temporal relationship. Indeed, there are not only spatial relationships that refer to the specular image when it begins to come alive and become the other incarnate; there is also a temporal relationship – I hasten to see myself like the other, failing which where will I be?

If, however, you take a look at my articles – those who keep abreast of my work know that I discussed the function of haste in logic in a little sophism, the three prisoners problem – you will see that I am being more prudent here. I have my reasons for not taking the formulation all the way. The function of haste – namely, the way a man runs headlong toward his resemblance to another man – is not anxiety. In order for anxiety to be constituted, there must be a relationship at the level of desire. This is why I am leading you by the hand today to the level of fantasy in order to broach the problem of anxiety.

In order to show you where we are headed, I am going to get well ahead of myself, after which we will backtrack, darting hither and thither like jackrabbits.

Where is the analyst situated in the subject's relationship to desire, in his relationship to an object of desire that we assume, in this case, to be an object that brings with it the threat in question, the threat that determines the *zu Verdrängen*, the [fact that it] "must be repressed"? It goes without saying that none of this is definitive, but since we are broaching the problem in this way, let us raise the following question: when faced with a dangerous object, since that is what is involved here, what would a subject ordinarily expect from someone who would dare occupy the place of his companion? The subject would expect his companion to give a danger signal, a signal that, in the case of a real danger, would lead the subject to get the hell out of there.

What I am introducing here is something that people complain that Freud did not include in his dialectic, for it was truly something that needed to be done. I say that the internal danger is altogether comparable to an external danger, and that the subject strives to avoid it in the same way that we avoid external dangers. Look at what this provides us by way of an effective articulation if we consider what actually happens in animal psychology.

Everyone has heard about the role played by signals among social animals like those that live in herds. When a predator shows up, the cleverest animal, or the one in the herd that is keeping watch, notices, smells, and locates it. Gazelles and antelopes raise their muzzles, make a little bellowing sound, and without delay the whole herd dashes off in the same direction. A signal as a reaction to a danger in a social complex, at the biological level, can thus be grasped in an observable society. Well, the same is true of anxiety as a signal – the subject can receive the signal from the alter ego, from the other who constitutes his ego.

You have heard me warn you at length against the dangers of altruism. I have explicitly told you to beware the pitfalls of *Mitleid* or pity, that which stops us from harming the other, the poor girl [*la pauvre gosse*], leading us to marry her and to both of us being bored for a long time to come – I am abbreviating here. However, if it is merely humane to alert you to the dangers of altruism, it does not mean that this is the final mainspring; and it is, moreover, in this respect that I am not, with respect to whomsoever I am speaking on a particular occasion, playing devil's advocate. The latter would bring him back to a healthy egoism and steer him away from this truly likable direction that involves not being mean. For, in fact, this precious *Mitleid* or altruism merely covers over something else, and you can always find it, assuming that you look at it psychoanalytically.

428

He who is suffocated by this *Mitleid* is the obsessive, and the first step is to notice – using what I point out to you and what the whole tradition of moralists allows us to assert in this case – that what he respects, what he is unwilling to violate in the other's image, is his own image. If the inviolability of this image were not carefully preserved, what would arise would truly be anxiety.

Anxiety when faced with what? Not when faced with the other in whom he sees himself, the one I called "the poor girl" earlier, who is poor only in his imagination, for she is always much tougher than you might think. When faced with "the poor girl," he is scared to death of being faced with the other *a* – not the image of himself, but the object of his desire.

I will illustrate this with the following point, which is quite important. Anxiety is undoubtedly produced topographically in the place defined by $i(a)$ – in other words, as Freud articulated it in his last formulation, in the place of the ego. But there is no anxiety as a signal except insofar as it is related to an object of desire, inasmuch as the latter disturbs the ideal ego – that is, the $i(a)$ that originates in the specular image.

Anxiety as a signal has an absolutely necessary connection with the object of desire. Its function is not exhausted in the warning that one must take off. Even as it serves this function, a signal preserves one's relationship with an object of desire.

This is the key to and the mainspring of what Freud accentuates in this text – as well as elsewhere, repeatedly and with the same accent, with the same choice of terms, and with the same incisiveness that is illuminating in his work – by distinguishing the situation of anxiety from that of danger and from that of *Hilflosigkeit* [helplessness or distress].

When in *Hilflosigkeit* or distress, the subject is purely and simply overwhelmed by a situation that irrupts, which he cannot cope with in any way. Between that and taking flight – flight which, not to be heroic here, Napoleon himself considered the truly courageous solution when it came to love – there is another solution and it is what Freud points out to us by underscoring the *Erwartung* character of anxiety.

This is its central feature. True, we can secondarily construe it to be a reason to take off, but that is not its essential characteristic. Its essential characteristic is *Erwartung*, and I designate it by telling you   429
that anxiety is the radical mode by which a relationship to desire is maintained.

When the object disappears – for reasons of resistance, defense, or other ways of canceling out the object – there remains what can remain, which is *Erwartung*. In other words, what remains is a pointing toward the object's place, a place where the object is now missing, where we are no longer dealing with anything but an *unbestimmte Objekt* [an uncertain, undecided, or indefinite object], or again, as Freud says, an object with which we are in a relationship of *losigkeit* [not having it]. When we are at this stage, anxiety is the final or radical mode in which the subject continues to sustain his relationship to desire, even if it is an unbearable mode.

3

There are other ways to sustain one's relationship to desire that concern the unbearable nature of the object. This is why I tell you that hysteria and obsession can be defined on the basis of the two statuses of desire that I call "unsatisfied desire" and "impossible desire" – that is, desire instituted in its impossibility.

But it suffices that you cast your eyes now on the most radical form of neurosis, phobia, around which all of Freud's discourse revolves here, to see that it cannot be defined otherwise than by the following: phobia is designed to sustain a relationship to desire in the form of anxiety.

There is but one thing that must be added in order to fully define it, just as in the complete definition of hysteria and obsession one must add the metaphor of the other, at the point at which the subject sees himself as castrated, confronted with the Other with a capital *O*. In the case of Dora, for example, it is by means of Herr K. that Dora desires, yet she does not love him – she loves Frau K. It is by means of the man she desires that she finds her way toward the woman she loves. We must, similarly, complete our formulation of phobia.

Phobia involves the maintenance of a relationship to desire through anxiety, with a more precise supplement: the place of the object, insofar as it is aimed at by anxiety, is occupied by what I explained to you at length regarding little Hans – the function of the phobic object, namely, Φ, capital *Phi*. In the phobic object, it is clearly the phallus that is at stake, but it is a phallus that takes on the value of all signifiers, occasionally even the value of the father.

430

What is remarkable in the case of little Hans is both the absence [*carence*] and the presence of the father – absence in the form of the real father, presence in the form of the symbolic father, who is invasive. If all of this can take place at the same level, it is because the phobic object has the infinite possibility of serving a certain missing or deficient function; the latter is precisely what would make the subject succumb were anxiety not to arise in that function's place.

Having taken this roundabout pathway, we can now grasp in what respect the function of anxiety as a signal warns about something, something very important in psychoanalytic practice and clinical work. The anxiety to which your patients are exposed is not at all, or is not only, as people think and as you always seek to confirm, as it were, internal to the subject. What is characteristic of the neurotic is to be, in this regard, according to André Breton's expression, a communicating vase. The anxiety your neurotic has to deal with, anxiety as energy, is an anxiety that he is in the serious habit of seeking with a magnifying glass, to the right and to the left, in one or the other of the Others with a capital *O* he deals with. Their anxiety is just as valid and useful to him as his homegrown variety is. If you do not take it into account in the economy an analysis, you will go very far astray. In many a case, you will be scratching your head, trying to figure out where a little resurgence of anxiety comes from when you least expect it. It is not necessarily his, and is not necessarily the anxiety you are already aware of owing to the prior months of analysis. There is also the anxiety of his neighbors that counts, not to mention your own.

Naturally, you imagine that you will find your way. You know that you have already received warnings on this score. I'm afraid that this does not alert you to much, for what these warnings imply is that your own anxiety must not enter into the picture. The analysis must be aseptically free of your own anxiety.

What can this mean at the level where I am trying to get you to stay this year, the synchronic level which does not provide the same ease as diachrony? The fact that you have largely gone beyond anxiety in your own prior analysis resolves nothing, for what we must know is in what current state you must be, as concerns your desire, so that not only anxiety as a signal, but anxiety itself does not arise from you in an analysis. For if it arises, it is quite capable of being transferred to your patient's economy – and this all the more so the further along he is in his analysis, in other words, the more he seeks out the path of his desire at the level of the Other with a capital *O* that you are for him.

Be that as it may, in order to come full circle, we have to bring in the function of the Other with a capital *O* concerning the possibility of the arising of anxiety as a signal.

My earlier reference to animal herds clearly shows that signals operate within a necessary function of imaginary communication, and it is here that I want you to sense that, if anxiety is a signal, what this means is that it can come from someone else. The fact remains that, insofar as what is involved here is a relationship to desire, a signal is not exhaustively covered by the metaphor of the danger posed by the herd's enemy. Indeed, what distinguishes a human herd from an animal herd is – as everyone, except for the shakers and movers in group [*collective*] psychology, knows – that each subject himself is the enemy of the herd.

We find an interesting transposition, in this reference to the reality of the herd, of what Freud articulates for us as an internal danger. We find here the exact confirmation of what I always tell you – the universal, individual, and collective are situated at one and the same level. What is true at the individual level, this internal danger, is also true at the collective level. The danger that is internal to the subject is the same as the danger that is internal to the herd.

This is related to the originality of the very nature [*position*] of desire. Insofar as desire emerges in order to make up for a lack of

431

certainty or for the lack of a guarantee, the subject finds himself confronted with what is significant to him insofar as he is not simply an animal in a herd. He may be an animal in a herd, except that every elementary action on his part, which surely exists, is seriously disturbed owing to the fact that it is included – both at the collective and at the individual level – in his relationship to the signifier.

At the moment at which a social animal takes off upon hearing a signal given by a guard animal or some other animal, he is the herd. A speaking being, on the other hand, is essentially the want-to-be that has arisen out of a certain relationship to discourse – that has arisen from a kind of poetry, if you will. The subject can only fill this want-to-be, as I have already indicated, through an action that – you will sense this better in the context of the parallel I am drawing – very easily takes on, indeed perhaps always radically takes on, the quality of a headlong flight.

But this action, which involves neither the level of coherence nor that of collective defense, does not in any way help out the herd. In short, the herd does not take very well to the subject's action, in theory, not to say that it wants nothing to do with it. And it is not simply the herd – reality wants nothing to do with his action either, because reality is precisely the sum total of certainties accumulated by adding up a series of prior actions. A new action is always unwelcome.

This is what allows us to correctly situate – in other words, in a way that intersects psychoanalytic practice – the nevertheless surprising fact, which is still more or less obvious, of the slight lifting of anxiety that occurs every time the subject's desire is truly at work. Here we are dealing both with the everyday level of experience and with what is essential – that is, with what is at the heart and root of our practice.

If psychoanalysis has not succeeded in getting men to understand that their desires, first, are not the same thing as their needs and, second, are in themselves of a dangerous nature, threatening to the individual – this is shed light on by the fact that their desires are obviously threatening to the herd – then I wonder what purpose psychoanalysis has ever served.

The point is to follow a certain upward path, and since we are already on our way, we are going to continue by raising an insidious question: "What must the analyst's *Versagung* be?" Here, frankly, I haven't yet taken things much further, but I ask you this: doesn't the analyst's fruitful *Versagung* consist in the fact that he refuses to give his own anxiety to the patient and leaves empty the place he is called upon to occupy as the other who is [expected] to give anxiety as a signal?

We can see highlighted here what I already pointed out last time when I said that the analyst's pure place, insofar as we can define it in and through fantasy, is that of pure desirousness [*désirant pur*].

The function of desire is always produced somewhere, whether the subject comes to occupy the place of *erómenos* or *erómenon*. This is why I had you engage in extensive deciphering of the theory of love in Plato's *Symposium* at the beginning of this academic year. We must now manage to conceptualize how a subject can occupy the place of pure desirousness – in other words, abstract or subtract himself, in the relationship to the other, from any supposition of being desirable. What you have read of the statements made and responses given by Socrates in the *Symposium* must give you a glimpse of what I am telling you now.

If something is incarnated in and signified by the episode with Alcibiades, it is clearly the following: on the one hand, Socrates asserts that he knows nothing except about matters of love, and everything we are told about him is that he is desirous through and through and inexhaustibly so; yet, on the other hand, when it comes time for him to take up the position of he who is desired when faced with Alcibiades' public, scandalous, out-of-control, and drunk aggression, he literally is not up to it. I'm not saying that this resolves the matter, but it at least illustrates what I am talking to you about – it has a meaning that was at least incarnated somewhere.

I am not the only one to whom Socrates appears to be a human enigma, a one-of-a-kind case about which we know not what to do, with what kind of tweezers we can try to pick him up and examine him. Everyone has thought as much, whenever they genuinely raised the following questions: "How was this guy put together?" "And why did he create such chaos wherever he went simply by showing up and telling little stories that seem to be about everyday matters?"

I would like us to dwell a little while on the status of the place of the desirer [*désirant*]. It resonates or rhymes with what I will call the place of the entreater [*orant*] in prayer, for in prayer the entreater sees himself in the process of praying [*orer*]. There is no such thing as a prayer in which the entreater does not see himself praying.

This morning I thought of Priam [in the *Iliad*]. He is the very epitome of entreaters, having demanded that Achilles give him back the body of the last, or almost last, of his sons. In any case, he is attached to Hector.

What does he tell Achilles? He does not say much to him about Hector, first of all because it is not easy for him to talk about Hector given the state he is in at that moment, and second because it seems that whenever the living Hector is at stake, Achilles – who is hard to handle, not being master of his own impulses – begins to grow

433

furious, even though he has received divine instructions via his
mother, Thetis, who came to tell him the following: the big boss
came to see me expressly to tell me that he wants you to return
Hector to his father, Priam.

Priam is not very sophisticated, psychologically speaking. Owing
to the fact that he is in the position of the entreater, he exemplifies
in his request the very figure of the entreater. His prayer has reso-
nated since the beginning of our age, for even if you have not read
the *Iliad*, the episode cannot be utterly unfamiliar to you given all
the other models it has engendered. In his prayer, Priam's character is split in two, being accompanied by an other who is described
and inserted into his prayer in the form of someone who is not
there, namely, Peleus, Achilles' father. It is Priam who prays, but
his prayer must necessarily involve another person. He does not
simply invoke Achilles' father, but the figure of a father who is,
perhaps, quite annoyed at that very moment because his neighbors
are harassing him, but who knows he at least still has one son left,
Achilles. In every prayer, you can thus find what I call the place of
the entreater within the very discourse of the person who prays.

The desirer [*le désirant*] is not the same, which is why I am taking
this roundabout route. The one who desires [*le désirant*] as such can
say nothing about himself without abolishing himself as desiring.
This is what defines the pure place of the subject qua desiring. Any
attempt to explain oneself is, in this context, futile. Even a breaking
off of speech can say nothing [*syncope du langage est impuissante à
dire*] because, as soon as the subject speaks, he is no longer anything
but a beggar [*quémandeur*] – he shifts to the register of demand,
which is a horse of a different color.

This is no less important when the point is to formulate what
traces out the specific form of the analyst's place in the response to
the other that psychoanalysis constitutes.

I will end today on a point that will perhaps add yet another dead-
end formulation to all those that I seem to have already served up
to you. Here is the formulation, and it is of some interest since it
brings together the elements I have just gone over: if anxiety is what
I told you it is, a relationship that props up desire where the object
is lacking, then by inverting the terms, we see that desire is a remedy
for anxiety.

We observe this constantly in psychoanalytic practice. Anyone
who is slightly neurotic knows as much about it as you do, if not even
more. The support found in desire, as awkward as desire may be
given all the guilt that accompanies it, is still much easier to maintain
than the position of anxiety. The upshot is that, overall, for someone

434

who is a bit astute and experienced – I am speaking here about the analyst – it is good to always have within reach a little well-polished desire so as not to be prone to bringing into play in the analysis a quantum of anxiety that would be neither opportune nor welcome.

435

Is this where I mean to lead you? Certainly not, for it is not easy to locate the walls of a hallway by feeling our way along with our hands. Our concern here is not with desire as an expedient but, rather, with a certain relationship to desire which must not be sustained merely from day to day.

Next week, I will return to the distinction, which I began talking about last time, between the subject's relation to the ideal ego and to the ego-ideal. This will allow us to find our way in the true topography of desire, thanks to the function of the *einziger Zug*, which fundamentally characterizes the ego-ideal and thus allows us to define the function of the object in relation to narcissism.

This is what I hope to be able to accomplish in the next class, placing it under the heading of Pindar's formulation, "A dream of a shadow is man," as he writes in the last verses of his eighth *Pythian Ode*.

June 14, 1961

XXVI

"A DREAM OF A SHADOW IS MAN"

A fly in the field of the Other.
With an analyst, man awakens.
Abraham and partial love.
From narcissism to the object.
The fox and the tip of his nose.

Today we are going to try to talk a bit about the subject of identification inasmuch as we are led to it – as I hope you have figured
out – as the terminus of the precise question around which my
attempt to elucidate transference this year has revolved.

I announced last time that I would take things up again this time
using as an epigraph Pindar's famous ejaculatory proclamation,
found in his eighth *Pythian Ode* written for Aristomenes, the wres-
tler from Aegina who was the winner at the Pythian Games:

Επάμεροι·τί δέ τις ; τί δ' οὐ τις ; σκιᾶς ὄναρ ἄνθρωπος.
[Creatures of a day! What is someone? What is no one?]
A dream of a shadow is man.

I intentionally stress the need to distinguish between two different concrete levels of identification, making an obvious distinction
that is phenomenologically within everyone's ken: the ideal ego is
not to be confused with the ego-ideal. Psychologists [like Lagache]
can discover this all by themselves, and they do not fail to do so,
moreover. The fact that this is just as important in the articulation
of Freud's dialectic is confirmed, for example, by the work I mentioned last time by Conrad Stein on primal identification, which
ends with the recognition of something that is still obscure – namely,
the difference between the two series of identifications that Freud
distinguishes and accentuates as ego identifications and ego-ideal
identifications.

1

Let us thus turn to the little optical schema [see Chapter XXIV above] that you are beginning to become familiar with, and that you will come across again when you work at your leisure on the sixth issue of the journal *La Psychanalyse*, which will be published shortly.

The illusion that is represented here, known as that of the inverted vase, can only be produced for eyes that are situated somewhere within the cone produced by the point that joins the edge of the spherical mirror with the focal point where the illusion is produced. You are aware that this illusion, which is a real image, serves to metaphorize for us what I call *i* of *a*, written *i(a)*, which designates the specular image as a function. In other words, it is the specular image as such, imbued with the tone and specific accent of the power of fascination, with its own characteristic cathexis in the libidinal register, that is clearly distinguished by Freud with the term "narcissistic cathexis." This function, *i(a)*, is the core function of narcissistic cathexis.

These words do not suffice to define all the relations and impacts in which this function appears. What I will say today will allow you to approach more closely what is at stake, for it is also what I call the ideal ego as a function insofar as it is distinct from the ego-ideal as a function and is, indeed, opposed to it.

I trace out the operationalizing [*mise en fonction*] of the Other insofar as he is the Other of the speaking subject, the Other insofar as through him, as the locus of speech, the impact of the signifier comes into play for every subject – for every subject we deal with as psychoanalysts. We can pinpoint there the place of what will begin to function as an ego-ideal.

In my little schema, as you will see it published in the journal [see *Écrits*, p. 675], you will perceive that S, which is there to figure the subject as a function, is purely virtual. This function is, as it were, a necessity of thought, the very one that is at the crux of the theory of knowledge – namely, that we cannot conceptualize anything as an object that is not propped up by a subject. But, as analysts, we call into question the real existence of this function. Indeed, we bring out the fact that the subject we deal with, owing to the fact that he is essentially a subject who speaks, cannot be confused with the subject of knowledge. It was truly a case of stating the obvious on my part when I reminded analysts that, to us, the subject is not the subject of knowledge, but the subject of the unconscious. We must not speculate about him as some sort of pure self-transparency of thought, since this is precisely what we contest. The idea that thought is transparent is a pure illusion.

439

I am aware that some of my comments get philosophers up in arms. Believe me, I have already had discussions with defenders of Descartes' position that went far enough for me to be able to say that there is room for possible agreement among us. But I will leave this debate to one side, since it is not what I am interested in today.

The subject who is indicated in my schema is thus in a position to accede to a grasp of the real image that is produced at $i(a)$ only by means of an artifice. This is so because he is not there and because it is only by means of the Other as a mirror that he can come to situate himself there. As he is nothing, he cannot see himself there. Thus it is not he himself qua subject that he looks for in this mirror.

A long time ago, shortly after the war, in my paper on psychical causality delivered in the town of Bonneval, I spoke of a "mirror [that] shows him a surface in which nothing is reflected" [*Écrits*, p. 188]. At the time, this enigmatic comment led people to confuse what I was saying with some kind of more or less mystical ascetic exercise. You should now realize what I meant, or more precisely, you should begin to sense that in the analyst's function as a mirror, it is not the mirror of specular assumption that is involved. I am speaking of the place that the analyst must occupy, even if it is in the mirror that the specular, virtual image must be produced.

The image that is found at $i'(a)$ is truly what the subject sees in the Other, but he only sees it insofar as he is situated in a place that cannot be confused with the place of what is reflected. No condition requires him to be at $i(a)$ in order to see himself at $i'(a)$.

Certain conditions nevertheless require him to be in a certain field, the field traced out by the lines delimiting a certain conical volume. Why then, in this original schema, did I place S in the spot where you will find it in the published figure? Nothing implies that he is there rather than elsewhere. He is there in theory because, with respect to the orientation of the figure, you see him appear in some sense behind $i(a)$, and because this position is not without having a phenomenological correspondent that is expressed rather well in the French expression – and it is no accident that it exists – *une idée derrière la tête* [literally, "an idea behind the head"; figuratively, "an idea in the back of one's mind"]. Why would ideas that are generally the ones that sustain us be qualified as "ideas behind the head"? It is no accident that analysts sit behind their patients. We will turn again later today to the topic of what is in front and what is behind.

Be that as it may, the position of S in the field of the Other – that is, in the virtual field that the Other develops, owing to its presence, as a field of reflection – can only be located here at the point designated by capital I, insofar as it is distinct from the place where $i'(a)$ is projected. It is inasmuch as this distinction is not merely possible but ordinary that the subject can apprehend what is fundamentally illusory about his narcissistic identification. There is the shadow, *der Schatten*, as Freud says somewhere [*SE* XIV, p. 249], precisely as regards the *verlorenes Objekt*, of the lost object, in the work of mourning. If *der Schatten* – the shadow or essential opacity that narcissistic structure brings to the object relationship – is surmountable, it is insofar as the subject can identify with something else.

I have figured the Other here in a form in which it is legitimate for us to figure it – as a mirror. It is the form in which existentialist philosophy grasps it, grasping it in that form to the exclusion of any other, and this is precisely what constitutes its limitation. The Other, that philosophy tells us, is he who sends our own image back to us. Now, if the Other is nothing but he who reflects my own image back to me, I am, in fact, nothing but what I see myself as. Literally, I am the Other with a capital *O* insofar as he himself, if he exists, sees the same thing as me. He, too, sees himself in my place. How am I to know if what I see myself as over there is not all there is? It is truly the simplest hypothesis to assume the Other to be a living mirror, such that when I gaze at him, it is him in me that gazes at himself, and who sees himself in my place, in the place that I occupy in him. Assuming he is nothing but his own gaze, he is the one who grounds the truth of this gaze.

In order to dissipate this mirage, something suffices, something is required, and something occurs every day that I represented to you earlier on as the movement of the small child's head when he turns around toward the person who is carrying him. It doesn't take much – a lightning flash (but that is already saying too much, for flashes of lightning have always been taken to be no less than emblematic signs of the Father of the gods, and I am not bringing this up at random) or even just a fly buzzing about that passes into this field – for me to locate myself elsewhere, to lead me outside of the conical field in which $i(a)$ is visible.

441

Don't think that by bringing in a fly, wasp, or anything else that makes noise and surprises us, I am just kidding around – because, as you very well know, even such a diminutive insect can be the elective object that suffices to constitute what I call the signifier of a phobia. Such an object can take on the altogether sufficient, operative function of calling into question the reality and consistency of the ego as an illusion. It is enough for anything that serves as a prop for the subject to move within the field of the Other for the Other's consistency – or more precisely, the consistency of what is there qua field of narcissistic cathexis – to be called into question by one of these deviations [*écarts*].

Indeed, if we rigorously follow Freud's teaching, although the field of narcissistic cathexis is central and essential – and it is around this field that the entire fate of human desire is played out – it is not the only field. The proof thereof is that, at the very moment at which Freud introduces this field in his *Einführung* ["On Narcissism: An Introduction"], he distinguishes it from another field: that of the relationship to the archaic object, the nourishing field of the maternal object. This other field – which, in Freud's dialectic, takes on the value of being of an altogether different order, and which is, if I understood Conrad Stein correctly, what the latter identified in his work by the term "primal identification" – is, to my way of thinking, and this is something new that I am introducing, structured in an original, radical way by the presence of the signifier as such.

If I am introducing this notion, it is not for the sheer pleasure of contributing a new articulation of what is truly still the same field, but because the function of the signifier is decisive here. It is thanks to its function that what comes from this field allows the subject the possibility to exit from his pure and simple captivity in the narcissistic field. And it is only by pointing out that the function of signifying elements is essential that we can introduce clarifications and make possible distinctions that are imperiously necessitated by clinical questions that are as concrete as possible, as I will show you. It is only by introducing the articulation of the signifier in structuring the field of the Other that clinical questions can be resolved that have hitherto remained unresolved, leading for this reason to irreducible confusions.

In other words, σκιᾶς ὄναρ ἄνθρωπος, "A dream of a shadow is man." It is on the basis of my dream, it is by moving about in the field of dreams insofar as it is the field of the wandering of signifiers, that I can glimpse the possibility of dissipating the effects of the shadow and know that it is merely a shadow. Naturally, there is something that I may for a long time still not know, which is that I am dreaming. But it is already at the level of dreams and in the field of dreams, assuming I know how to question them and articulate them, that I can not only triumph over the shadow but that I have my first access to the idea that there is something more real than the shadow – that there is, first of all and at the very least, a reality [*réel*] of desire that this shadow separates me from.

You will tell me that the world of reality [*réel*] is not the world of my desires. But Freud's dialectic also teaches us that I only proceed in the world of objects along the pathway of the obstacles placed before my desire. The object is *ob*. The object is found through objections. If the first step toward reality is made at the level of dreams and in dreams, I still have to wake up to get to this reality. But it does not suffice to topologically define this awakening by saying that what wakes me up is when there is a little too much reality in my dream. In fact, I awaken when the satisfaction of demand appears in my dream. It is not the most common occurrence, but it happens.

The psychoanalytic path toward the truth about man has taught us what awakening is, and we glimpse what becomes of demand. The analyst articulates what man demands. With an analyst, man awakens. He realizes that for the million years that the human species has been here, it has not ceased to be necrophagous. This is the final word of what Freud articulates with the term "primal identification," the first type of identification: man has never ceased to eat his dead, even if he dreamt for a short space of time that he had definitively repudiated cannibalism.

It was important here for me to point out that it is precisely along the pathway whereby we are shown that desire is an oneiric desire – that desire has the same structure as dreams do – that the first correct step was made regarding the pathway toward reality.

It is because of dreams and in the field of dreams that we first prove to be stronger than the shadow.   443

2

Now that I have articulated the relations between $i(a)$ and I – although I am sorry that I have done so in such a way that you cannot already see their clinical implications – I am going to show the relations between this couple of terms and little a, the object of desire. This is what is important to me, and my prior discourse implies it, inasmuch as it suffices to guide us in the relations [between a and] $i(a)$.

I will return later to what, apart from the overall experience of dreams, justifies the emphasis I have placed on the signifier's function in the field of the Other. Whenever identifications with the ego-ideal are mentioned – for example, in the introjection involved in mourning around which an essential part of Freud's conception of identification revolves – you will see that, if we look closely at the clinical picture, we never encounter a global identification, the kind that would, with respect to the narcissistic identification that it combats, involve the enveloping of one being by another.

In order to illustrate what I have just said, consider the image we find in Christian icons: the mother with the child that she holds before her on her lap. Believe me, this figuration of the mother enveloping her child is no accident. If this were the crucial opposition between identifications, then compared to narcissistic identification, anaclitic identification should be like a vase containing within it a more limited world.

I will tell you right away that one of the most demonstrative texts on this topic is the *Versuch einer Entwicklungsgeschichte der Libido* by Karl Abraham. You must read his "Short Study of the Development of the Libido," which came out in 1924.

In his article, what is constantly at stake is to draw out the consequences of what Freud had just contributed regarding the mechanism of mourning and the identifications that it involves. Among the very numerous clinical illustrations Abraham provides of the reality of this mechanism, there is not a single example that does not unambiguously give you the impression that the kind of introjection involved is not the introjection of the reality of another person as enveloping, overflowing, or all-inclusive, or even as a hodgepodge at times, but always the introjection of *ein einziger Zug*, a single trait. The illustrations of this that he supplies go very far, since in reality, despite his title, *Versuch*, an "essay" or "short study" on the development of the libido, what he talks about is the function of that which is partial in identification, and he does this alongside his study of development and under the aegis of this study, unless the latter is merely the excuse for the former, or perhaps even a sub-division of it.

Indeed, it is in this article that Karl Abraham introduced the notion that is incorrectly referred to as that of the "partial object," which has since circulated throughout psychoanalytic work, becoming the foundation on which quite a lot of theorization concerning the neuroses and perversions has been constructed. I will show you what it is actually about before returning to the brilliant illustrations he provides of it.

It will suffice for me to indicate to you exactly where you can find these things in the text, and you will see that there is nothing to object to in what I am formulating here. For Abraham's article has no meaning or import except insofar as it illustrates on every page what characterizes identification inasmuch as it is an ego-ideal identification – it is an identification via isolated traits, each of which is unique and has a signifying structure.

This is also what obliges us to look a bit more closely at what must be distinguished from it, assuming we wish to see clearly. Indeed, in the same context, and for good reason, Abraham introduces what is designated as the function of the partial object. This is precisely what is involved in the relations between $i(a)$ and a.

If you read Abraham's essay, you will find the following term, *Partialliebe*, partial love, used in connection with the object: partial love for the object. The object of this love, the more than exemplary object, the only true object – although others can be inscribed in the same structure – is the phallus. This is what

Abraham stresses. How does he conceptualize in his text the break or disjunction that gives the phallus its value as a privileged object? On every page, he manages to produce for us what is at stake in the following manner.

What does partial love for the object mean according to Abraham? It is not love for what goes by the name phallus that falls away in the process. It is truly love that is close to acceding to the normal object, love for the opposite sex, the kind of love tied to the capital, structuring, and structural stage that we call the "phallic stage." It is truly love for another person, a person who is as complete as possible – minus the genitals.

445

By way of clinical examples, Abraham provides two cases of hysterical women [pp. 483–94] who have with their fathers certain relations that are entirely based on variations in the relationship [to the object]. In the first case, following a traumatic experience involving her father [at age six, she witnessed her parents having sexual intercourse and saw her father's naked body; p. 483], the father was no longer apprehended by the patient for anything other than his phallic value; but later on in the treatment, he appeared in her dreams with his complete image, except that this image was censured at the level of the genitals – he appeared devoid of pubic hair [p. 494]. All of Abraham's examples run along these lines: partial love for the object – that is, love for the object minus the genitals – provides a foundation for the imaginary separation of the phallus, insofar as the latter intervenes henceforth as a central and exemplary function.

The phallus is the pivotal function, I would say, in that it allows us to situate what is distinguished from it, namely *a* and, in little *a* qua little *a*, the general function of the object of desire. At the heart of the little *a* function – allowing us to group together the different modes of possible objects that intervene in fantasy – is the phallus. The latter is the object, as I have said, that allows us to situate the series of possible objects, their point of origin, what comes before and what comes after.

The crucial point is articulated on page 89 of the original edition [p. 495 in the English], where Abraham points out in a footnote that love for the object, with the exclusion of the genitals, appears to analysts to be the stage of psychosexual development that temporally coincides with the stage of phallic development. He adds that the two are linked not only because they coincide temporally, but also because they have much closer internal relations; in addition, he indicates that hysterical symptoms can be understood as the negative of the function that is defined as the exclusion of the genitalia.

I had not reread this text in a long time, having left it to two of you to do so for us. Perhaps it would not be a bad thing for you to realize that the algebraic formula that I gave for the hysteric's fantasy is manifest in Abraham's text. For the time being, it is something else that I wish to get you to see, which is also found in the text, but which I think no one has thus far noticed.

Abraham raises the following question: whence comes the struggle [*réluctance*] and, in short, raging will [*rage*] – a term that I am introducing, but that is justified by his preceding lines – to castrate the other in the living flesh, a raging will that already wells up at the imaginary level? He answers this by saying: "*Wir müssen ausserdem in Betracht ziehen, dass bei jedem Menschen das eigene Genitale stärker als irgendein anderer Körperteil mit narzisstischer Liebe besetzt ist.*" "We must thus take into consideration the fact that in every man, the genitals, strictly speaking, are more cathected than any other part of the body in the narcissistic field." And so that there will be no mistaking what he thinks, Abraham indicates that this corresponds precisely to the fact that anything but the genitals must be cathected when it comes to the object.

I am not sure if you truly realize what such a modification implies, a modification that is not isolated here as if it were a mere slip of the pen; everything goes to show that this is what underpins all of Abraham's thought. I cannot in good conscience quickly glide over this point as if it were an everyday truth. Despite the obviousness and necessity of such an articulation, I do not believe that it has hitherto been pointed out by anyone.

Let us try to understand this with the help of the blackboard. [Lacan begins drawing a schema.] Here is the field of one's own body – in other words, the narcissistic field. The only reason for having brought in narcissism here is to show us that the process of cathexis' progress depends on the transformations of narcissism. Let us try to draw something that corresponds to what Abraham tells us – namely, that cathexis is never stronger than when it comes to the genitals. We arrive at the following graphic representation, where this [the uppermost squiggly line] represents the profile of narcissistic cathexis.

446

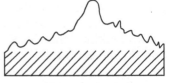

Narcissistic cathexis   Object cathexis

Now what can we say about object cathexis? Abraham's sentence – if we are to take it seriously – implies that, as opposed to what we might at first think, the energy that is going to be transferred to the object is not subtracted from the summit, from the spot where there is maximal cathexis. It is not the regions that are the most cathected that lose some of their charge in order to begin to provide a little cathexis to the object. In Abraham's conceptualization, insofar as it is necessitated by the whole of his book – otherwise his book has no meaning whatsoever – it is, on the contrary, at the lowest levels of cathexis [of one's own body] that energy is taken so as to be used for object cathexis.

Abraham explains this to us in the clearest manner possible: it is inasmuch as the subject's own genitals remain cathected, that the object's genitals are not cathected.

There is absolutely no other way to understand what he says.

3

447

Doesn't it seem, if you give this a little thought, that it leads us to an observation that has far more importance than we might think?

Indeed, there is something that it seems people don't realize about the mirror stage and the function of the specular image. If the kind of communicating, reversal, deflection [*déversement*], or interchanging [of libido] that takes place between the narcissistic object and the other object is regulated at the level of specular relations, mustn't we show a bit of imagination and give importance to what results from it? If, in the imaginary, the organizing center of the relationship to the other as sexual, or as not sexual, is situated in man at the specular stage, isn't it worth our while to dwell for a moment on the following point, that no one ever mentions? This economy has an intimate relationship with faces, with the "face-to-face relationship."

We often employ this term, emphasizing it in a certain way, but it does not seem that we have ever entirely emphasized what is original about it: we call the genital relationship that takes place *a tergo* a relationship *more canis*. It should not be good enough for cats, if you catch my drift. It would suffice for you to think of cat-like women to tell yourself that there is perhaps something decisive in imaginary structuring which is such that, for the vast majority of species, the relationship with the object of desire being structurally destined to come from behind, this relationship consists in covering or being covered. Rare are the species for which this thing must take place from the front. In our species, the sensitive moment of the apprehension of the object is decisive, assuming you lend credence to both the experiential results of the mirror stage and what I have tried to find in it. I am speaking of an object that is defined by the fact that, in animals that have an erect posture, something essential happens with the appearance of their ventral side. This is of capital importance.

It seems to me that people have never yet clearly brought out the full range of consequences of what I will call the various fundamental positions of eroticism. It is not that we do not see features of them here and there, or that psychoanalytic authors have not for a long time observed that almost all primal scenes evoke and reproduce the witnessing of coitus that occurs *a tergo*, and are connected to that. Why? I will not dwell here on a certain number of notations that could be put into some kind of order in this way, because I want to indicate to you that it is rather remarkable that the objects that turn out to have an isolated value in the imaginary composition of the human psyche, especially as partial objects, are not only situated in front, but stick out, as it were.

If we take as our frame of reference a vertical surface that is parallel to the surface of a mirror, and gauge in some sense the depth of what is at stake in the specular image, we can measure what comes forward with respect to this depth, as emerging from libidinal immersion. I am not speaking merely of the phallus, but also of the essentially fantasmatic objects known as the breasts.

I recently remembered, in this context, an episode in a book by the marvelous Madame Gyp, which is entitled *Petit Bob*. In it, Little Bob, who is an inimitable clown, notices two little sugar loaves, as he puts it, on a woman who is floating on her back in the water at the seaside; he discovers their appearance with wonder – and we sense some indulgence here on the author's part.

I believe that it is never a waste of time to read works by authors who take the trouble to transcribe for us what children say. This comment was surely a direct quote. The fact that Madame Gyp – who was the mother of a late lamented neurosurgeon, who may well have been the prototype of Little Bob – was, we must admit, a bit of an idiot, certainly does not mean that reading her work is any less profitable to us; quite the contrary.

We will thus perhaps see better now the true function that should be ascribed to the object relation to the nipple.* The tip of the breast also has a gestalt-like relationship insofar as it is set off from or isolated against a background. Owing to this, it is in a position of exclusion with respect to the profound relationship with the mother which is that of breast-feeding. Were it not so, perhaps one would not so often have such trouble getting infants to latch on to their

448

mothers' nipples. And perhaps the phenomena of anorexia nervosa   449
would also take a different shape.

You should thus keep in mind the little schema concerning the mainspring of the two-way link between narcissistic cathexis and object cathexis, a link that justifies its name and allows us to isolate its mechanism. Not every object must be defined, purely and simply, as a partial object – far from it – but the central characteristic of the relationship between one's own body and the phallus conditions the relationship to the most primitive objects after the fact, *nachträglich*. The fact that they are separable objects, that they are objects that can possibly be lost, and that they function as lost objects – all of these features would not be laid out in the same way were there not at the center the emergence of the phallic object as a blank spot on the body image.

Think of the islands you see on sailors' maps; what there is on the islands is not represented in the slightest, but merely the outlines. Well, the same is true for objects of desire in general. I will try to show this to you next time: the genital is like an island, and it is not enough to say that later on we will sketch in what there is on the island, that the thing will be taken care of, and that we will then enter thoroughly into genitality. No one has ever done the drawing. To characterize the object as genital does not suffice to define its relationship with the body. Nor does it suffice to qualify one's entry into the genital stage as post-ambivalent – no one has *ever* entered into it.

I will conclude here with a little image designed to get you to remember what is new in what I wished to add to your mental imagery today.

While I was contemplating the relationship between men and animals, it occurred to me that I should read up on hedgehogs to find out how they make love. It is clear that to do so *a tergo* must be rather inconvenient for them. I must give Jean Rostand a call to ask him what they do. But I will not dwell on this point. Hedgehogs figure in literature. Archilochus says the following in his *Epodes*: "The fox knows lots of tricks, the hedgehog only one – but it's a winner." Well, what is at issue here concerns the hedgehog.

Whether or not he was thinking of Archilochus, Jean Giraudoux   450
reveals the lightning-flash style of someone who also has a winning trick up his sleeve, which he attributes to the fox. He says – and it is possible that an association of ideas played a role here – perhaps the hedgehog, too, knows this particular trick. It would, in any case, be urgent for him to know it, for it has to do with the way to get rid of vermin, an operation that is more than merely problematic for the hedgehog.

Giraudoux's fox proceeds in the following manner. He wades very slowly into the water, going in tail first. He slips in slowly, letting the water envelop him until nothing remains above the surface but the tip of his nose. Then he dives in, in order to be thoroughly washed clean of everything that has infested him.

I hope this image will illustrate for you the relationship that I brought out today – namely, that everything that is narcissistic must be conceptualized as at the root of castration.

June 21, 1961

MOURNING THE LOSS OF THE ANALYST

The little *a* of desire.
The Sadean line.
"I desire."
The relationship between I and *a*.

As I was preparing this last class of the year for you, Plato's invocation at the beginning of the *Critias* came to mind. He speaks there about tone as an essential element in the measure of what must be said. Would, indeed, that I could know how to maintain the right tone.

In order to do so, Plato mentions the topic he is going to discuss in this unfinished text, which is no less than the birth of the gods [106a–b]. This coincidence of topics did not displease me, since, tangentially no doubt, we came quite close to the same one, to the point of hearing someone – who professes, you may think, to be an atheist in certain ways – speak of the gods as that which is found in the real.

It turns out that, every week, more and more of you hear what I tell you as especially addressed to you. Not that I privately address whomsoever I please, since many of you, if not all of you, hear it. Nor is what I say addressed to you as a group either, for I observe that what each person hears leaves room among yourselves for dissent, if not discordance. A lot of room is thus left for different views. Perhaps this is what is known, strictly speaking, as "a voice crying in the wilderness" [*parler dans le désert*].

I can certainly have no reason to complain about having been deserted this year. As everyone knows, there can practically be a crowd of people in the desert, for a desert is not constituted by emptiness. What is important is the following that I dare to hope: that it is to some degree in the desert that you have come to find me. Let us not be too optimistic, nor too proud of ourselves; but let us say, all the same, that you have had, all of you have had, some concern about where the desert ends.

452   This is why I ensure that what I tell you is never, in fact, cumbersome as concerns the role that I must play with some of you, which is that of your analyst. This is precisely related to what my Seminar this year aims at – namely, the position of the analyst. We are concerned with what is at the heart of the response that the analyst must provide in order to be equal to the power of the transference. I characterize this position by saying that the analyst must abstain from having any notion of an ideal analyst in the very place that is his. I believe that respecting this condition is likely to permit the necessary reconciliation of the two positions I hold for a number of you, being both your analyst and someone who speaks to you about analysis.

In various ways and under various headings, one can of course formulate something along the lines of ideals as regards the analyst. There are qualifications the analyst must have, and they already suffice to constitute a core of ideals. The analyst must not be altogether ignorant of a certain number of things, that is for sure. But this is not at all what is involved in his essential position.

Naturally, the ambiguity of the word "knowledge" [*savoir*] comes in here. If, in his invocation at the beginning of the *Critias*, Plato refers to knowledge as the sole guarantee that what he will broach will remain measured, it is because at his time, this ambiguity was much smaller. The meaning the word "knowledge" has for him is much closer to what I am aiming at when I try to articulate for you what the analyst's position is, and it is here that the choice I made this year to begin with the exemplary image of Socrates is truly justified.

1

Last time I arrived at what I believe to be a turning point in what I will have to articulate hereafter: the function of little object *a* in my schemas. It is, indeed, the function that I have thus far elucidated the least.

I broached it last time regarding the object qua part, a part that presents itself as separate – the "partial object," as they say. And, directing you to a text that I entreat you to peruse carefully during
453   the upcoming summer vacation, I pointed out that Karl Abraham, he who introduced the notion of the partial object, quite categorically means by it a love for the object from which a part is excluded. A partial object is an object minus this part.

Such is the foundation of the experience around which the

introduction of the partial object revolves, and you are aware of the interest that has since been granted it, in particular in Winnicott's speculations – those that are related, in the final analysis, to the meditations of the Kleinian circle.

Those who listen to me, assuming they hear me, have been able to have for a long time, it seems to me, more than just a suspicion of the formal fine-tuning that we can perform regarding the partial nature of the object, insofar as it is very closely related to the function of metonymy. The latter lends itself to the same equivocations in grammar. There, too, you can hear that metonymy is "the part taken for the whole," a definition that allows for everything – both truth and error. Truth, if this part taken for the whole is transformed in the process in order to become a signifier. Error, if we consider only the part-like face – in other words, if we look only to a reality-based reference in order to understand it. I have already underscored this elsewhere sufficiently not to return to it here.

What is important is that you recall to mind the schema I presented last time, as well as the schema of the mirror [the optical schema in Chapter XXIV], which I am going to take up again today in a simplified form. It is important for you to know what relationship there is between, on the one hand, the object of desire – whose essential feature in psychoanalytic practice, namely, its structure as a partial object and its function as fundamentally obstructing, I have always stressed – and, on the other hand, what libidinally corresponds to it. The latter is what I brought out last time; it is what remains most irreducibly cathected at the level of one's own body: the basic fact of narcissism and its central core. The sentence by Abraham that I discussed involves this: it is inasmuch as the real phallus remains, unbeknown to the subject, that around which the maximum cathexis is preserved, that the partial object turns out to be elided or left blank in the image of the other qua cathected.

The very term "cathexis" [*investissement*] takes on all of its meaning from the ambiguity that we find in the German term *Besetzung*. What is involved is not merely a charge, but something that surrounds a central blank. If we must, in this context, latch onto something obvious, then let us take an image that seems, we might say, to stand erect at the height of desire's fascination, the image that is renewed with the same form of Plato's theme by Botticelli's brush: the birth of Venus – that is, Heavenly Aphrodite – Venus rising from the waters, her body erect above the waves of bitter love. Venus – or even Lolita. What does this image teach us as analysts?

We have been able to identify it with the symbolic equation, to employ Fenichel's words, "Girl = Phallus."* The phallus is not

454

articulated here in a different way but, strictly speaking, in the same way. Where we symbolically see the phallus is precisely where it is not. Where we assume it to be behind a veil, having manifested itself in the erection of desire, is to the left side of the mirror in the [following] schema. If it is there before us, to the right, in the dazzling body of Venus, it is precisely insofar as it is not there. Whereas this form is invested, in the sense that I mentioned earlier, with all of the attractions, all the *Triebregungen* that surround it on the outside, the phallus, along with its charge, is located to the left of the mirror, within the narcissistic enclosure. This is why where it is, is also where it is not.

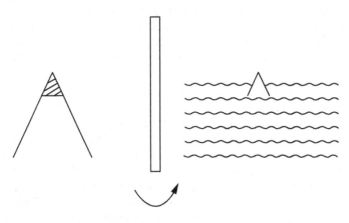

What emerges as a fascinating form turns out to be invested with libidinal waves. These waves come from the place where it [the phallus] was withdrawn – namely, from the narcissistic foundation, as it were, from which everything that comes to form the object's structure (as such, we might say, on the condition that we respect its relations and elements) is drawn. What constitutes the *Triebregung* at work in desire – desire in its privileged function as distinguished from demand and need – has its seat in the remainder, to which the mirage corresponds in the image, the mirage owing to which the image is identified with the part that is missing from it and whose invisible presence gives beauty its shine [*brilliance*]. This is what is meant by Antiquity's term ἵμερος (*hímeros*), which I have mentioned many times here, going so far as to play on its equivocation with ἡμέρα (*iméra*), meaning day.

455

This is the central point around which what we must conceptualize as regards the function of little *a* is played out.

Be so kind as to recall the myth that I devised for you when we were talking about the *Symposium*, the myth of the hand that reaches out toward a log. In order for the myth to be true, this hand must bring some rather amazing heat with it if the object is to burst into flames at its approach. It is a pure miracle, against which all kind souls rise up in protest. For however rare this phenomenon may be, it must still be considered both unthinkable and nevertheless unstoppable, in any case. It is indeed an utter miracle that, at the level of this induced fire, another hand appears. It is quite an ideal image, a phenomenon one can only dream of, like that of love. We all know that love's fires burn invisibly; we all know that a damp wooden beam can burn on the inside for a long time without anything being revealed on the outside; and, in short, we all know that, in the *Symposium*, it is left to the most complete simpleton [Eryximachus] to articulate in an almost derisive way that the nature of love is the nature of that which is humid, which essentially means the same thing as what is shown here on the board – that the reservoir of object love, insofar as it is love for what is alive, is the *Schatten*, the narcissistic shadow.

I announced the presence of this shadow last time, and I will go so far today as to call it a moldy stain [*tache de moisi*] – this is perhaps a better name for it than we might think, since the word *moi* [me or ego] is included in it. I would go so far as to intersect tender Fénelon's speculations on the ego – he, too, was wavy or slippery [*ondoyant*], as they say. He makes the ego into the sign of some sort of political maneuvering between the MRP and God. I would be just as capable as anyone else to take this metaphor very far, even so far as to make of my Seminar a message for your bed sheet. Must we not see an essentially human sign in the smell of dead rats that emanates from your laundry if you leave it on the edge of your bathtub for too long? If my style as an analyst emphasizes more willingly what people qualify or stigmatize with the term "abstraction," it is not simply the effect of a preference but perhaps simply in order to accommodate your sense of smell that I could tickle as well as anyone else.

Whatever the case may be, you can see behind this the outline   456
of the mythical point of libidinal development that psychoanalysis, without ever really knowing how to situate it on the scale, has termed the "urinary complex," with its obscure relationship to fire. These are antonymic terms, the one struggling against the other, which animated our primitive ancestors' play; as you know, psychoanalysis discovered that man's first playful reflex when faced with flames must have been to piss on them, an exploit that we find anew in *Gulliver's Travels*. The profound relationship between *uro*, I am burning, and *urina*, urine, is inscribed in the foundation of childhood experience – the operation of drying the sheets, dreams of laundry that is enigmatically starched, or erotic thoughts about

the laundress, which are familiar to those who were able to go see the splendid staging by Visconti of all possible whites [*blancs*, which also means "blanks"], materializing for us the fact that Pierrot is dressed in white as well as the question as to why.

In short, it is a small, clearly human environment that sets off a chain reaction around the ambiguous moment between enuresis and the first stirrings [*émois*] of the phallus. It is here that the dialectic of love and desire, in its most palpable roots, is played out.

How does the central object, the object of desire, present itself? Not wishing to take any further here the myth that is placidly incarnated in what we call the little geographical map, or little Corsica, that every analyst knows well, let us say that the object of desire presents itself, at the center of this phenomenon, as an object that has been saved from the waves of your love. Its place must be situated precisely – and this is the function of my myth – in the midst of the same burning bush in which "I am what I am" was one day announced, in the form of an opaque answer – at the very point we are still at when, not knowing who is speaking, we hear the question "*Che vuoi?*" proffered by the strange head of a metaphorical camel, out of which might just as well come the little faithful dog of desire.

This is the acme around which revolves what we deal with as regards the little *a* of desire.

2

We deal with this little *a* throughout the structure [of desire], for it is never superseded as regards its libidinal attraction.

457   Let us consider what precedes it in development – namely, the first forms of the object qua separate.

Breasts only take on their function in desire *nachträglich*, after the fact, inasmuch as they have already played their role in the same place in the dialectic of love, on the basis of early demands, on the basis of the *Trieb* [drive] involved in feeding, which is instated right from the outset because the mother speaks. At the level of oral demand, there is, in effect, an appeal to something beyond what can be satisfied by the object known as the breast. And the breast, which is quickly distinguished from its background, immediately takes on an instrumental value. It is not simply that which is taken, but also that which is pushed away or refused because one already wants something else.

I have already demonstrated what comes before what in the anal relationship, where the appeal to the mother's being goes beyond anything she can provide by way of an anaclitic prop, a function in which being and having meld.

Lastly, it is on the basis of the advent of the phallus in this dialectic that the way is paved for the distinction between being and having, precisely insofar as they previously were combined.

Beyond the phallic object, the topic of the object opens up – and this is the right word for it – otherwise. To consider this emergence of what I would almost call the most sublime island – this fantasy, reflection, or image – in which the object is incarnated as an object of desire, the one that I brought to the fore earlier, it is clear that the phallus is incarnated precisely in that which is lacking in the image. The entire subsequent relationship between the subject and the object of desire originates therein.

The horizon of the relationship to the object is not, above all, that of a relationship that preserves. The point is to investigate what the object has under the hood, so to speak, from what cloth it is cut. This can be done along the lines by which we try to isolate the function of little a, the characteristically Sadean line, whereby the object is investigated to the very depths of its being, and made to turn itself inside out to show what is most hidden inside it, in order to fill in this empty form insofar as it is fascinating.

To what degree can the object bear such questioning? Perhaps to the point where the final want-to-be is revealed, to the point where the questioning merges with the very destruction of the object. Such is the endpoint – and this is why there is a barrier here that I situated for you last year, the barrier of beauty or form. The requirement to preserve the object reflects back on the subject himself here.

458

Rabelais shows us Gargantua leaving home for war. "Keep this, which is most beloved, safe," his wife says to him, pointing with her finger at what, back then, it was much easier to designate unambiguously than in our own times, since the piece of clothing known as the fly or codpiece was quite glorious at the time. This means, first of all, that it cannot be safeguarded at home. But the second signification is just as full of the sapience that we never fail to find in Rabelais' statements – throw all of your forces into the battle, but keep this irreducibly at the center. Do not place this at risk.

This allows us to change the course of our dialectic. Indeed, all of this would be very pretty were it so easy to conceptualize desire on the basis of the subject, and we had to find anew at the level of desire a myth that developed at the level of knowledge, to turn the world into a sort of vast web extracted from the stomach of the subject qua spider.

Wouldn't it be simpler for the subject to say "I desire"? But it is not so simple to say so. It is much less simple, as you know from experience, than to say "I love," oceanically, as Freud expresses himself so prettily in his critique of religious effusion. I love, I soak, I wet, I flood, and I drool to boot – all of which is, moreover, pure drivel – and most often barely enough to moisten a handkerchief, especially since such effusion is becoming rarer and rarer these days.

The great crybabies [*humides*] have been disappearing from this earth since the middle of the nineteenth century. If anyone can show me someone today who is like Louise Colet [1810–76], I would go out of my way to see her. It seems, rather, that this truly leaves the *I* in abeyance. It leaves it so well glued [*collé*], in any case, in fantasy that I defy you to find this *I* of desire anywhere else than where Jean Genet points it out in *The Balcony*.

I already spoke to you about Jean Genet – dear Genet – one day when I discussed him at length here [Seminar V, pp. 263–8]. You can easily find the passage where he admirably indicates what call-girls know full well, namely that, whatever the fanciful ideas of men may be who are thirsting to have their fantasies fulfilled, one feature is common to all of them: in the enactment, there must be one feature that seems *untrue*, because otherwise, perhaps, were it to become altogether true, they would no longer know which way is up. The subject would perhaps no longer have any chance of survival. This is the place of the barred signifier, which is necessary in order for us to know that it is merely a signifier. This indication of something inauthentic is the place of the subject qua first person in fantasy.

The best way I have found to indicate it, as I have suggested several times, is to restore the subject to his true form. The cedilla of *ça* in French is not a true cedilla, but rather an apostrophe – it is the apostrophe from *c'est*, the first person of the unconscious. You can even cross out the *t* at the end: *c'es* is a way of writing the subject at the level of the unconscious.

We must not say that this is well designed to facilitate the shift from the object to object-relatedness [*objectalité*]. As you know, people even speak, on this score, of the shifting of certain lines within the spectrum. In fact, the gap between the object of desire and the real object, insofar as we can aspire to it, is fundamentally determined by the negative [non-included] or included nature of the appearance of the phallus. I was aiming at nothing else earlier when I sketched out for you a brief trajectory of the object from its archaic forms to the horizon of its destruction – that is, from the orificial or "anificial" object, were I to dare to put it thus, of our infantile past, to the object of the fundamentally ambivalent aim that persists right up to the endpoint of desire's aim. It is a pure lie, which has no theoretical necessity whatsoever, to speak [as Abraham does] about a supposedly post-ambivalent stage in our relationship to the object of desire.

It is thus solely by establishing an order in the ascending and concording scale of objects with respect to the phallic summit that we can understand the link between the different levels involved, for example, in sadistic attacks, insofar as they in no wise involve the pure and simple satisfaction of a supposedly elemental aggression, but rather a way of questioning the object as to its being and drawing forth from it the split – the either/or – introduced between being and having on the basis of the phallic summit.

The fact that we find ourselves, after the phallic stage, "highly ambivalent like before," is not the worst outcome imaginable. Looking at things from such a vantage point will never get us very far. There is always a moment where we lose our grip on the object, qua object of desire, because we do not know how to take the question any further. To force a being – because this is the essence of little a – beyond life is not within the grasp of all and sundry.

This is not simply to allude to the fact here that there are natural limits to coercion and to suffering itself. Even to force a being to have pleasure is not a problem that we can solve so easily, and for a very good reason: we are the ones who run the show and we are the ones who are involved. Everyone wonders at the fact that Sade's Justine is able to indefinitely bear up under all kinds of ill treatment, to the point that Jupiter himself must intervene, supplying a thunderbolt to put an end to it. But the fact of the matter is that, in truth, Justine is but a shadow. Juliet is the only one who exists. She is the one who dreams, and as such, as dreaming, she is the one who must necessarily – read the story – run all the risks endemic to desire, which are no slighter than those that Justine runs. Obviously, we hardly consider ourselves to be worthy of such company, for she takes things very far. We should not make too much of them in high-society conversations. People who care only about their own little selves can find scant interest in this.

Which brings us back to the subject. How can the whole dialectic of desire be based on the subject if this subject is nothing but an apostrophe, inscribed in a relationship that is, above all, a relationship to the Other's desire?

It is here that the function of capital I – the function of the signifier of the ego-ideal – comes in.

460

3

The ego-ideal as a function preserves $i(a)$, the ideal ego.

What is involved? What is involved is the precious thing with which we try to capture moisture [*de l'humide*], a ceramic bowl or a little pot, which has always been the symbol of that which is created [by humankind], in which everyone tries to give himself some measure of consistency. Many other shapes and models help out here [*y concourent*]. A prop must necessarily be constructed in the Other, the Other who determines whether the flower is enclosed or not [by the opening of the vase]. Why is this? It is because there is no other way in which the subject can subsist.

Doesn't psychoanalysis teach us, in this regard, that the radical function of the image in phobia is clarified analogically by what Freud uncovered in the ethnographic work of his time under the heading of totems? The latter has undoubtedly been considerably revised since then, but if something remains of it, it is the following: we are willing to risk everything for pleasure, for a fight, or for prestige, including life itself, but we are not willing to risk a certain liminal image, not willing to risk the dissolution of the very riveting, the dissolution of that which rivets the subject to this image – a fish or a tree. The fact that a Bororo is not a macaw is not a macaw phobia, even if it apparently involves similar taboos. The sole common factor between phobia and totemism is the image itself in its function of isolating and discerning the object – namely, the ideal ego.

The metaphor of he who desires [*désirant*] in just about anything can always, in fact, become urgent again in an individual case. Think of Little Hans. It is at the moment at which he who is desired finds himself defenseless – with respect to the Other's desire that threatens $i(a)$ – [that is,] the riveting or limit that the eternal artifice reproduces – that the subject pulls himself together and appears to be locked in the bearskin before having killed it. But in reality it is a bearskin that has been turned inside out, and it is on the inside of it that the phobic defends [*défend*] the other side of the specular image.

Of course, the specular image involves cathexis, but it also involves defense. It is a dam against the Pacific of motherly love. Let us simply say that the cathexis of the Other is, briefly stated, prohibited [*défendu*] by the ideal ego. The final cathexis of the phallus itself is, in a certain way, defended against by the phobic. I would go so far as to say that phobia is the luminous signal that appears to warn you that you are running on the last little bit of libido left in the tank. You can keep driving for a little while on it. This is what phobia means and this is why the phallus as a signifier is its prop.

461

I need not remind you of everything that, in our past discussions, illustrates and confirms this way of envisioning things. Recall simply the dream related by Ella Sharpe that I commented on for you. Remember the little cough with which the subject alerted his analyst to his presence before entering her office, and everything that was hidden behind it, and which came out along with his usual reveries.

What would I do, he said, if I were someplace where I would not want people to know I was? I would make a little barking sound and the people there would tell themselves, "Oh, it's only a dog." The patient had this association to his cough also owing to a dog that once began to masturbate on his leg [pp. 130–2]. What do we find in this exemplary story? That the subject, who was more than ever in a defensive posture at the moment he entered the analyst's consulting room, was pretending to be a dog. He pretended to be one, but it was everyone else who was a dog before he entered, and he was wanting them to don anew their human appearance before he entered. Don't go imagining that this suggested some kind of special interest in dogs on his part. In this example, as in every other, to be a dog had but a single meaning: it meant that one goes "bowwow," and nothing else. I would bark and the people would say to themselves, "It's a dog." The words "It's a dog" had the value there of an *einziger Zug*.

462

Consider the schema in Freud's *Massenpsychologie* [*Group Psychology and the Analysis of the Ego*] with which he shows us the origin of the kind of identification that is characteristic of the ego-ideal. How does he do so? He does so via group psychology. What thus happens, he asks, prefacing in this way Hitler's grand explosion onto the scene, such that everyone enters into a sort of fascination that allows them to be taken as a mass, as a kind of amorphous gel, as what is known as a crowd? In order for all those subjects to collectively have, at least for a moment, the same ideal, which allows virtually anything to happen for a rather short period of time, all external objects must, he explains, be taken to have a common trait, an *einziger Zug*.

Why is this of interest to us? It interests us because what is true at the collective level is also true at the individual level. The relationship between the subject and outside objects revolves around the function of the ideal. In the world of a subject who speaks – in other words, in what we call the human world – we purely and simply encounter a metaphorical attempt to attribute a trait in common to all objects; it is purely and simply by decree that we can try to attribute a common feature to their diversity. As concerns the animal kingdom, in which the psychoanalytic tradition has shown the exemplary play of defensive identifications, the subject can – in order to subsist in a world where his *i(a)* is respected – decree that everything, whether dogs, cats, skunks, or deer, goes "bowwow." This is the function of the *einziger Zug*.

It is essential to keep it structured in this way, for outside of this register, it is impossible to conceptualize what Freud means when he talks about the psychology of mourning and melancholia. What distinguishes mourning from melancholia?

In mourning, it is quite clear that its length and difficulty stem from the metaphorical function of the traits attributed to the love object insofar as they are narcissistic privileges. In a manner that is all the more significant, since he says it in a way that seems to surprise even him, Freud clearly emphasizes what is at stake: mourning consists in authenticating the real loss little by little, piece by piece, sign by sign, element capital I by element capital I, until they are all exhausted. When that is done, the mourning is over.

But what does this imply if the object was a little *a*, an object of desire? The object is always masked behind its attributes, it is almost trivial to say so. Naturally, the matter only begins to become serious when it becomes pathological – in other words, when we are talking about melancholia. There the object is, curiously enough, much harder to get a handle on, even though it is certainly present and triggers infinitely more catastrophic effects. For these effects go so far as to dry up what Freud calls the most fundamental *Trieb*, the one that makes you want to go on living.

It is necessary to study this text and grasp what Freud indicates in it regarding some kind of disappointment that he is hard-pressed to define but that is nevertheless there. With an object that is so thoroughly veiled, masked, and obscure, what traits show through? The subject cannot investigate any traits of an object that cannot be seen, but we analysts, insofar as we work with the subject, can identify some of them via those that he criticizes in himself. "I am nothing, I am nothing but rubbish."

Observe that his specular image is never involved in his self-criticism. The melancholiac never tells you that he looks bad, that his face is at its worst, or that it is contorted; instead he tells you that he is the lowest of the low, that he brings on one catastrophe after another for his entire family, and so on. In his self-accusations he remains entirely within the realm of the symbolic. Let us add "having" to the list – he is broke. Doesn't this help put us on the scent?

I will merely indicate it to you today by designating a specific point which, in my eyes, at least for the time being, is a point where mourning and melancholia meet up. It is a question of what I will call, not mourning, nor depression owing to the loss of an object,

463

but remorse of a certain type triggered by a dénouement that involves something along the lines of suicide on the part of the object. Remorse, thus, regarding an object that has entered in some way into the field of desire and that, owing to its own actions or some risk it took in a venture, has disappeared.

Analyze such cases. The path is traced out for you by Freud when he indicates that, already in normal mourning, the drive that the subject turns against himself could well be an aggressive drive toward the object. Plumb the dramatic remorse when it arises. You will perhaps see that it turns against the subject a maelstrom of insults that may be akin to what we find in melancholia. Its source lies in the following: if the object who has thus disappeared went so far as to destroy himself, it was not worth my while to have taken so many precautions with him; it was useless for me to have turned away from my own true desire for his sake.

As extreme as this example may be, it is not so very rare. The same disposition is encountered when a certain loss arises after the long embraces between desiring subjects that we call the oscillations of love.

This brings us to the heart of the relationship between capital I and little *a*, at a point of fantasy where the safety provided by the limit is always called into question; we must know how to get the subject to stay away from this limit. This requires, on the analyst's part, a complete comprehension of the function of the signifier, regarding which he must grasp by what mainspring or means, in what roundabout manner, the function of the signifier is always involved when the position of the ego-ideal is at issue.

But there is still something else that, arriving now at the end of my talk today, I can merely indicate, which concerns the function of little *a*.

What Socrates knew and what the analyst must at least glimpse is that at the level of little *a*, the question is entirely different from the question of access to some ideal. Love can only surround this island, this field of being. And the analyst cannot help but think that any object whatsoever can fill it. This is where we analysts are led to vacillate, regarding the limit where – with any object whatsoever, once it has entered into the field of desire – the following question arises: "What are you?" There is no object that is of any greater value than another – this is the mourning around which desire for the analyst [*le désir de l'analyste* also means "the analyst's desire"] is centered.

At the end of the *Symposium*, consider who Socrates is going to praise – he is going to praise the idiot of idiots, the most idiotic of them all, and even the only thoroughgoing idiot [*con*] in the place [Agathon]. And think about the fact that this idiot is the one who

464

was given the job of saying, in a ridiculous form, what is truest about love. He does not know what he is saying, he utters stupidities, but no matter, he is nevertheless the beloved object. And Socrates says to Alcibiades, "Everything that you have just said to me was for his ears."

This is the analyst's function, along with what it brings with it by way of a certain mourning. We meet up here with a truth that Freud himself left outside of the field of what he could understand.

Oddly enough – and this is probably owing to reasons of comfort, the reasons that I exposed to you today by formulating the need to preserve the pot or vase [*potiche*] – people do not seem to have realized that this is what is meant by "Thou shalt love thy neighbor as thyself."

People do not want to translate this, because it probably would not be Christian, in the sense of a certain ideal – and believe me, Christianity has not yet said its last word – but it is a philosophical ideal.

This means that, regarding anyone, you can raise the question whether desire is totally destructive. With anyone, you can try to determine how far you will dare to go in questioning a being – at the risk to yourself of disappearing.

June 28, 1961

Translator's Endnotes

In these notes, the numbers in parentheses refer first to the page number of the present English edition and then, after a comma, to the paragraph number (note that partial and short paragraphs are counted, as are chapter titles and the block of subheadings, counted as one paragraph, located just below each chapter title).

Chapter I – In the Beginning Was Love

(3,3) The announcement can be found in the journal *La psychanalyse* 6 (1961): 313.

(3,4) As an adjective, *impair* (uneven) means odd, odd-numbered, or unpaired.

(4,5) Lacan discusses John's "In the beginning was the Word" at length in an interview found in *The Triumph of Religion* (Cambridge: Polity, 2013).

(4,6) "In the beginning was the deed" is from Goethe, *Faust*, Part I; it is quoted on the last page of Freud's *Totem and Taboo*.

(4,7) "Praxis" is an obvious reference to Marx.

(4,11) *Confus* (jumbled) can also mean confused or embarrassed.

(5,3) *Kern unseres Wesen* (the core of our being) is found in *SE* V, p. 603, and *SE* XXIII, p. 197.

(7,1) Lévi-Strauss' inaugural lecture was published in English as Chapter 1 ("The Scope of Anthropology") of *Structural Anthropology*, vol. 2, trans. M. Layton (Chicago, IL: University of Chicago Press, 1983).

(8,3) This version of Breuer's story comes from Freud and Jones (see *The Life and Work of Sigmund Freud*, vol. I, pp. 222–6), but it is contested by Breuer's biographer, Albrecht Hirschmüller (1978/1989). Hirschmüller admits, however, that Jones had access to letters that he himself never saw. One of the only convincing points Hirschmüller makes is that, whereas Jones claims that the result of the second honeymoon in Venice was the conception of Breuer's youngest daughter, Dora, she was actually born on March 11, 1882, thus three months *before* Anna O.'s treatment ended.

(9,1) See *The Interpretation of Dreams*, *SE* IV, pp. 106–21 and *passim*; on p. 107, Freud says, "she showed signs of recalcitrance"; in *GW* II/III (1942), he writes, "*Dabei zeigt sie etwas Sträuben wie die Frauen*" (p. 111), and "*Sie sträubt sich*" (p. 115), "She was recalcitrant" (p. 110 in the English). The German cited in the text of the seminar appears to be erroneous.

(9,2) Aristophanes often uses the Greek term for "weasel" (in French, *belette*) –
       see, for example, *Peace, The Frogs, The Wasps, Ecclesiazusae* (or *The
       Assemblywomen*), *The Acharnians*, and *The Clouds* – to refer to girls (or
       prostitutes) and, by extension, to the female genitalia.

(10,4) Cf. Freud's comment that life is but a long detour on the way to death
       in *Beyond the Pleasure Principle, SE* XVIII, pp. 38–9. Other versions
       would have us read: "We must distinguish between the idea of eternal
       death – the death that makes being itself into a detour, we being unable
       to know whether or not it makes sense – and the second death, that of
       the body" instead of "The idea of eternal death must be distinguished
       here from death insofar as it makes being itself into a detour – we being
       unable to know whether or not it makes sense. The idea of eternal death
       must be distinguished from the other death as well, the second, that of
       the body."

(10,5) A possible allusion to the River Styx.

(11,3) Lacan is paraphrasing a children's nursery rhyme here: "*Je te tiens, tu me
       tiens, par la barbichette. Le premier de nous deux qui rira aura une tapette.*"
       There is a game that accompanies it in which two children hold each
       other by the chin, and sing this little song: "I hold you, you hold me, by
       the chinny chin chin; the first one of us who laughs will get a little slap."
       Whoever laughs first during or after the end of the song receives a little
       slap [*tapette*] on the cheek. Lacan changes the *tapette* into a *soufflet* – a real
       slap – and qualifies it as "well-deserved."

(11,4) Alternative readings for the last sentence of this paragraph (*Les erreurs
       ne seront jamais que des erreurs judiciaires*): "Errors will never be anything
       other than judicial errors" or "Errors are never just judicial errors." Other
       versions add "regardless of personal motives" at the end of this sentence
       instead of at the beginning of the next sentence.

(12,1) *La relation berger-bergère* (Dick and Jane relationships): all lovers became
       associated with shepherds and shepherdesses in French eighteenth-century
       literature, and even much earlier. See, for example, Jehan de Brie's 1379
       treatise, written at the request of King Charles V, "Le vray regime et
       gouvernement des bergers et bergères" in which he teaches the practice
       of "L'art de Bergerie" (as mentioned in Marguerite Favier's *Christine de
       Pisan: Muse des cours souveraines*. Lausanne: Editions Rencontre, 1967,
       p. 142). One might also say "boy/girl relationships" or "man/woman
       relationships."

(12,2) Other versions read: "poker, the theory of which is not discussed" instead
       of "poker, theory as poker, is not discussed." The reference here is to J. von
       Neumann and O. Morgenstein's *Theory of Games and Economic Behavior*
       (Princeton, NJ: Princeton University Press, 1953).

(12,3) *Prendre une telle attitude* (adopt a certain attitude) could, alternatively, be
       rendered as "strike a certain pose" or "adopt a certain posture (or stance)."

(12,4) *S'enferrer* (to impale himself) could also be rendered as "to run himself
       through," "to sabotage himself," "to get himself stuck," or "to fall into
       his own trap." *Le tourner* (roast him on the spit) could also be rendered as
       "shape him on the lathe" or "turn him inside out."

(12,5) Lacan himself discussed intersubjectivity in "Function and Field" in *Écrits*.

(13,1) On analysis and bridge, see "Direction of the Treatment" in *Écrits*,
       pp. 589–91. On this "two-body psychology," see John Rickman, *Selected*

Contributions to Psycho-Analysis (New York: Basic Books, 1957; Glasgow: The University Press, 1957), above all Chapters 19, 21, and 22.

(13,2) "Interpsychology" is a reference to Lev Vygotsky (1896–1934), who lived during the Russian Revolution. His work was largely unknown in the West until it was published in 1962.

(13,4) One might read "movement of questioning" instead of "moment of questioning."

(14,7) "Bracketing" is a term borrowed from Edmund Husserl. Other versions read "what the body is" instead of "what this bracketing is."

(15,1) *Contrainte par corps* (bodily coercion) is a legal term for imprisonment for unpaid debts (in debtors' prison). One might perhaps read *étreinte* (embrace) or *contacte* (contact) here instead of *contrainte*.

(15,6) *En tant qu'aimant* (insofar as he loves) could also be rendered here as "insofar as he begins to love." *Amare est velle bonum alicui* means "To love is to wish another well." Cf. Aristotle, *Nicomachean Ethics*, 1156a (regarding friendship).

(16,2) See Anders Nygren, *Agape and Eros* (Philadelphia: Westminster Press, 1953).

Chapter II – Set and Characters

(21,3) In 212c, Aristophanes is starting to comment on what Socrates said in 205e that alluded to his own speech (188c and following).

(21,5) *Nekuía* refers to a sacrifice associated with the conjuring up of the dead in order to learn about one's future; it can be found in the title of Book XI in the *Odyssey*, rendered by Robert Fitzgerald as "A Gathering of Shades" and by others as "Trip to the Dead." On *prótos erastés*, see Plato's *Alcibiades I* (103a).

(22,2) The *hermaí* were heads of the god Hermes on a plinth with a phallus.

(24,3) Lacan is perhaps referring here to a French Orientalist (1883–1962), Louis Massignon, a professor at the prestigious *Collège de France* and then at the *École des hautes études*, who wrote a number of works on Islamic mysticism. Though married, he was nevertheless ordained as a preacher of the Melkite Church. Regarding "the Brothers variously ignoramus," Lacan is playing on the fact that a certain order of Catholic monks, those of the Order of St John of God, had, for humility's sake, taken on the name of *les ignorantins* or the *Frères ignorantins*. By inserting the word *diversement* between *Frères* and *ignorantins*, the brothers become ignorant to varying degrees.

(25,1) Lacan did, in fact, mention Marguerite de Navarre in the class of Seminar VII given on February 3, 1960 (p. 156/131).

(25,3) The "lady" in question was the Abbess of the Royal Abbey of Fontevrault, de Rochechouart-Mortemart.

(26,1) Socrates was accused by Meletus II, Anytus, and Lycon in 399 B.C., and was tried, convicted, and executed. Several years after the trial (i.e., in 393 B.C.), the orator Polycrates wrote an "Accusation of Socrates," which he put in Anytus' mouth as if it had been the case made by the prosecution at Socrates' trial. Xenophon, in his *Memorabilia*, was in part responding to Polycrates' accusation, even though it was not the actual speech given at Socrates' trial.

(26,2) *Le pavé de l'ours* (has truly got it all backward) is an expression from La

Fontaine: an unintentional mistake made in the attempt to be serviceable, whose effect is quite the opposite of that intended.

(28,2) In 177d and 209e, we find τὰ ἐρωτικά (*ta erotiká*), meaning erotics, love matters, or the art of love. The Greek *smikroú tinos* is from the *Theages* (128b).

(29,1) *Moyenne* (middling): Lacan is no doubt referring here to Socrates' situating of love as *metaxú*, in between or midway between mortals and immortals (202d–e). See further on.

(29,4) As Lacan indicates in Chapter III below, it is in Plato's *Protagoras*. See the beginning of Aristophanes' play, *Ecclesiazusae* or *The Assemblywomen*.

(30,3) A reference to Jacques II de Chabannes, lord of La Palice, in whose "honor" the word *lapalissade* – something that goes without saying, being so clearly self-evident – was forged, though not because he himself was prone to truisms. A ditty written about him by some soldiers who served under him was misunderstood owing to an ambiguity of writing: "*Hélas, s'il n'était pas mort,/ Il ferait encore envie*" was read as "*Il serait encore en vie*" (Alas, if he weren't dead,/ He'd still be alive).

(31,1) Other versions would have us read: "It involved nothing that we *cannot* situate within the register of regression on a societal scale" instead of "It involved nothing that we *can* situate within the register of regression on a societal scale."

(31,2) This may be a reference to the end of Seminar VI. Here is one possible rendition of the schema:

Neurosis	⟶	Culture	Greek Homosexuality
↑		↓	
Society	⟵	Perversion	Courtly Love, Sade

(33,1) The "great lunging thrusts with a sword into the curtains" is an obvious allusion to Hamlet and Polonius.

(33,7) Reading *notre investigation* (our investigation) for *votre* (your investigation). Love was first declared to be a comical feeling by Lacan in *Le séminaire, Livre V, Les formations de l'inconscient* [*Unconscious Formations*] (Paris: Seuil, 1998), p. 136.

(34,2) "Love is giving what you don't have" can be found in "Direction of the Treatment," a paper given by Lacan in 1958 and found in *Écrits*, p. 618.

Chapter III – The Metaphor of Love: Phaedrus

(36,1) The French title of this chapter, *La métaphore de l'amour*, could alternatively be translated as "Love as a Metaphor."

(37,2) Note that Lacan lost his own father shortly before he gave this class.

(37,3) *Semblable* (semblable) is often translated as "fellow man" or "counterpart," but in Lacan's usage it often refers specifically to the mirroring of two imaginary others (*a* and *a'*) who *resemble* each other (or at least see themselves in each other). Here that is perhaps not so much the case, but I have employed throughout the somewhat obsolete English "semblable" found, for example, in *Hamlet*, Act V, Scene II, line 124: "his semblable

is his mirror; and who else would trace him, his umbrage, nothing more."
Note that it was used by Virginia Woolf in *Between the Acts* (New York: Harcourt, Brace and Company, 1941).

(37,4) "Beeswax," to be understood as in the expression, "mind your own beeswax," meaning "mind your own business."

(38,3) "Observations on Transference-Love" is found in *SE* XII, pp. 159–71.

(38,4) "Know thyself" is the famous precept found at Delphi. See Plato, *Alcibiades I* (124b).

(39,1) See Freud's "Analysis Terminable and Interminable" in *SE* XXIII, pp. 250–3.

(39,3) Interestingly enough, *aimant* (lover) also means magnet.

(40,1) The word διαλεκτικεύεσθαι (*dialektikeúesthai*) is apparently known from only one source: Marcus Aurelius, *Meditations*, Book 8, Chapter 13.

(40,3) On the creation of meaning, see especially "Instance of the Letter" in *Écrits*.

(40,7) *Portée* has many meanings, including import, range, span, litter (of pups, for example), maximum weight, best throw, and stave (in music).

(42,4) As Lacan indicates in the next chapter, it should be *épainos* (commendation or praise) not *epaínesis* (praise for the fallen). *Enkómion* and *épainos* are found in the *Symposium* at 177b.

(43,5) See Jean Beaufret, *Le poème de Parménide* (Paris: PUF, 1955).

(45,3) *L'Astrée* is a gigantic pastoral novel by Honoré d'Urfé, published in 60 volumes between 1607 and 1627.

(47,2) See also ὑπεραποθανεῖν (*hyperapothanein*) at 179b.

(47,3) *Celui qui me suivra* (the one who will follow me [in death]); *epapothanein* means to die immediately afterward. Cf. Seminar III, *The Psychoses*, trans. R. Grigg (New York: Norton, 1993), Chapters 22–4, p. 315ff.

(48,4) The *Carte du Tendre* is a seventeenth-century map of the tender/amorous sentiments – perhaps a forerunner to Adam Smith's (1759) *Theory of Moral Sentiments* – drawn by Madeleine de Scudéry. It purported to trace out all the stages of love, all the stages of development of the tender feelings, as well as all of the obstacles and problems one might encounter along love's path such as jealousy and despair. It can be found in her 10-volume novel *Clélie* (1654–60). The map can be found in Joan DeJean's *Tender Geographies: Women and The Origins of the Novel in France* (New York: Columbia University Press, 1991).

(49,3) This seems to be a play on words, as the French *eromène* (which is not a real verb, but a Gallicized version of the Greek *erómenos*, which I have attempted to render in English by "eromenoses") could be seen to be composed of Eros, *errer* (to wander aimlessly, drift, or to make a mistake), and *mener* (to lead).

(49,6) *Imprimatur* means approval or authorization to print. Cf. Mark 19:24: "Again I tell you, it is easier for a camel to go through the eye of a needle than for a rich man to enter the kingdom of God."

Chapter IV – The Psychology of the Rich: Pausanias

(50,3) Certain versions indicate that Lacan wrote a line in Greek on the blackboard before this class that can be rendered more or less as follows: "Redoubled desire is love, but redoubled love turns into delusion."

(51,6) "The Freudian Thing" was originally published in *Évolution Psychiatrique* XXI/1 (1956): 225–52; it was republished in *Écrits*.

(52,2) Lacan clearly has in mind here the following writing (which is articulated at the end of this section as "*erastés* over *erómenos*"):

Erastés

Erómenos

(52,4) Lacan presumably meant to say, "the explosion of a log which bursts into flames," but apparently said, "the explosion of a hand which bursts into flames."

(54,1) See Jacque Prévert's poem, *La pêche à la baleine*.

(54,7) *Mythomane* (myth lover) can often be figuratively rendered as "pathological liar" or "inveterate taleteller," in the sense of someone who makes up stories that he or she tries to pass off as reality. If the second half of the word, "mane," is taken to derive from *manus*, meaning hand, it might instead be understood to imply a maker of myths. I have taken it to be constructed like *mélomane*, meaning "music lover" – hence "myth lover." Other versions of the Seminar provide *mythologue* (mythologist, a studier of myths) instead of *mythomane*.

(55,5) Léon Robin's translation of the *Symposium* (in French, *Le banquet*) can be found in Plato, *Oeuvres complètes*, Volume IV, Part 2 (Paris: Belles Lettres, 1966 [originally published in 1929]). It was published in the Collection des Universités de France, under the patronage of the Association Guillaume Budé.

(56,2) *Valeurs cotées* (listed values) literally refers to securities listed on a stock exchange. *Pollé spoudé* is sometimes rendered in English as "all this time and effort" or a "sad waste of attentions."

(56,3) *Postulance* (candidacy) means applying for a position, there being an implicitly competitive application/selection process.

(57,2) One finds χρηστοῦ (*chrestoú*) at 183e. *Chrestós* means "good" or "useful."

(58,4) *Cote* (level) is a financial term meaning valuation, rating, quotation, and so on. *Cote d'alerte* is usually rendered as "danger level." At the time, 50,000 francs a month was not much, by way of comparison.

(59,1) Lacan slightly abbreviates and modifies Léon Robin's translation of 184e–185b, p. 22 (See note to page 55, paragraph 5, above.) The passage runs roughly as follows: "In this case, even if one were to be completely deceived, there would be no dishonor. Suppose, in effect, that one had, in order to become rich, given one's favors to a lover believed to be rich, and been completely deceived, there being no pecuniary advantage as the lover turned out to be poor. [. . .] General opinion would have it that one has thereby shown one's true colors: a willingness to do anything at anyone's behest for money – not a pretty thing. Let us follow the same reasoning to its end: suppose that, having given one's favors to a lover one believes to be virtuous, hoping to improve oneself through his friendship, one is mistaken, and the lover in question turns out to be κακὸς (*kakós*) [in the text we find κακοῦ (*kakoú*)], fundamentally base, a villain lacking in all merit, possessing no virtue, it is nevertheless a fine thing to be deceived."

(59,5) Lacan is clearly extrapolating here, as this is not literally found at the end of Pausanias' speech.

(60,4) The book Lacan says he would like to get his hands on is likely *Sappho und Simonides. Untersuchungen über griechische Lyriker* (Berlin: 1913).

(62,2) The *Vermot Almanac* was founded by Joseph Vermot and first published in 1886. The volume in which Georges Courteline's very short play appears dates from 1911 (there is no English translation of which I am aware). Much, if not all, of the work appearing in the almanac was considered to be humorous. "Théodore cherche des allumettes," can be found in Courteline, *Théâtre complet* (Paris: Flammarion, 1961), pp. 287–97, where it is listed as having been performed at Grand-Guignol on October 10, 1897. Virtually the entire play takes place in the dark.

(62,5) Instead of διασχισθησόμεθα (*diaschisthisómetha*), the French edition reads διῳκίσθημεν (*dioikísthemen*), which I have been unable to find in any dictionary or edition of Plato's work. It also provides *dioecisme*, which at least in English (dioecism) refers to the fact that the male and female sexual organs are found in different individuals of a species. The Graph of Desire can be found in *Écrits*, p. 817.

Chapter V – Medical Harmony: Eryximachus

(66,3) Lacan erroneously suggests that the citation from Aragon comes from *Le Paysan de Paris*, whereas it is found in his *Traité du Style* (Paris: Gallimard, 1928), republished in *L'imaginaire* (Paris: Gallimard, 1980), p. 148. Here is the passage: "Avec le plus grand sérieux il se trouve des particuliers qui pour faire valoir leur romantisme de chevet prétendent que le digne pisseur de copie bien que n'ayant pu lire Freud a eu, comment dirais-je, le pressentiment de la sychanalisse, et tel est le génie de Prou, comme on prononce à droite."

(67,3) The name Plato chose for the doctor here, Eryximachus, is apparently a play on the words for "belch-fighter." See *Plato on Love*, p. 42 n. 59.

(68,3) Cnidus is sometimes also spelled Knidos. Lacan provides a name for Alcmaeon's school in Croton, the *Alcmeonides* (perhaps Alcmaeonidae in English, like the family in Athens), which I have been unable to confirm. Alcmaeon reputedly thought that health involved a harmony of, balance of, or state of equilibrium between opposites.

(68,4) *Accord* (concord) can mean concord, harmony, accord, agreement, attunement, and the like, while *accordé* can mean granted, agreed to, or in tune. I have translated *accord* and its derivatives as "concord" throughout Lacan's discussion of Eryximachus' speech, unless noted otherwise.

(69,2) See Georges Canguilhem, *The Normal and the Pathological*, trans. C. R. Fawcett, introduction by Michel Foucault (New York: Zone Books, 1991). The French edition was published by PUF in 1966 and was based on Canguilhem's 1943 doctoral dissertation in medicine.

(70,5) See Bertrand Russell, *Wisdom of the West: A Historical Survey of Western Philosophy in Its Social and Political Setting* (New York: Doubleday, 1959; London: Rathbone Books, 1959).

(72,3) Other English translations of ὥσπερ ἁρμονίαν τόξου τε καὶ λύρας include: "The One at variance with itself is drawn together, like harmony of bow or lyre" and "The One is united by disunion like the harmony of the bow and the lyre." This fragment by Heraclitus is found, for example, in Diels-Kranz, fragment B51; in G. S. Kirk and J. E. Raven, *The Presocratic Philosophers* (Cambridge: Cambridge University Press, 1957), p. 193, it is fragment 212.

(74,6) The auditor in question was apparently Paul Ricoeur.

(75,1) *N'être pas hétérogène* (not to be discordant) strikes me as erroneous in this context; my impression is that Lacan means that asking the gods to act as judges in matters of love *is discordant* with what follows in Plato's discourse. Unless, of course, he is referring to the fact that everything in the dialogue is said tongue-in-cheek.

(75,6) On Bororos and macaws, see *Écrits*, pp. 117–18.

(76,4) Reading *immatériel* (immaterial) instead of *matériel* (material).

Chapter VI – Deriding the Sphere: Aristophanes

(77,2) *Pitre* can mean fool, clown, or buffoon.

(77,3) This class took place on December 21, 1960, the date of the winter solstice.

(78,2) "Other civilizations" is a likely reference at least to Indian philosophies.

(78,5) The early "physical philosophers" are also known as "natural philosophers."

(79,2) Plato, *The Seventh Letter*, 341c. In Jowett's translation: "the matter itself." See Heidegger's *Being and Time* on *to prágma*.

(79,3) Lacan contrasted *die Sache* with *das Ding* in Seminar VII, during the class given December 9, 1959. Praxis (πράξις, *práxis*), the act of practicing something or putting something into practice, comes from πράσσω (*prásso*, to do), *to prágma* (neuter): affair, event, or praxis.

(79,4) On the notion of theory among the Greeks, see Arthur Koestler's *The Sleepwalkers*.

(80,5) See *Pourquoi des philosophes* (1957), a book by Jean-François Revel; it can be found in a recent edition of his works, *Jean-François Revel* (Paris: Robert Laffont, 1997); the book is also mentioned in *Écrits*, p. 516. The title might also be rendered as "Why are there philosophers?"

(81,5) The passage in the *Phaedo*, 117b, is sometimes rendered as "looking up at the man [who brought him the hemlock] with wide open eyes," but there is also some evidence that Socrates' eyes were set wide apart on his face, giving the impression that he could see like a bull or other animal with eyes set on either side of its head.

(83,2) *Santons* are Christmas nativity scene figurines that are especially popular in Provence.

(83,6) A *bateleur* is literally a juggler or tumbler, but can figuratively refer to a charlatan or fool.

(85,2) See Xenophon, *The Shorter Socratic Writings*, ed. R. C. Bartlett (Ithaca, NY, and London: Cornell University Press, 1996), p. 150; the passage is from *Symposium*, Chapter 4, pp. 27–8.

(85,6) William Arrowsmith renders the Greek here with "Bugger"; see *Three Comedies by Aristophanes: The Birds, The Clouds, The Wasps* (Ann Arbor, MI: University of Michigan Press, 1969), pp. 79–80.

(86,4) The Loeb edition gives "the mere amorous connection," while Jowett gives "desire of the other's intercourse." *Plato on Love* gives "the intimacy of sex" [192c].

(87,4) "The narcissistic overestimation of the subject" refers back to Lacan's discussion at the beginning of Chapter 3.

(88,6) The term *sphaíra* actually is not found in the *Symposium*, where one finds instead *strongúlos* (sphere) at 189e. It is likely that the reference here is to Empedocles and to Plato's *Timaeus* 33b–34a. In *Plato on Love*, 189e is rendered as "completely round, with back and sides in a circle."

(89,2) Christian von Ehrenfels introduced the term *Gestalt*. See his *Über Gestaltqualitäten*, "On the Qualities of Form," 1890.

(89,3) Kirk and Raven render this passage as "equal [to himself] from every side and quite without end, he stays fast in the close covering of Harmony, a rounded sphere rejoicing in his circular solitude" (fragment 421, pp. 325–6). Empedocles employs *sphairos* as a masculine noun; ancient Greek more generally uses the feminine form *sphaíra*.

(91,4) Arthur Koestler, *The Sleepwalkers* (New York: Grosset & Dunlap, 1959).

(92,2) The Greek ἄπειρον (*ápeiron*) means unlimited, infinite, or indefinite; from a- (without) and πεῖραρ (*peírar*) meaning end or limit.

(92,4) Reading *désexercer* (disexercise) instead of *désexorciser* (dis-exorcize), which does not seem to exist in French or English. One could possibly read instead *déséthiquer* (de-ethicize, that is, to dissociate from ethics, i.e., "the finest virtues" mentioned in the previous paragraph) or simply *exorciser* (exorcize).

(93,1) "All the other six [forms of motion] were taken away from him" (*Timaeus*, 34a). The French version of the *Timaeus* Lacan may have been using seems to equivocate about these six forms.

(93,2) It is thought, however, that the *Timaeus* was written *circa* 360 B.C., whereas the *Symposium* is thought to have been written *circa* 385–380 B.C. – that is, some 20 years earlier.

Chapter VII – The *Atopia* of Eros: Agathon

(96,3) *Poussée* (pressure) is the usual French translation of Freud's *Drang*, one of the four components of the drive; see *SE* XIV, p. 122.

(96,4) Lacan is likely referring here to "Remarks on Daniel Lagache's Presentation: 'Psychoanalysis and Personality Structure,'" the second paper he presented at the Royaumont Colloquium, held July 10–13, 1958. In *Écrits*, he tells us that the final redaction occurred over Easter vacation in 1960. It was first published in *La Psychanalyse* VI (1961): 111–47.

(97,1) *Ça* in French also means the id. *Tendance* (tendency [but also impulse or urge]) was an early French translation of Freud's *Trieb* (drive), which was later dropped, for the most part, in favor of *pulsion*. Lacan sometimes uses *pulsion* (drive), but often uses *tendance* where English would use "drive."

(102,2) See Paul Valéry, *Le cimetière marin* ("The Graveyard by the Sea" or "The Sailors' Cemetery").

(106,5) The verses in poetic meter may be rendered as follows:

[Love] gives peace to men and stillness to the sea,
Lays winds to rest, and careworn men to sleep. [197c]

(106,7) See Paul-Jean Toulet's *Les Contrerimes* (Paris: Gallimard, 1979), p. 152.

(107,2) Émile Benveniste, "Remarques sur la fonction du langage dans la découverte freudienne," *La Psychanalyse* 1 (1956). Reprinted in E. Benveniste, *Problèmes de linguistique générale* (Paris: Gallimard, 1966). In English, see "Remarks on the Function of Language in Freudian Theory," in *Problems in General Linguistics*, trans. M. E. Meek (Coral Gables, FL: University of Miami Press, 1971), pp. 65–75. On the SiRonga proverb, see "Function and Field," *Écrits*, p. 276. The quote is from the epigraph to Lévi-Strauss' on the SiRonga proverb, see *The Elementary Structures of Kinship*, where *cuisse* (thigh, or leg or shank, for a piece of meat, as we are talking about food here) is infelicitously rendered in the English translation as "hip."

(107,4) Love is said to be the "father of elegance, luxury, delicacy, grace, yearning, desire" (197d). *Minne* (or *Minnesang*) refers to the German courtly love tradition.

Chapter VIII – From *Epistéme* to *Mýthous*

(113,3) *Romancero* refers to a collection of Spanish epic poems in octosyllables.

(116,2) Keep in mind that Lacan often uses *le signifiant* (the signifier) to talk about the signifying system as a whole.

(116,4) On even and odd, see Seminar II, *The Ego in Freud's Theory and in the Technique of Psychoanalysis*, Chapters 15 and 16, and the "Seminar on 'The Purloined Letter'" in *Écrits*.

(119,4) W. Granoff gave a talk in October 1955 at the Société Française de Psychanalyse, entitled "Desire for children, children's desire," which was published in *La Psychanalyse* 2 (1956). *Désir du beau* can be rendered in English either as "desire for beauty" or "beauty's desire." I don't believe that "desire of beauty" can convey both of these simultaneously in English.

(120,1) *Goeteía* means witchcraft, sorcery, or trickery.

Chapter IX – Exit from the Ultra-World

(125,4) *Ktéma* means possession, having, good, property, or treasure.

(127,3) My sense is that Lacan's distinction here between *désir* du *beau* and *désir* de *beau* is designed to capture Diotima's shift from our desire for beauty, insofar as we wish to possess it – possess the person we find beautiful (forever) – to desire insofar as it is inspired by beauty, insofar as we are inspired, in the presence of beauty, to *poíesis*: to create speeches about virtue, for example. Beauty, in the latter case, seems to be desire's muse.

(127,4) *Époptie* may strike the reader as strange here, since in the Greek we find ἐποπτικά (*epoptiká*), which is the neuter plural adjective meaning "the Mysteries." However, in Robin Léon's commentary on the passage, we find "*Alors l'initié contemple* (époptie) *et adore*," which could be rendered as "Then the initiate contemplates and adores." *Époptie* thus seems to be a Gallicized version of the Greek verb, which Lacan employs too.

(129,5) The English in 202a reads, "for what hits on the truth cannot be ignorance" or "for how could what hits the truth be ignorance?"

(130,4) *Écrits*, pp. 506–7. See Victor Hugo, *La Légende des siècles*, Booz endormi. In French and English, see *The Penguin Book of French Poetry, 1820–1950*, ed. W. Rees (London: Penguin Books, 1990), pp. 62–8. On metaphor, see Seminar III, Chapters 17 and 18.

(131,6) Lacan seems to get the story backward here: Cronus castrates his father, Uranus. Cronus is overthrown by his son, Zeus, not castrated (although in some versions, his stomach is cut open). Yet the French versions read: "The billhook with which Cronus was castrated . . ."

(134,2) On transitivism, see "The Mirror Stage" in *Écrits*.

(134,3) Lacan mistakenly refers here to Renoir's *La Règle du jeu*.

Chapter X – *Ágalma*

(136,3) "There are two others here" is a likely reference to the notion that it takes three to love, and possibly to the three prisoners problem in "Logical Time"; see Lacan's comments on the latter in Seminar XX, *Encore*. See also his comments on Rosencrantz and Guildenstern and on Goethe in *Écrits*, p. 506 n. 1.

(139,3) Regarding *Che vuoi?*, see "Subversion of the Subject" in *Écrits*, p. 815. "*Che vuoi?*" (not "*Chè vuoi?*" as found in my translation of *Écrits*) is the spelling used by Jacques Cazotte in *Le Diable amoureux et la Patte du chat* (Geneva: Editions de Crémille, 1968), p. 18. See, also, the annotated French edition by Annalisa Bottacin (Milan: Cisalpino-La Goliardica, 1983), pp. 56–7. In English, see *The Devil in Love* (New York: Houghton Mifflin, 1925).

(140,1) Leto was a lover of Zeus', and the mother of Apollo and Artemis. An English translation of the passage reads as follows: "Or to an island home, sped on my way in grief by an oar plied in the brine, to spend a life of misery in the house, there where the date palm, first of all its line, and the laurel tree sent up their holy shoots as an adornment dear to Leto to grace the birth of her children by Zeus? Shall I with the maidens of Delos sing in praise of the golden headband and bow of the goddess Artemis?" from *Euripides: Children of Heracles, Hippolytus, Andromache, Hecuba* (Cambridge, MA: Harvard University Press, 1995), p. 441.

(140,2) Lacan may be alluding here to the so-called maternal phallus and its role in fetishism. *Cet objet infantile* (this infantile object) might also allude to the infant as a (phallic) object.

(141,4) "Articulated language" is not found in the *Cratylus* but is discussed by the French translator, Louis Méridier, who mentions "ἔναρθρον ἔχειν ἔπος [*énarthron échein épos*], avoir une parole articulée," in a footnote of his edition (Paris: Les Belles Lettres, 1969 [originally published much earlier]).

(143,1) For *agálmata*, see Homer's *Odyssey*, Book III, verse 274. Reading, in the last sentence of the paragraph, *seins* (breasts) instead of *saints* (saints), which are perfect homonyms in French. Lacan might be playing off the two meanings. Useful information on the use of the term *ágalma* can be found in Catherine M. Keesling's *The Votive Statues of the Athenian Acropolis* (Cambridge: Cambridge University Press, 2003).

(143,2) It seems there may be a problem of transcription here, Lacan perhaps having said *galer* or *gala*. *Galant* is the present participle of the verb *galer*, meaning to have fun, have a good time. *Gala* comes from the Old French *gale*, meaning pleasure or rejoicing (*réjouissance*). The idea of *éclat* is not found in the *Dictionnaire étymologique* by Bloch et von Wartburg, which is Lacan's favorite for Old French.

(143,4) Pausanias (*c.* 180 A.D.). The passage referred to by Lacan is found in Book IX, Chapter 11, entitled Boiotia: "Here are portraits of women carved in relief; the carvings are already rather faint [*amudrótera éde ta agálmata*]. The Thebans call them the Witches and say they were sent by Hera to interfere with Alkmene's birthpains. They were preventing the birth [*tais ôdisin*], but Teiresias' daughter Historis thought up a trick against them: she yelled with triumph for them to hear, as if the baby was born; the legend is that the witches went away deceived, and Alkmene had her baby." Pausanias, *Guide to Greece*, vol. 1, trans. P. Levi (Harmondsworth: Penguin, 1971), pp. 330–1.

(144,1) "Oblativity" is a supposed tendency to give to others selflessly or disinterestedly that was discussed in French analytic texts of the 1950s (the adjectival form is "oblative"). The term was introduced by Laforgue in 1926 and was rendered as "self-sacrifice" in Lacan's "Some Reflections on the Ego," *IJP* XXXIV 1 (1953): 17. It's often a synonym for altruism. On the so-called genital stage, see "Direction of the Treatment," *Écrits*, pp. 605–7.

(148,3) We could alternately read: "And we shall see that it is only via the other and for the other that Alcibiades, like each and every one of us, wants to make Socrates realize how much he loves Alcibiades [*veut faire savoir à Socrates son amour*]."

Chapter XI – Between Socrates and Alcibiades

(149,2) I have left out the first heading included by the editor here, finding no connection between it (*L'état de perversion*, The state of perversion or The perverse state) and this particular chapter of the Seminar.

(150,5) English has the term "encomium" with which the Greek ἐνκώμιον (*enkómion*) is generally rendered.

(151,1) We saw *to cheíre* earlier (213d), and it was translated there as "slapping me around."

(152,1) There may be a play on words here, since while literally a *flûtiste* is a piper or flautist (and the satyr Marsyas was a well-known piper), figuratively it refers to someone who is not serious, a "joker" we might say colloquially in American English, and *flûter* can imply that when you speak no one listens to what you say.

(153,2) Lacan may be referring to the fact that Léon Robin begins this section with the subtitle "Socrate: sa maîtrise de lui-même" (Socrates' self-mastery) in his first translation of the *Symposium* in Plato, *Oeuvres complètes*, Volume IV, Part 2 (Paris: Belles Lettres, 1989 [originally published in 1938]), p. 80; or with the subtitle "La spiritualité de l'amour chez Socrates" (The spirituality of Socrates' love) in his later translation in *Plato, Oeuvres complètes* (Paris: Gallimard, 1950), p. 755.

(157,2) *Noli me tangere* is usually rendered as "touch me not" or "do not hold on to me" (John 20:17).

(157,4) On the "repudiation of femininity," see Freud (1937), "Analysis Terminable and Interminable," *SE* XXIII, p. 250.

(158,5) The English translation of 222d provides the following: "Well, we were not deceived; we've seen through your little satyr play."

(159,2) The French here (*il donne satisfaction à Alcibiade*) literally implies that Socrates gives Alcibiades satisfaction, and it can also mean that Socrates compensates or grants redress to Alcibiades, or rules in his favor. In bygone days, *donner satisfaction* meant to agree to fight a duel.

(159,5) *Leurre* means illusion, decoy, or deception. *Être leurré* means to be deluded, deceived, or taken in.

(159,6) On the little schema of the spherical mirror, see *Écrits*, pp. 675ff, and Chapter 24 in this Seminar.

(160,9) *Hímeros* and *enargés* can be found in Sophocles' *Antigone*, verses 795–6; compare *Phaedrus* 251c–e.

(161,3) The reference here is to Flaubert's Monsieur Homais in *Madame Bovary*.

(161,5) Lacan is referring here to Jean Giraudoux's 1929 play entitled *Amphitryon 38*.

(162,4) John the Scot is also known as John Scottus Eriugena. See, for example, Dermot Moran, *The Philosophy of John Scottus Eriugena: A Study of Idealism in the Middle Ages* (Cambridge: Cambridge University Press, 1989). In French, see Maieul Cappuyns' *Jean Scot Erigène: Sa vie, son oeuvre, sa pensée* (Louvain, 1933).

(163,7) Lacan here provides a play on words in Greek: ἡμέρα (*heméra*) means day; ἥμερα (*hémera*) means gentle or tame; and ἵμερος (*hímeros*) means longing, desire, or love. Cf. Plato's *Cratylus*, 418c–d.

Chapter XII – Transference in the Present

(169,2) On the Graph of Desire, see "Subversion of the Subject," *Écrits*, p. 817.

(169,4) *L'au-delà* (the beyond) can sometimes be translated instead as the "hereafter."

(173,8) "The Action of Suggestion in Psychotherapy" – first published in 1910 in *The Journal of Abnormal Psychology*, vol. 5 – is Chapter 12 of the fourth edition of Jones' *Papers on Psycho-analysis*, pp. 241–82; the paper was not included in the fifth edition.

(174,5) See Daniel Lagache, "Le problème du transfert" ["The Problem of Transference"] (Paper given at the 14th Conference of French-speaking Psychoanalysts on November 1, 1951), *RFP* XVI/1–2 (1952): 5–115.

(174,6) The Zeigarnik effect is the psychological tendency to remember an uncompleted task rather than a completed one. See Bluma Zeigarnik, "Das Behalten erledigter und unerledigter Handlungen," *Psychologische Forschung* IX (1927): 1–85. In English, see "On Finished and Unfinished Tasks," in W. D. Ellis, ed., *A Source Book of Gestalt Psychology* (New York: Harcourt-Brace, 1938).

(176,6) On *Aidós*, see "Signification of the Phallus," *Écrits*, p. 692. "Its aim is the fall of the Other, A, into the other, *a*" – that is, its aim is to get the partner to fall from the position of Other to that of *a*, to fall off a certain kind of pedestal.

(179,6) Here it is quite clear that desire is a question. The "analysand's constitutive desire" is the question, "What does the analyst want?"

Chapter XIII – A Critique of Countertransference

(180,5) "For it is not necessary to know the floor plan of a house to bang one's head against its walls: indeed, one can do so very well without it" (*Écrits*, p. 608). See Georges Courteline, "Théodore cherche des allumettes" [Theodor searches for matches], *Théâtre complet* (Paris: Flammarion, 1961), pp. 287–97. Virtually the entire play takes place in the dark.

(182,3) "Reserve unconscious" (*inconscient-réserve*) implies there is some leftover unconscious material (or stock) that can serve as a sort of backup.

(186,4) On the death drive, see *Beyond the Pleasure Principle, SE* XVIII, pp. 38–9.

(186,6) *Un mort* means both a dead person and a dummy in the game of bridge. See *Écrits*, p. 589.

(187,2) In this passage, Lacan is presumably pointing to a schema he has put up on the board, which is related to the L Schema (*Écrits*, p. 53; see also Seminar II, p. 134/109). There seems to be little agreement about how to read the passage and what the schema on the board might have looked like; see J.-A. Miller's proposed reconstruction from notes taken by Paul Lemoine in his "Editor's Notes" at the end of this volume.

(188,2) Paula Heimann, "On Counter-transference," *IJP* XXXI (1950): 81–4.

(189,2) Money-Kryle never actually says "a demanding superego" in this article. He mentions "the severity of [the analyst's] superego [. . .] which a demanding patient may sometimes come to represent" (p. 361).

(190,2) Lacan seems to confuse some general comments Money-Kryle makes with the details of his interactions with this one specific patient (see pp. 362–3).

(190,3) The dream in question was not actually recounted during the session that day; Money-Kryle merely recalled that the patient had had a certain dream on what Money-Kryle thought was a similar occasion (p. 362).

(191,2) "The analyst effectively becomes the patient" – "patient" to be understood here in the sense of a person who suffers.

(191,6) Heimann says that the analyst "must use his emotional response as a key to the patient's unconscious. [. . .] This, however, is his private affair, and I do not consider it right for the analyst to communicate his feelings to his patient" (p. 83).

(192,1) According to Money-Kryle, the patient's reaction was as follows: "For the first time in two days, he became quiet and thoughtful. He then said this explained why he had been so angry with me yesterday: he had felt that all my interpretations referred to my illness and not to his" (p. 363).

(192,3) "Analytic setting" is more common in contemporary English than "analytic situation," but *situation analytique* could be construed to be a direct translation of Richard Sterba's term "analytic situation" – a term also found in Freud's work (*SE* XII, p. 161, and *SE* XIX, p. 274) – in "The Fate of the Ego in Analytic Therapy," *IJP* XV/2–3 (1934): 117, or a reference to Melanie Klein's use of the word in the expression "total situation" in her "The Origins of Transference," *IJP* XXXIII (1952): 433–8.

(194,4) It is Money-Kryle who, in the same article Lacan discussed earlier, presents these two drives.

Chapter XIV – Demand and Desire in the Oral and Anal Stages

(197,8) One could potentially read *conscient* (conscious) instead of *concret* (concrete).

(198,3) *Défilés* (defiles) should probably be understood in the sense of a narrow, difficult path. Since the French also means procession or succession, however, it could perhaps imply consequence or aftermath. Cf. Freud's "defile of consciousness" in *SE* II, p. 291.

(198,7) *Automatismes de répétition* (repetition automatisms): Lacan rarely employs the more usual French translation of Freud's *Wiederholungszwang* (generally translated into English as "repetition compulsion"), which is *compulsion de répétition*.

(199,4) The *Standard Edition* reads as follows: "As a rule the physician cannot spare the patient this phase of the treatment; he must necessarily make him re-experience a certain portion of his past life, and must see to it that he remains to some degree above it all so that he remains cognizant at every turn that what appears to be reality is in truth the refracted image of a forgotten past" (*Beyond the Pleasure Principle*, *SE* XVIII, pp. 18–19).

(200,2) Lacan quotes here from Samuel Jankélévitch's French translation of the work known in English as *Beyond the Pleasure Principle* (Paris: Payot, 1920), which was purportedly read over by Freud prior to its publication.

(200,5) *L'Autre-on* might literally be translated as "the one-Other" or (in a more Heideggerian vein as) "the they-Other," but this would eliminate Lacan's attempt to make it sound like neutron, proton, electron, and so on.

(200,6) Reading *Autre* (Other) instead of *autre* (other) at the end of the first sentence of the paragraph.

(201,3) Or one "cannot admit to the most primordial Other . . ." The French here, *tué le désir*, could just as easily (and perhaps more grammatically) be transcribed as *tuez le désir* or *tuer le désir*, meaning "kill desire" or "kill what I desire."

(203,3) *Excédent sexuel* (surplus sexuality) is a French translation for a term found in Freud's early work on trauma: *sexual über*. According to Freud, a child experiences excessive sexuality, a surplus or overload of sexual feeling or pleasure, and is revolted by it (in hysteria) or later comes to feel guilty about it (in obsession). *Sexual über* is translated in *The Origins of Psychoanalysis* (New York: Basic Books, 1954) as "surplus of sexuality" (pp. 163–4, letter dated May 30, 1896); the French translate it as *excédent de sexualité* or *excédent sexuel*, that is, excess of sexuality or sexual excess; see *La Naissance de la psychanalyse* (Paris: Presses Universitaires de France, 1956), p. 145.

(203,4) *Débordements* (excesses) might also be understood here as "accidents."

(203,6) *Vertige* (giddiness) literally means "vertigo," but might also be rendered here as "whirlwind."

(204,2) The wording Lacan uses here, "*Le désir, littéralement, s'en va aux chiottes*" (Desire, literally, goes down the tubes), plays on the French expression "*aux chiottes!*" (go to hell, to hell with it, or screw it) and on the slang meaning of *chiottes*, which is shithouse, latrine, crapper, or can.

(204,6) *Une compréhension à la limite* (a liminal understanding) is somewhat vague and perhaps could alternatively be rendered by "a possible understanding," "a quasi-understanding," "an understanding at the fringes," or "a being on the verge of understanding."

(205,1)   "Must appear as an existence offered up to this gap" – that implies, I think, that the imaginary other (or semblable) is someone who is offered up to the devouring Other in the subject's stead.

(206,1)   Lacan is likely referring to the famous phrase in *Les mariés de la Tour Eiffel* (1921, to which Jean Cocteau contributed), "*Puisque ces mystères nous dépassent, feignons d'en être l'organisateur.*"

(206,2)   Reading *à l'organe qui est* (to the organ that is) instead of *à ce qui est* (to what is).

(206,5)   Reading *métathèse* (metathesis) instead of *métastase* (metastasis).

(207,2)   *Toute compréhension de la demande, en effet, l'implique si profondément que nous devons y regarder à deux fois avant d'aller à sa rencontre* (Every understanding of his demand, in effect, implicates him so profoundly that we must look twice before broaching it) is quite ambiguous: (1) some versions include *formulation* instead of *compréhension* and *sa demande* instead of *la demande*, (2) the *l'* could refer to the other, his demand, or even anality, and (3) *aller à sa rencontre* could also imply going out and looking for the understanding or formulation, broaching it, or joining with or agreeing to it.

(208,1)   Some versions give *marge de l'incompréhensible* (space occupied by what is incomprehensible) instead of *marge de l'incompréhension*.

(208,2)   The book one can feed on is a reference to the phrase in Revelation 10:9–10, "eat the book," discussed in Seminar VII, pp. 340/294 and 371/322.

(208,4)   Reading *qui s'incarna* (that became incarnate) instead of *qui s'incarne* (that becomes incarnate or that is incarnated). One could potentially read *Poros endormi* (sleeping Poros) instead of *parole endormie* (sleeping speech).

Chapter XV – Oral, Anal, and Genital

(209,5)   *Passe à s'articuler* (gets articulated) could also be understood here as "manages to get articulated" or "is conveyed because it gets articulated."

(210,1)   In the singular, *Lust* is used by Freud in the sense of pleasure, but in the plural in the sense of desires, appetites, or cravings. See Freud's (1905) comment on the term in his *Three Essays on the Theory of Sexuality*, in *SE* VII, p. 212 n.1; there he indicates that *Lust* has two meanings, being "used to describe the sensation of sexual tension ('*Ich habe Lust*' = 'I should like to,' 'I feel an impulse to') as well as the feeling of satisfaction." See also *SE* VII, p. 135 n. 2. *La déviation quant au but se faire en sens inverse de l'objet d'un besoin* (a deviation in aim occurring in a way that does not happen when it comes to the object of need) is rather elliptical, but seems to me to imply that whereas need can suffer no deviation in object or aim, sublimation can.

(210,2)   Reading *seulement après coup* (only after the fact) instead of *non seulement après coup* (not only after the fact).

(210,5)   Henri Ey's work on animal perversions was eventually published in book form as *Psychiatrie animale* (Paris: Desclée de Brouwer, 1964).

(211,2)   *Subjectiviser* (subjectivize) can be understood here in the sense of to make a human subject of something or to anthropomorphize.

(211,3)   *Elle* (this jouissance) could alternatively refer to the praying mantis, as could *elle* (it) in the next sentence.

(211,5)   Reading *effets* (effects) instead of *efforts* (efforts). See *Écrits*, p. 95. On the sexual maturation of pigeons, see L. Harrison Matthews, "Visual Stimulation and Ovulation in Pigeons" in the *Proceedings of the Royal Society*, Series B, 126 (1939): 557–60. On the development of the migratory locust, see R. Chauvin's work in *Annales de la Société entomologique de France* (1941, third quarter): 133, 272. These and other references are provided in Lacan's paper "Some Reflections on the Ego," *IJP* XXXIV, 1 (1953): 11–17, and in "Remarks on Psychical Causality" in *Écrits*, pp. 189 and 190–1.

(213,1) Some versions provide *le partenaire* (the male partner) instead of *la partenaire* (the female partner).

(213,2) *Son anatomie* (her anatomy) could alternatively be rendered as "his anatomy."

(213,6) Reading *l'homme* (man) instead of *le sacré* (the sacred). Caillois' first book was entitled *Le mythe et l'homme* (Paris: Gallimard, 1938); his second book was entitled *L'homme et le sacré* (Paris: Gallimard, 1939).

(214,1) Lacan may be referring here to *koine* Greek (also known as Alexandrian dialect, common Attic, or Hellenistic Greek), which was the widespread form of spoken and written Greek during Hellenistic and Roman Antiquity. It spread following Alexander the Great's conquests in the fourth century B.C., and served as the common *lingua franca* for much of the Mediterranean region during the following centuries. *Koine* Greek is also known as "Biblical," "New Testament," or "patristic Greek." Certain versions provide *telos* instead of *Gelüst*.

(214,5) The church, Santa Maria degli Angeli, is located on the island of Murano in the Venetian Lagoon. Carpaccio's *Saint George and the Dragon* is currently housed in the Scuola di San Giorgio degli Schiavoni of Venice; Lacan could possibly be referring to a different canvas: *The Triumph of Saint George*. It is not clear to me what *morceaux de pavillon d'anatomie* (panoply of anatomical morsels) actually means. See Jacques Cazotte, *Le Diable amoureux et la Patte du chat* (Geneva: Editions de Crémille, 1968).

(216,3) Freud uses the term "hominization" in *SE* XXIII, pp. 75 and 153; it refers there to the process of becoming human. Lacan is probably referring here to the theologian Pierre Teilhard de Chardin (1881–1955); cf. *Écrits*, pp. 88 and 684. The Scandinavian (Danish) name is referred to again in Seminar XIII, *The Object of Psychoanalysis* (class given on December 8, 1965).

(216,5) Jones used the Greek term *aphanisis* to refer to the "total, and of course permanent, extinction of the capacity (including opportunity) for sexual enjoyment"; see "Early Development of Female Sexuality" (1927), in *Papers on Psycho-Analysis*, 5th edition (Boston: Beacon, 1961), p. 440. According to Jones, the fear of *aphanisis* is more fundamental than that of castration in both sexes, castration being only a "special case" of *aphanisis* in boys. Cf. Lacan, *Écrits*, p. 687, and Seminar XI, *The Four Fundamental Concepts of Psychoanalysis*. Some versions do not include the term *aphanisis* in this passage; hence: "the starting point of desire." *Laisse faire quelque chose* (be allowed to do something); one could possibly read *fasse* (be made) instead of *laisse* (be allowed).

(217,7) The someone here is Marie-Antoinette. She said this at her trial on October 14, 1793, when she was accused of having incestuous relations with her son.

(218,3) See *Écrits*, pp. 627 and 730.

(218,4) *Traite sur l'avenir* (promissory note) literally implies betting or taking a gamble on the future; it relates to a document (like an IOU) concerning a possible exchange to take place in the future, and can, in some contexts, be rendered by having "a lien against" something.

(218,5) Reading *habeo* (I have) instead of *habeum* (we have).

(219,1) *Ce qui manque à l'Autre pour être l'A noétique* (what the Other is missing because it is the noetic A) could alternatively be understood, perhaps, as "what the Other is missing [and would have to have] in order to be the noetic A."

(219,2) *Manque de réponse* (lack of response) could perhaps also be rendered in this context as "failure to respond" or "lack of answers." Lacan seems to be saying here that *phi* is at the root of barred A – that is, "the Other as designated by the lack of a signifier."

Chapter XVI – Psyche and the Castration Complex

(224,3) Reading *se terminerait là si* (would end there were) instead of *veut donc dire que* (thus means that).

(225,1) Lacan is alluding here to Hegel's *unglückliches Bewusstsein*, sometimes rendered in English as "troubled conscience" (more literally as "unhappy consciousness"). See Jean Wahl, *Le Malheur de la conscience dans la philosophie de Hegel* (Paris: PUF, 1951). Cf. *Écrits*, p. 589.

(226,1) Other versions suggest we read: "turns out to illustrate what I can designate today only as the point at which two registers converge," the two being the instinctual dynamic and the castration complex. Keep in mind that "the signifier" is very often shorthand in Lacan's work for "the system of signifiers" or "the signifying system."

(227,3) *Instances du savoir* (knowledge's entreaties) could be alternatively understood as "agencies (or authorities) of knowledge." Lacan might have been thinking here of Freud's *Wissentrieb* (the child's drive for knowledge of sexual matters). In *SE* VII, p. 194, *Wissentrieb* is translated as "instinct for knowledge," and in *SE* X, p. 245, as "epistemophilic instinct."

(228,2) See René de Monchy, "Oral Components of the Castration Complex," *IJP* XXXIII (1952): 450–3.

(228,5) Reading "congenital reaction schemes" (as in Monchy's article, p. 450) instead of "releaser mechanisms." Lacan may have mentioned Lorenz and von Uexküll here as those who first named them in German (as *angeborene Reactionsschema*). I have modified a number of terms in this discussion based on Monchy's article. Note that Monchy never actually mentions the "biting reflex" in his own name, quoting only the term "biting" from Susan Isaacs.

(229,2) All of Lefèvre-Pontalis' summaries can be found in the 2011 issue of *Bulletin de psychologie* LXIV, 516 (6): 503–57; the one referred to here is "Le désir et son interprétation" (pp. 541–57), originally published in *Bulletin de psychologie* XIII, 172 (6), dated January 20, 1960. Lacan himself reviewed and approved these summaries. On Ella Sharpe's patient, see Seminar VI, Chapters 8–12. The dream can be found in Ella

Sharpe's *Dream Analysis* (London: Karnac, 1988 [originally published in 1937]).

(230,1) See, for example, Matthew 22:30.

(230,7) "Double symbolization" is perhaps a reference to Lévi-Strauss.

(231,6) See "Remarks on Daniel Lagache's Presentation: 'Psychoanalysis and Personality Structure,'" in *Écrits*, pp. 647–84; Lacan had initially discussed this in Seminar I, Chapter 7 (February 24, 1954).

(232,1) The quotes in this passage are from Pontalis' summary of Seminar VI (the class given on February 11, 1959) found in *Bulletin de psychologie* XIII, 172 (6): 334. Cf. Seminar VI, p. 258.

(233,1) Lacan quotes here from Rabelais' *Pantagruel*, Book 8; cf. *Écrits*, p. 632. *Conscience* can mean both conscience and consciousness, and *science sans conscience* is usually translated as "science without conscience."

Chapter XVII – The Symbol Φ

(234,6) Other versions read: "The idea is not that one mustn't say everything, but that to speak accurately we cannot say all that we could formulate."

(235,3) *Se produit le manque de signifiant* (the lack of a signifier occurs) might also be understood as "a lack in the signifying system appears."

(239,4) See Seminar VII, pp. 33–4/24–5.

(240,1) The first intersection is likely at A and the second at s(A) in Graph 2 in *Écrits*, p. 808.

(240,2) Regarding the ideal ego, see the point labeled *i(a)* on Graph 2, *Écrits*, p. 808.

(240,3) Regarding the ego-ideal, see the point labeled I(A) in Graph 2 in *Écrits*, p. 808.

(241,2) "What do you want?" is a likely reference to "*Che vuoi?*" in Graph 3, *Écrits*, p. 815.

(241,3) "*Qu'est-ce que ça veut là-dedans?*" ("What does the old coconut want?") is a highly colloquial way of speaking that avoids any mention of "you" (as in "what do you want?"), using *ça* (it, or in psychoanalytic parlance, id) instead. *Là-dedans* refers to the head, in particular: the noggin, nut, coconut, bean, lemon, melon, or skull, as you like.

(245,4) The French here (*elle préfère que son désir soit insatisfait à ceci, que l'Autre garde la clé de son mystère*) is quite ambiguous, and could possibly be rendered as "she prefers having her own desire go unsatisfied to having the Other hold the key to her mystery." Other versions propose: *elle préfère que son désir soit insatisfait afin* (or: *et*) *que l'Autre garde la clé de son mystère*: "she prefers to let her own desire go unsatisfied in order to (or: and) let the Other keep the key to her [his?] mystery."

(246,7) On "phallophany," see Seminar VI, p. 419. In English, see Lacan, "Desire and the Interpretation of Desire in *Hamlet*," trans. J. Hulbert. *Yale French Studies* 55/56 (1977): 11–52.

Chapter XVIII – Real Presence

(249,3) The following quotes are from *Gulliver's Travels*, Part III, Chapter VI.

(249,6) *Substantifique moëlle* (heart of the matter) is from Rabelais and means something like the very substance, "the real stuff"; more literally, the marrow or quick.

(250,2) The "news" most likely concerned Algeria. The newspaper *Le Figaro* apparently announced on April 26 that Salan had committed suicide, only to indicate later that Challe, Salan, and Jouhaud had left Algiers. I have been unable to find *reflet de la beauté* (reflection of beauty) in Seminar VII; one does, however, find *effet de la beauté* (effect of beauty), a close homonym in French, in the class given on May 25, 1960 (p. 291/249).

(250,6) Reading φ in the formula for the obsessive's fantasy, as in the 1991 edition of the Seminar (p. 295), instead of Φ; note, however, that other versions read Φ. (The discussion further on in this section suggests to me that the formula should contain φ, not Φ.). In the published edition, the formula for the obsessive's fantasy is not included in the prior class.

(253,4) Other versions read: "other who observes him" instead of "Other who observes him."

(254,2) Note that *défaut* can mean fault, defect, absence, or lack.

(255,4) *Prise au ventre* (public displays) might alternatively be understood as "grabbing around the middle"; Lacan's meaning strikes me as quite unclear here.

(256,1) *Est tout phallicisme* (is all about phallicism) could alternatively be rendered as "to be all phallic." On "isolation," see *SE* XX, pp. 120–2.

(256,4) *Se dégonfler* (deflating) also means backing down (when one has supposedly decided to do something courageous, for example) or caving (giving into someone else's demands).

(257,3) See Bouvet's "Incidences thérapeutiques de la prise de conscience de l'envie de pénis dans des cas de névrose obsessionnelle féminine," *RFP*, XIV, 2 (1950): 215–43.

(258,7) Other versions propose: "insofar as the object in question would be objectivity itself."

(260,5) *Prégnant(e)*: full of implicit meaning, full of consequences. In psychology: something that imposes itself or forces itself upon the mind. In linguistics: a term or construction whose meaning is not entirely enunciated. Lacan earlier suggested that Psyche's slim stature, for example, allowed one to see her as representing or standing in for the (erect form of the) phallus. The "profound choice" is perhaps that of girl=phallus, or of the phallus as the sign of desire.

Chapter XIX – Sygne's No

(266,1) *Partialité* (is only partial) is often translated as "bias," but it is also related to *partial*, which is an alternate spelling of *partiel* (meaning partial as opposed to whole).

(266,4) The French expression *y couper* means skip out on, avoid, or shirk (a responsibility).

(267,6) Claudel glosses the distinction between habit and *habitus* in his letter to Gide dated September 1, 1910. See *Correspondance: Claudel–Gide, 1899–1926* (Paris: Nouvelle Revue Française/Gallimard, 1949). In English, see *The Correspondence (1899–1926) between Paul Claudel and André Gide*, trans. J. Russell (Boston: Beacon Press, 1952), p. 138.

(268,4) Cf. *Écrits*, p. 814. According to the *Trésor de la langue française*, "The distinction between a subjective genitive and an objective genitive is based on the transposition of a verb phrase into a noun phrase such that, in the first case it is the subject function that is transposed and in the second it is the object function that is transposed." For example, in English, the phrase "the love of a child," as a subjective genitive, means the love a child has or feels for something or someone; as an objective genitive, it means the love something or someone has for the child. Other versions of the second sentence of this paragraph read differently, but are not any clearer.

(269,2) *Ça* (that) also means "id." *Il* (it) in this passage should perhaps be rendered instead by "he" (i.e., the patient).

(270,1) On "mediocre" analysts, see *Écrits*, pp. 484 and 491. The author is Maurice Benassy.

(270,4) *S'en serait payé* could also be rendered as "made up for lost time." See M. Benassy, "Les fantasmes [Fantasies]," *Bulletin de Psychologie* XIV, 192 (1960–1): 12.

(271,7) This typography problem is discussed in Claudel's letters dated November 22, 1910 (p. 143), and February 25, 1911 (p. 151), and in Gide's letters dated February 22, 1911 (p. 149), and [February 1911] (p. 152).

(272,3) Claudel refers to *The Hostage* as likely to be viewed as reactionary in his letter to Gide dated June 2, 1910 (p. 125 in the English edition). In the letter dated June 17, 1910, he proposes to put just his initials P.C. on the play in order to get around the rule that all publications be authorized. In his letter dated September 16, 1910, he calls it overly "royalist, feudal, and reactionary," adding that "No government official could sign it" and proposing to sign it "Paul C" (pp. 140–1 in the English edition).

(272,5) Napoleon I (Napoleon Bonaparte) was Emperor of the French from 1804 to 1815. Sygne is said to be under 30 on p. 34/24; in my notes (and in the text in brackets) I give first the page number in the French Folio edition, *L'otage suivi de Le pain dur et de Le père humilié* (Paris: Gallimard, 1979), and then, after a slash, the page number of the English translation: *Three Plays: The Hostage, Crusts, The Humiliation of the Father*, trans. J. Heard (Boston: John W. Luce, 1945).

(274,1) Printed in May 1911, the play finally came to the stage in 1913 in London. Henri Charles Ferdinand Marie Dieudonné d'Artois (September 29, 1820–August 24, 1883) was the Duke of Bordeaux and the Count of Chambord.

(274,7) Reading *son cousin* (her cousin [male]) instead of *sa cousine* (her cousin [female]).

(275,4) The "second death" is literally mentioned in Claudel's *The Hostage* (p. 97/58).

(276,1) Reading *le beau* (beauty) for *le bien* (the good); see Seminar VII, pp. 278ff/237ff. Regarding the Greek, see Seminar VII, p. 311/267–8.

(277,5) Reading Haemon instead of Creon.

(277,6) A second, alternative ending is provided by Claudel in the French edition (pp. 149–53), but the English edition does not include it.

(277,7) Epinal images were popular prints that told a story, and were often designed for people who could not read. They provided a traditional, naïve vision of things, showing only the positive side of things. Figuratively, the term means "cliché."

(279,3) In Seminar VII, Lacan provides the following translation of the passage: "a means by which to bring about, through pity and fear, the catharsis of passions like this one" (p. 286/244); he glosses it again a few pages later: "by means of pity and fear, we are purged of . . . the imaginary" (p. 290/247–8). See Aristotle, *Poetics* 1453b12–14; see also *Rhetoric* III, 16; 1417a13.

Chapter XX – Turelure's Abjection

(280,4) Other versions suggest that Merleau-Ponty himself wanted Lacan to occupy this podium, even though Lacan was reluctant to do so.

(281,3) See Hegel, *The Phenomenology of Mind*, Section 734 or Chapter 7, Section B, subsection c: "The spiritual work of art" (p. 738); *The Phenomenology of Spirit* (p. 445); and Jean Hyppolite's French translation (p. 248). *Versöhnung* is also sometimes rendered by "appeasement." Other versions read *tout Bien* (every Good) instead of *tout lien* (all bonds).

(282,1) The someone here is Ernest Jones; see his book entitled *Hamlet and Oedipus* (New York: W. W. Norton & Co., 1976 [original work published 1919]), p. 25.

(282,4) Lacan is referring here to his discussion in Seminar VI (classes given on March 4 and May 27, 1959); see *Ornicar?* 24 (1981): 7–31, and *Le Séminaire, Livre VI, Le désir et son interpretation* (Paris: La Martinière, 2013), pp. 286 and 479 (on p. 479 one finds *jardin*, not *verger*; in other versions, one finds both). In English, see "Desire and the interpretation of desire in *Hamlet*" (J. Hulbert, trans.). *Yale French Studies* 55/56 (1977): 11–52.

(283,4) In a more modern vein, we might refer to cartoon images that ask, "Where's Waldo?"

(284,1) I follow the English translation in the longer passages (for example, in Chapter 21 below), but try to provide English renderings that fit better with Lacan's commentary elsewhere. The little monk tends bees and used to tend sheep (pp. 354–5/183).

(285,3) See Paul Reboux and Charles Muller, *À la manière de . . .* (Paris: Grasset & Fasquelle, 2003 [shorter edition in 1914]). *Il n'y a pas de petites économies* (a penny saved is a penny earned) is an expression akin to "every little bit helps" in English, and literally means "there's no such thing as small savings." The French expression is often completed by the following: *Il n'y a que de grandes pertes* ("There are only big losses"). Cf. *Écrits*, p. 477.

(286,2) *Avoir la peau de quelqu'un* also means "to fix him good."

(286,3) The English translation here reads as follows: "He's as unbusinesslike as he is stingy, and, at that, he isn't as stingy as he is crooked" (p. 90).

(287,3) There is perhaps a play on words here, as *carrée* can mean bedroom and "adult" matters.

(288,4) On games with four players, see Lacan's discussion of bridge in *Écrits*, p. 551.

(290,2) *Le Sapeur Camember* is a cartoon series by Marie-Louis-Georges Colomb, known as Christophe. The French here reads as follows: "*Regarde, dit-il, c'te lettre elle n'est pas chargée . . . ce n'est pas que le général n'en ait pas les moyens, mais elle n'est pas chargée, eh bien ça n'va pas l'empêcher de partir tout de même !*" See Christophe, *Les facéties du sapeur Camember* (Paris: Livre de Poche, 1965).

(291,5) Boniface de la Mole was decapitated on April 30, 1574, and it is said that Marguerite de Navarre, Queen of France, asked the executioner if she could have his head, he having been her lover.

(293,1) Other versions would have us read: "saying that they aspire to put an end to it and that they pursue the sharing by all of the only thing that is real, which is jouissance."

(295,4) *Point mort* means neutral, as in a car's gearbox.

Chapter XXI – Pensée's Desire

(300,1) *Le désir de Pensée de Coûfontaine* (Pensée de Coûfontaine's desire) could also be rendered as "desire for Pensée de Coûfontaine."

(300,3) *Surimposition* (superimposing) could alternatively be rendered as "overtaxing."

(300,7) The noun *Versagung* is often rendered as denial or privation (or deprivation), but in the *Standard Edition* of Freud's work is often translated as "frustration." What Lacan says in this passage (evoking the English verb "to renege") might apply better to the transitive verb *versagen* (to deny somebody or oneself something, refuse somebody or oneself something) than to the noun *Versagung*.

(301,2) One could possibly read, "it is refusal regarding perdition," instead of just "perdition."

(301,3) On the words *me phunai* in *Oedipus at Colonus*, see Seminar VII, pp. 292/257 and 353/305–6. On the so-called pleonastic or expletive *ne*, see Seminar VII, pp. 79 and 353/64 and 305–6. See also B. Fink, *The Lacanian Subject* (Princeton: Princeton University Press, 1995), pp. 38–41.

(301,4) On debt, see *Écrits*, p. 278; there Lacan refers to Rabelais' Panurge, who says that he has always believed debts to be "a sort of connecting-link between Heaven and earth, a unique interrelationship of the human race – I mean without which all humans would soon perish – peradventure to be that great soul of the universe, which, according to the Academics, gives life to all things"; if we imagine a world without debts, "There, among the stars, there will be no regular course whatever. All will be in disarray. Jupiter, not thinking himself a debtor to Saturn, will dispossess him of his sphere . . . The moon will remain bloody and dark: on what ground will the sun impart his light to her? He was in no way bound to. The sun will not shine on their earth, the stars will exert no good influence there, for the earth was desisting from lending them nourishment by vapors and exhalations, by which [. . .] the stars were fed." See *The Complete Works of François Rabelais*, trans. Donald M. Frame (Berkeley: University of California Press, 1991), pp. 267–73 (*Tiers livre*, Chapters 3 and 4).

(302,2) The French *reprochée* (reproached) includes *proche* (proximate). Other versions add *d'y céder* (for giving into it) after "debt" in the last sentence of this paragraph.

(303,8) The passage Lacan is referring to (p. 381 in the French) is not included in the English edition (p. 196).

(304,1) The passage Lacan is referring to (p. 381 in the French) is not included in the English edition (p. 196).

(305,2) Lacan is referring here to Victor Hugo's poem entitled "Booz endormi." In French and English, see *The Penguin Book of French Verse*, 3 (Baltimore: Penguin Books, 1957), pp. 69–73. See Lacan's commentary on the poem in *Écrits*, pp. 506–8.

(306,3) "Homodarmes" might be heard to include *homme d'armes* (man-at-arms) and *homme aux dames*, which reminds us of *homme à femmes* (womanizer), among other things. Sir Thomas Pollock Nageoire appears in Claudel's play entitled *L'échange* ("The Exchange"). *Nageoire* means fin, as in a fish's fin. See André Breton's 1924 "Introduction au discours sur le peu de réalité" in *Point du Jour* (Paris: Gallimard, 1970); in English, see "Introduction to the Discourse on the Paucity of Reality" in *Break of Day*, trans. M. Polizzotti and M. A. Caws (Lincoln, NE: University of Nebraska Press, 1999), pp. 3–20.

(306,6) Lacan is likely referring to the end of Seminar VI (pp. 492–504), where he discussed exhibitionism and voyeurism on June 3 and 10, 1959.

(307,1) One could possibly translate, "that it is thus the very desire that sustains its function in fantasy that veils from the subject her role in the activity," instead of, "that it is thus the very desire that sustains its function in fantasy that veils from the subject his role in the exhibitionistic or voyeuristic activity."

(307,2) In ancient myth, Actaeon, coming upon Diana during her bath, is turned by her into a stag which is then chased and killed by Actaeon's own dogs. Cf. *Écrits*, p. 412.

(307,5) The French here, *on ne s'entend pas là où l'on s'entend*, is very ambiguous, and could be understood in several other ways: we do not hear ourselves where others hear us, we do not hear ourselves where we are heard, or we do not hear our own thoughts being heard.

(307,6) See Lacan's discussion of Psyche in Chapter 16 of this Seminar (class given on April 12, 1961).

(308,1) The figure of the Synagogue is apparently found in the south transept (not the portico) of the cathedrals in both Reims and Strasbourg.

(308,4) "Second *temps-pire*" is a play on "Second Empire" and literally "worse time." Other versions suggest a different reading: *second en pire*, a pun attributed to Victor Hugo regarding Napoleon III that plays on "Second Empire" and the "second that is worse."

(309,4) See Claudel, *Two Dramas: Break of Noon & The Tidings Brought to Mary*, trans. W. Fowlie (Washington, D.C.: Henry Regnery Company, 1960).

(309,6) On anamorphosis, see Seminar VII, pp. 161–3/135–6, 169–70/140–2, and elsewhere; see also Seminar XI.

(309,8) The allusions to crucifixion are not included in the English edition; they should appear on pages 157 and 223. Doña Prouhèze appears in *Le soulier de satin*; in English, see *The Satin Slipper; or, The Worst Is Not the Surest*, trans. J. O'Connor, in collaboration with Paul Claudel (New York: Sheed & Ward, 1945).

(310,1) In English, see *Tête d'Or: A Play in Three Acts by Paul Claudel*, trans. J. S. Newberry (New Haven, CT: Yale University Press, 1919).

(310,2) The passage on page 439 in the French is not included in the English edition (p. 223). Lacan seems to conflate two scenes here, one at the very beginning and one at the very end of Act IV (pp. 415 and 439).

(310,4) The poet Lacan has in mind here may be Goethe.

(310,5) The "four terms" here are those of the L Schema; the L Schema is found in *Écrits* (pp. 53 and 548) and in Seminar II, p. 284/243.

(311,6) Some versions read *lacune* (lacuna) instead of *blessure* (wound).

(311,7) *Points d'écartèlement* (quartering points) is somewhat obscure, but may refer to the four corners of the L Schema (*a*, *a'*, S, and A) mentioned half a page earlier. It might more figuratively be rendered as "points of fracture."

(311,8) The someone in question is André Gide. The usual French expression, *les extrêmes se touchent* (the extremes meet up or come together), is a much older one and may be the one intended by Lacan here. It is attributed to M. de Marivetz, author of *La physique du monde*.

Chapter XXII – Structural Decomposition

(313,5) The author whose work Lacan is most averse to here is Sacha Nacht; Lacan paraphrases his article, "La thérapeutique psychanalytique," which is included in *La Psychanalyse d'aujourd'hui* ["Contemporary Psychoanalysis"] (Paris: PUF, 1956). He also comments on it in *Écrits*, p. 587. The actual passage reads as follows: "Thus I sometimes maintain that what is of prime importance in an analysis is not so much what the analyst says or does as what he is. What he says or does is informed by the education he has received. But how he makes use of this education depends in large part on his personality" (p. 135).

(317,1) See Lacan's paper, originally published in French in 1953, "Le mythe individuel du névrosé ou poésie et vérité dans la névrose," *Ornicar?* 17/18 (1979): 289–307. In English, see "The Neurotic's Individual Myth," trans. M. N. Evans, *Psychoanalytic Quarterly* XLVIII, 3 (1979): 405–25.

(318,4) See Sigmund Freud, *The Origins of Psychoanalysis: Letters to Wilhelm Fliess* (New York: Basic Books, 1954), and *The Complete Letters of Sigmund Freud to Wilhelm Fliess, 1887–1904* (Cambridge, MA: Harvard University Press, 1985).

(319,5) See E. Jones, (1931). "The Concept of a Normal Mind," in *Papers on Psychoanalysis*, fifth edition (Baltimore: Williams and Wilkins, 1948), pp. 201–16.

(319,6) Other versions provide *ratiocinations* instead of *vaticinations*.

(320,4) Recall that "the signifier" is often a shorthand in Lacan's work for "the signifying system as a whole."

(322,2) *Se refuser* could be rendered as "deny himself something" or "deprive himself of something" and *refus* as "self-denial," "self-deprivation," or "self-refusal."

(322,3) *Préjudicielle* (prerequisite) is a legal term, describing questions and costs associated with a legal judgment that must be handed down *prior* to the principal suit. It could also be translated as "preliminary" or "prior."

(323,3) The second half of the passage quoted here (p. 325/167) is not included in either the French or English editions referred to here.

(325,2) The French here, *juste le temps qu'il ne soit plus qu'un soldat du Pape, mais froid* (for just as long as he is no longer anything but one of the Pope's defenders, albeit a cold [or tepid?] one) strikes me as quite obscure.

Chapter XXIII – Slippage in the Meaning of the Ideal

(330,3) See Ernest Jones, *The Life and Work of Sigmund Freud*, 3 vols. (New York: Basic Books, 1953, 1955, 1957).

(330,4) See Freud's letters to Eitingon dated October 22 and November 23, 1919, as cited in Jones' *Life and Work of Sigmund Freud*, vol. 2, p. 154. Cf. *Écrits*, p. 486, footnotes 11, 12, and 13.

(331,2) See L. Jekels and E. Bergler, "Übertragung und Liebe," *Imago* XX, 1 (1934); in English, "Transference and Love," *Psychoanalytic Quarterly* XVIII (1949): 325–50.

(331,3) See Seminar I, pp. 127–42.

(331,5) See "Remarks on Daniel Lagache's Presentation: 'Psychoanalysis and Personality Structure'" in *Écrits*.

(332,2) The example is found in the case that Lacan discusses at the end of this class. One could alternatively understand *accrochage* (get started) here as "sticking point": hence "this perhaps becomes the true sticking point of certain analyses."

(332,3) Words are missing in the stenography here, as indicated by [. . .].

(334,1) This may be a reference to Freud's 1910 paper, "The Future Prospects of Psycho-analytic Therapy," *SE* XI, pp. 141–51.

(334,5) Reading *points stables et ondes fixes* (stable points and fixed waves) instead of the virtually homonymous *besoins stables et zones fixes* (stable needs and fixed zones). See H. Nunberg, "The Synthetic Function of the Ego" (1930), in *Practice and Theory of Psychoanalysis* (New York: International Universities Press, 1960).

(334,6) Other versions suggest *artefacts* (artifacts) instead of "acting out" here.

(335,6) Lacan is likely referring here to "The Direction of the Treatment and the Principles of Its Power," the first of two papers he presented at the Royaumont International Colloquium held July 10–13, 1958, at the invitation of the Société Française de Psychanalyse. It was published in *La Psychanalyse* VI (1961): 149–206, and was republished in *Écrits*.

(337,3) See Jekels and Bergler, "Transference and Love," pp. 335–7.

(337,4) Other versions read *gênant* (bothersome or annoying) instead of *nanan* (simplistic).

(338,4) See Jekels and Bergler, p. 325.

(341,3) Other versions propose "brings together well-meaning authority and all that is narcissistically beneficial" instead of just "brings together all that is narcissistically beneficial."

(342,2) See "Observations on Transference-Love," *SE* XII, pp. 166–7, where Freud refers to certain women who seem unable to "preserve the erotic transference for the purposes of analytic work without satisfying it," "who refuse to accept the psychical in the place of the material, [and] who, in the poet's words, are accessible only to 'the logic of soup, with dumplings for argument.'" The poet here is Heinrich Heine, and the poem is entitled *Die Wanderratten* ("The Roving Rats"), which includes the term *Knödelgrunden* (dumpling grounds or reasons). More idiomatically put, "a morality based on dumplings" might be rendered as "a meat-and-potatoes morality."

Chapter XXIV – Identification via *"ein einziger Zug"*

(345,2) Note that the published French edition provides the complete version of the optical schema, as it is found in *Écrits* (p. 675), whereas other versions provide several different schemas, each corresponding to a specific section of Lacan's commentary here.

(345,3) Lacan had already discussed this optical schema in Seminar I, Chapter 11, and Seminar VI, *Desire and Its Interpretation*.

(346,1) This passage likely refers to a schema without the vertical mirror A and the virtual image it allows for (shown in the right half of the complete schema). The eye, then, would be situated at the extreme right of the schema, not at the left.

(347,5) Cf. Jekels and Bergler's term "neutral zone" in "Transference and Love," *Psychoanalytic Quarterly* XVIII (1949): 328 and 330.

(348,1) One could possibly translate "a distinct libidinal energy" instead of "an energy that is distinct from the libido."

(348,2) See Freud's 1915 paper entitled "Instincts [or Drives] and their Vicissitudes," *SE* XIV, pp. 117–40. The French tend to translate *Schicksal* as *sort*, meaning "destiny" or "fate."

(350,2) See Jekels and Bergler, pp. 334, 336, 337, and 339; cf. *Écrits*, p. 853.

(350,5) Reading schema here (or possibly montage) instead of description.

(351,1) The model referred to here may be that introduced by Jekels and Bergler, or even by Freud.

(353,5) Other versions add, after "that is effectively desired or not desired," the words, "by the person toward whom the child turns"; *à* (to) might instead be rendered here by "in."

(354,1) Other versions read *das echte Ich* instead of the *authent-Ich*.

(354,4) Cf. *Écrits*, p. 339, where Lacan translates *Einfühlung* as "connivance."

(354,6) In Strachey's translation of *Group Psychology and the Analysis of the Ego*, the German Lacan cites is rendered as "typically masculine" (*SE* XVIII, p. 105).

(355,4) On Dora, see Freud's "Fragment of an Analysis of a Case of Hysteria" (1905), *SE* VII, pp. 7–122. See Lacan's extensive discussion of the Dora case in "Presentation on Transference," *Écrits*, pp. 215–26.

(357,5) *Grisélidis* is an opera by Jules Massenet, based on the medieval tale – taken up by many authors, including Chaucer, Boccaccio, and Petrarch, for example – of "patient Grissil" (also known as Grizzel or Griselda).

(357,7) The French here is quite ambiguous and could potentially be understood as follows: "rich people act temperately at home or, to be more exact, give themselves a thousand excuses for avoiding their party-giving function."

(357,8) A possible reference to Matthew 19:23–4.

(358,2) *La femme pauvre* was first published in 1897.

Chapter XXV – The Relationship between Anxiety and Desire

(360,4) Certain authors prefer to render *angoisse* in English with "angst" or "anguish"; note that French also has the word *anxiété*, which is generally translated into English as "anxiety." Lacan never uses the latter in this Seminar. Cf. *Inhibitions, Symptoms and Anxiety, SE* XX, p. 92, where Freud raises the question: "Where does the energy come from which is employed for giving the signal of unpleasure?"

(360,5) Lacan is referring here to Freud's *Gesammelte Werke*, XIV (S. Fisher Verlag, 1948: London: Imago Publishing Co.). In *SE* XX, pp. 92–3, Strachey renders this as follows: "The ego withdraws its (preconscious) cathexis from the instinctual representative that is to be repressed and uses that cathexis for the purpose of releasing unpleasure (anxiety)."

(361,2) The perhaps unfamiliar ring to Descartes' phrase (often rendered "I think, therefore I am") is due to the English translation of Descartes' *Philosophical Writings* by J. Cottingham (Cambridge: Cambridge University Press, 1986).

(361,4) Or "could grab hold of himself" (instead of "could grasp himself").

(362,3) As Freud puts it, "the ego is the actual seat of anxiety" (*SE* XX, p. 93).

(362,6) See, for example, *SE* XVI, p. 398, where we find "expectant anxiety" and "anxious expectation"; *SE* XVIII, the beginning of Chapter 2; and *SE* XX, pp. 164–8. See also *GW* XIV, pp. 197–200, and Seminar VI, p. 502.

(363,4) See "Logical Time and the Assertion of Anticipated Certainty: A New Sophism" in *Écrits*.

(364,1) See, however, *Inhibitions, Symptoms and Anxiety*, where it seems that Freud says exactly the same thing: "Here we may be assisted by the idea that a defence against an unwelcome *internal* process will be modelled upon the defence adopted against an *external* stimulus, that the ego wards off internal and external dangers alike along identical lines" (*SE* XX, p. 92).

(364,3) *Mitleid* also means "compassion" or "sympathy."

(364,5) Lacan seems here to be trying to bring his audience to grasp the difference between *a* as the imaginary, specular other, and *a* as object *a*, the cause of desire, in fantasy.

(365,1) This is a likely reference to the complete Graph of Desire, *Écrits*, p. 817.

(365,6) Reading *losigkeit* (an ending meaning something like "lessness," as in senselessness) – though perhaps we should read *Hilflosigkeit* (helplessness or distress) – instead of *Löslichkeit* (solubility). Lacan seems to be referring to *GW* XIV, pp. 197–200, where we find the following: "*Es haftet ihr ein Charakter von Unbestimmtheit und Objektlosigkeit* [objectlessness] *an* [. . .]"; Strachey translates this as "It [anxiety] has a quality of indefiniteness and lack of object" (*SE* XX, p. 165). The same pairing of terms is found again in *GW* XIV, p. 199: "Its [anxiety's] connection with expectation [*Erwartung*] belongs to the danger-situation, whereas its indefiniteness and lack of object [*Unbestimmtheit und Objektlosigkeit*] belong to the situation of helplessness [*Hilflosigkeit*]" (*SE* XX, p. 166).

(366,1) On "unsatisfied desire," see, above all, "Direction of the Treatment" in *Écrits*.

(366,3) Other versions provide here the following formula:

$$\frac{a}{(-\varphi)} \ \lozenge\, A$$

Herr K. seems to be associated here with the other with a lowercase *o* and Frau K. with the Other with a capital *O*.

(366,5) *Carence* also means "lack" or "deficiency."

(366,6) Reading *à la loupe* (with a magnifying glass) instead of *à la louche* (with a ladle, literally; in abundance, figuratively).

(368,1) Other versions read *relation* (relationship) instead of *action* (action).

(368,6) Reading *de l'analyste* (the analyst's) instead of *de l'analyse* (psychoanalysis').

(369,1) Other versions add "*erastés* or *erón*" at the end of this sentence.

(369,3) Reading *Socrate affirme ne rien connaître qu'aux choses de l'amour* (Socrates asserts that he knows nothing except about matters of love) rather than *Socrate affirme ne rien connaître aux choses de l'amour* (Socrates asserts that he knows nothing about matters of love). Perhaps we should read "confession" in this paragraph instead of "aggression."

(369,5) *Orant* also means "praying figure," as in statuary.

(370,2) See *The Iliad*, Chapter 24, where Priam says, "Think of your father, O Achilles like unto the gods, who is such even as I am, on the sad threshold of old age. It may be that those who dwell near him harass him, and there is none to keep war and ruin from him. Yet when he hears of you being still alive, he is glad, and his days are full of hope that he shall see his dear son come home to him from Troy; but I, wretched man that I am, had the bravest in all Troy for my sons, and there is not one of them left."

(370,3) *La syncope du langage est impuissante à dire* seems rather ambiguous to me: it may suggest that even a breaking off of speech, or skipping certain letters or syllables as one speaks (a linguistic syncope), is powerless to say or convey anything. Other versions would have us read: "Any attempt to explain oneself leads to nothing but a breaking off of speech and an inability to speak, because . . ." *Quémandeur* implies that he is a beggar, not a desirer, someone who begs for something, not someone who desires.

(371,4) The fuller passage reads as follows: "Creatures of a day! What is someone? What is no one? A dream of a shadow is man," verses 95–6, p. 337, in Pindar, *Pindar I: Olympian Odes, Pythian Odes*, ed. and trans. W. H. Race (Cambridge, MA: Harvard University Press, 1997 [Loeb Classical Library]).

Chapter XXVI – "A Dream of a Shadow Is Man"

(372,6) C. Stein, "L'identification primaire [Primal identification]," *RFP* XXVI (1962): 257–65. Lacan had apparently mentioned it in the initial part of the class that is missing. See J.-A. Miller's summary notes of that missing section in his Editor's Notes at the end of this Seminar.

(373,5) It is not entirely clear whether we should read S instead of S here and on the next pages as well.

(374,2) The subject referred to here, if he is indeed S and not S, is no more than a gaze (the eye in the optical schema); in the vertical mirror (A) this subject does not see himself, but rather the (virtual image of the) vase with the flowers in it.

(374,3) There seems to be a problem with the transcription here, because in his paper on psychical causality, Lacan writes, "a dull mirror shows him a surface in which nothing is reflected" (*Écrits*, p. 188), whereas the text of the Seminar reads a "mirror without a surface in which nothing is reflected."

(374,4) Lacan is likely pointing to the different parts of the schema in Chapter 24 in the course of this discussion; $i(a)$ corresponds to the bouquet to the left where the real image of the vase containing the flowers would be produced if the eye were located at I, all the way to the right, instead of at S, all the way to the left, and the vertical mirror (A) were removed (see *Écrits*, p. 680, Figure 3).

(375,1) There may be a problem here with the transcription of the Seminar, for the passage by Freud reads: "*Der Schatten des Objekts . . . das verlassene Objekt*," in *GW* X, p. 435. "*Das verlassene Objekt*" is rendered by Strachey as "the forsaken object"; *verlassene* could also be translated as "abandoned" or "deserted." But *verlorene* is used by Freud elsewhere in the German edition (pp. 199 and 209). Other versions add "via the Other" at the end of this paragraph.

(375,4) It is not clear whether the *écarts* (deviations) in question are those of the object that moves or those of the eyes that follow it.

(377,2) "Primal identification" is a likely reference to the first type of identification mentioned by Freud at the beginning of Chapter 7 of *Group Psychology and the Analysis of the Ego*: identification with the father.

(377,6) Narcissistic identification, involving the ideal ego, is enveloping or all-encompassing; non-narcissistic (or symbolic) identification, involving the ego-ideal, is not enveloping or all-encompassing, relying as it does on a single trait.

(378,1) See Karl Abraham's *Versuch einer Entwicklungsgeschichte der Libido* (Leipzig, Vienna, and Zurich: Internationaler Psychoanalytischer Verlag, 1924). In English, see "A Short Study of the Development of the Libido, Viewed in the Light of Mental Disorders," in his *Selected Papers on Psycho-Analysis* (London: Hogarth Press, 1927). Page numbers included in brackets in the text refer to the English edition.

(379,4) This may be a reference to the formula Lacan provided for obsession in Chapter 18:

$$\text{A} \Diamond \varphi \, (a, a', a'', a''', \dots)$$

(379,5) Here is the passage and footnote that Lacan is referring to: "Freud pointed out that hysterics reject the normal, genital sexual aim, and put in its place other, 'perverse' aims. We shall remain in agreement with his view in proposing to set up a stage of object-love with the exclusion of the genitals." Abraham then adds a footnote: "Such a stage of object-love with genital exclusion seems to coincide in time with Freud's 'phallic stage' in the psychosexual development of the individual, and moreover to have close internal relations with it. We may look upon hysterical symptoms as the obverse of those libidinal impulses which belong to object-love with genital exclusion and to the phallic organization" (p. 495).

(380,1) This may be a reference to the formula Lacan provided for hysteria in Chapter 18:

$$\frac{a}{(-\varphi)} \Diamond \text{A}$$

The left-hand side can be read, at least at one level, as "the object minus the genitals."

(380,2) In physics, *réluctance* (struggle) is a measure of the opposition to magnetic flux, which is analogous to electrical resistance; it is the resistance to magnetic flux offered by a magnetic circuit, determined by the permeability and arrangement of the materials of the circuit. Its use here seems somewhat curious, even if it is actually an Anglicism. In *Selected Papers on Psycho-Analysis*, the German is rendered as follows: "We must not forget, too, that the genitals are more intensely cathected by narcissistic love than any other part of the subject's own body" (p. 495).

(380,3) Other versions give *notification* instead of *modification*.

(380,4) In the left-hand schema, the summit may represent the maximum cathexis of a specific part of the subject's own body: the genitalia.

(381,5) *Déversement* (deflection) could alternatively be rendered as "spilling over."

(381,6) Lacan is perhaps alluding here to the idiomatic expression, *"C'est bon pour les chiens,"* suggesting that something is rotten or spoiled now and only good enough for dogs to eat, cats being presumably above that or pickier eaters. He might, however, be alluding to *"Ce n'est pas fait pour les chiens"* (it's meant to be used by humans) or *"C'est de la bouillie pour les chats"* (said of a text that is confused and unintelligible).

(382,2) Note Abraham's use of the words "stuck out" in his comment about the other "hysterical patient" he describes, patient Y: she had "a desire to bite off everything that 'stuck out'" (p. 485).

(382,4) In English, see Gyp's *Petit Bob* (Whitefish, MT: Kessinger Publishing, 1887/2008); in French, see *Petit Bob* (Paris: Calmann-Lévy, 1929), p. 177. *Complaisance* (indulgence) could, instead, be rendered by "smugness."

(382,6) Note that French does not have a very commonly used word for "nipple" (hence Lacan's use here of the English word); the circumlocution often used in French is *"bout de* (or *du) sein,"* tip of the breast; *mamelon* is a somewhat scientific term, more often used in anatomy than in everyday speech.

(383,3) On a "post-ambivalent" object love, see Abraham's terms *"ambivalenzfrei (nach-ambivalent)"* in the German (Laplanche and Pontalis' *Language of Psycho-analysis* gives the wrong German terms in its entry concerning "ambivalence, pre-ambivalence, post-ambivalence"), "free from ambivalence, or post-ambivalent" (p. 481 in the English; see also p. 452).

(383,5) Jean Rostand was a well-known French biologist. Archilochus' epodes can be found in *Greek Lyric Poetry*, trans. M. L. West (New York: Oxford University Press, 1993). This is the edition cited in the text (p. 5).

Chapter XXVII – Mourning the Loss of the Analyst

(385,1) The title of this chapter, *L'analyste et son deuil*, is ambiguous and could instead be rendered as "The Analyst and His Mourning." The same ambiguity is found at the end of the chapter, it being unclear whether it is the analyst who mourns or the analysand who mourns the loss of the analyst.

(385,3) Few if any published English translations of the *Critias* mention "tone" at the beginning (106a–b), mentioning instead striking the right or wrong note or being in or out of tune. "Tone" is, however, explicitly mentioned in the French translation included in the Pléiade collection: *Platon, Oeuvres complètes* (Paris: Gallimard, 1950).

(385,4) See, above, Chapter 3, section 2. Lacan is thus presumably referring to himself!

(385,5) The French, *parler dans le désert* ("a voice crying in the wilderness") literally means "speaking in the desert," and more figuratively, "talking to a brick wall."

(387,4) The German term *Besetzung* can take on the meanings of filling, casting, stocking, team, side, and occupation.

(388,1) *Triebregungen* (drive movements, stirrings, or flickerings) strikes me as odd in this context, where Lacan seems to be providing a German term for the French *attraits* (attractions or charms). One might possibly read instead *Anziehungen*.

(388,2) Again, one might possibly read *Anziehung* instead of *Triebregung*. As indicated in a translator's note to Chapter 11, *hímeros* (meaning want or desire) can be found in Sophocles' *Antigone*, verses 795–6; compare *Phaedrus* 251c–e. Recall Lacan's final words in Chapter 11: "I will conclude my talk today with these words, καλήμερα (*kalémera*), good day [*bonjour*], καλήμερος (*kalémeros*), good day and beautiful desire."

(389,1) The French *à bas bruit* (invisibly) is a medical term meaning that nothing (of a viral condition, for example) shows on the outside or even during an examination. It might, alternatively, be rendered figuratively as "at a low boil."

(389,2) As J.-A. Miller indicates in his editor's notes, the MRP (*Mouvement républicain populaire*) was the Christian Democratic Party during the Fourth Republic.

(390,1) Lacan may be referring here to Luchino Visconti's production of John Ford's play entitled '*Tis Pity She's a Whore* (*Dommage qu'elle soit une p. . .*) at the Théâtre de Paris in 1961; the word "white" appears in numerous contexts in the play. He might, alternatively, be referring to Visconti's 1961 film *Rocco and His Brothers*. Pierrot, a figure from the Commedia dell'Arte, is always dressed in white (as a sign of innocence?) and his face is usually whitened (to indicate the pallor of death?).

(390,2) Other versions suggest that a shift (*bascule*) occurs here, not a chain reaction (*cascade*).

(390,3) Other versions add, after "little Corsica," the words "on the sheets," thereby suggesting the outline on the child's sheets of a little pool or trace of urine (likened here to the shape of Corsica on a map). On "I am what I am," see Seminar VII, p. 98/81.

(390,8) See Chapters 14 and 15 earlier on.

(391,6) See Rabelais' *Tiers Livre*, Chapter 8, where we find the following:

> *Celle qui veid son mary tout armé,*
> *Fors la braguette aller à l'escarmouche,*
> *Luy dist. Amy, de paour qu'on ne vous touche,*
> *Armez cela, qui est le plus aymé.*
> *Quoy? tel conseil doibt il estre blasmé?*
> *Ie diz que non: Car sa paour la plus grande*
> *De perdre estoit, le voyant animé,*
> *Le bon morceau, dont elle estoit friande.*

(392,1) See Freud, *Civilization and Its Discontents*. One could understand *cela* (such effusion) as referring to "handkerchiefs" instead.

(392,2) *Humides* (crybabies) might, alternatively, be rendered as "tearjerkers" in this context.

(392,3) Other versions read: "the barred signifier S" – in other words, $\math{S}$.

(392,5) Lacan is possibly referring here to his discussion of fantasy in *Écrits*, p. 825.

(393,3) *Forcer un être* (to force a being) could also be rendered as "to coerce a being" or "to flush a being out."

(393,4) See *The Marquis de Sade: Three Complete Novels: Justine, Philosophy in the Bedroom, Eugénie de Franval and Other Writings* (New York: Grove Press, 1965), pp. 741–2.

(394,3) Reading here and in the next paragraph *rivetage* (riveting, in the sense of joining things together with rivets) instead of the near homonym *rivage* (shore). "Shore" could make sense if we think of it as the limit of the image (an island or object).

(394,4) Other versions read *avant de vous avoir tué* (before having killed you) instead of *avant de l'avoir tué* (before having killed it), which may or may not have been a slip of the tongue on Lacan's part. The usual French expression is *vendre la peau de l'ours avant de l'avoir tué* (literally, to sell the bearskin before you have killed the bear; figuratively, to count one's chickens before they're hatched). *Défend* (defends) also means "prohibits."

(395,1) See Seminar VI, Chapters 8 and following (starting on p. 112), and Ella Sharpe, *Dream Analysis*, Chapter 5, entitled "Analysis of a Single Dream" (London: Hogarth, 1937), pp. 125–48.

(395,2) For example, in a room where his brother was with his girlfriend (p. 131).

(396,4) "An object of desire" – that is, not simply a love object.

(398,3) I have assumed that *potiche* here refers back to *pot* (pot) earlier on. *Potiche* also means "puppet"; *la conservation de la potiche* might potentially be rendered instead as "to preserve appearances."

(398,5) This might be understood to imply that, assuming the analysis goes far enough, the analyst as an object (for the patient) is eventually destroyed by the patient's desire.

Editor's Notes

(434,4) Assuming this should be spelled Sapho and not Sappho (the Greek poetess), there are several possible references:

- Madeleine de Scudéry, who sometimes published work under the pen name Sapho.
- Renée Vivien, a British poet who wrote in French.
- The novel by Alphonse Daudet entitled *Sapho*.

Editor's Notes

The article that is mentioned on page 345 as soon to be published was included in *Écrits*; it was entitled "Remarks on Daniel Lagache's Presentation: 'Psychoanalysis and Personality Structure.'"

I indicated on page 360 that the beginning of Class XXV is missing. Here is the text of some notes that were taken at the time by my friend Dr. Paul Lemoine, who was one of the most attentive participants at the Seminar and is now sorely missed. His notes allow us to partially fill this gap:

> Conrad Stein gave a very fine presentation on primal identification. What I will talk about today will show him that his work was well oriented. We are going to try to make headway now. I intended to read Sapho to find things in it that could enlighten us.[1] This will lead us to the heart of the function of identification. As we are still concerned with locating the analyst's function, I thought it would not be a bad idea to reexamine certain things. Freud wrote *Hemmung, Symptom und Angst* [*Inhibitions, Symptoms and Anxiety*] in 1926. It was the third stage of his thought, the first two being constituted by the *Traumdeutung* [*The Interpretation of Dreams*] and the second topography.

I would like to thank Prof. Jacques Body, who was kind enough to search for the fox in Giraudoux's work that is mentioned on pages 383–4. This fox was not found. Should you locate it, please write me care of the publisher, Editions du Seuil; the same goes for any possible corrections. Note that I have not been able to locate the otter and the weasel mentioned on page 9.

Editions du Seuil assigned the preparation of the manuscript to Paul Chemla, who paid particularly close attention to the material quoted, and Evelyne Cazade-Havas worked alongside him – my hearty thanks to both of them.

I have asked Judith Miller to henceforth direct with me the collection entitled "Le Champ freudien" that was founded by Jacques Lacan.

J.-A. M.

Notes to the Second Edition

Paul Lemoine's notes taken at the Seminar have allowed me to improve in certain places the text that I established some ten years ago. A few points should be highlighted here:

1 The term invented by Aragon that is quoted on page 66 is found in his *Traité du style*.
2 The film by Renoir that is mentioned on page 134 is *La Grande Illusion*.
3 The schema that is discussed on page 187 can be reconstituted on the basis of the notes as follows:

$$i(a) \quad \begin{matrix} \text{A } i(a)^2 \\ \\ \$ \end{matrix} \quad \text{S}$$

4 The book by Roger Caillois that is mentioned on page 213 is *Le Mythe et l'homme*.
5 The church mentioned on page 214 is the Scuola di San Giorgio degli Schiavoni.
6 The simplified [version of the complete] schema that is provided here on page 345 showed, according to Lemoine's notes, to the left of the [vertical flat] mirror, the real image of the vase, $i(a)$, surrounding the flowers, a.
7 On page 389 the abbreviation MRP designates the Christian Democratic Party during the Fourth Republic, known as the *Mouvement républicain populaire* [Popular Republican Movement]; *apparentement* (political maneuvering) was a procedure that was authorized at the time that allowed for a partial alliance between different electoral lists, which isolated the extremists in order to benefit the centrists.

469

I am grateful to Gennie Lemoine, who was kind enough to allow me to consult Paul Lemoine's notes. I would also like to thank Evelyne Cazade, who once again worked alongside me on this project.

J.-A. M.

Index